LABRST 1A03

TABLE OF CONTENTS
& ACKNOWLEDGEMENTS

PAGE

Unfair Masters and Rascally Servants? Labour Relations Among Bourgeois, Clerks and Voyageurs in the Montréal Fur Trade, 1780-1821

Carolyn Podruchny

THE HISTORY OF WORKING PEOPLES in the fur trade has recently become a subject of concentrated interest.[1] The publication of Edith Burley's *Servants of the Honourable Country*, which explores the master and servant relationship between Orkney workers and Hudson's Bay Company (HBC) officers stands as an important development in focussing attention squarely on the workers themselves, and demonstrates the extent of their power through insubordination and resistance.[2] A

[1]Some broader studies of labour and capital in early Canadian history briefly mention fur trade workers, such as H. Clare Pentland, *Labour and Capital in Canada, 1650-1860* (Toronto: James Lorimer & Co. 1981), 30-3; and Bryan D. Palmer, *Working-Class Experience: Rethinking the History of Canadian Labour, 1800-1991* (Toronto: McClelland & Stewart 1992), 35-6. European labourers first received significant examination by Jennifer S.H. Brown, *Strangers in Blood: Fur Trade Families in Indian Country* (Vancouver: University of British Columbia Press 1980). Native labourers have been subject to some examination by Carol M. Judd, "Native Labour and Social Stratification in the Hudson's Bay Company's Northern Department, 1770-1870," *Canadian Review of Sociology and Anthropology*, 17, 4 (November 1980) 305-14.

[2]Edith I. Burley, *Servants of the Honourable Company: Work, Discipline, and Conflict in the Hudson's Bay Company, 1770-1879* (Toronto, New York and Oxford: Oxford University Press 1997); Philip Goldring first began to compile information on labourers in *Papers on the Labour System of the Hudson's Bay Company, 1821-1900*, Volume I, Manuscript Report Series, no. 362, Parks Canada, (Ottawa: Ministry of Supply and Services 1979). Also see Ron C. Bourgeault, "The Indian, the Métis and the Fur Trade: Class, Sexism and Racism in the Transition 'from 'Communism' to Capitalism," *Studies in Political Economy: A*

Carolyn Podruchny, "Unfair Masters and Rascally Servants? Labour Relations Between Bourgeois and Voyageurs in the Montréal Fur Trade, 1770-1820," *Labour/Le Travail*, 43 (Spring 1999), 43-70.

general pattern of master and servant relations existed among most fur trade companies and their labour forces which was similar to other 18th-century labour contexts. Servants signed a contract for several years, agreeing to be obedient and loyal to their master in exchange for food, shelter, and wages.[3] However, labour relations were highly influenced by local conditions. The personality of individual masters, the availability of food resources, the difficulty of work, and the cultural conventions of the labour force all affected the nature of the master-servant relationship. As many fur trade scholars have contended, there was never just one fur trade: it varied tremendously in different contexts.[4] The same can be said of labour relations in the fur trade. Process and flexibility were dominant characteristics in the relationships between masters and servants.

French Canadian *voyageurs*[5] working in various Montréal-based fur trade companies developed a distinct culture which emerged in the early 18th century and lasted to the mid-19th century. During the most active period of the Montréal trade, the labour force grew from 500 men in the 1780s, to over 2000 by the time the North West Company (NWC) merged with the HBC in 1821. As voyageurs travelled from their homes in Lower Canada to the Native interior, they underwent continuous transformations in identity and their culture came to be shaped by liminality.[6] Voyageur culture was also structured by masculinity. The cluster of values that permeated voyageur culture and became markers of the ideal man

Socialist Review, 12 (Fall 1983), 45-80 and Glen Makahonuk, "Wage-Labour in the Northwest Fur Trade Economy, 1760-1849," *Saskatchewan History*, 41 (Winter 1988), 1-17.

[3]For a brief report of master and servant law in a colonial setting see Douglas Hay and Paul Craven, "Master and Servant in England and the Empire: A Comparative Study," *Labour/Le Travail*, 31 (Spring 1993), 175-84.

[4]Daniel Francis and Toby Morantz, *Partners in Furs: A History of the Fur Trade in Eastern James Bay, 1600-1870* (Montréal and Kingston: McGill-Queen's University Press), 167.

[5]Louise Dechêne uses the term *voyageur* to identify the small-scale independent fur traders, working alone or in small groups, with some financial backing from merchants, from the late 17th century to the mid-18th century. Louise Dechêne, *Habitants and Merchants in Seventeenth-Century Montréal*, trans. Liana Vardi, (Montréal: McGill-Queen's University Press 1992), 94. Later, the term came to be used more widely to refer to contracted labourers, or *engagés*. I use the term *voyageur* interchangeably with *engagé*, servant, and worker.

[6]The term "liminal" is used by cultural anthropologists to mean interstitial, implying both margins and thresholds, and a transitional state. The concept was first suggested by Arnold van Gennep in his work *The rites of passage*, trans. by Monika B. Vizedom and Gabrielle L. Caffee, (London: Routledge and Kegan Paul 1909). The concept was further developed by Victor Turner, *The Ritual Process: Structure and Anti-Structure* (Chicago: Aldine, 1969), 94-5 and *Blazing the Trail: Way Marks in the Exploration of Symbols* (Tuscon: University of Arizona Press 1992), 48-51. For a theoretical discussion and cross cultural comparisons of *communitas* or the development of community in liminal spaces see Turner, *The Ritual Process*, 96-7, 125-30 and *Blazing the Trail*, 58-61.

included being tough, daring, risk-taking, hard-working, jovial, and carefree.[7] The voyageurs made direct links between their work and their gendered identity as men. This was a means in which to ground themselves in their passage out of French Canadian society as adolescents, and into the adult world of the exotic and dangerous *pays d'en haut* or "Indian country" where they had to become courageous and tough adventurers. Their masculine identity was influenced by their French Canadian peasant and Catholic upbringing, the Native peoples they met in the interior, and of course the hegemonic rule of their masters. Although many voyageurs became freemen (independently trading and living off the land[8])and joined Native families or emerging métis communities[9], their occupational culture remained distinct from these groups. Voyageur culture was also different from that of other labour forces, such as the Kahnawake Iroquois, and Orcadians. The men from these groups did not often work together, and language barriers prevented close communication.

As the fur trade in North America varied tremendously during its long history and expansive presence, it is not surprising that its paternalistic structure also varied tremendously.[10] Patterns between regions and among different companies changed over time. Fur trade historian Jennifer Brown contends that the managers of Montréal companies had greater difficulty in controlling their servants than did the HBC officers. The more fortunate HBC officers could rely on the London committee to lay down the standard rules of conduct which served as a basis for governing their men's behaviour. The Montréal companies not only lacked this central disciplining influence, but they also had further obstacles with which to contend. Discipline was not easy to administer while voyageurs traded *en derouine* (out on their own among Native peoples), or on long journeys requiring their support and assistance. Brown goes on to assert that not only were Montréal masters outnumbered by French Canadian voyageurs, but:

> they also generally lacked the vertical social integration that helped to hold the Hudson's Bay men together. Differences of status, without the mitigating prospect of promotion, and of ethnic background meant that relations between the two groups were often characterized more by opposition, bargaining, and counter-bargaining, than by solidarity. In addition, the

[7]My understanding of masculinity as a category for historical analysis is informed by Joan Scott, "Gender: A Useful Category of Historical Analysis," *American Historical Review*, 91, (December 1986), 1053-75 and R.W. Connell, *Masculinities* (Berkeley and Los Angeles: University of California Press 1995), 67-92.

[8]John E. Foster, "Wintering, the Outsider Adult Male and the Ethnogenesis of the Western Plains Métis," *Prairie Forum*, 19, 1 (Spring 1994), 1-13.

[9]See Jacqueline Peterson and Jennifer S.H. Brown, eds., *The New Peoples: Being and Becoming Métis in North America* (Winnipeg: University of Manitoba Press 1985) and Gerhard J. Ens, *Homeland to Hinterland: The Changing Worlds of the Red River Métis in the Nineteenth Century* (Toronto: University of Toronto Press 1997).

[10]See Palmer, *Working-Class Experience*, 41-51.

French Canadians could draw on a long tradition of independent behaviour, social and sexual, in the Indian country.[11]

The particular form of paternalism in the post-Conquest Montréal fur trade was shaped by the high degree of control exercised by voyageurs in the labour system. Flexibility in contracts, frequent labour shortages, and continual re-postings gave the voyageurs bargaining power. Voyageurs' power was also augmented by isolation which increased their masters' dependence on them.

Burley challenges Brown's characterization of the HBC workforce as more rigidly controlled and less independent than the French Canadian voyageurs. She contends the Orcadians opposed and bargained with their masters like the voyageurs.[12] Although the culture of voyageurs was distinct from other fur trade labourers, all engaged in similar types of resistance and agency. These correlations are worth serious note, but the fractured nature of the sources prevents scholars from arguing convincingly that voyageurs were either more or less independent and 'rascally' than other fur trade labourers. The partners and clerks in the NWC did not keep detailed or consistent reports of their activities at fur trade posts, and they commented less on the behaviour of their men. It is thus difficult to compare quantitatively the extent to which voyageurs and other fur trade labourers resisted the rule of their masters. This paper instead focuses on the nature and patterns of voyageur and master relations, providing comparisons with other fur trade labourers where possible.

After the 1763 conquest of New France, the fur trade operating out of Montréal reorganized under the direction of Scottish, English, American, and a few French Canadian managers who called themselves *bourgeois*.[13] These companies, which eventually merged into the NWC, hired French Canadian men mainly from parishes around Montréal and Trois Rivières to transport goods and furs from Montréal to the North American interior during the summer months. They were also hired to work year-round at the company posts and handled trading with Native peoples. There is no question that the job of voyageurs was difficult. They performed near miraculous feats of transporting goods and furs over immense distances and undertook challenging canoe routes. Work at the interior posts was easier than that on the summer canoe brigades, but voyageurs were responsible for a tremendous range of duties, which included construction, artisan crafts, hunting, fishing, and trading. Threats to voyageurs' well-being, including starvation and physically debilitating overwork, came mostly from the harsh environment, but hostile Native peoples and cruel masters could contribute to the misery. Despite the harsh working

[11] Brown, *Strangers in Blood*, 88.

[12] Burley, *Servants of the Honourable Company*, 15-16.

[13] The term "bourgeois" was used in 18th and 19th-century Canada to refer to the Montréal fur trade merchants and managers, which included company partners and all but the most junior clerks.

and living conditions, voyageurs developed a reputation as strong, capable, and cheerful, although sometimes unreliable, servants. The writings of the bourgeois and clerks working in the trade reveal a deep admiration for their skill and effectiveness as workers, and a tolerance for petty theft and minor insolence.[14] This article concerns itself with two questions: why did voyageurs put up with their tough lot without overt revolt, and what was the substance of the relationship between voyageurs and their masters? Because voyageurs were primarily non-literate and left little record of their experiences, we must rely on the writings of a diverse group of literate outsiders, including the powerful fur trade partners, lowly clerks, and assorted travellers to the north-west interior. A close and extensive examination reveals a complex network of accommodation and resistance in the master and servant relationship. This article maps out some patterns in the period from 1780 to 1821, which was the height of competition between trade companies and the expansion into the interior.

The Montréal fur trade labour system was organized around indentured servitude, paternalism, and cultural hegemony. The fur trade managers and clerks acted as paternal masters directing the labour of voyageurs. Voyageurs signed a legal contract, or *engagement*, which established the framework for the paternal relationship. The principal tenet of the contract dictated that servants obey their masters in exchange for board and wages. Voyageurs and their masters, however, interpreted the contract differently in particular contexts. Their diverging and situational "readings" of the legal contract led to the emergence of a "social contract" which constituted the actual working relationship between the two groups. The "social contract" was expressed in the customs which came to characterize the fur trade workplace and the dialogue between servants and masters over acceptable working conditions. Masters tried to enforce obedience, loyalty, and hard work among voyageurs, while the voyageurs struggled to ensure that their working conditions were fair and comfortable, and that masters fully met their paternal obligations. Voyageurs exercised relative cultural autonomy on the job, and often controlled the workpace and scope of their duties. Their masters, however, maintained ultimate authority by exercising their right to hire and fire voyageurs and by successfully profiting in the trade.

Although masters and servants can be understood as constituting two loose but distinct "classes" within the fur trade, it is important to be aware of the ranges within each class in terms of power, authority, and duty. Some masters were junior clerks, bound in a paternal relationship with senior clerks and partners. These clerks were paid a smaller annual salary than senior bourgeois, and did not hold shares in the partnerships which made up the Montréal fur trading companies. Partners were granted voting privileges in business meetings, in addition to their company shares

[14]For a representative example see W. Kaye Lamb, ed., *Sixteen Years in Indian Country: The Journal of Daniel Williams Harmon, 1800-1816* (Toronto: The MacMillan Company of Canada 1957), 197-98.

and higher salaries.[15] *Engagés* also had varying status. At the bottom were seasonally employed summer men, referred to as *mangeurs du lard*, or Porkeaters, who paddled between Montréal and the Great Lakes. Wintering *engagés*, or *hommes du nord*, who paddled canoes to and worked at the interior posts, scorned these greenhorns. Within the canoe, paddlers called middlemen or *milieu*, were subject to the authority of the foreman and steersman, or *devant* and *gouvernail*, who usually acted as canoe and brigade leaders. Some estimates suggest that these *bouts* could earn from one third to five times as much as paddlers.[16] Interpreters and guides, paid usually twice or three times as much as other *engagés*, also assumed more authority by their greater wealth and knowledge.[17]

Although the ethnic divisions did not entirely follow occupational lines, the Montréal bourgeois became more and more British after the 1763 Conquest, while the voyageurs were primarily French Canadians. British discrimination against French Canadians, and fellow-feeling among voyageurs contributed to the social distance between masters and servants. Voyageurs lived within a different cultural ethos than that of the bourgeois, one which emphasized independence, strength, courage, and cultural adaptation rather than profit, obedience, and cultural supremacy. These different frames of reference distanced voyageurs from their masters, and frequently impeded harmonious workplace relations. Despite the range of roles within each group, the division between bourgeois and voyageur, or master and servant, served as a basic social organization of the fur trade.[18] Class, ethnic, and

[15]Toronto, Ontario Archives (hereafter OA), North West Company Collection (hereafter NWCC), MU 2199, Box 4, No. 1 (photostat of original), "An Account of the Athabasca Indians by a Partner of the North West Company, 1795," revised 4 May 1840 (Forms part of the manuscript entitled "Some Account of the North West Company," by Roderick McKenzie, director of the North West Company. Original at McGill Rare Books (hereafter MRB), Masson Collection (hereafter MC), C.18, Microfilm reel #22. Photostat can also be found at National Archives of Canada (hereafter NAC), MC, MG19 C1, Vol. 55, Microfilm reel #C-15640); 51.

[16]George Heriot, *Travels Through the Canadas, Containing a Description of the Picturesque Scenery on Some of the Rivers and Lakes; with an Account of the Productions, Commerce, and Inhabitants of those Provinces* (Philadelphia: M. Carey 1813), 254; and MRB, MC, C.27, Microfilm reel #13, Roderick McKenzie, Letters Inward [all the letters are from W. Ferdinand Wentzel, Forks, McKenzie River], 1807-1824, pp. 3, 23.

[17]"An Account of the Athabasca Indians by a Partner of the North West Company, 1795," pp. 51; and Alexander Mackenzie, Esq., "A General History of the Fur Trade from Canada to the North-West," *Voyages from Montréal on the River St. Laurence through the Continent of North America to the Frozen and Pacific Oceans in the Years 1789 and 1793 with a Preliminary Account of the Rise, Progress, and Present State of the Fur Trade of that Country*, (London: R. Noble, Old Bailey 1801), 34.

[18]Brown, *Strangers in Blood* 35, 45-8. Also see E.P. Thompson's discussion of "patricians" and "plebs" in *Customs in Common: Studies in Traditional Popular Culture* (New York: The New Press 1993), 16-17.

cultural differences operated in conjunction to create a paternalistic and hegemonic labour system.

Masters and servants accepted their positions as rulers and ruled. Voyageurs could challenge the substance and boundaries of their jobs and loyalty to their masters without contesting the fundamental power dynamics. Voyageurs' acceptance of their masters domination was based on a deeply held belief in the legitimacy of paternalism. Voyageurs certainly became discontented, resisted their masters' authority, and sometimes revolted, but it was outside of their conception of the world to challenge the hegemonic culture.[19] Thus, the structure of cultural hegemony was not inconsistent with the presence of labour strife. Although voyageurs participated in the formulation of the master and servant relationship, they challenged the terms of their employment and contracts without fundamentally challenging their position in the power relationship. Voyageurs, clerks and bourgeois engaged in a dialogue of accommodation and confrontation as a means of constructing a workable relationship.[20] To assert the power and agency of the voyageurs does not deny the framework of subordination; rather it looks within it. Hegemony did not envelop the lives of the voyageurs and prevent them from defending their own modes of work, play, and rituals. Hegemony offered, in the words of E.P. Thompson, writing of the 18th-century English plebians, a "bare architecture of a structure of relations of domination and subordination, but within that architectural tracery many different scenes could be set and different dramas enacted."[21]

What "scenes of rule" were enacted in the north-west fur trade? The mutuality intrinsic to paternalism and hegemony governed social relations and made up the substance of the "social contract" between the bourgeois and voyageurs in the north west. Each party accepted their roles and responsibilities in the master and servant relationship, but they pressed the boundaries, and tried to shape the relationship to best suit their desires and needs. The difficulty masters encountered in enforcing authority, and the precariousness of survival meant they had to be particularly responsive to their servants. Part of hegemony involved appearances.[22] Masters often engaged in self-consciousness public theatre, while voyageurs offered their own form of counter-theatre. Through this means of communication masters and servants came to accept common ideas of the way things should work. The formula laid out in the labour contracts served as the crux from which both parties tried to digress. In the "social contract," or "ritual theatre," masters attempted to evade their provision of welfare, and the voyageurs tried to ease the strain of their work and to

[19]For a discussion on cultural hegemony and the consent of the masses to be ruled, see T. J. Jackson Lears, "The Concept of Cultural Hegemony: Problems and Possibilities," *American Historical Review*, 90 (June 1985), 567-593.

[20]Edith Burley also found that the relationship between masters and servants in the HBC was constantly subject to negotiation. Burley, *Servants of the Honourable Company*, 110-11.

[21]Thompson, *Customs in Common*, 85-6.

[22]This is suggested by Thompson, *Customs in Common*, 45-6.

control aspects of the workplace. A dialogue of resistance and accommodation kept the paternalistic relationship fluid and flexible, which was crucial to its resilience. Paternalistic hegemony was constantly being negotiated and, in the fur trade, management authority never came close to being absolute or ubiquitous.

Because the NWC and XY Company (the second most significant of the Montréal companies, hereafter XYC) were co-proprietorships, contracts were made in the names of the various firms or individuals comprising the shareholders and joint partnerships. No engagements were issued specifically in the name of the NWC or XYC, as all of the outfitting was carried out by shareholder partners and firms.[23] The labour contracts of all partnerships, both within and outside of the NWC, however, were remarkably similar. Contracts reveal voyageurs' names, parishes of origin, destinations in the north west, job positions, lengths of term, and salaries. The language of most contracts underscored the paternal nature of the relationship, requiring voyageurs to obey their masters, to work responsibly and carefully, to be honest and well-behaved, to aid the bourgeois in making a profit, and to remain in the service. For example, a contract form for the firm McTavish, McGillivrays & Co., and Pierre de Rocheblave, Ecuïer clearly instructs the *engagé*:

> to take good and proper care, while on routes, and to return to the said places, the merchandise, provisions, furs, utensils, and all the things necessary for the voyage; to serve, obey and to faithfully carry out all [orders] of the said Bourgeois, or all others who represent the Bourgeois, which are required by the present contract, he lawfully and honestly commands, to make his profit, avoid misfortune, warn him if you know of danger; and generally do all that a good and loyal servant must and is obliged to do, without doing any particular trading; do not leave or quit the said service, under the pain carried by the laws of this Province, and the loss of your wages.[24]

Masters were bound to pay the voyageurs' wages and provide them with equipment. The substance of the equipment, and the provision of food and welfare for the *engagé*, were rarely specified in contracts, and thus provided one of the few places for obvious negotiation between the masters and servants.[25] Custom came to dictate that equipment consisted of one blanket, one shirt, and one pair of trousers.[26]

[23]Lawrence M. Lande, *The Development of the Voyageur Contract (1686-1821)* (Montréal: McLennan Library, McGill University 1989), 41.
[24]Winnipeg, Provincial Archives of Manitoba (hereafter PAM), Fort William Collection (hereafter FWC), MG1 C1; fo. 33, contract form for McTavish, McGillivrays & Co. My translation.
[25]For examples see Joseph Defont's 1809 contract with the North West Company, PAM, FWC, MG1 C1, fo. 32-1 and the contract of Louis Santier of St. Eustache with Parker, Gerrard, Ogilvy, & Co. as a *milieu* to transport goods between Montréal and Michilimackinac, 21 Avril [sic] 1802, NAC, MG19 A51.
[26]Mackenzie, "A General History," 34.

In order to enforce the terms of the legal contracts, bourgeois tried to regulate their servants through legal and state sanctions. In January 1778, an official of the NWC sent a memorandum to Governor Guy Carleton asking him "that it be published before the Traders and their Servants that the latter must strictly conform to their agreements, which should absolutely be in writing or printed, and before witnesses if possible, as many disputes arise from want of order in this particular." The memorandum goes on to ask that men be held to pay their debts with money or service and that traders hiring men already engaged to another company should purchase their contracts.[27] Lower Canadian law eventually recognized the legality of notarial fur trade contracts, and a 1796 ordinance forbade *engagés* to transgress the terms or desert the service.[28] In Lower Canada, the legislature empowered Justices of the Peace (JPS) to create and oversee the rules and regulations for master and servant relations.[29]

Bourgeois on occasion turned to the law to enforce the terms of the contract. Voyageurs were charged with breaking contracts, mainly for deserting, rather than for insolence or disobedience.[30] The files of the Court of Quarter Sessions in the District of Montréal reveal a range of cases: voyageurs accepted wages from one employer while already working for another, they obtained advance wages without appearing for the job, and they deserted the service.[31] Cases of voyageur desertion and theft can also be found in the records of the Montréal civil court.[32] In 1803, the British government passed the Canada Jurisdiction Act by which criminal offenses committed in the "Indian territories" could be tried in Lower Canada, and the five

[27]NAC, Haldimand Papers, "Memorandum for Sir Guy Carleton," 20 January 1778, cited by Harold Adams Innis, *The Fur Trade in Canada* (Toronto: University of Toronto Press 1956, first published in 1930), 221.

[28]*Ordinances and Acts of Quebec and Lower Canada*, 36 George III, chpt. 10, 7 May 1796.

[29]Grace Laing Hogg and Gwen Shulman, "Wage Disputes and the Courts in Montreal, 1816-1835," in Donald Fyson, Colin M. Coates and Kathryn Harvey, eds., *Class, Gender and the Law in Eighteenth- and Nineteenth-Century Quebec: Sources and Perspectives* (Montréal: Montréal History Group, 1993), 129.

[30]For one example see Montréal, McCord Museum of Canadian History, North West Company Papers, M17607, M17614, Deposition of Basil Dubois, 21 June 1798, and Complaint of Samuel Gerrard, of the firm of Parker, Gerrard and Ogilvie against Basil Dubois.

[31]Montréal, Archives nationales de Québec, dépot de Montréal (hereafter ANQM), Court of Quarter Sessions of the District of Montréal, TL32 S1 SS1, Robert Aird vs. Joseph Boucher, 1 April 1785, JP Pierre Foretier; Atkinson. Patterson vs. Jean-Baptiste Desloriers dit Laplante, 21 April 1798, JP Thomas Forsyth; and Angus Sharrest for McGillivray & Co. vs. Joseph Papin of St. Sulpice, 14 June 1810, JP J-M Mondelet. These cases were compiled by Don Fyson as part of a one in five sample of the whole series.

[32]ANQM, Cours des plaidoyers communs du district de Montréal (hereafter CPCM), Cour du samedi (matières civiles superieurs), TL16 S4 /00005, pp. 37, 27 mars 1784, JPs Hertelle De Rouville and Edward Southouse; and TL16 S4 /00002, no page numbers, 2 Avril 1778, JPs Hertelle De Rouville and Edward Southouse.

JPs named were all prominent fur trade bourgeois, although the court's power remained limited.[33] It is difficult to determine the effectiveness of court action to control workers, especially since prosecution rates have not survived in most of the records. Presumably the bourgeois would not continue to press charges if their efforts did not pay off. Yet pressing charges against voyageurs did not seem to deter them from continuing to desert, cheat contract terms, and steal from their employers.

Other efforts to control workers included cooperation between companies to limit contract-jumping and blacklisting deserters. In 1800 NWC officer William McGillivray wrote to Thomas Forsyth of Forsyth, Ogilvy and McKenzie:

> I agree with you that protecting Deserters would be a dangerous Practice and very pernicious to the Trade and fully sensible of this when any Man belonging to People opposed to The North West Company have happened to come to our Forts, we have told the Master of such to come for them and that they should not be in any way wise prevented from taking them back.

McGillivray assured Forsyth that he was not protecting one of their deserters and had told his master to come and claim him. He went on to discuss the case of the NWC *engagé*, Poudriés, who was allowed to return to Montréal because of ill health on the understanding that he was to pay his debt in Montréal or return to the north west to serve out his time. McGillivray explained that when the NWC discovered that Poudriés engaged himself to Forsyth, Ogilvy & McKenzie they attempted to arrest him. McGillivray accused Forsyth of protecting him, and requested that he be returned to NWC service or that his debt be paid, continuing:

> With regard to paying advances made to Men I wish to be explicit, we have alwise made it a practice and will continue so to do to pay every shilling that Men whom we hire may acknowledge to their former Master such Men being free on the Ground. We hire no Men who owe their Descent considering this a principle not to be deviated from in determining to adhere strictly to it we cannot allow others to treat us in a different manner- if a Man was Free at the Point au Chapeau we do not consider him at liberty to hire until he has gone to it.[34]

[33]The JPs were William McGillivray, Duncan McGillivray, Sir Alexander Mackenzie, Roderick McKenzie, and John Ogilvy. Marjorie Wilkins Campbell, *The North West Company* (Toronto: MacMillan Company of Canada 1957), 136-7.
[34]NAC, North West Company Letterbook, 1798-1800 (hereafter NWCL), MG19 B1, vol. 1, pp. 131, William McGillivray to Thomas Forsyth, Esq., Grand Portage, 30 June 1800.

McGillivray decided to purchase voyageurs' engagements from their previous masters rather than paying their wages, and warned other fur trade companies against hiring any deserters.[35] The other fur trade companies soon followed suit.[36]

Voyageurs occasionally took their employing masters to court, most often to sue for wages.[37] Cases of this kind were widespread in all sorts of labour contracts in New France and Lower Canada, so it is not surprising that voyageurs followed suit. However, servants were not usually successful in claiming wages for jobs which they had deserted, or where they had disobeyed their masters.[38] The colonial government and legal system supported fur trade labour contracts, but the contracts were difficult to enforce because of the limits of the policing and justice systems in the north west. Masters thus relied more on the "social contract" which they were constantly negotiating with their servants.

Masters and voyageurs had different views of their "social contract," which frequently resulted in rocky negotiations. They agreed that servants were supposed to obey their masters' requirements to trade successfully in exchange for fair board and wages. Their divergent readings of "the deal" were based on different ideas of what was fair. Establishing a mutual understanding of obligations was easier if servants respected their masters. Servants respected those masters who they regarded as tough but evenhanded.

How did masters command and maintain their authority? In many historic circumstances, masters turned to physical might or the law as a principal vehicle for hegemony. But at the height of fur trade competition, the arm of the law was short and the high value of labour discouraged masters from physically intimidating their workers. Masters relied on paternalistic authority as an accepted ideology to justify and bolster their might. The ideology was expressed in the "theatre of daily rule."[39] Bourgeois and clerks imposed their authority believing that they were superior and were obliged to control their inferior servants. Masters also contributed to a dominant public discourse of their superiority, or enacted the "theatre of rule" in material ways. They ensured their access to more and better food, fancier

[35]NAC, NWCL, MG19 B1, vol. 1, pp. 152-3, William McGillivray to McTavish, Frobisher and Company, Grand Portage, 28 July 1800.

[36]NAC, Letterbook of Sir Alexander McKenzie and Company, kept by Daniel Sutherland (hereafter LAMC), pp. 40, D. Sutherland to Henry Harou, 15 May 1803.

[37]ANQM, CPCM, Cour du vendredi (matières civiles inferieurs), TL16 S3 /00001, pp. 41, 314-25, 3 juillet 1770 and 3 juillet 1778, JPs Hertelle De Rouville and Edward Southouse; and TL16 S3 /00008, no page numbers, 13 janvier 1786, JPs Hertelle De Rouville and Edward Southouse, 6 octobre 1786 (followed by several other entries later in the month), JPs John Fraser, Edward Southouse and Hertelle De Rouville, and 27 octobre 1786, JPs Edward Southouse and Hertelle De Rouville; and Eliot Coues, ed. *New Light on the Early History of the Greater Northwest: The Manuscript Journals of Alexander Henry* (Minneapolis: Ross and Haines 1897), vol. 2, 860-1, Sunday, 27 March 1814.

[38]Hogg and Shulman, "Wage Disputes and the Courts in Montréal" 128, 132, 135-40, 141-3.

[39]Thompson, *Customs in Common*, 43, 45-6.

clothing, and better sleeping conditions than voyageurs.[40] Further in the interior, away from the larger fur trade administrative centres, bourgeois and clerks had to rely on inexpensive symbols and actions to enforce their authority. Carefully maintained social isolation, differential work roles, control over scarce resources, reputation, and ability all symbolized masters' authority.[41]

Differentiation in work roles was very apparent in travel. Bourgeois were usually passengers aboard canoes, and only helped their men paddle and portage in cases of extreme jeopardy. At times the rituals of travel situated bourgeois at the head of a great procession. In his reminiscences of a fur trading career, Alexander Ross described how the light canoe, used for transporting men and mail quickly through the interior, clearly positioned the bourgeois as a social superior:

> The bourgeois is carried on board his canoe upon the back of some sturdy fellow generally appointed for this purpose. He seats himself on a convenient mattress, somewhat low in the centre of his canoe; his gun by his side, his little cherubs fondling around him, and his faithful spaniel lying at his feet. No sooner is he at his ease, than his pipe is presented by his attendant, and he then begins smoking, while his silken banner undulates over the stern of his painted vessel.[42]

HBC surveyor Philip Turnor, both envied and criticized that the NWC

> give Men which never saw an Indian One Hundred Pounds pr Annum, his Feather Bed carried in the Canoe, his Tent which is exceedingly good, pitched for him, his Bed made and he and his girl carried in and out of the Canoe and when in the Canoe never touches a Paddle unless for his own pleasure all of these indulgences.[43]

At posts, bourgeois and clerks did not participate in the vigorous round of activities which kept the post functioning smoothly, such as constructing and maintaining houses, building furniture, sleighs and canoes, gathering firewood, hunting, and preparing food. Rather, these masters kept accounts, managed the wares and provisions, and initiated trade with Native peoples.

Bourgeois and clerks were encouraged to keep a distance from their labourers. Junior clerks in particular, whose authority in isolated wintering posts was threat-

[40]Elizabeth Vibert, *Traders' Tales: Narratives of Cultural Encounters in the Columbia Plateau, 1807-1846* (Norman and London: University of Oklahoma Press 1997), 110-12.
[41]James Scott Hamilton, "Fur Trade Social Inequality and the Role of Non-Verbal Communication," Ph.D. Thesis, Simon Fraser University, 1990, 138, 261-3.
[42]Alexander Ross, *Fur Hunters of the Far West; A Narrative of Adventures in Oregon and the Rocky Mountains* (London: Smith, Elder and Co. 1855), 1: 301-2.
[43]J. B. Tyrrell, ed. *Journals of Samuel Hearne and Philip Turnor* (Toronto: Champlain Society 1934), Journal III, "A Journal of the most remarkable Transactions and Occurences from York Fort to Cumberland House, and from said House to York Fort from 9th Septr 1778 to 15th Septr 1779 by Mr Philip Turnor," 15 July 1779, 252.

ened by experienced labourers, had to establish firm lines of control. When the NWC clerk George Gordon was still a novice, he received advice from a senior clerk, George Moffatt, to be independent, confident, very involved in the trade, and

> Mixt. very seldom with the Men, rather retire within yourself. than make them your companions.- I do not wish to insinuate that you should be haughty- on the contrary- affability with them at times, may get You esteme, while the observance of a proper distance, will command respect, and procure from them ready obedience to you orders.[44]

In 1807, John McDonald of Garth was sent out as a novice to take over the NWC's Red River Department which was notorious for its corruption and difficult men. A French Canadian interpreter, who had long been in the district managing to secure great authority among voyageurs and Native peoples, had to be reminded by McDonald: "you are to act under me, you have no business to think, it is for me to do so and not for you, you are to obey."[45]

Probably the greatest challenges the bourgeois and clerks faced in asserting authority and controlling workers came from the circumstance of the fur trade itself— the great distances along fur trade routes and between posts, and the difficulties of transportation and communication. The arduous job of traversing an unfamiliar and inhospitable terrain led to frequent accidents. The incomplete nature of the sources obscure any measurement of mortality rates, but the writings of the bourgeois are filled with literally hundreds of cases of trading parties losing their way along routes, injuring themselves or perishing in canoeing accidents, being attacked by bears, and starving, to name a few of the mishaps.[46]

[44]OA, George Gordon Papers, MU 1146G, Moffatt, Fort William, to George Gordon, Monontagué, 25 July 1809. See also Hamilton, "Fur Trade Social Inequality," 135-6. Burley found a similar pattern in the HBC, Burley, *Servants of the Honourable Company*, 122-3.

[45]NAC, Autobiographical Notes of John McDonald of Garth, 1791-1815, written in 1859, photostat, MG19 A17, pp. 119-21. The original can be found at MRB, MS 406, and a typescript can be found at the OA, MU 1763.

[46]For a few examples of becoming lost see MRB, MC, C.8, microfilm reel #14, Alexander McKenzie, Journal of Great Bear Lake, 18-26 June 1806, pp. 20; MRB, MC, Journal of John MacDonell, Assiniboines-Rivière qu'Appelle, 1793-95, Thursday, 13 March 1794 and Monday, 8 December 1794, pp. 11, 22; and OA, Company of Temiscamingue, Microfilm #MS65, Donald McKay, Journal from January 1805 to June 1806, Thursday, 12 September 1805, pp. 32 (I added page numbers). For examples of canoeing accidents see NAC, MC, MG19 C1, vol. 1, microfilm reel #C-15638, Charles Chaboillez, "Journal for the Year 1797," Wednesday, 16, 19 and 31 August 1797, pp. 4, 6; NAC, MC, MG19 C1, Vol. 4, Microfilm reel #C-15638, William McGillivray, "Rat River Fort Near Rivière Malique...," 9 September 1789 to 13 June 1790 (written transcript precedes original on reel, both badly damaged), pp. 73-4; and NAC, MC, MG19 C1, Vol. 8, Microfilm reel #C-15638, W. Ferdinand Wentzel, "A Journal kept at the Grand River, Winter 1804 & 1805," 9 October 1804, pp. 9. On bear attacks see Toronto, Metropolitan Reference Library, Baldwin Room (hereafter *MRL BR*),

Masters and voyageurs dealt with the danger which infused the fur trade in a particular way. Both social groups idealized strength, toughness, and fortitude. Voyageurs competed with each other to perform awesome feats of dexterity and endurance.[47] They played rough and risk-taking games and tried to push themselves beyond their limits. In doing so, they tried to distract themselves from, and desensitize themselves to the risks inherent in fur trading and the deaths, accidents, and illnesses around them. Rather than being overwhelmed by the danger and tragedy, they made a virtue of necessity and flaunted their indifference. By incorporating manly violence and aggression into daily life, in their competitions and brawling, men could toughen themselves for the challenges of their jobs.[48] For example, in August of 1794, the Athabasca brigade raced the Fort George brigade from the south side to the north side of Lake Winnipeg. Duncan McGillivray, in charge of the Fort George crew, explained that

> The Athabasca Men piqued themselves on a Superiority they were supposed to have over the other bands of the North for expeditions marching [canoeing], and ridiculed our men *a la facon du Nord* for pretending to dispute a point that universally decided in *their* favor.

S13, George Nelson's Journal "No. 7", describing the Lake Winnipeg district in 1812, written as a reminiscence, pp. 283-4; NAC, MG19 A17, Autobiographical Notes of John McDonald of Garth, 1791-1815, written in 1859 (photostat), pp. 54-5, 65-6; and "First Journal of Simon Fraser from April 12th to July 18th, 1806," Appendix B, *Public Archives Report for 1929*, pp. 109-45, (transcript from a copy at University of California at Berkeley, Bancroft Collection, Pacific Coast Mss., Series C, No. 16; copy also at NAC, MG19 A9, Simon Fraser Collection, Vol. 4; originals at the Provincial Archives of British Columbia), Sunday 13 July 1806, pp. 143-4. On starvation see MRB, MC, C.24, Microfilm reel #2, Archibald Norman McLeod, Journal kept at Alexandria, 1800, Thursday, 19 February 1801, pp. 22; NAC, MG19 A14, Microfilm reel #M-130, John Stuart, Journal kept at North West Company Rocky Mountain House, 1805-6 (original at Provincial Archives of British Columbia), Saturday, 1 February 1806, pp. 20; and MRL BR, S13, George Nelson's Journal "No. 5," June 1807 - October 1809, written as a reminiscence, dated 7 February 1851, pp. 209-10.

[47]Coues, ed., *New Light*, 1: 11 August 1800, pp. 30-1; MRL BR, S13, George Nelson's diary of events on a journey from Cumberland House to Fort William, part in code, 3 June - 11 July 1822 (notes taken from a transcription made by Sylvia Van Kirk); Tuesday, 9 July 1822; *ibid.*, Nelson's diary of events on a journey from Fort William to Cumberland House, 21 July - 22 August 1822 (notes taken from a transcription made by Sylvia Van Kirk); Monday, 19 August 1822; and Alexander Ross, *Fur Hunters of the Far West; A Narrative of Adventures in Oregon and the Rocky Mountains*, (London: Smith, Elder and Co. 1855), II: 236-7.

[48]Elliot J. Gorn describes this pattern as well in "Gouge and Bite, Pull hair and Scratch: The Social Significance of Fighting in the Southern Backcountry," *American Historical Review*, 90 (Feb. 1985), 18-43.

Despite the fact that the Fort George crew was more heavily loaded than the Athabasca crew, the two groups were evenly matched. They pressed on for 48 hours before agreeing to call a truce and set up camp on shore. Not surprisingly, McGillivray was delighted with their progress.[49] During a return trip to Montréal in 1815, John McDonald's crew of Canadians raced McGillivray's crew of Iroquois all day. The Canadians allowed the Iroquois to pull ahead at the start of the day, but they raced past them in the evening.[50]

Bourgeois encouraged the 'rugged' ethos of the voyageurs, which conveniently suited their agenda for quick, efficient, and profitable fur trade operations.[51] In some instances, bourgeois had to remind voyageurs of their manly pride in skill and endurance. During a particularly difficult journey, Alexander Mackenzie began to hear murmurs of discontent. The desire to turn back increased when one of the canoes was lost in a stretch of rapids. In order to encourage them to continue, Mackenzie

> brought to their recollection, that I did not deceive them, and that they were made acquainted with the difficulties and dangers they must expect to encounter, before they engaged to accompany me. I also urged the honour of conquering disasters, and the disgrace that would attend them on their return home, without having attained the object of the expedition. Nor did I fail to mention the courage and resolution which was the peculiar boast of the North men; and that I depended on them, at that moment, for the maintenance of their character.... my harangue produced the desired effect, and a very general assent appeared to go wherever I should lead the way.[52]

Whether or not Mackenzie's "harangue produced the desired effect," it seems clear that both bourgeois and voyageurs valued the strength and courage required to paddle farther into the north west.

Accommodation among voyageurs, clerks and bourgeois made up part of the master and servant relationship. They worked closely for long periods of time, often shared living quarters, and faced many calamities and adventures together. As many disputes were caused by shortages of provisions, the surest way in which bourgeois and clerks could ensure loyalty was to provide plenty of good food for their men. Bourgeois and clerks fostered accommodation by meeting other paternal duties,

[49]Arthur S. Morton, ed., *The Journal of Duncan McGillivray of the North West Company at Fort George on the Saskatchewan, 1794-5* (Toronto: The MacMillan Company of Canada Limited 1929), 11.

[50]NAC, Autobiographical Notes of John McDonald of Garth, 215.

[51]In a different case, Gunther Peck found that middle class commentators condemned miners' penchant for risk-taking in late 19th century Nevada. Gunther Peck, "Manly Gambles: The Politics of Risk on the Comstock Lode, 1860-1880," *Journal of Social History*, 26 (Summer 1993), 701-23.

[52]See entries Friday, 31 May 1793 and Thursday, 13 June 1793, Mackenzie, *Voyages from Montréal*, 285, 295-6, 322-6.

such as attempting to protect their men from dangers in the workplace, providing medicines, and treating men with respect. Masters also solidified their hegemony through generosity and kindness, reminiscent of a kind of feudal largesse. Extra rations of alcohol and food, known as *regales*, were provided on significant occasions, such as settling accounts and signing new engagements.[53] Routine "rewards," such as the customary provision of drams at portages, were also incorporated into the more tedious aspects of fur trade work.[54] Sometimes masters' generosity was self-interested. When McKay gave his men moose skin to make themselves shoes, mittens, and blankets to last them through the winter, he warned them that "we have a strong opposition to contend with this year" and that they must be ready to go at a moment's notice.[55] His gifts no doubt consolidated his authority, but they also helped the voyageurs to perform their duties more effectively.

Despite these points of accommodation, harmony in the workplace was continually under stress as voyageur resistance to master authority characterized labour relations in the fur trade. Voyageurs' discontents focused on such unsuitable working and living conditions as poor rations, or unreasonable demands by masters. Voyageurs turned to strategies such as complaining to their bourgeois and attempting to bargain for better working conditions to highlight their concerns and initiate change. Like the Orcadians working for the HBC, individual action was a more common form of worker resistance than was organized collective protest.[56]

Complaining by the voyageurs became a form of "counter-theatre," which contested bourgeois hegemonic prerogatives. Just as the bourgeois often asserted their hegemony in a theatrical style, especially with canoe processions, the voyageurs also asserted their presence by "a theatre of threat and sedition."[57] In one illuminating example in the summer of 1804, while trying to travel through low water and marshes, Duncan Cameron's men ceaselessly complained about the

[53]For examples see Coues, ed., *New Light*, vol. 1, 10, 243, 23 July 1800 and 6 May 1804; Lamb, ed., *Sixteen Years*, 105, Sunday, 19 July 1807; and Ross Cox, *Adventures on the Columbia River* (New York: J. & J. Harper 1832), 304-5, 19 September 1817.

[54]For examples see NAC, MC, MG19 C1, vol. 1, microfilm reel #C-15638, pp. 3, Friday, 11 August 1797, Charles Chaboillez, "Journal for the Year 1797"; NAC, MC, MG19 C1, Vol. 9, Microfilm reel # C-15638, pp.16, Unidentified North West Company Wintering Partner, "Journal for 1805 & 6, Cross Lake," Sunday, 10 November 1805; MRB, MC, C.1, microfilm reel #55, pp. 66, Duncan Cameron, "The Nipigon Country", with extracts from his journal in the Nipigon, 1804-5, (also found in the OA, photostat, MU 2198 Box 3, Item 3; and in triplicate typescript, MU 2200, Box 5 (a-c)); and Mackenzie, *Voyages from Montréal*, 325, Thursday, 13 June 1793.

[55]Approximately 20 June 1807, described in TMRL, BR, S13, pp. 186, George Nelson's Journal "No. 5," June 1807 - October 1809, written as a reminiscence, dated 7 February 1851.

[56]Burley, *Servants of the Honourable Company*, 118-20.

[57]E.P. Thompson, *Customs in Common*, 67.

miserable conditions and difficulty of the work. They cursed themselves as "Blockheads" for coming to "this Infernal Part of the Country", as they called it, damning the mud, damning the lack of clean water to quench their thirst, and damning the first person who chose that route. Cameron tried to be patient and cheerful with them, as he knew that complaining was their custom.[58] Voyageurs sometimes chose to limit the theatre of resistance to a small, and perhaps more effective scale by complaining to their bourgeois in private, so that they would not appear weak in front of the other men. During a difficult trip from Kaministiquia to Pembina, Alexander Henry the Younger commented that little or nothing was said during the day when the men had "a certain shame or bashfulness about complaining openly," but at night everyone came to complain about bad canoes, ineffective co-workers, and shortages of gum, wattap, and grease.[59] Often voyageurs restricted their complaining in front of their bourgeois to avoid losing favour. If they approached the bourgeois or clerk individually with strategic concerns, their demands were more likely to be met than if they openly abused their masters for unspecified grievances.[60]

When labour was scarce, men often bargained for better wages, both individually and in groups. In a large and organized show of resistance in the summer 1803, men at Kaministiquia refused to work unless they received a higher salary.[61] However, these types of group efforts to increase wages were more rare than the relatively common occurrence of men trying to individually bargain for better remuneration or conditions. Daniel Sutherland of the XYC instructed his recruiting agent in Montréal, St. Valur Mailloux, to refuse demands made by a couple of *engagés* for higher wages, and to appease the men with small presents. One *engagé* named Cartier caused turmoil by telling the XYC wintering partners that Mailloux was hiring men at significantly higher wages and by asking for his pay to be increased to that amount. Sutherland became angry with Mailloux, warning him "Always [offer more to] oarsman and steersman, but never exceed the price that I told you for going and coming [paid to the paddlers]."[62] Voyageurs could refuse to do tasks outside the normal range of their duties without extra pay as a means of

[58]Cameron, "The Nipigon Country," 38-39.

[59]Coues, ed. *New Light*, 1: 247-8, 28 July 1804.

[60]A blacksmith named Philip earned the wrath of his bourgeois, McKay, when he abused him both behind his back and to his face. Nelson, Journal "No. 5", 2 (labelled pp. 186). George Nelson felt pressured by the continual complaints made by his men about their rations. He worried that his men were spreading discontent among each other and preferred them to approach him directly with their concerns. Nelson, "A Daily Memoranda," pp. 8, Friday, 10 February 1815.

[61]Mentioned in Coues, ed., *New Light*, 1: 247, 1 July 1804.

[62]NAC, LAMC, 1802-9, vol. 1, MG19 A7, pp. 18-19, 25-26, D. Sutherland to Monsr. St. Valur Mailloux, Montréal, 10 November 1802, 29 November 1802, and 20 December 1802, (originals in the Seminaire de Quebec). My translation.

increasing their wages.[63] They also frequently demanded better working conditions. Most often their concerns centred on safety, and they could refuse to take unreasonable risks.[64] Men with valued skills and knowledge, such as interpreters and guides, were in the best position to bargain for better working conditions and more pay.[65] Because fur trade labour was frequently scarce, and the mortality rate was high, skilled men were valued. Masters often overlooked servant transgressions and met servant demands in an effort to maintain their services.

Voyageurs also attempted to deceive their masters by pretending to be ill, or by lying about resources and Native peoples in the area to evade work. It is difficult to judge the extent to which voyageurs tried to trick their masters, especially when they were successful. However, hints of this practice, and suspicions of bourgeois and clerks emerge frequently in fur trade journals, suggesting that the practice was widespread. In December 1818, stationed near the Dauphin River, George Nelson became frustrated with one of his men, Welles, who frequently sneaked in "holiday" time by travelling slowly or claiming to be lost.[66] Less suspecting bourgeois probably did not catch the "dirty tricks" more careful voyageurs played on them regularly. Some masters, however, questioned their men's dubious actions and sent out "spies" to ensure that voyageurs were working honestly.[67] Other deceptions were of a more serious nature. Alexander Mackenzie was suspicious that his interpreters were not telling prosepective Native trading partners what Mackenzie intended, which could have serious repercussions for the trade.[68]

When efforts to deceive their masters were frustrated, voyageurs could become sullen and indolent, working slowly and ineffectively, and even openly defying bourgeois orders. In one case in the fall 1800, while trying to set out from Fort Chipewyan, James Porter had to threaten to seize the wages of a man who refused to embark. When the voyageur reluctantly complied he swore that the devil should

[63]For one example of men demanding their pay be doubled for extra duties see Chaboillez, "Journal for the Year 1797," 49, Tuesday, 20 March 1798.

[64]MRB, MC, C.27, Microfilm reel #13, pp. 2, Athabasca Department, Great Slave Lake, W.F. Wentzel to Roderick McKenzie, Letters Inward, 1807-1824, 5 April 1819.

[65]NAC, MC, MG19 C1, vol. 3, microfilm reel # C-15638, pp. 8-15, François-Antoine Larocque, "Missouri Journal, Winter 1804-5"; and Nelson, "A Daily Memoranda," pp. 30-2, Saturday, 8 April 1815.

[66]See entries Monday, 2 November 1818, and from Tuesday, 1 December 1818 to Wednesday, 30 December 1818, OA, MU 842, pp. 10-11, 18-23, Diary of George Nelson, in the service of the North West Company at Tête au Brochet, 1818-19.

[67]NAC, MC, MG19 C1, Vol. 15, Microfilm reel #C-15638, pp. 7, Fragment of a journal, attributed to W. Ferdinand Wentzel, kept during an expedition from 13 June to 20 August 1800, Friday, 26 June 1800.

[68]MRB, MC, C.8, microfilm reel #14, pp. 125, Alexander Mackenzie, Journal of Great Bear Lake, March 1806.

take him for submitting to the bourgeois.[69] More serious breaches of the master and servant contract included stealing provisions from cargo. Though Edward Umphreville kept up a constant watch over the merchandise in his canoes, a father and son managed to steal a nine gallon keg of mixed liquor.[70] George Nelson described the pilfering of provisions as routine.[71] Men also sometimes stole provisions to give extra food to their girlfriends or wives.[72] For the Orcadians working in the HBC service, Burley characterizes this type of counter-theatre—working ineffectively and deceiving masters—as both a neglect of duty and as an attempt to control the work process.[73] The same applies to the voyageurs.

One area of particular unease between voyageurs and masters was the issue of voyageurs freetrading with Native peoples. Unlike the HBC, the Montréal fur trading companies did not prohibit voyageurs from trading with Native peoples on the side to augment their income; some masters even expected them to do so as long as they did not abuse the privilege.[74] However, masters were often upset to find their men

[69]On trip from Athabasca to the McKenzie River, NAC, MC, MG19 C1, Vol. 6, Microfilm reel #C-15638, pp. 50, James Porter, Journal kept at Slave Lake, 18 February 1800 to 14 February 1801, 29 September 1800. Porter quotes the man as saying "Si Je avait Point des gages que le Diable ma aport si vous ma Soucier Embarker." See also John Thomson, who records that this man, named Bernier, gave further trouble to Porter on the trip. Thompson's interpretation of Bernier's swearing is "swearing the Devel myte take him if he had stirred a Step." See entries Monday, 29 September 1800 to Saturday, 4 September 1800, MRB, MC, C.26, Microfilm reel #15, pp. 1-2, John Thompson, "Journal, Mackenzies River alias Rocky Mountain, 1800-1."

[70]OA, NWCC, MU 2199, pp. 8, photostat of original, Edward Umfreville, "Journal of a Passage in a Canoe from Pais Plat in Lake Superior to Portage de L'Isle in Rivière Ouinipique," June to July 1784, Wednesday, 23 June 1784. Forms part of the manuscript entitled "Some Account of the North West Company," by Roderick McKenzie, director of the North West Company. Typescripts can be found also in the OA, NWCC, MU 2200, Box 5, Nos. 2 (a), (b), and (c). Photostats and typescripts can also be found in NAC, MC, Vol. 55, Microfilm reel #C-15640; the MRB, MC, C.17; and the MHS, P1571. For other examples of theft see MRB, MC, C.24, Microfilm reel #2, pp. 5, Archibald Norman McLeod, Journal kept at Alexandria, 1800, Friday, 28 November 1800; OA, Angus Mackintosh Papers; MU 1956, Box 4, pp. 2-3, Journal from Michilimackinac to Montréal via the French River, summer 1813. 16 July 1813; and NAC, MC, MG19 C1, Vol. 2, microfilm reel # C-15638, pp. 10, Michel Curot, "Journal, Folle Avoine, Riviere Jaune, Pour 1803 & 1804," Lundi, 11 octobre 1803.

[71]TMRL, BR, S13, pp. 9, George Nelson's Journal "No. 1," written as a reminiscence, describing a journey from Montréal to Grand Portage, and at Folle Avoine, 27 April 1802 - April 1803, (a typescript can also be found in the George Nelson Papers of the TMRL, BR).

[72]Coues, ed., *New Light*, 1: 25, 6 August 1800.

[73]Burley, *Servants of the Honourable Company*, 139-44.

[74]Mackenzie, "A General History," 34. On the HBC prohibition of private trading see Burley, *Servants of the Honourable Company*, 24-25. However, Burley suggests that the lack of reporting on this offense may indicate that the officers tacitly allowed their men to do so (144-52).

trading with Native peoples, because they wanted to concentrate the profit into their company's hands, and considered freetrading as "contrary to the established rules of the trade and the general practice among the natives."[75] In an 1803 trial over trading jurisdiction, John Charles Stuart, a NWC clerk, testified that when any men brought skins from the wintering grounds for the purpose of trading on their private account, "it was by a Special Favour" granted by their bourgeois, supported in the clause "Part de pactons" in their contracts. Although the practice was customary, the bourgeois retained the right to grant or refuse it.[76] After the 1804 merger of the XYC and NWC, the bourgeois decided to restrict private trade to increase profitability in the newly reformed company. Any man caught with more than two buffalo robes or two dressed skins, or one of each, would be fined 50 livres NW currency, and any employee caught trafficking with "petty traders or Montréal men" would forfeit his wages. The bourgeois were able to enforce this new restriction because the merger had created a surplus of men, so that employment became tenuous, and many voyageurs were concerned that their contracts would not be renewed.[77] In the minutes of the 1806 annual meeting, NWC partners agreed to ban men from bringing furs out of the interior in order to discourage petty trading.[78]

Voyageurs sometimes moved out of the "counter-theatre of daily resistance" to engage in "swift, direct action" against their masters' rule. Deserting the service was an outright breach of the master and servant contract.[79] Desertion should not be viewed as the single and straightforward phenomenon of voyageurs quitting their jobs. Rather, voyageurs deserted for a variety of purposes. Temporary desertions could provide a form of vacation, a ploy for renegotiating terms of employment, and a means of shopping for a better job. Men deserted when they were ill and needed time to recuperate.[80] Men also deserted when they thought their lives might be in danger, as was the case in March 1805, when servants of both the NWC and XYC ran off from the fishery at Lac La Pluie because they feared the Native people there wanted to kill them.[81] Voyageurs felt they could desert because they had a

[75]Described by Ross, *Fur Hunters*, 1: 159.

[76]MHS, GLNP, Folder 7, P791, pp. 2, NWC Letters, 1798-1816, Dominique Rousseau and Joseph Bailley v. Duncan McGillivray, (originals from the Judicial Archives of Montréal).

[77]Campbell, *The North West Company*, 155.

[78]Wallace, W. Stewart, ed., *Documents Relating to the North West Company* (Toronto: Champlain Society 1934), Minutes of the Meetings of the NWC at Grand Portage and Fort William, 1801-7, with Supplementary Agreements (originals in Montréal, Sulpician Library, Baby Collection), 216, 15 July 1806.

[79]For an example see MRB, MC, C. 7, microfilm reel #4, pp. 4, Journal of John MacDonell, Assiniboines-Riviere qu'Appelle, 1793-95, (typescript copy in NAC, MC, MG 19 C 1, vol. 54, microfilm reel #C-15640), 5 December 1793 to 6 December 1793.

[80]McLeod, Journal kept at Alexandria, pp. 40, Saturday, 30 May 1801; and "The Diary of John Macdonell" in Charles M. Gates, ed., *Five Fur Traders* of the Northwest (St. Paul: Minnesota Historical Society 1965), 72, 1 June 1793.

[81]"The Diary of Hugh Faries" in Gates, ed., *Five Fur Traders*, 233-34, Monday, 25 March 1805.

clear notion of their rights as workers which was instilled by the reciprocal obligations of paternalism. This may be one of the more significant differences between Orcadians working for the HBC and the voyageurs. Orcadians did not desert very often because of the lack of "desirable places to go." Orcadians would most often desert to NWC posts, while voyageurs more often became freemen, joined Native families, or returned to the St. Lawrence valley.[82]

As part of the continual negotiation of the master and servant "social contract," bourgeois and clerks responded to voyageurs' counter-theatre with intense performances of authority. They disciplined their men for transgressions of the master and servant contract, and sought to encourage voyageur obedience. Servant privileges, such as the provision of regales or sale of liquor might be curtailed or denied.[83] Bourgeois and clerks also frequently humiliated and intimidated their men. In one case during a journey to the Peace River in summer 1793, Alexander Mackenzie was confronted with a man who refused to embark in the canoe. He wrote:

> This being the first example of absolute disobedience which had yet appeared during the course of our expedition, I should not have passed it over without taking some very severe means to prevent a repetition of it; but as he had the general character of a simple fellow, among his companions, and had been frightened out of what little sense he possessed, by our late dangers, I rather preferred to consider him as an object of ridicule and contempt for his pusillanimous behaviour; though, in fact, he was a very useful, active, and laborious man.[84]

He also confronted the chief canoe maker during the same trip about his laziness and bad attitude. Mackenzie described the man as mortified at being singled out.[85] This kind of ritualized public shaming reinforced masculine ideals of effectiveness and skill. On an expedition to the Missouri in 1805, one of Larocque's men wished to remain with Charles McKenzie's party. Larocque became angry and told the man his courage failed him like an old woman, which threw the man into a violent fit of anger.[86] On occasion, a voyageur could be whipped for delinquency,[87] and

[82] Burley, *Servants of the Honourable Company*, 153-4.

[83] For example, see McLeod, Journal kept at Alexandria, 15, Friday, 2 January 1801.

[84] Mackenzie, *Voyages from Montréal*, 329, Saturday, 15 June 1793.

[85] *passim*, pp. 373-4, Saturday, 29 June 1793.

[86] MRB, MC, C.12, Microfilm reel #6, pp. 41, Charles McKenzie, "Some Account of the Missouri Indians in the years 1804, 5, 6 & 7," addressed to Roderick McKenzie, 1809. Photostat and typescript copies can be found in NAC, MC, MG19 C1, Vol. 59, Microfilm reel #C-15640 and OA, NWCC, MU2204, Vol. 3 and MU2200 Box 5 - 4 (a), and the account is published by W. Raymond Wood and Thomas D. Thiessen, eds., *Early Fur Trade on the Northern Plains: Canadian Traders Among the Mandan and Hidatsa Indians, 1738-1818; The narratives of John Macdonell, David Thompson, François-Antoine Larocque, and Charles McKenzie* (Norman: University of Oklahoma Press 1985).

[87] For one example see McLeod, Journal kept at Alexandria, Saturday, 22 November 1800.

bourgeois and clerks sometimes used the fear of starvation as a means of asserting authority over their men.[88]

In cases of severe dereliction, bourgeois could take the liberty of firing their employees.[89] In some cases, voyageurs were happy to be let go because they desired to become freemen. Nelson fired Joseph Constant, for example, for his "fits of ill humour without cause and Constant went on to become a prosperous independent trader."[90] However, it was a very serious matter when voyageurs decided to quit. Bourgeois and clerks made efforts to recoup deserters, and could punish them with confinement.[91]

The usual difficulties of the weather, accidents, and the constant challenge of the strenuous work could lead to high levels of stress and to anxieties among bourgeois, clerks, and voyageurs. Voyageurs' blunders, lost and broken equipment, and voyageur insolence often exacerbated tensions.[92] Alexander Henry the Younger grew frustrated with one of his men named Desmarrais for not protecting the buffalo he shot from wolves. He grumbled:

> My servant is such a careless, indolent fellow that I cannot trust the storehouse to his care. I made to-day a complete overhaul, and found everything in the greatest confusion; I had no idea matters were so bad as I found them.... Like most of his countrymen, he is much more interested for himself than for his employer.[93]

On rare occasions violence punctuated the generalized tension of master-servant relations in the fur trade. Mutual resentments could lead to brawls between the masters and servants.[94]

More typically tensions in the master and servant relationship were expressed in nastiness and unfairness, rather than violence. Motivated by the desire to save money and gain the maximum benefit from their workers, bourgeois pushed their men to work hard, which could result in ill will. Most serious cases of ill will and injustice concerned bourgeois selling goods to voyageurs at inflated prices and encouraging voyageurs to go into debt as soon as they entered fur trade service. It is difficult to find many instances of "bad faith" in bourgeois writings, as they would

[88]Nelson, Journal No. 1, pp. 43, Saturday, 17 November 1809.
[89]Nelson, "A Daily Memoranda," 8, Friday, 10 February 1815; and "The Diary of Hugh Faries," pp. 235, Tuesday, 2 April 1805.
[90]TMRL, BR, S13, pp. 14-15, George Nelson's Coded Journal, 17 April - 20 October 1821, entitled "A continuation of My Journal at Moose Lake," (notes made by Sylvia Van Kirk), Thursday, 10 May 1821. Constant had been threatening to desert the service for years, and he did make arrangements with another bourgeois, William Connolly, to leave the service. *ibid.*, Thursdays, 10 and 24 May 1821, pp. 14-15, 20.
[91]"The Diary of Hugh Faries," pp. 206, Sunday, 26 August 1804.
[92]Coues, ed., *New Light*, 1: 114, 9 October 1800.
[93]*passim*, pp. 99-100, 18-19 September 1800.
[94]Cox, *Adventures*, 166-7.

not likely dwell on their cruelty as masters, nor reveal their unfair tricks. However, travellers, critics of fur trade companies, and disgruntled employees provide clues. The French Duke de La Rouchefoucault Liancourt, travelling through North America in the late eighteenth century, commented that the NWC encouraged vice among their men by paying them in merchandise, especially luxuries and rum, so that none of them ever earned a decent wage.[95] Lord Selkirk, certainly no fan of the NWC, criticized the bourgeois further for exploiting their men, pointing out that *engagés* often left their French Canadian families in distress, and were unable to provide for them because the cost of goods in the interior was double or triple the price in Lower Canada, and men were usually paid in goods rather than cash. The NWC saved further costs on men's wages by encouraging addiction to alcohol, and then paying wages in rum at inflated prices. The Company placed no ceiling on its men's credit, so that many of them fell deeply into debt.[96]

Despite Selkirk's obvious bias against the NWC, he was not alone in his misgivings about Montréal fur trade company labour practices. As a new clerk in the XYC, George Nelson was instructed to provide any trade goods his men might ask for, and to encourage them to take up their wages in any of the trade goods on board the canoe. Nelson was initially uneasy with this mode of dealing,

> for thought I what is there more unnatural, than to try to the get the wages a poor man for a few quarts of rum, some flour & sugar, a few half fathoms of tobacco, & but verly little Goods who comes to pass a few of his best years in this rascally & unnatural Country to try to get a little money so as to settle himself happily among the rest of his friends & relations.

Eventually Nelson came to justify his participation in this system of exploitation because he felt that the men would ruin themselves anyway, and that most of them were disobedient "blackguards" for whom slavery was too good.[97] Nelson was also surprised that these men could live such a carefree existence while deeply in debt and with few material possessions.[98] His comment reveals one of the deep cultural fissures between masters and servants.

Voyageur responses to the cruelty of bourgeois and clerks could reach intense heights in the ongoing counter-theatre of resistance. Ill will between servants and masters could impede work. Sometimes the tensions were so strong that voyageurs refused to share the fruits of their hunting and fishing with their masters.[99] The

[95] *Voyages dans l'Amerique par la Rouchefoucould Liancourt*, Vol. II, 225, Paris, An. 7.; cited by Thomas Douglas, Earl of Selkirk, *A Sketch of the British Fur Trade in North America; with Observations Relative to the North-West Company of Montréal*, 2nd edition (London: James Ridgway 1816), 36-7.

[96] Selkirk, *A Sketch of the British Fur Trade*, 32-47.

[97] Nelson, Journal, 13 July 1803 - 25 June 1804, 1-2, 34, Friday, 15 July 1803.

[98] TMRL, BR, S13, pp. 7-9, George Nelson, Tête au Brochet, to his parents, 8 December 1811.

[99] Nelson, "A Daily Memoranda", pp. 17-18, 40-1, Thursday, 9 March 1815, Tuesday, 23 May 1815 and Wednesday, 24 May 1815.

more outrageous instances of masters abusing servants could lead to collective resistance among the voyageurs in the form of strikes or mass desertion. When a voyageur named Joseph Leveillé was condemned by the Montréal Quarter Sessions to the pillory for having accepted the wages of two rival fur-trading firms in 1794, a riot ensued. A group made up largely of voyageurs hurled the pillory into the St. Lawrence River and threatened to storm the prison. The prisoner was eventually released and no one was punished for the incident.[100] Voyageurs seemed to have developed a reputation for mob belligerence in Lower Canada. Attorney general Jonathan Sewell warned in a 1795 letter to Lieutenant Colonial Beckworth that officers in Lower Canada should be given greater discretionary power to counter the "riotous inclinations" of the people, especially of the "lawless band" of voyageurs.[101]

Instances of mass riots or collective resistance were not unknown in New France and Lower Canada. However, the small population, diffuse work settings, and not too unreasonable seigneurial dues usually restricted expressions of discontent to individual desertions or localized conflicts.[102] Yet, the instances of collective action could have created a precedent and memory for future mass protest.[103] On occasion voyageurs deserted en masse during cargo transports or exploration missions. In these cases men worked closely in large groups doing essentially the same difficult and dangerous tasks. Communication, the development of a common attitude to work, and camaraderie fostered a collective consciousness and encouraged collective action. In the summer of 1794 a Montréal brigade at Lac La Pluie attempted to strike for higher wages. Duncan McGillivray explained:

> A few discontented persons in their Band, wishing to do as much mischief as possible assembled their companions together several times on the Voyage Outward & represented to them how much their Interest suffered by the passive obedience to the will of their masters, when their utility to the Company, might insure them not only of better treatment, but of any other conditions which they would prescribe with Spirit & Resolution.

[100]NAC, 'Civil Secretary's Letter Books, 1788-1829', RG7, G15C, vol. 2, CO42, vol. 100, Sheriff Edward Gray to Attorney General James Monk, 9 June 1794; J. Reid to same, 12 June 1794; T.A. Coffin to James McGill, 21 July 1794; cited by F. Murray Greenwood, *Legacies of Fear: Law and Politics in Quebec in the Era of the French Revolution* (Toronto: University of Toronto Press 1993), 80, 285.

[101]NAC, Jonathan Sewell Papers, MG23 GII10, Volume 9, pp. 4613-14, Jonathan Sewell to Lieutenant Colonel Beckworth, 28 July 1795. Donald Fyson brought this reference to my attention.

[102]Terence Crowley, "'Thunder Gusts': Popular Disturbances in Early French Canada," *Canadian Historical Association Historical Papers* (1979), 11-31; and Jean-Pierre Hardy et David-Thiery Ruddel, *Les Apprentis Artisans à Québec, 1660-1815* (Québec: Les Presses de L'Université du Québec 1977), 74-80.

[103]Jean-Pierre Wallot, *Un Québec qui Bougeait: trame socio-politique du Québec au tournant du XIXe siècle* (Montréal: Boréal 1973), 266-7.

When they arrived at Lac La Pluie the brigade demanded higher wages and threatened to return to Montréal without the cargo. The bourgeois initially prevailed upon a few of the men to abandon the strike. Soon after most of the men went back to work, and the ringleaders were sent to Montréal in disgrace.[104]

Efforts at collective action in the north west did not always end in failure. In his third expedition to the Missouri Country in fall 1805 and winter 1806, Charles McKenzie's crew of four men deserted. They had been lodged with Black Cat, a chief in a Mandan Village, who summoned McKenzie to his tent to inform McKenzie of their desertion. The men had traded away all of their property to Native people and intended to do the same with McKenzie's property, but Black Cat secured it. When McKenzie declared he would punish his men, Black Cat warned that the Native people would defend the voyageurs. When McKenzie tried to persuade the men to return to service, they would not yield.[105] Men who spent their winters in the *pays d'en haut* became a skilled and highly valued labour force and felt entitled to fair working conditions; they were not afraid to work together to pressure the bourgeois.[106]

Despite the occasions of mass actions, voyageurs more often acted individually than collectively. Their most powerful bargaining tool in labour relations was the option of desertion. The decision to desert could be caused by any number of poor working conditions, such as bad food, an unfair master, and difficult journeys. Voyageurs used desertion often as a means of improving their working conditions rather than quitting their jobs. Although bourgeois took voyageurs to court for deserting their contracts, the measure had little effect as voyageurs continued to desert anyway. The option to desert acted as a safety valve, relieving pressure from the master and servant relationship. If voyageurs were very unhappy with their master, they could leave to work for another company, return to Lower Canada, or become freemen. This safety valve worked against a collective voyageur consciousness. Collective action was also hindered because voyageurs valued independence.[107] They left farms where feudal relationships prevailed to enter into contracted servitude, but part of their pull to the north west may have been the promise of a more independent way of life than that on the Lower Canadian farm. Voyageurs idealized freemen and many chose this path, becoming independent hunters and petty traders, living primarily off the land with their Native families.[108]

[104]Morton, ed., *The Journal of Duncan McGillivray*, 6-7.

[105]Charles McKenzie, "Some Account of the Missouri Indians," 72, 77-8.

[106]MRB, MC, C.5, Microfilm reel #5, abridged version on Microfilm reel #6, pp. 75, 79, Alexander Henry the Younger, travels in the Red River Department, 1806, Saturday, 26 July 1806 and Thursday, 7 August 1806.

[107]Alexander Ross, *Fur Hunters of the Far West; A Narrative of Adventures in the Oregon and Rocky Mountains*, 2 vols. (London: Smith, Elder and Co. 1855), II: 236-237.

[108]Toronto; Metropolitan Reference Library; Baldwin Room; S13; George Nelson, Tête au Brochet, to his parents, 8 December 1811; pp. 9-11; and Ross, *Fur Hunters of the Far West*, I: 291-93.

Some permanent deserters maintained a casual relationship with fur trading companies, serving the occasional limited contract, or selling furs and provisions. One man, Brunet, was forced to desert because his Native wife insisted on it. He rejoined the company under a freer contract. His wife began again to pressure him to desert the company and live with her Natives relatives.[109] Another man named Vivier decided to quit his contract in November 1798 because he could not stand living with Native people, as he was ordered to do by his bourgeois, John Thomson:

> he says that he cannot live any longer with them & that all the devils in Hell cannot make him return, & that he prefers marching all Winter from one Fort to another rather than Live any Longer with them.

Thomson refused to give him provisions or equipment because in the fall he had provided him with enough to pass the winter. Thomson was frustrated with his behaviour all season, as he had refused to return to the fort when ordered. Vivier had become so disenchanted with the trade that he offered his wife and child to another voyageur, so he could return to Lower Canada, but his wife protested. Thomson finally agreed to provide him with ammunition, tobacco and an axe on credit, and Vivier left the post. It is unclear whether he remained with his Native family. A month and a half later Vivier returned to the post, and appeared to take up work again.[110] Voyageurs may have returned to work for fur trade companies because they could not find enough to eat, or desired the protection that a post provided. Fear of starvation and the dangers of the north west may have discouraged voyageurs from deserting in the first place. In one case, Alexander Henry the Younger came across a pond where André Garreau, a NWC deserter, had been killed in 1801 with five Mandans by a Swiss party.[111]

Although it is difficult to quantify the occurrence of turbulence and accommodation in the relations between masters and servants, negotiations over acceptable labour conditions dominated the north-west fur trade. Masters controlled the workforce by ensuring that all men immediately became indebted to their company, and by being the sole providers of European goods in the interior. Masters also capitalized on the risk-taking and tough masculine ethos to encourage a profitable work pace. However, their best way to maintain order was to impress their men with their personal authority which was garnered by a strong manner, bravery, and effectiveness. Formal symbols, such as dress, ritual celebrations, access to better provisions, and a lighter work load reminded voyageurs of the superior status and power of their bourgeois. This "theatre of daily rule" helped to lay out the substance

[109]Nelson, Journal, 13 July 1803 - 25 June 1804, pp. 22-3, Monday, 31 January 1804, Monday, 14 February 1804, Tuesday, 15 February 1804, and Thursday 17 February 1804.
[110]NAC, MC, MG19 C1, Vol. 7, Microfilm reel #C-15638, pp. 19-24, John Thomson, "A Journal kept at Grand Marais ou Rivière Rouge, 1798," Sunday, 18 November 1798, Monday, 19 November 1798, Tuesday, 20 November 1798, and Friday, 4 January 1799.
[111]Henry, Travels in the Red River Department, pp. 50, Wednesday, 23 July 1806.

of the hegemonic structure of paternal authority. Masters also turned to the courts to prosecute their men for breaches of contract, and attempted to cooperate with other companies to regulate the workforce, but these methods were far from successful in controlling their voyageurs. The "social contract" overshadowed the legal contract between masters and servants, establishing an effective working relationship that was key to ensuring a well-functioning trade and high profits.

In turn, voyageurs asserted their cultural autonomy and resisted master authority. Their "counter-theatre" shaped the working environment. Voyageurs generally had very high performance standards for work, which were bolstered by masculine ideals of strength, endurance, and risk-taking. Nonetheless, voyageurs created a space to continually challenge the expectations of their masters, in part through their complaining. They also set their own pace, demanded adequate and even generous diets, refused to work in bad weather, and frequently worked to rule. When masters made unreasonable demands or failed to provide adequate provisions, voyageurs responded by working more slowly, becoming insolent, and occasionally freetrading and stealing provisions. More extreme expressions of discontent included turning to the Lower Canadian courts for justice, but, like the bourgeois and clerks, voyageurs found that their demands were better met by challenging the social, rather than the legal, contract. Their strongest bargaining tool proved to be deserting the service, which they sometimes did *en masse*. Overall, voyageurs acted more individually than collectively, as the option to desert the service acted more as a safety valve against the development of a collective voyageur consciousness.

The master and servant relationship was thus a fragile balance, constantly being negotiated. Ruling-class domination was an on-going process where the degree of legitimation was always uneven and the creation of counterhegemonies remained a live option. E.P. Thompson's emphasis on theatre and the symbolic expression of hegemony ring true for the voyageurs and bourgeois, whose power struggles were as often about respect and authority as about decent wages and provisions.[112] The difficult working conditions, regular fear of starvation, and absence of a police force positioned labour mediation in the forefront of the trade and strengthened the symbolic power of the "theatre of daily rule." The "social contract" between the masters and servants overshadowed their legal contract, and determined the day-to-day relations between the two groups. Frequently, accommodation allowed the fur trade to run smoothly, and voyageurs and bosses cooperated, especially in the face of external threats. Yet just as often, labour disputes and power struggles characterized the trade.

[112]Thompson, *Customs in Common*, 74-5.

I wish to thank the Social Sciences and Humanities Research Council of Canada, the Imperial Order of the Daughters of the Empire, and the History Department at the University of Toronto for financial assistance during the research and writing of this article. I would also like to thank Allan Greer, Ian Radforth, Sylvia Van Kirk, Catherine Carstairs, and Eva Plach for their helpful comments on earlier drafts of this article.

PARDEVANT les Temoins, soussignés ; fut présent

lequel s'est volontairement engagé et s'engage par ces présentes à MESSRS. WILLIAM M'GILLIVRAY, SIMON M'GILLIVRAY, ARCHIBALD NORMAN M'LEOD, THOMAS THAIN, et HENRY MACKENZIE, de Montréal, Négocians et Associés, sous le nom de M'TAVISH, M'GILLIVRAYS & Co. et PIERRE DE ROCHEBLAVE, Ecuier, à ce present et acceptant pour hiverner pendant l'espace de

en qualité de

avoir bien et duement soin, pendant les routes, et étant rendu aux dits lieux, des Marchandises, Vivres, Pelleteries, Ustensiles, et de toutes les choses nécessaires pour le voyage ; servir, obéir, et exécuter fidèlement tout ce que les dits Sieurs Bourgeois, ou tout autre représentant leurs personnes, auquels ils pourraient transporter le présent engagement, lui commanderont de licite et honnête, faire leur profit, éviter leur dommage, les en avertir s'il vient à sa connaissance ; et généralement tout ce qu'un bon et fidèle engagé doit et est obligé de faire, sans pouvoir faire aucune traite particulière ; s'absenter ni quitter le dit service, sous les peines portées par les loix de cette Province, et de perdre ses gages. Cet engagement ainsi fait pour et moyennant la somme de

argent de Grand Portage,

avec un équipement,

qu'ils promettent et s'obligent de bailler et payer au dit engagé, un mois après son retour à Montréal, où le présent engagement finira, au bout des dits années. Car Ainsi, &c. Promettant, &c. Obligeant, &c. Renonçant, &c. FAIT ET PASSE' à

et ont signé à l'exception du dit engagé, qui ayant déclaré ne le savoir faire, de ce enquis, a fait sa marque ordinaire, après lecture faite.

"*Engagement* or contract signed by servants entering into service for fur trade partnership McTavish, McGillivrays & Co. and Pierre de Rocheblave." *Winnipeg, Provincial Archives of Manitoba, Fort William Collection*, MG1 C1/33.

Chapter 9

Gender at Work at Home: Family Decisions, the Labour Market, and Girls' Contributions to the Family Economy

Bettina Bradbury

Introduction

"Gender at work" can be read in two ways. In the first, work is a noun, and the central question is "How do definitions of skill, of appropriate work for men and women get negotiated within the workplace by men and women, workers and capital?" Recent discussions of the sexual division of labour in diverse industries, of "gender at work," the social construction of skill and of the role of unions in perpetuating women's unequal position in the workforce have made major contributions to our understanding of the complexities of the relationships between gender and class, between patriarchy and capitalism. Historical research in this field is rich and fascinating, and is reshaping both women's history and working-class history in Canada as elsewhere.[1]

"Gender at work" can also be read, if my grammar is correct, as a verb. Here the question posed would be "How does gender work as a process in society which means that men and women end up with different work and life experiences?" To answer this question involves consideration of factors other than those found in the workplace. In this paper I would like to argue that while workplace centred approaches go a long way toward explaining sex segregation within specific trades, they ignore different levels of decision making and other institutions that have already gendered the workforce before it arrives at the factory gate.[2] Equally, while approaches stressing the strength of patriarchal ideology or the importance of domestic labour help explain why married women remained out of the workplace they fail to grasp the complex interactions between patriarchy and capitalism. Furthermore they are more difficult to apply when dealing with the work of daughters rather than their mothers.

Within families decisions were made about who should stay home to look after children and do housework and who should earn wages which had wide reaching impact on the composition

Gregory S. Kealey and Greg Patmore, eds., *Canadian and Australian Labour History* (Sydney: Australian-Canadian Studies, 1990),119-40.

of the workforce. Such decisions were never made in an ideological or economic vacuum, they represented a complex and often unconscious balance between basic need, existing ideology and practise regarding gender roles, the structure of the economy, and the particular economic conjuncture. Schools taught specific skills and implanted tenacious ideas about future roles. At its broadest level this paper represents a simple plea to those looking at divisions of labour in the workplace to also consider the work done by historians of the family and education. In Canada such work offers some clues about this broader process, although little research systematically examines the question. [3] To the extent that historians interested in how gender is worked out within the workplace and in the unions ignore what happens prior to men and women's arrival at work, their explanations will fail to consider the wider and deeper sexual division of labour, which not only relegated women to jobs defined as less skilled in workplaces shared with men and to feminine ghettos, but also determined that large numbers would simply not enter the workforce or would do so only sporadically.

More specifically the paper focuses on one aspect of the question, namely how family decisions in interaction with the nature of local labour markets influenced sons' and in particular daughters' contribution to the family economy. [4] The paper concentrates on the micro-level, examining what I have been able to deduce about family decision-making processes regarding which family members should seek wage labour in two Montreal working-class wards between the 1860s and 1890s. A brief description of the major sectors employing males in Montreal is followed by an assessment of the importance of additional wage earners to working-class families. The respective work of sons and daughters within the family economy is evaluated.

The sexual division of labour within the family, and the need for additional domestic workers as well as extra wage labourers, I argue meant that the context, timing, and contours of boys' and girls' participation in wage labour were different. By looking at the role of girls in the family economy and not just in the labour market. [5] we can better see how the major changes accompanying the emergence of industrial capitalism in Montreal did not modify the dominant sexual division of labour.

Montreal Families and Wage Labour, 1860-90

The years 1860 to 1890 were characterised by the growing dominance of industrial capital in the economic structure of Montreal, the increasing dependence on wage labour of a major proportion of its population. Canada's first and largest industrial city, "the workshop" of Canada, had a wide and complex array of industries. Most important were those relating to rail and water transportation, shoemaking, clothing, and food and beverages. The metallurgy sector, dominated by production for the railroads, provided jobs for skilled immigrants from Great Britain, and some French Canadians with a long tradition of working in metal. In shoemaking and dressmaking, as in numerous other smaller trades, artisanal production was rapidly, if unevenly giving way to production in large factories. Minute divisions of labour accompanied the utilisation of new types of machinery throughout the period, drawing immigrants and French

Canadians new to the city into the myriad of largely unskilled jobs that were being created. Broadly speaking, the male workforce was divided into four groups. Best paid and most secure were the relatively skilled workers involved in the new trades that emerged with the industrial revolution—the engineers, machinists, moulders and others who worked in the foundries and new factories. More subject to seasonal and conjunctural unemployment were skilled workers in the construction trades. A third group comprised those workers in trades undergoing rapid deskilling and re-organisation, most important amongst these were the shoemakers. General unskilled labourers made up the other major sub-group within the working class. About twenty-five cents a day separated the average wage of each of these groups, setting the stage for potential differences in their standard of living, and their family economy.[6] Women and girls worked largely in separate sectors of the economy, particularly as domestic servants, dressmakers and in specific kinds of factory work. In virtually every sector, their wages were half those of males or less.[7]

The Importance of Additional Earners in the Family Wage Economy

These disparities of approximately twenty-five cents a day had the potential to separate the working class into identifiable fractions each capable of achieving a different standard of living in good times, each vulnerable in diverse ways to the impact of winter, cyclical depressions and job restructuring. Throughout most of the period the most skilled had more flexibility in their budget and a greater chance of affording to eat and live at a level that may also have helped to ward off the diseases that spread only too quickly through the poorly constructed sewers and houses of the City. This greater margin of maneouvre which higher daily wages, greater job security, and the possession of skills that were scarce and usually in demand gave to the skilled, was not constant. It was particularly likely to be eroded in times of economic depression or of rapid transformations in the organisation of work.

While some skilled workers organised successfully during this period, the major element of flexibility in the family income, for skilled and unskilled alike, lay not so much in the gains that organisation could offer, but in the ability to call on additional family members to earn wages, to gain or save money in other ways, or to limit the necessity of spending cash. Decisions about who additional family workers would be, were therefore crucial in determining the contours of the family economy and of the labour force. An examination of the importance of secondary wage earners, and of who they were in terms of their age and sex allows a better grasp of the interaction between family labour deployment decisions, the "gendering" of the workforce and the structure of the economy. This section therefore assesses the importance of additional wage earners in families headed by men in different types of occupations.[8] The following section then attempts to determine who such workers were.

The average number of workers reported by the families of the two working-class areas studied here, Ste. Anne and St. Jacques wards, fluctuated over the family life cycle. Amongst young couples who had not yet borne children, the wife would occasionally report an occupation, sometimes another relative lived with the couple, contributing to the number of workers in the household, so that until 1881 families averaged just over one worker at this first stage of a couple's married life. Most families then passed through a long period of relative deprivation as children were born, grew, and required more food, clothing and larger living premises. Between the time when the first baby was born and some children reached twelve or thirteen, the families of Ste. Anne and St. Jacques continued to have only slightly more than one worker. Then children's contribution began to make up for the difficult years. In 1861, families where half the children were still under fifteen averages 1.34 workers; once half were fifteen or more they averaged 1.97. In subsequent decades the expansion of wage labour made children's contribution even more important. Whereas in 1861 the average family with children over the age of eleven had only .48 of them at work, in 1881 it had 1.16. By 1871 the average family with offspring aged fifteen or more had nearly as many children living at home and working as there had been total number of workers a decade earlier. From .85 children at work, the number reported increased to 1.85. The total number of family workers increased from an average of under two at this stage in 1861 to nearly three a decade later. Children's wages became more and more important as children came to constitute a wage-earning family's major source of security.

The prosperity that this number of workers could have secured was temporary. It depended largely on the ability of parents to keep their wage earning children in the household. As older sons or daughters began to leave home to work or marry, the average dropped down again. If both members of a couple survived they would find themselves struggling again in their old age on a single wage, or no wage at all. For aged working-class widows and widowers, the situation was particularly bleak if there were no children able to help. [9]

Over these years the patterns of the working-class and non-working-class families diverged. In 1861 the non-working class, particularly in St. Jacques, included a high proportion of artisans and shopkeepers, men whose family economy required not the wages, but the work of wives and children. As a result, the average number of workers and of children at work in their families was higher than in all other groups except the unskilled. Over the next two decades, artisans became less and less common. Family labour was increasingly limited to enterprises like small corner groceries. Professionals and some white collar workers became more important among the non-working-class populations. After 1871, the reporting of jobs by children was least likely amongst this group.

It was within the working class family economy that the most dramatic changes occurred over this period, although there were significant and changing differences between the skilled, the unskilled and those in the injured trades. The inadequacy of the $1.00 a day or less that a labourer could earn remained a constant throughout this period. As a result, unskilled families consistently relied on additional workers when they were able to. In 1861 they averaged 1.45 workers, compared to 1.27 among the skilled. Over the next two decades the growing number of jobs available allowed them to increase the average number of family workers to 1.62 then

1.66. Amongst those with working age offspring, the average number at work increased by 123 percent from .60 in 1861 to 1.34 two decades later.

For these unskilled workers the period before children were old enough to work was the most difficult. It is worth examining how some such families managed at the critical stage of the family life cycle and later as children matured. Olive Godaire, wife of labourer Pierre, worked, probably at home as a dressmaker in 1861, to help support their three children aged two to eight. Ten years later, it was her eighteen-year-old daughter who was taking in sewing, while a ten-year-old boy was apprenticed to be a tinsmith. [10] In the case of labourer John Harrington's family, the period when the father was the only earner within the nuclear family lasted for at least eighteen years. When John and Sarah's children were under ten, they took in boarders and had John's fifty-year-old father, also a labourer, living in the household. Whatever money these extra family and household members contributed would have helped compensate for John's low wages or irregular work and they continued to take in boarders over the next ten years. Their oldest son, Timothy was still going to school in 1871 and the family was cramped in a rear dwelling where rent was minimal. Somewhere between 1871 and 1881, the boys joined their father in seeking general labouring jobs. For the first time the family lived alone, without additional household members, and with three wage earners, even three labourers, must have enjoyed a standard of living that was relatively high compared to the previous year.

The degradation of work conditions and lower wages that typified trades like shoemaking appear to have been counteracted by sending growing numbers of family members to seek steady work. In 1861 such families had only 1.08 workers—fewer than any other group. By 1881 they averaged 1.62 workers. Most dramatic was the increased importance of the contribution of children resident at home. The average number of children reporting a job amongst those families with children of working age, nearly tripled over the two decades from .55 to 1.51. At that date a few families like that of Angeline and Alexis Larivière had four workers. Their two daughters, twenty-two year old Josephine and sixteen year old Marie-Louise worked as general labourers. The twenty year old son Charles was a stone-cutter. [11]

The relative superiority of the wages of skilled workers seems clear in 1861 when they appear to have been able to manage with fewer workers than other groups—averaging only 1.27. A decade later, with 1.5 workers, they still needed fewer than the rest of the working class. The depression which hit in 1874, however, appears to have eroded much of the superiority of the skilled workers. In 1881 after seven years of major depression, which was only just lifting and which must have left many a family heavily indebted, the pattern of family labour deployment was similar to that of the unskilled and those in the injured trades.

This convergence of experiences within the working class over this period is not surprising, given the impact of the depression, combined with the degeneration of work conditions in some skilled trades. In the metal working trades, for example, trade was said to be dead in the winter of 1878. Half the local unionised workers were said to be "working at any kind of labouring work." Two years earlier, a moulder drew attention to the desperate condition of

Montreal mechanics, "working on a canal at 60 cents per day, men who have served years in securing a trade, the wages they receive being only a mockery of their misery." [12]

Families clearly attempted to shape their own economies by adjusting the numbers of wage earners to fit their expenses when they were able to do so. Additional wage earners were not only needed, but were used by all fractions of the working class, with differences stemming from the economic conjuncture, the nature of the labour market, their own life cycle and earning power. In so doing they influenced the city's labour pool and enhanced their own survival. The increasing availability of wage labour in the factories, workshops and construction sites of Montreal meant that even in times of depression more and more sons and daughters could and did find work. The reliance of employers in certain sectors on women and youths resident at home depressed male wages generally, while offering families the opportunity to counter a father's low earnings.

Economic transformation thus interacted dialectically with family needs reshaping the labour market, the family economy and the life course of children. This interaction is clearest in the case of workers in those sectors undergoing most dramatic transformation. The continued re-organisation of production in trades like shoemaking was reflected not only in the greater increase in the number of children seeking waged work over the period but also in a tendency to delay marriage and reduce family size. In the labour market in general, children living at home became a much more significant proportion of workers. [13] In the sewing trades, for example, one quarter of the workers had been co-resident children in 1861, by 1881 55% were.

Age, Gender and Additional Family Earners

To try and grasp the decision making processes behind these patterns of change in the average numbers of family members reporting work over this period, it is necessary to determine who the family workers were in terms of age and gender and to examine the families from which they came.

Older sons living at home were the most usual second earners in a family. The number of really young children or married women reporting a job was insignificant beside the importance of children in their late teens or twenties, despite the attention focussed on such young workers by contemporaries. [14] Once sons in particular reached 15 or 16 they were expected to work. "In our culture," reported Alice Lacasse, the daughter of a French Canadian immigrant to New Hampshire, "the oldest children always went to work." [15] Wage labour for boys over 15 became the norm in this period as more and more were drawn into the labour force. Growing numbers of girls did report a job, but the proportion of boys at work remained consistently higher than that for girls in all age groups. And, the pattern of involvement over a girl's life course continued to be completely different from a boy's.

By the age of fifteen or sixteen, 30 per cent of the boys who lived at home, in these two wards were reporting a job in 1861. Others no doubt sought casual labour on the streets, working from time to time, at other times roaming together in the gangs of youths which dismayed middle class contemporaries and filled up the local police courts. In 1871, when times were good, and industrial capitalism more entrenched, nearly 46% of boys this age could find a job, while in the depression of the 70s and early 80s the percentage dropped back to 37%. After the age of 16, and increasingly over the period, boys involvement with wage labour or other work would grow steadily as they aged. At ages 17 to 18, 50% reported a job in 1861, nearly 68% two decades later. By age twenty-one nearly 90% of boys listed a job at the end of the period.

Among the girls of Ste. Anne and St. Jacques wards, the work found and the pattern of job reporting over their lives was very different from that of the boys. Once boys passed their early teens they found work in a wide variety of jobs in all sectors and workplaces of Montreal. Girls, in contrast, remained concentrated within specific jobs and sectors. For girls as for boys, the chances of finding work clearly expanded with the growth of Montreal industry. At ages 15 to 16, for instance, only 13% reported a job in 1861 compared to 30% in 1881. At the peak age at which girls reported working, 19-20, 25% worked in 1861, nearly 38% did so in 1871, then 35% in 1881. Even then, however, the visible participation rate of girls was only half that of boys.[16] After age 20, the experiences of boys and girls diverged quickly and dramatically, as most, but never all women, withdrew from the formal labour market while most men found themselves obliged to seek work for the rest of their lives.

For those girls who did earn wages, then, paid labour was apparently undertaken for a brief period of their lives prior to marriage. At any one time, most girls aged fifteen or more who remained at home with their parents in these wards reported no job at all. Joan Scott and Louise Tilly have suggested that within the "industrial mode of production" "single women are best able to work, *since they have few other claims on their time.*"[17] The discrepancy in the formal wage labour participation rates for boys and girls in these two Montreal wards suggests to me that single women did, in fact, have other claims on their time. In particular, the heavy and time consuming nature of nineteenth century housework, the prevalence of disease, the wide age spread amongst children in most families, and the myriad of other largely invisible pursuits and strategies necessary to survival for the working-class family, meant that many of these girls were needed by their mothers to help with work at home. Their role in the division of labour within the family is highlighted on one census return where members' roles were explicitly described. Louis Coutur, a carter who was fifty in 1861, reported that his twenty-one-year-old son was a shoemaker, his wife's job was "housework."[18] It seems fair to assume, making allowance for the under-enumeration of steady labour and casual work among daughters, that most of the girls who listed no job or school attendance, worked periodically, if not continually, at domestic labour as mother's helpers in and around the home. It is thus in the light of family decisions about the allocation of labour power at home, as well as in the structure of jobs available in the marketplace, that the patterns of children's wage labour as well as of their schooling must be interpreted.

At home, girls served an apprenticeship in the reproduction of labour power—in baby-sitting, cleaning, mending, sewing, cooking, and shopping, and by the end of the century in nursing and hygiene.[19] Religious leaders were explicit about the need for mothers to educate their daughters in their future roles. "Apply yourselves especially to the task of training your daughters in the functions they will have to perform for a husband and family, without neglecting your other children," wrote Père Mailloux in a manual for Christian parents that was republished several times between the middle and end of the nineteenth century.[20] When girls attended school, the subjects learned were not very different. Education for females, except in a few expensive academies, out of reach of the working class, taught only the most basic and general of subjects and housekeeping-type skills. Whereas boys' schools offered bookkeeping and geography, girls' schools offered music, needlework, and sewing.[21] Curriculums aimed to prepare girls for their future role as housekeeper, wife, and mother.[22] The minister of education was explicit. He feared that too many young women were being educated above their station in life, and suggested that bookkeeping and domestic economy constituted the best basis of female education.[23] In separate schools, with curriculum that moulded life roles based on gender distinctions, girls were not going to reshape their futures dramatically by slightly increasing the average number of years that they spent at school and in the workplace over this period.

Girls then, did become secondary wage earners within the working-class family economy, were increasingly likely to do so over this period, but remained less likely to report a job than were boys. The importance of their contribution to domestic labour, the lower wages they could make in the formal labour market, or an ideological repulsion to girls' labour either within the working class or amongst capitalists, constitute partial explanations for their lower rate of participation. In the absence of interviews or written memoirs, it is important to examine the work patterns of specific families more closely to see what reasons can be deduced from the evidence.[24]

Even among the families apparently in greatest need, sons seem to have been sent out to work in preference to daughters. If any families needed to draw on as many workers as possible, it should have been those headed by the labourers or shoemakers of these wards. In such families, food costs alone for a family with several growing children rapidly outstripped a man's incoming wages. Yet even these families appear to have avoided sending girls out to work, if possible. Among labourers' families in Ste. Anne in 1881, for example, 66 percent of those who had boys over ten reported having a son at work, while only 28 percent of those with girls the same age did so. If older brothers were working, girls generally did not. Girls of age twenty or more would stay at home while a teenage son worked. Their respective roles seem clearly defined. Twenty-six-year-old Ellen Mullin, for example, reported no occupation. Two brothers, aged nineteen and twenty-three worked as carters. Ellen's role was to help her mother with the domestic labour for the three wage earners and her fourteen-year-old younger brother.[25]

In Ste. Anne, even families without sons, or with young sons only, seem to have been either unwilling to send girls to work or unable to find work that was seen as suitable in the neighbourhood. Forty-two-year-old Octave Ethier must surely have had trouble supporting his four daughters aged one to seventeen and his wife on his labourer's wages. Yet neither seventeen-year-old Philomène, nor fifteen-year-old Emma reported having a job. [26]

The girls in labourers' families who did report an occupation fell into two categories. Half were the oldest child, either with no brothers or only brothers who were much younger than they were. Nineteen-year-old Sarah Anne Labor, for instance, was the oldest in a family of six children. The closest brother was only seven. She worked as a soap maker. Her wages, and the fact that the family shared the household with several other families, must have helped make ends meet. [27]

The second group of girl workers in Ste. Anne and St. Jacques came from labourers' families that sent almost all their children to work regardless of gender. Catherine Harrigan, for instance, was fourteen. She worked as a servant. Her two brothers aged fifteen and twenty were labourers like their father. In the family of St. Jacques labourer Damase Racette, four girls aged seventeen to twenty-five were all dressmakers, as was his wife, Rachel. A twenty-seven-year-old son, was a cigar maker. [28] This latter group of families appears the most desperate, perhaps because of recurrent illness, or the habitual drunkenness of a parent. When Commissioners Lukas and Blackeby were examining the work of children in Canadian mills and factories in 1882, they reported finding too many cases in the cities and factory districts where parents with "idle habits" lived "on the earnings of the children, this being confirmed" in their eyes by one instance where three children were at work, having a father as above described. [29] Yet, such a family could simply have been taking advantage of the fact of having more children of working age to make up for years of deprivation on the inadequate wages most family heads could make. Two years later, reports made to the Ontario Bureau of Industries stressed the inadequate wages of family heads as the major cause of children working, while mentioning that dissipation of the husband or father was less often a cause. [30] When a father was chronically ill, or a habitual drunkard, the wages of several children would indeed have been necessary to support a family. The use of daughters and of children aged ten to twelve to earn wages in this minority of labourers' families contrasts with the absence of such workers in other labourers' families, highlighting the relative infrequency of a daughter's work, even among those in greatest need.

Was it in part working-class ideology that kept girls at home if at all possible, seeing the workplace as unfit for them, or was it rather a pragmatic response to the fact that boys wages rapidly outstripped those of girls? Pragmatism, made necessary by the exigencies of daily existence, must certainly have played an important part. It made good sense to have boys earn wages rather than girls, for while young children of each sex might earn a similar wage, once they reached fifteen or sixteen, girls' wages were generally half those of a young man. On the other hand, when there was work available that girls could do, more were likely to report a job. Thus the labourers of St. Jacques were more likely to have daughters at work than those of Ste. Anne. An equal percentage of those with children eleven or over had girls at work as had boys. The fact that nearly 80 percent of these girls worked in some branch of the sewing industry shows how advantage was taken of the availability of this kind of work in the neighbourhood.

Family labour deployment decisions, then, were forged in the context of their own needs, invariably arising partly from the size, age, and gender configurations of the family, as well as from the kind of work the family head could find. They were realised in relationship with the structure of the local labour market, of job possibilities, and of local wage rates for men and women, boys and girls. And they were influenced by perceptions, ideologies, and gut reactions about what was appropriate for sons and daughters. Thus, it was not just the fact that sewing was available in St. Jacques ward that made this such a popular choice for daughters living in that ward, for putting out could theoretically operate anywhere in the city or the surrounding countryside. It was, I suspect, the very fact that it could be done at home that was crucial. For, while domestic service no doubt took some young women from families in these wards away from their own families and into the homes of others, sewing usually kept daughters working at home.[31]

Home-work offered parents, and mothers in particular, several advantages. Firstly, they could oversee their daughters' work and behaviour, avoiding the individualism that working in a factory might encourage, and skirting the dangers and moral pitfalls that at least some contemporaries associated with factory work for young, unmarried women.[32] More importantly, girls sewing at home, like their mothers, could combine stitching and housework, could take care of younger children, run odd errands or carry water as needed, because they were right there and were always paid by the piece.

The clustering of two to five family members, all seamstresses, commonly found in the census returns for St. Jacques ward suggests very strongly that here was a centre of the home-work that was crucial to Montreal's sewing and shoemaking industries during this period. It was not uncommon to find three to four sisters, ranging in age from eleven to twenty-eight all working, presumably together, as sewing girls. In the Mosian family of St. Jacques ward, for instance, four daughters worked as seamstresses in 1871. The father was a labourer, and although the wife reported no occupation, she probably also did some sewing at home at times.[33] In 1881, the family of Marie and Michel Guigère had reached a relatively secure stage in their family life cycle. With nine children at home aged two to twenty-three, this joiner's family reported seven workers. Four of the girls, aged thirteen to twenty-three were seamstresses, one son worked as a labourer, and the thirteen-year-old son was an apprentice. The girls could combine sewing with helping their mother keep house for other workers, caring for the younger children, shopping, cooking, cleaning, and also looking after her husband's seventy-year-old father who lived with them. Marie too probably helped sporadically with sewing.[34]

Some parents with the liberty to choose must have been reluctant to expose their daughters to the long hours, continual supervision, exhausting work, and brutal forms of discipline that existed in some of Montreal's workshops and factories. Work at home could counteract such factors of "repulsion"[35] in some of the sectors employing girls. Cigar-making factories provided jobs for girls and boys in Ste. Anne and St. Jacques alike. While some manufacturers appear to have been decent men, neither fining nor beating their employees, others, in an apparently desperate attempt to control their youthful workforce resorted to physical violence, heavy fines, even locking up children as they strove to mould this young generation of workers to industrial work. Children, like adults, in these factories worked from six or seven in the morning until six at night, and sometimes later.[36] Unlike adult males, they were subject to a vast array of disciplinary measures aimed at making them more productive and more responsible as workers. One child reported:

> If a child did anything, that is, if he looked on one side or other, or spoke, he would say: I'm going to make you pay 10 cents fine, and if the same were repeated three or four times, he would seize a stick or a plank, and beat him with it.[37]

Mr. Fortier's cigar-making factory was described as a "theatre of lewdness." There was said to be "no such infamous factory as M. Fortier's ... nowhere else as bad in Montreal." There, one cigar maker described apprentices as being "treated more or less as slaves."[38] It was the evidence of the treatment of one eighteen-year-old girl that really shocked both the public and the commissioners examining the relations between labour and capital in 1888. Georgina Loiselle described how Mr. Fortier beat her with a mould cover because she would not make the 100 cigars as he demanded.

> *I was sitting, and he took hold of me by the arm, and tried to throw me on* the ground. He did throw me on the ground and beat me with the mould cover.
>
> Q. Did he beat you when you were down?
>
> A. Yes, I tried to rise and he kept me down on the floor.[39]

The case of Mr. Fortier's cigar factory was not typical. It created a sensation when the evidence was heard. At least some of the mothers of girls working there got together, perhaps encouraged by Mr. Fortier, to give evidence to counteract the impact of such bad publicity. "I am the mother of a family and if I had seen anything improper I would not have stayed there," explained a Mrs. Levoise. "I have my girl working there."[40]

While conditions in other Montreal factories were not as extreme, there was sufficient evidence of beatings, other draconian forms of discipline and heavy fines to explain why many girls and their parents may have wished to avoid factory labour. In cotton factories there was some evidence of boys and girls being beaten. Furthermore, fines in at least one Montreal cotton factory could reduce pay packages by between $1.00 and $12.00 in two weeks. Work there began at 6:25 a.m. and finished at 6:15 p.m. When extra work was required, employees had to stay until 9 p.m., often without time off for supper. [41] There were some perks to work in the textile industry. Nineteen-year-old Adèle Lavoie explained that the girls were accustomed to "take cotton to make our aprons." Apparently this was usually allowed, but on at least one occasion she was accused by the foreman of having taken forty to fifty yards. When a search of her house produced no results, she reported that the foreman returned to the factory to insult and harrass her sister. When she did not produce the cotton, "he stooped at this time and raising the skirt of my sister's dress, he said she had it under her skirt." [42]

Airless, hot, dusty factories, such sexual abuse by foremen, work conditions, and the long hours, were all factors that may have discouraged parents from sending girls into factory work. More significant were the wages they earned. For children under fourteen or so, wages varied little by sex. After that, male and female differentials hardened. Girl apprentices in dressmaking, mantlemaking, and millinery sometimes earned nothing for several years until they learned the trade; then they received around $4.00 a week only. "Girls" in shoe manufactories received $3.00 to $4.00 compared to the $7.00 or $8.00 earned by men. A girl bookbinder made between $1.50 and $6.00 weekly, compared to an average of $11.00 for male journeymen. Even on piece-work, girls and women generally received less than men. In general, wage rates for women were approximately half those of men. [43]

Duties at home and low wages, whether they worked in or outside the home, meant that whereas over this period more and more working-class boys would have reached manhood accustomed to wage labour, their sisters were much more likely to move backwards and forwards between paid work and housework in response to the family's economic needs, and their position in the household. Once boys, and particularly those who had been fortunate enough to acquire a skill in demand in the marketplace, reached their late teens, their earning power might rival that of their father. Wage labour offered such children potential freedom from their family in a way that had not been possible in family economies based on shared work and the inheritance of property. Such freedom was seldom possible for girls, unless they were willing to complement wage labour with prostitution.

Age, Gender, and Changing Patterns of Residence, Schooling, and Domestic Labour

Yet, boys in general do not appear to have taken dramatic advantage of such potential freedom. Nor did girls. [44] In 1861, living with others was still an important stage in the lives of some young people of both sexes. Amongst the seventeen-year-old girls residing in Ste. Anne and St. Jacques, 35 percent were boarding with other families, living with relatives or working and living in as a servant. Twenty years later, only 12 percent of girls that age were not living with their parents, and half of these were already married. Amongst boys aged eighteen 34 percent were not living with their parents in 1861 compared to only 17 percent two decades later. Living longer at home with their parents was a fundamental change in the life cycle of boys and girls alike during this period of industrial expansion. [45]

Behind the percentages of children living with their parents or elsewhere lies a complex history of tension between family needs and individual desires, of children balancing off the advantages of the services offered at home against the relative independence that living with strangers, or even relatives might offer.[46] For all families who had passed through at least fifteen years of budget stretching, house sharing, and debt building while their children were young, the relative prosperity that several workers could offer was to be jealously guarded. It was precisely "because young adults could find jobs" that it "was in the interest of parents to keep their children at home as long as possible."[47] The patterns of residence of children suggest that, whatever conflicts there were overall, in these two wards of Montreal between 1861 and 1881 it was increasingly the parents who were the winners.

The motives behind individual decisions, the weight of traditions of family work, are difficult to grasp in the absence of written records. The factors constraining or encouraging one choice or another are clearer. Most children would have left home once they had a job only if their wages were adequate to pay for lodgings and they felt no commitment to contributing to the family income.[48] Clearly more older boys earned enough to pay for room and board than did girls. Thus, in 1871, when work was readily available, 29 percent of the twenty-three-year-old males living in these wards were boarding or with relatives; 39 percent were living with their parents and 32 percent had married. Amongst girls the same age, the low wages they could make severely limited their options. Only 15 percent were boarding; 41 percent were still with their parents, and 44 percent were already married. The contraction of work and lower wages that accompanied the Great Depression, which hit in 1874, limited the possibility of leaving home to lodge with others or to marry. In 1881, the percentage of twenty-three-year-old boys married had dropped to 25 percent; only 10 percent were boarding or living with relatives. Sixty-five percent remained at home with their parents, presumably pooling resources to survive the difficult times. The depression appears to have hastened the decline of this stage of semi-autonomy. What occurred in subsequent years remains to be determined.

The different roles of boys and girls in the family economy are confirmed in the different patterns of school attendance by age and sex. In general, school and work appear to have been complementary rather than in competition. Some children began school at four years old. By age seven approximately 60 percent of boys and girls were receiving some education. In 1881 this percentage rose to a peak of 78 percent for eight- and nine-year-old boys, and of around 80 percent for girls aged nine to twelve, then fell off rapidly once both sexes reached thirteen. The proportion of children receiving some schooling increased, but not dramatically, between 1861 and 1881. Age, gender, and the economic conjuncture created variations within this overall trend. Most important was the more erratic pattern in the attendance of boys that hints at relationships between age, gender, schooling, and wage labour that require further investigation. Overall the percentage of ten- to fourteen-year-old girls at school increased slowly but steadily from 57 percent in 1861 to 68 percent in 1881.[49] The increase was greater in St. Jacques than Ste. Anne, but the pattern was similar. Amongst boys in each ward, in contrast, the proportion at school was lower in 1871 than any other year, and the proportion of ten- to nineteen-year-olds at work increased. In Ste. Anne, in particular, the factories, workshops, and general labouring jobs attracted growing numbers of these youths. The percentage of fifteen- to nineteen-year-old boys reporting working in that ward increased from thirty-eight in 1861 to sixty-four a decade later. While a certain number of families appear to have taken advantage of boom periods to draw their sons, in particular, out of school, the majority of families appear to have got the best of both worlds. Most working-class boys went to school for varying lengths of time before they reached thirteen or so, and then sought wage labour.

These figures confirm the greater importance of a son's wage contribution to the family economy. Girls' role is clear in the high proportion that continued to report neither a job, nor school attendance. Transformations of the economy and the passage of time were slow to modify this gender difference in the relationship between girls' and boys' schooling, and their roles in the family economy. A study conducted in Quebec in 1942, just before schooling was finally made compulsory in that province, found that among children quitting school before the age of sixteen, 61 percent of girls gave as their reason, "Maman avait besoin de moi," while 50 percent of boys stated, "Ma famille avait besoin d'argent." Only 10 percent of girls gave that reason.[50] The centrality of girls' domestic labour in a different Canadian city, Toronto, is corroborated by evidence showing that potential foster parents in that city at the turn of the century were four times more likely to seek girls than boys, specifically for their usefulness as domestics and nursemaids.[51]

Conclusion

Gender was clearly at work in both senses of the word in nineteenth-century Montreal. On the one hand, the labour market was characterised by a sexual division of labour which, despite the rapid and dramatic changes occuring in the period, limited the numbers of jobs where capitalists considered employing women. This was not immutable, as the cases where "girls" were used as strikebreakers made clear. Montreal's labour market included major sectors, particularly sewing and shoemaking, that employed large numbers of girls and women. Yet, the figures of labour-force participation rates for the two wards studied here, suggest strongly that girls and women seldom entered the workforce in proportions equivalent to their brothers or boys the same age, and that over their life courses their participation was totally different.

The reasons why lie at least partially within the workings of the family wage economy. Working-class families in Montreal clearly both needed and used additional family workers to counteract low wages, and to improve their standard of living. The number of extra workers varied with the skill of the family head, and the worth of that skill in the labour market. Thus, while in good times, skilled workers managed with fewer family workers than the unskilled or those in injured trades, economic depression eroded such superiority. Yet whatever complex and probably tension-loaded decisions were made about who would seek what kind of work, boys were much more likely to be the auxiliary wage earners than girls.

To explain why brings us, in a sense, to the heart of the debate about the relative importance of patriarchy and capitalism in explaining women's oppression. [52] That the domestic labour of wives has been crucial both to family survival and to women's inequality has long been recognised both empirically and theoretically. But where do daughters fit in? Fathers, one could argue, by keeping girls at home along with their mothers to serve their daily need for replenishment, ensured that the work of all women was viewed as intermittent and secondary to that of the major wage earners. [53] Alternatively, the accent can be put on the nature of specific industries, or more generally on the capitalist labour market, which, by setting women's wage rates at half those of men, made it logical to send boys to work rather than girls. [54] Unequal access to work on the same terms as men thus not only perpetuated women's position in the home, but tragically disadvantaged those single women and widows who alone, or supporting children or elderly parents, had to live on such wages.

Clearly a dialectic is at work here. Neither empirically, nor theoretically, can the workings of patriarchy, or of capitalism be neatly separated from each other. [55] The nature of the interaction between the two and the weight of one over the other will vary historically and geographically. Among Montreal families, decisions were made in part in relation to existing jobs and wage rates, and such decisions perpetuated, reified the idea that women's work was temporary, performed before marriage or in moments of family crisis. [56] Admitting the dialectic adds complexity to the explanation but remains, I suspect, insufficient. It does so, because the emphasis remains on the formal, wage-earning labour market. Domestic labour in the nineteenth century was fundamental to family survival, to the transformation of wages into a reasonable standard of living, and to the reproduction of the working class. Historians have recognised the importance of this job for the working-class wife and mother, the role of daughters has been examined less explicitly. [57] Yet, for nineteenth-century mothers whose children were widely spaced in age, in whose homes technology had made virtually no inroads to lighten their labour, the help of daughters was invaluable. Housewives had no control over the amount of wages the husband earned, and little over how much was turned over to them. Housework was labour intensive and time consuming. One of the only ways in which wives could control the content and intensity of their work was to get children to help. Wherever possible, once girls reached an age where they could be of use to the mother, they were used to babysit, to run errands, to clean, sew, and cook. If this could be combined with wage earning activities, as in the case of home-work in the sewing industry, then such girls did work more formally. If there were no brothers of an age to earn, daughters might work in factories, offices, shops or as domestics. But the need of mothers for at least one helper at home would mean, that the rate of formal labour-force participation for girls would generally be lower than that for boys. [58] Patriarchal ideas within the working class, elements of male pride and self-interest, economic pragmatism and the daily needs of mothers and housewives thus interacted, creating a situation in which most girls served an apprenticeship in domestic labour prior to, or in conjunction with, entering the workforce. [59] In cities and towns where the labour market was completely different, where whole families or women were explicitly sought by employers, this division of labour, indeed, the very institutions of marriage and the family could be modified. The question of how to ensure that the necessary domestic labour was performed, however, would remain fundamental.[60] The working out of roles by gender at home would continue to influence the configurations of gender at work.

Endnotes

1 Heidi Hartmann, "Capitalism, Patriarchy, and Job Segregation by Sex", *Signs* 1 (Spring, 1976): 137-69; Judy Lown, "Not So Much a Factory, More a Form of Patriarchy: Gender and Class During Industrialisation" in E. Garmarnikow et. al., *Gender, Class, And Work* (London, 1983); Sonya O. Rose, "Gender at Work: Sex, Class, and Industrial Capitalism" *History Workshop Journal* 21 (Spring, 1986): 113-31; Nancy Grey Osterud, "Gender Divisions and the Organization of Work in the Leicester Hosiery Industry" in Angela V. John, *Unequal Opportunities, Women's Employment in England 1800-1918* (Oxford: Basil Blackwell, 1986), 45-70. Sylvia Walby, *Patriarchy at Work: Patriarchal and Capitalist Relations in Employment* (Minneapolis: University of Minnesota Press, 1986); Ruth Milkman, *Gender at Work: The Dynamics of Job Segregation by Sex during World War II* (Urbana: University of Illinois Press, 1987). For Canadian articles touching the question see: Gail Cuthbert Brandt, "The Transformation of Women's Work in the Quebec Cotton Industry, 1920-1950" in *The Character of Class Struggle: Essays in Canadian Working Class History, 1840-1985*, ed. Bryan D. Palmer (Toronto: McClelland and Stewart, 1986); Mercedes Steedman, "Skill and Gender in the Canadian Clothing Industry, 1890-1940" in *On the Job: Confronting the Labour Process in Canada*, ed. Craig Heron and Robert Storey (Montreal: McGill-Queen's University Press, 1986), 152-76; Marta Danylewycz and Alison Prentice, "The Evolution of the Sexual Division of Labour in Teaching: A Nineteenth-Century Ontario and Quebec Case Study," *Histoire sociale/Social History* 6 (1983): 81-109; Marta Danylewycz and Alison Prentice, "Teachers, Gender, and Bureaucratising School Systems in Nineteenth-Century Montreal and Toronto," *History of Education Quarterly* 24 (1984): 75-100; Jacques Ferland, "Syndicalisme parcellaire et syndicalisme collectif: Une interpretation socio-technique des conflits ouvriers dans deux industries québecoises, 1880-1914," *Labour/Le Travail* 19 (Spring 1987): 49-88.

2 This argument is obviously not mine alone. It is fundamental to much of the discussion of the workings of patriarchy and to the domestic labour debate, where too often it remains at an abstract theoretical level or based on cursory historical data. It is worth making here because much theoretical work places too much emphasis on either capitalist relations or reproduction and patriarchy, simplifying the complexity of relations between the two, while historical literature on the workplace or the family tend to treat the relation between the two simplisticly.

3 Joy Parr's recent articles offer the first major sustained analysis in which decisions and conditions in the home and in the workplace and the relationship between the two are constantly and systematically examined. See especially "Rethinking Work and Kinship in a Canadian Hosiery Town, 1910-1950," *Feminist Studies* 13, 1 (Spring 1987): 137-62; and also "The Skilled Emigrant and Her Kin: Gender, Culture, and Labour Recruitment," *Canadian Historical Review* 68, 4 (Dec. 1987): 520-57, reprinted in Veronica Strong-Boag and Anita Clair Fellman, eds., *Rethinking Canada: The Promise of Women's History*, 2nd ed. (Toronto: Copp Clark Pitman, 1991), 33-55. Gail Cuthbert-Brandt does so in a different sense in "Weaving It Together: Life Cycle and the Industrial Experience of Female Cotton Workers in Quebec, 1910-1950," *Labour/Le Travailleur* 7 (Spring 1981). Mark Rosenfeld's recent article "'It Was a Hard Life': Class and Gender in the Work and Family Rhythms of a Railway Town, 1920-1950," *Historical Papers* (1988), and reprinted in the volume, carefully unravels how the rhythms of work in the running trades structured the family economy and gender roles in Barrie, Ontario, a railway town.

4 No Canadian works directly confront this question either in the econometric sense in which Claudia Goldin poses

it in "Family Strategies and the Family Economy in the Late Nineteenth Century: The Role of Secondary Workers," in Theodore Hershberg, *Philadelphia, Work, Space, Family and Group Experience in the Nineteenth Century* (New York: Oxford University Press, 1981), 277-310, or in the more feminist and qualitative way that Lynn Jamieson poses it in "Limited Resources and Limiting Conventions: Working-Class Mothers and Daughters in Urban Scotland c. 1890-1925" in *Labour and Love: Women's Experience of Home and Family, 1850-1940*, ed. Jane Lewis (Oxford: Basil Blackwell, 1986), 49-69.

5 Marjorie Cohen makes a similar argument without elaborating on its implications for daughters in stating that "the supply of female labour was limited by the labour requirements of the home." *Women's Work, Markets, and Economic Development in Nineteenth-Century Ontario* (Toronto: University of Toronto Press, 1988), 139. Her insistence on the importance of domestic production and women's work in the home for rural and urban families alike and for an understanding of the wider economy represents an important contribution to economic history as well as to the history of women and the family in Canada.

6 On the average, in the early 1880s, for example, a labourer earned around $1.00 a day, a shoemaker $1.25, a carpenter $1.50, and various more highly skilled workers anything from $1.75 (blacksmith) up. See Bettina Bradbury, "The Working-Class Family Economy, Montreal, 1861-1881" (Ph.D. diss., Concordia University, 1984), 18; *Canada*, Parliament, Sessional Papers, 1882, Paper No. 4, Appendix 3, Annual Report of the Immigration Agent, 110-11, lists wages in a variety of trades.

7 In this, Montreal and Canada were little different from other cities and countries, nor has much of the discrepancy been eliminated today.

8 The figures used in this paper are derived from research done for my Ph.D thesis, currently under revision for publication. A 10 percent random sample was taken of households enumerated by the census takers in Ste. Anne and St. Jacques in 1861, 1871, and 1881. This resulted in a total sample of 10,967 people over the three decades. They resided in 1,851 households and 2,278 families as defined by the census takers.

9 For a brief and preliminary examination of how widows of all ages survived, see my "Surviving as a Widow in Nineteenth-Century Montreal," *Urban History Review* 17, 3 (1989): 148-60, reprinted in *Rethinking Canada*, 2nd ed., ed. Strong-Boag and Fellman.

10 These life histories were recreated by tracing families between the censuses of 1861, 1871, and 1881.

11 Mss. Census, St. Jacques, 1881, 17, p.110.

12 *Iron Moulders Journal*, Jan. and June, 1878, Report of Local 21; *Iron Moulders Journal*, Jan. 1876, Report of Local 21 and open letter from local 21 to the editor, cited in Peter Bischoff, "La formation des traditions de solidarité ouvrière chez les mouleurs Montréalais: la longue marche vers le syndicalisme, 1859-1881," *Labour/ Le Travail* 21 (Spring 1988): 22. Bischoff suggests, sensibly, that amongst moulders the homogenising experience of these years of depression left them more open to the idea of including less skilled workers in their union in the 1880s. The widespread appeal of the Knights of Labor could be seen in the same light.

13 In 1861, for example, only 16 percent of those reporting jobs in these two wards were children residing at home; twenty years later nearly one-third of all reported workers were offspring living with their parents. Peter Bischoff found a similar trend amongst moulders. The percentage of moulders for the entire city of Montreal that were sons living with their parents rose from 25 percent in 1861 to nearly 40 percent in 1881. Peter Bischoff, "Les ouvriers mouleurs à Montréal, 1859-1881" (M.A. thesis, Université de Québec à Montréal, 1986), 108.

14 There is no doubt that the wage labour both of young children and married women was under-enumerated. However, as no labour laws existed in Quebec until 1885, and education was not compulsory until 1943, it is unlikely that fear of repercussions would have inhibited parents from responding as it might have elsewhere. It seems fair to assume that the under-reporting of children's jobs, and probably married women's, would have been no greater in Montreal than in other cities of Canada, England, or America, and possibly less.

15 Tamara K. Hareven and Randolph Langenbach, *Amoskeag: Life and Work in an American Factory City* (New York: Pantheon Books, 1978), 262.

16 Caution has to be exercised when using reported jobs for women and children. There is a tendency now in some of the literature on the subject to suggest that gender differentials in work-force participation are largely a result of women s work not being adequately enumerated.

While I am sure that some under-enumeration of women's work occurred in Montreal, as elsewhere, I don't think that under-enumeration can explain away the differential. Nor is the phenomenon easy to measure. More important, I think, was the nature of women's work, which because of its lack of regularity, its more informal nature, was less likely to be reported. On the problem of under-reporting see, in particular, Sally Alexander, "Women's Work in Nineteenth-Century London: A Study of the Years 1820-1850" in *The Rights and Wrongs of Women*, ed. Juliett Mitchell and Ann Oakley (London: Penguin Books, 1976), 63-66; Karen Oppenheim Mason, Maris Vinovskis, and Tamara K. Hareven, "Women's Work and the Life Course in Essex County, Massachusetts, 1880," in Tamara K. Hareven, *Transitions: The Family and the Life Course in Historical Perspective* (New York: Academic Press, 1979), 191; Margo A. Conk, "Accuracy, Efficiency and Bias: The Interpretation of Women's Work in the U.S. Census of Occupations, 1890-1940," *Historical Methods* 14, 2 (Spring 1981): 65-72; Edward Higgs, "Women, Occupations, and Work in the Nineteenth-Century Censuses," *History Workshop* 23 (Spring 1987).

17 Joan Scott and Louise Tilly, *Women, Work, and Family* (New York: Holt, Rinehart and Winston, 1979), 231.

18 Mss. Census, 1861,. St. Jacques, 11, p. 7750.

19 By the end of the century the need for this kind of education of daughters was being explicitly preached by Montreal doctors and by church representatives, and was formalised in Quebec with the creation of écoles menagères after the 1880s. Carole Dion, "La femme et la santé de la famille au Québec, 1890-1940" (M.A. thesis, Université de Montréal, 1984).

20 A. (Père) Mailloux, *Le manuel des parents Chrétiens* (Quebec, 1851, 1910), cited in Carole Dion, "La femme et la santé de la famille," 60-65.

21 L.A. Huguet-Latour, *L'Annuaire de Ville Marie: Origine, utilité, et progrès des institutions catholiques de Montréal* (Montreal, 1877), 165-70.

22 Marie-Paule Malouin, "Les rapports entre l'école privée et l'école publique: L'Academie Marie-Rose au 19e siècle" in *Maîtresses de maison, maîtresses d'école*, ed. Nadia Fahmy-Eid and Micheline Dumont (Montreal: Boreal Express, 1983), 90.

23 Québec, *Documents de la Session*, 1874, "Rapport du Ministre de l'instruction publique," vii.

24 In Lynn Jamieson's study of working-class mothers and daughters in Scotland, which is based on interviews, she makes it clear that mothers made different demands upon boys and girls in terms of the contributions they should make to the family economy. Mothers "pre-occupied with their housekeeping responsibilities" were much more likely to keep girls home from school to help with housework than to encourage boys to go out and earn. If a father died, for example, daughters or sons might enter full-time paid employment, but if a mother died "only daughters left school early to become full-time housekeepers," "Working-Class Mothers and Daughters in Scotland" in *Labour and Love*, 54, 65.

25 Mss. Census, Ste. Anne, 1881, 5, p. 1.

26 Mss. Census, Ste. Anne, 1881, 5, p. 1.

27 Mss. Census, Ste. Anne, 1881, 9, p. 208

28 Mss. Census, St. Jacques, 1881, 17, p. 340.

29 "Report of the Commissioners Appointed to Enquire into the Working of the Mills and Factories of the Dominion and the Labour Employed therein," Canada, Parliament, *Sessional Papers*, 1882, Paper No. 42, p. 2.

30 Annual Report of the Ontario Bureau of Industries, 1884, cited in Cohen, *Women's Work*, 128.

31 The fact that domestic service was Montreal's leading employment for girls, and that it usually involved living in, complicates this analysis of the work of children. Girls could work away from home as a domestic and contribute their pay to their parents; they would not, however, figure among the average number of workers found in census families, nor would their experience be captured in the proportion of girls having a job. On the other hand, neither is that of any boys who left to find work in construction shanties, lumbering camps, railroad work, etc. The figures given in the text are always the percentages of those living in the ward, and with their parents who reported a job. Those who lived and worked elsewhere are thus always removed from both the numerator and the denominator.

32 On the commissioners' concerns about this see Susan Mann Trofimenkoff, "One Hundred and Two Muffled Voices," in Susan Mann Trofimenkoff and Alison Prentice, *The Neglected Majority: Essays in Canadian Women's History* (Toronto: McClelland and Stewart, 1977). How the working class viewed these morality issues requires examination.

33 Mss. Census, St. Jacques, 1871, 6, p. 137.

[34] Mss. Census, St. Jacques, 1881, 12, p. 101.

[35] Sydney Pollard, *The Genesis of Modern Management: A Study of the Industrial Revolution* (London: Edward Arnold, 1965),162.

[36] *Quebec Evidence*, evidence of Wm. C. McDonald, tobacco manufacturer, p. 529.

[37] RCRLC, *Quebec Evidence*, anonymous evidence, p. 42.

[38] RCRLC, *Quebec Evidence*, pp. 44-47.

[39] RCRLC, *Quebec Evidence*, p. 91.

[40] RCRLC, *Quebec Evidence*, evidence of Mrs. Levoise.

[41] RCRLC, *Quebec Evidence*, evidence of a machinist, Hudon factory, Hochelaga, pp. 273-74.

[42] RCRLC, *Quebec Evidence*, evidence of Adèle Lavoie, pp. 280-82.

[43] RCRLC, *Quebec Evidence*, evidence of Patrick Ryan, cigar maker, p. 37; machinist Hudon Mills, p. 271; Samuel Carsley, dry goods merchant, p. 15; Oliver Benoit, boot and shoemaker, p. 365; Henry Morton, printer, p. 297; F. Stanley, foreman at the Star, p. 331.

[44] Here I am referring to the percentage of children at home as opposed to boarding, living with relatives, or living in someone else's house as a servant. The samples taken in each census do not allow me to follow children over time and identify those who actually left home.

[45] The same process occurred in Hamilton, and in other cities that have been studied. See Michael Katz, *The People of Hamilton*, 257, 261; Mary P. Ryan, *The Cradle of the Middle Class: The Family in Oneida County, New York, 1790-1865* (New York: Cambridge University Press, 1981), 168-69; Richard Wall, "The Age at Leaving Home," *Journal of Family History* 8 (Fall 1983), 238.

[46] For a careful analysis of the relationship between women's wages, costs of board, and decisions about where to live see Gary Cross and Peter Shergold, "The Family Economy and the Market: Wages and Residence of Pennsylvania Women in the 1890s," *Journal of Family History* 11, 3 (1986): 245-66.

[47] Paul Spagnoli, "Industrialization, Proletarianization and Marriage," *Journal of Family History* 8 (Fall 1983), 238.

[48] Michael Anderson's careful analysis of which children left home shows that boys in Preston, Lancashire, were more likely to do so than girls. He believes children made "a conscious calculation of the advantages and disadvantages, in terms of the standard of living which they could enjoy," based on the wages they could make, their father's wage and the amount they were required to hand over to their parents. *Family Structure*, 67, 127-29.

[49] A similar, but greater, increase in girls' school attendance is described for Hamilton by Michael B. Katz and Ian E. Davey in "Youth and Early Industrialization" in *Turning Points: Historical and Sociological Essays on the Family*, ed. John Demos and Sarane Spence Boocock.

[50] "Le problème des jeunes qui ne fréquènt plus l'école," *École Sociale Populaire* 351 (April 1941), 26, cited by Dominique Jean, "Les familles québécois et trois politiques sociales touchant les enfants, de 1940 à 1960: Obligation scolaire, allocations familiales et loi controlant le travail juvenile" (Ph.D. diss., Université de Montréal, 1988).

[51] "First Report of Work Under the Children's Protection Act," p. 26; "Third Report of Work Under the Children's Protection Act," p. 10, cited in John Bullen, "J.J. Kelso and the 'New' Child-Savers: The Genesis of the Children's Aid Movement in Ontario" (Paper presented to the CHA Annual Meeting, Windsor, Ont., June 1988), 35-38.

[52] The usefulness of taking a category of women other than wives and mothers to test the soundness of contemporary feminist theory on this question is clear in the article of Danielle Juteau and Nicole Frenette who start with an examination of the role of Nuns in late nineteenth- and early twentieth-century Quebec, and use their insights to critique much contemporary feminist theory. "L'évolution des formes de l'appropriation des femmes: des religieuses aux 'meres porteuses,'" *Canadian Review of Sociology and Anthropology* 25, 2 (1988).

[53] One of the great advantages of the domestic labour debate was its recognition of the importance of housework and reproduction of labour power to capitalism. Less clear in much of the writing was the failure of most writers to acknowledge the interest of men in the perpetuation of domestic labour. For an elaboration of this critique see Walby, *Patriarchy at Work*, 18-19.

[54] Ruth Milkman criticizes labour segmentation theory, early Marxist feminist writing as well as Hartmann's description of patriarchy for paying insufficient attention to the effect of industrial structure on the sexual division of labour and struggles over "woman's place" in the labour market. Looking much more concretely than theorists have done at specific industries, she argues that "an industry's pattern of employment by sex reflects the economic, political, and social

constraints that are operative when that industry's labour market initially forms." *Gender at Work*, 7.

[55] Herein lies the problem of the "dual systems" approach of Hartmann and others. Heidi Hartmann, "Capitalism, Patriarchy and Job Segregation by Sex," *Signs* (1977); Varda Burstyn, "Masculine Dominance and the State" in Varda Burstyn and Dorothy Smith, *Women, Class, Family, and the State* (Toronto: Garamond Press, 1985), Sylvia Walby succeeds better than others in drawing out the links between the two, but insists on their relative autonomy in *Patriarchy at Work*.

[56] Canadian historians, whether in women's history or working-class history are only just beginning to unravel this complex, dialectical relationship between the structure of the economy and the needs of the family, in interaction with both capital and labour's definitions of gender roles. It is an unravelling that must continue if we are to understand how gender was at work and continues to work outside the workplace as well as within it.

[57] Some of the problems faced by feminist theoreticians grappling with the relationship between women's oppression by males within marriage, their subordination in the labour market, and the wider forces of patriarchy, stem from the assumption that only wives perform domestic labour. This seems to me a profoundly a-historical view, and one that downplays the importance of the family as a place of socialization and training.

[58] Here would be an example of mothers making choices that made their lives easier, but which in the long run perpetuated, even exaggerated, men's more privileged position in the marketplace. On this see Gerder Lerner, *The Creation of Patriarchy* (Oxford: Oxford University Press, 1986), cited in Bonnie Fox, "Conceptualizing Patriarchy," *Canadian Review of Sociology and Anthropology* 25, 2 (1988): 165.

[59] Psychological, Freudian theories about gender identity seem less important here than the practical day-to-day experience in the home and the role model of the mother. Nancy Chodorow, *The Reproduction of Mothering* (Berkeley: University of California Press, 1978).

[60] For a superb description of the complex ways in which women in Paris, Ontario—a knitting town where job opportunities for women were much greater than for men—dealt with domestic labour see Joy Parr, "Rethinking Work and Kinship in a Canadian Hosiery Town, 1910-1950," *Feminist Studies* 13, 1 (Spring 1987): 137-62.

Chapter 5

The Honest Workingman and Workers' Control: The Experience of Toronto Skilled Workers, 1860-1892

Gregory S. Kealey

And now Canadian workingmen,
Arise and do your duty;
Behold these massive towers of stone,
In all their wondrous beauty.
Who builds those lovely marble towers,
Who works and makes the plans?
'Tis he who sleepless thinks for hours—
The honest workingman.

From "The Toilers" written for
The Ontario Workman, 17 July 1873.

Skilled workers in the nineteenth century exercised far more power than we have previously realized. Well on into the industrial period craftsmen through their trade unions played important roles in community affairs, in the world of politics and especially on the job. In Toronto work places, craftsmen employed their monopoly on skill and experience to dictate terms to their employers in a wide array of areas which, in modern parlance, gave to these late nineteenth century craftsmen a high degree of workers' control of production. In this paper I will describe the practice of three Toronto unions from the 1860s to the early 1890s to illustrate the extent of this power.

The three unions under discussion have been chosen to exemplify significant variants of trade union power in Toronto. They include: the relatively little known Coopers International Union, Ontario No. 3, which played an important role in the Nine Hour Movement and the establishment of the Toronto Trades Assembly; the extensively studied International Typographical

Union No. 91; and the Iron Molders International Union No. 28, employed in Toronto's heavily capitalized stove, machinery and agricultural implements industry. This great diversity of experience demonstrates that the crafts analyzed here, although each unique, are nevertheless not atypical of other Toronto skilled unions of this period. Other crafts could have been chosen and although the details would differ the overall patterns would remain much the same.

To date most discussion of artisanal resistance to the arrival of industrial capitalism has focussed on the maintenance of pre-industrial work habits, the tenacious hold of ethnic cultural ties, and on the deep suspicion craft workers felt for "the new rules of the game" demanded by the advent of the market economy.[1] This analysis applies to workers undergoing the process of industrialization and will account for the Coopers' early Toronto experience but in studying the history of Toronto moulders and printers we will need other explanations.

David Montgomery has suggested that we must look beyond pre-industrial cultural forms if we are to understand the behaviour of skilled workers in late nineteenth century America. These workers often were "veterans of industrial life" who "had internalized the industrial sense of time, were highly disciplined in both individual and collective behaviour, and regarded both an extensive division of labour and machine production as their natural environment."[2] This was the world of Toronto moulders; Toronto printers, or rather Toronto compositors, occupied a position somewhere between the experience of the cooper and that of the moulder. The world of moulders and printers certainly drew on old craft traditions but it also transcended them. Although drawing on "residual" cultural categories there was much about their world that was "emergent," if we can borrow the important theoretical distinction drawn by Raymond Williams.[3] In the late nineteenth century Toronto skilled workers came to terms with the new industrial society but the terms they arrived at were those of constant resistance and struggle. The successes that they and other workers achieved forced management and government to devise entirely new strategies which have become commonly known as "scientific management" and "progressivism." Those innovations remain, however, subjects for other papers; here we will limit ourselves to an analysis of how the workers struggled, often successfully, for control of the work place.[4]

I

The experience of coopers in Toronto and throughout Ontario in the late 1860s and early 1870s provides a classic case of the artisan response to industrial capitalism. Elsewhere I have described the confrontation that occurred between Toronto shoe manufacturers and the Knights of St. Crispin.[5] Although less dramatic in their response than the Crispins' Luddism, the coopers shared with the shoemakers the unfortunate fate of watching the destruction of their craft by a combination of mechanization, the rise of factory production, the depression of the 1870s, and an all-out employer offensive.

Originally organized on a shop basis, coopers enjoyed all the prerogatives of the skilled artisan. One vivid description of the old time cooper's life style follows:

> Early on Saturday morning, the big brewery wagon would drive up to the shop. Several of the coopers would club together, each paying his proper share, and one of them would call out the window to the driver, "Bring me a goose egg," meaning a half-barrel of beer. Then others would buy "Goose Eggs" and there would be a merry time all around .... Saturday night was a big night for the old time cooper. It meant going out, strolling around town, meeting friends usually at a local saloon, and having a good time generally after a hard week's work. Usually the good time continued over Sunday, so that on the following day he usually was not in the best condition to settle down to the regular day's work. Many coopers used to spend this day sharpening up their tools, carrying in stock, discussing current events and in getting things in shape for the big day of work on the morrow. Thus Blue Monday was something of a tradition with the coopers, and the day was also more or less lost as far as production was concerned. "Can't do much today, but I'll give her hell tomorrow," seemed to be the Monday slogan. But bright and early Tuesday morning "Give her hell" they would, banging away lustily for the rest of the week until Saturday, which was pay day again, and new thoughts of the "Goose Eggs." [6]

However these older artisanal traditions were coming under attack at mid-century from trade unionists as well as efficiency-minded manufacturers. A St. Louis cooper's 1871 letter depicts both the tenacity of the old tradition and the new attitudes of skilled workers:

> The shops are paid off every two weeks, on which occasion one of these shops is sure to celebrate that time-honoured festival, Blue Monday. When Blue Monday falls it usually lasts for three days. And the man who succeeds in working during the continuance of this carnival is a man of strong nerve and indomitable will. Mr. Editor, did you ever hear of Black Monday? Perhaps not. But I tell you wherever Blue Monday is kept, there is also Black Monday. The only difference is, Blue Monday is celebrated at the shop, while Black Monday is observed at the cooper's home. The man celebrates Blue Monday, but the wife and family observe Black Monday. [7]

In 1870 craftsmen created the Coopers International Union in order, as the Chicago *Workingman's Advocate* so aptly put it, to avoid the fate of the ship caulkers and ship carpenters, artisanal victims of the new age of iron and steam. [8] The new union with head-offices in Cleveland was "in many ways the model of a successful organization of skilled mid-nineteenth century American craftsmen." [9] Its leaders were deeply embedded in the labour reform tradition which found its organizational expression through the National Labor Union in the U.S. In Canada the Cooper's international Vice-President John Hewitt, played an active role in organizing the

Toronto Trades Assembly and the Canadian Labour Union and was one of the major theorists of the nine hour movement of 1872. The C.I.U. created a union structure which provided sick and death benefits, an international strike fund, and a card system for tramping members. Entering Canada in 1870 the union organized 24 branches in the first two years of its existence. [10] In early 1872 on a visit to Chicago John Hewitt announced that "the coopers in Canada were alive and active and increasing their organization rapidly." [11] Their decline was to be equally precipitous but let us first examine the basis of their strength.

Coopers, like most skilled workers in the late nineteenth century, can best be described as "autonomous workmen." This term, usefully defined by Benson Soffer, describes workers who possess:

> Some significant degree of control over the quantity and quality of the product; the choice and maintenance of equipment; the methods of wage payment and the determination of individual wages and hours; the scheduling and assignment of work; recruitment, hiring, lay-off and transfer; training and promotion of personnel; and other related conditions of work. [12]

A reading of *The Coopers' Journal*, the excellent newspaper of the C.I.U., provides copious evidence that Canadian coopers enjoyed most of these prerogatives.

As was the case with most unions of skilled workers in the nineteenth century wages were not the subject of collective bargaining. The union met together, arrived at the "price" of its labour, informed management of its decision and either accepted the new rate with gratitude or struck if the boss refused. Local unions had no trouble dictating terms in prosperous times as can be seen in the report of the Brantford local of August 1871 which simply notes that they had imposed a new price list and expected no trouble. [13] In January of 1872 representatives from seven of the fifteen existing Ontario C.I.U. locals met in Toronto to arrive at a province-wide price list. [14] This document imposed not only prices but also called for a maximum ten-hour day province-wide. It dictated prices for 37 different categories of piece work and added a day rate of $1.75 for work not included on the list.

In addition to assuming control of hours and wages coopers also restricted production especially when work was short. In this way they could spread the work around and also prevent speed-ups or other infringements of their shop-floor control. In the Ontario reports stints are mentioned by locals in St. Catharines, Seaforth, Oshawa and London. [15] This union-dictated, restriction of output was of course the greatest evil in the eyes of the manufacturer. Coopers also struggled to control the methods of production as in this Brantford case:

> H. W. Read, a boss cooper of this place, has shown his dirty mean spirit by discharging three flour bbl. [barrel] makers from his shop; they were making bbls. at nine cts. jointed staves and circled heading. The boss took

> the jointer boy away, so that the hands had to join their own staves, which they did until noon, when they refused to make anymore barrels, unless the staves were jointed for them or they were paid extra. For thus demanding their rights, Boss Read discharged them .... But we fear him not, for no respectable cooper will take a berth in his shop under the circumstances.[16]

The union also enforced personnel decisions in the shop. The monitor of each shop assured that new workers' union cards were clear if members and that "nons" would abide by the shop rules. "Nons" who refused often found themselves moving on to the next town sooner than anticipated. In Brantford in 1891 for example:

> A scab in one of our shops, by the name of David Clawson, made himself very obnoxious to our men by his persistent abuse of the Union. At our last meeting it was ordered that the shop should strike against him, which was accordingly done, the consequence of which was that the mean tool of a man trampled and our men were out but half a day.[17]

One year later in Seaforth:

> J. Carter (who was suspended in Jan. 1872) got a berth at Ament's shop .... The monitor of the shop immediately went to him and asked him to pay up his dues .... And also that if he did not pay up, either he or they should not work there. [After he refused] the monitor of the shop went to the boss and told him that he must either sack Carter or they would take their tools out of the shop .... [When he refused] they did instantly.[18]

Equally the coopers controlled admission to the craft and their ritual pledged them to "allow no one to teach a new hand" in order "to control the supply of help."[19] Use of helpers and apprenticeship rules were tightly supervised by the union.[20]

But perhaps more striking even than the presence of workers' control is the pervasiveness of appeals to manliness evidenced throughout the coopers' materials. David Montgomery has argued that this was a crucial component of "the craftsmen's ethical code."[21] Skilled workers carried themselves with pride and felt themselves to be the equal of their boss. C.I.U. President Martin Foran's novel, *The Other Side*[22] illustrates this theme well. The hero is a proud and respectable workman surrounded by unscrupulous capitalists and unmanly workers who have given up their self-respect in order to carry out the evil tasks of the monopolistic bosses. Foran in discussing his didactic novel claimed that:

> The main incidents of the story are founded upon "notorious fact," so notorious that anyone wishing it can be furnished with irrefragable,

> incontestable proofs in support of all the charges made against the typical employer, Revalson; that working men have been—because being trade unionists—discharged, photographed on street corners, driven from their homes, hounded like convicted felons, prevented from obtaining work elsewhere, arrested at the beck of employers, thrown into loathesome prisons on ex parte evidence, or held to bail in sums beyond their reach by subsidized, prejudiced, bigoted dispensers of injustice, & in every mean dishonourable manner imaginable, inhumanly victimized and made to feel that public opinion, law & justice were Utopian "unreal mockeries" except to men of position and money ....[23]

Canadian coopers saw "manliness" as the keystone of their struggle and for them honour and pride were sacrosanct. "Owls" or "nons" who broke pledges or violated oaths were less than men:

> At our last monthly meeting, the name of George Morrow was erased from our books, it having been proven beyond a shadow of a doubt that he had violated his obligations by making known the business of our meetings to his boss. This thing Morrow, for I cannot call him a man, has never been of any use to us, he has not only betrayed us, but degraded himself in the estimation of every good man in our community.[24]

The Hamilton corresponding secretary went on to describe Morrow as a "compromise between man and beast."[25]

The traditions of autonomous work and the culture which grew from it made the coopers men to be reckoned with. Yet if the rise of the C.I.U. was rapid its decline was even more precipitous.

By late 1873 only seventeen locals remained and by 1875 this number had plummetted to approximately five.[26] The Canadian case was in no way unique and from a peak membership of over 8,000 in 1872 the union's total membership had declined to 1,500 by 1876. In that year *The Coopers' Journal* suspended publication.

This disastrous decline was related both to the depression of the mid-1870s and to a concerted employers' assault on the trade. The best account of the coopers' demise describes the displacement of the hand cooper by machines in the Standard Oil works in New York and Cleveland. These cities, which contained the largest concentrations of coopers in North America, saw an epic struggle as Standard Oil moved to crush the C.I.U., the one remaining obstacle in its path to modernization and total monopoly.[27]

A similar process took place in Ontario. Coopering began to break out of its artisanal mold in the late 1860s in Ontario when the need for well-made, tight oil barrels in Western Ontario led the London firm of R. W. and A. Burrows to introduce stave making and stave dressing machinery.[28] Until then the entire process had been performed by hand. This innovation was adopted by larger cooperages in the province such as those at distilleries in Windsor and Toronto. These three shops, Burrows, Walker's and Gooderham's, also differed from the old-time cooper's shop due to their larger size; they resembled small manufactories far more than artisans' shops. Gooderham, for example, employed forty coopers in Toronto while the next biggest Toronto shop in 1871 held only seven. [29]

Although creating some problems for the C.I.U. these early machines did not abolish the need for skilled workers. Skill and knowledge were still important components of barrel making. Thus as late as 1871, Martin Foran was taking consolation in the cooper's skill:

> Many of our members place far too much significance on machinery as a substitute for their labour. I have given the subject much thought and consideration, and am unable to see any serious cause for apprehension in barrel machinery .... Ours is a trade that cannot be reduced to the thumbrule of unfailing uniformity. To make a general marketable piece of work, of any kind peculiar to our trade, it requires tact, judgement and discrimination on the part of the maker ... when the friends of barrel machinery succeed in inventing a thinking machine they will succeed in making a success. [30.]

Within two years of this statement Standard Oil's version of "a thinking machine" was a complete success.

The process was less revolutionary in Ontario but the effects of increased mechanization can be seen in the reports of the Toronto local. Gooderham's defeated the union between 1870,[31] when hours and wages were dictated by the workers and C.I.U. President Martin Foran acclaimed "Gooderman's [sic] shop as without exception the finest cooper shop [he had] ever seen,"[32] and late 1872 when John Hewitt reported that the shop:

> contained the most inveterate set of owls to be found on this continent and the few good men we have there, not being able to control the shop, have concluded to sacrifice their principles and work on for whatever price the great Godderham [sic] chooses to pay. [33]

At its peak strength in March of 1872 the Toronto local had had complete control over the trade.[34] The ability of the coopers to dictate terms was seriously undermined elsewhere in Ontario by the advent of machinery. In 1874 the Seaforth local noted that the installation of two barrel machines would throw a great number of coopers out of work. [35] Six months later they reported their failure to control the machines due to non-union coopers taking their jobs at low rates.[36] By the 1880s the struggle was over; the cooper's craft was dead. In 1887 a

Windsor cooper argued before the Labour Commission that machinery had "killed the trade" and that there no longer was "a man in the world who would send his son to be a cooper." [37]

The power that coopers had possessed as artisans they tried to adapt to the industrial age. Old models of the trade practices of independent craftsmen were transformed into union rules and struggled over with new style bosses. However one base of their power was disappearing rapidly in the 1870s as technological innovation stripped them of "their monopoly of particular technical and managerial skills." [38]

Yet we should always be careful in positing technological change as the crucial factor for other workers, as we shall see here, were more successful than the coopers. A Seaforth cooper, P. Klinkhammer, recognized this only too clearly:

> The men here have much to say about the barrel machine. The machine is not to blame. If the union men had been supported by the nons last fall and the latter had not taken the berths vacated by the union men and worked at 4 cents the machine would not be making barrels now. [39]

Their one real hope was to ally with other workers as Klinkhammer suggested. Their important role in the U.S. National Labor Union and the Toronto Trades Assembly, the Canadian Labour Union, and the Nine Hour Movement were steps in the right direction but craft particularism remained very strong in the 1870s. However unionism did not disappear totally from the barrel factory with the demise of the C.I.U. Like the shoemakers, the coopers learned from their experience. Toronto coopers retained an independent union after the demise of the C.I.U. and were successful in raising their rates in the spring of 1882. [40] The next year they participated in attempts to create a new International. [41] In 1886 the Toronto local joined the Knights of Labor as "Energy Assembly," LA 5742. [42] This path was followed by many other coopers' locals throughout Canada and the U.S.

II

Workshop control traditions were extremely strong in foundry work. Late nineteenth century moulders displayed all the characteristics that Soffer and Montgomery identify as typical of "autonomous workmen." Two things distinguish them from the coopers. First is their impressive success in tenaciously maintaining these traditions on into the twentieth century. Second was their presence from the start of this period at the centre of the industrial capitalist world. Moulders were not artisans working in small shops reminiscent of pre-industrial society. In Toronto, Hamilton and throughout Ontario, moulders worked in the important stove, machinery and agricultural implements industries. These firms, among the largest in nineteenth century Ontario, led Canadian industry in attempting to fix prices and later to create multi-plant firms. Not surprisingly, these companies were also continually in the forefront of managerial innovations regarding labour.

Moulders in Toronto were first organized into a local union in 1857. [43] This local joined the Iron Molders International Union, organized in 1859, some time in 1860. [44] The International made clear its position on questions of shop floor control from its inception. The original constitution claimed for the union the power "to determine the customs and usages in regard to all matters pertaining to the craft." [45] This gave the union control over the price of the moulders' labour. In stove shops, the union shop committee would meet and discuss the price to charge for moulding new patterns as the boss brought them in. The committee would meet with the boss or foreman and arrive at a mutually acceptable overall price for the whole stove but as there were always a number of pieces involved in the assembly of any stove the committee would then decide amongst itself how to split this price among its members working on the different castings. This "board price" once established was considered to be almost non-negotiable and these prices very quickly became recognized as part of the established customs and usages that were the union's sole prerogative. This price was not the only source of the moulders' wages for there was a second element termed the "percentage" which was a supplement paid in addition to the piece rate. This percentage was negotiable and wage conflicts in the industry generally revolved around the "percentage" for very few bosses made the mistake of trying to challenge the "board price." [46]

This was one considerable area of strength for the union but there were others. The shop committee also dictated the "set" or "set day's work" which was the number of pieces that a member was allowed to produce in one day. Thus production control was also taken out of the boss' hands. It was of course in the union's self-interest to "set" a reasonable amount of work which an average craftsman could perform. Craft pride would dictate against "setting" too low, but equally craft strength could prevent any attempt at a speed-up. [47] Peterborough moulders enforced the "set" and brought charges against members who "rushed up work." [48] Generally part of each local's rules, the "set" was made a part of the International Constitution at the 1886 convention in London: "Resolved that all molders working at piece work be not allowed to make over $3.50 a day." In 1888 this was struck from the Constitution and was again left to the discretion of each local. Canadian locals continued to enforce this control over production. In Peterborough, in June 1891 "Brother Burns brought a charge against Brother Donavan for earning over $3 a day." [49]

An additional area in which the union dictated terms was hiring. Members who made the mistake of applying to the foreman instead of to the shop committee were often fined. [50] In one such case in Toronto moulders directly recruited by stove manufacturer Edward Gurney were casually turned away by the shop committee whom they had been directed to by the workers after asking for the foreman. [51] The number of apprentices allowed in a shop was also set by the union. The Peterborough local in 1889 refused to allow "Mr. Brooks to bring in any more apprentices" and in 1891 reasserted that the union would "allow no more than the regular number of apprentices, one for every shop and one to any eight moulders." [52] The union also controlled the use of "bucks" or "berkshires" (unskilled labourers). When used they were traditionally paid directly by the moulder out of his wages and thus were employed by the craftsman not the employer. Later when bosses tried to use "bucks" to perform some of the work customarily performed by moulders, the latter did all in their power to prevent it.[53] This was the greatest area of contention with Toronto employers. Finally the union struggled to impose a closed shop on its employers and refused to work with non-union moulders. Thus in the moulding industry large areas of control in the setting of price, productivity and hiring resided with the union.

The extent of the control that the union established was neither won nor maintained without constant struggle. Manufacturers used every device in their power to break the moulders' shop floor control. In 1866 the newly founded employers' association in the industry passed a resolution to

> proceed at once to introduce into other shops all the apprentices or helpers we deem advisable and that we will not allow any union committees in our shops, and that we will in every way possible free our shops of all dictation or interference on the part of our employees.[54]

The "Great Lock-out of 1866" that followed the employer's posting of the above "obnoxious notice" which extended into Canada, culminated in a costly victory for the union. Canadian stove manufacturers also organized and were active in the 1870s in fixing prices, advocating increased protection and most significantly in pressing a concerted effort to deal the union a smashing defeat.[55] In this they too failed.

In the Toronto moulding industry, the union's claim to control was the central issue. Strikes were fought at least fourteen times in the years between the founding of Local No. 28 and 1895.[56] The moulders engaged in the major strikes to resist demands by the manufacturers that the customs and usages of the craft be sacrificed. Thus in 1867 McGee demanded that he be allowed to hire as many apprentices as he wished;[57] in 1870 Gurney tried to force his moulders to work with "bucks;"[58] in 1890 both Gurney and Massey offered their moulders a choice of either a substantive cut in the previously unchallenged board price or accept "bucks;"[59] in 1892 Gurney demanded that his moulders not only accept a reduction on the percentage rate but also commit themselves to this rate for a year, a new scheme to prevent their raising the "percentage" as soon as the economic climate changed.[60] The same battles were to be fought yet again in 1903-1904.[61]

These strikes were not minor struggles in the history of the Toronto working class. In the general employers' offensive of the late sixties and early seventies to counter the emergence of a strong and newly self-confident working class movement the boss moulders used various techniques in their attempt to defeat the union. In this period they resorted most often to coercion, falling back on outmoded statutes and the power of the law. The frequently cited case of George Brown and the Toronto printers of 1872 was preceded in Toronto by numerous uses of the courts by stove manufacturers. In 1867 McGee charged six Buffalo moulders with deserting his employment. Recruited by his foreman for a one-year term they quit work when they discovered that they were being used as scabs. The magistrate claimed he was being lenient due to the implicit deception used and fined them only $6.00 each. [62] Two apprentices who left McGee's before their terms were up because of the union blacklist of the shop were not so lucky. They received fifteen days in jail for deserting his employment. [63] Three years later Gurney, a large Toronto and Hamilton stove manufacturer, made use of the courts to fight the union in a slightly different way. He had two union members charged with conspiracy and assault for trying to prevent scabs from filling his shop after he turned out the union men for refusing to work with "bucks" and a large number of apprentices. After the men were found guilty the Toronto Grand Jury commented that:

> It is with sincere regret that the Grand Jury have had before them ... two persons charged with assault and conspiracy acting under the regulations of an association known as the Molders Union and they feel it their duty to mark in the most emphatic terms their disapproval of such societies being introduced into our new country calculated as they are to interfere with capital and labour, cramp our infant manufactures and deprive the subject of his civil liberty .... [64]

During another strike that same summer Beard charged ten of his apprentices with "unlawfully confederating to desert his service with the intent to injure the firm in their business." Their real offense had been seeking a wage increase and then using the traditional moulders' weapon of restricting their output to enforce their demand. On their last day on the job they all did the same limited amount of work. They were found guilty. [65] Nevertheless the founders' tactics failed. The victory that the moulders won here was especially sweet given the force brought to bear against them. This victory was quite clearly contingent on their monopoly of skill and their ability to control the labour market. Thus it was reported that Gurney was forced to resort to employing moulders such as "John Cowie who quit one job to go scabbing in Gurney's shop where he had never worked in before, simply because he was of so little account they would never hire him—circumstances sometimes make strange companions." [66] The union "defied anyone to produce such a lot of molders as were in Gurney." [67] But if the victory over Gurney was pleasing, that over Beard was valued even more highly:

> It appears that for a year or two past, Beard and Co. of Toronto, have been running an independent scab shop refusing to be "dictated to by the Union as they felt competent to conduct their business in their own way." They found that reliable men were all union men, they found that the sober men were all union men, and what was of more importance, they found that all the good moulders were union men and they were obliged to take the off-scourings of creation, all the drunken scallawags and botch workmen, that found their way to Toronto .... Their scab

> foreman was not equal to the situation and they found that their trade was fast leaving them and to save themselves from utter ruin the nauseous dose had to be swallowed ... [68]

The 1880s saw the maturing of the system of industrial relations that was only emerging in the 1860s and 1870s. The foundrymen mounted no challenges to the basic rights of the union in 1880s and only the percentage came under consideration. In 1880 moulders sought and gained a 10% increase but when the economy turned in late 1883 they were forced to accept a 20% reduction. In 1886 they won a 12.5% advance but in 1887 their request for a 10% increase was resisted by Gurney and after a nine-week strike a compromise 5% advance was accepted. In early 1887 the Ontario branches of the I.M.I.U. came together to form a District Union. The thirteen Ontario locals with over 1,000 members were brought together to organize more efficiently and to run joint strikes more effectively. [69] In 1887 for example the Hamilton moulders' strike against Gurney spread to Toronto when Gurney locked out his moulders there. Later in 1890 moulders at the Massey Hamilton plant refused to mould while their Toronto brothers were locked out. But perhaps the major example of these cross-industry strikes was the Bridge and Beach Strike of 1887 in the U.S. In March of that year moulders struck the Bridge and Beach Manufacturing Co. in St. Louis with the sanction of the International. Immediately the new Stove Founders National Defense Association attempted to manufacture the required patterns for the Company. Their moulders in turn refused to work on the patterns from the struck foundry. This process spread until at its height almost 5,000 moulders were locked out in fifteen centres. Finally in June, the Defense Association called the patterns in and supplied the St. Louis company with a force of non-union moulders and work resumed as before at the other shops. Both sides claimed victory but most important was that each side had demonstrated to the other their respective strength and staying power. Almost immediately after the end of this strike negotiations were commenced which were to lead to the establishment of national conciliation in the industry through conferences of the contending parties. [70]

The Canadian industry did not take part in these conferences nor did conciliation apply to the machinery moulding branches of the trade. Until these industry-wide agreements in stove foundries the strength of the moulders depended entirely on their skill and control of the work process and their ability through their union to maintain this and to exercise some degree of control over the labour market. This labour market control was of great importance and has been admirably discussed before with reference to the moulders. [71] The importance of the union card to the moulder has been summarized: " ... within the jurisdiction of his own local a union card was a man's citizenship paper; in the jurisdiction of other locals it was his passport." [72]

The early 1890s saw a new employer offensive in Hamilton and Toronto as Gurney and Massey both attempted to smash the moulders' continuing power in their plants. The Gurney strike which commenced in February 1890 lasted an amazing sixteen months before local 28 ended it. The Massey strike covered ten months from October 1890 to July 1891. [73] In both cases the companies pursued a similar strategy. They shut down their moulding shops ostensibly for repairs and, after a considerable lapse of time, called in the shop committees and asked them to accept either a sizeable reduction or work with "bucks." [74] In both cases the moulders refused for "union rules did not permit 'bucks' and the men thought they saw in it their eventual displacement by these labourers and a menace to their trade." [75] Both Gurney and Massey claimed that they could no longer afford union rates and compete successfully but the moulders suspected "a long conceived plan in the attempt at a reduction." In each case management and labour settled down for a protracted struggle. David Black, the secretary of local 28, wrote after five months on strike:

> Our fight with Gurney still continues and bids fair to last quite a while longer, we succeed very well in relieving him of his good men, but he has plenty of money and it will take hard fighting and time to beat him. [77]

The Toronto local spared no expense or risk in this struggle and a number of their members were arrested and tried for intimidating scabs. [78] In September the local issued an appeal "To the Canadian Public" which complained they had been locked out "because they refused to make their work cheaper than for any other employer in the same line in the city; and thus assist them to destroy their competitors and monopolize the Canadian market at our expense." The public was called on to buy only union made goods since:

> By this means our victory over monopoly will be assured; our right to organize and obtain fair wages for our labour will be vindicated; while the superior quality of your purchase will amply repay your preference. [79]

The union lost both these struggles but the cost to capital was also high. Gurney, in early 1891, when his victory seemed sure brayed triumphantly that "the only change resulting from the strike is that he now controlled his shop." However when he continued to claim that things were excellent, the *Globe* reporter noted that, faced with the open incredulity of the union representatives present, Gurney modified his statement mentioning "that of course the whole year had not been as smooth." The key in these struggles in the early 1890s was control. As capital entered a new stage where it recognized the necessity of supervising more closely the process of production it had to confront and defeat its "autonomous workmen." This gives Gurney's parting chortle added significance:

> The men must work for someone else until they come to one of my proposals. I do not think (with a smile) that there is any likelihood of my going to local 28 and asking them to come and take control of my foundry. [80]

Gurney's last laugh was too precipitous however for the I.M.I.U. came back strong in Toronto in the late 1890s and a new wave of struggle broke over the foundry business in 1902-

1904.[81] It is not the purpose of this paper to detail that struggle but it is important to emphasize that the power of the moulders was not broken in the struggles of 1890-1892. Gurney and Massey delivered only a partial defeat and the moulders came back strong. J. H. Barnett, Toronto I.M.I.U. secretary, described one 1903 struggle:

> Just after adjourning the meeting this afternoon the foreman of the Inglis shop, R. Goods, came to the hall and informed us that he had discharged all the scabs in his shop and that he wanted the union men in on Monday, that the firm was tired of the scabs and was willing to give the nine hours ....[82]

One year later in yet another struggle with Toronto foundrymen now supported by the National Foundry Association, Barnett wrote again of the continued monopoly on skill that the moulders enjoyed:

> They are having greater losses in the foundry now than when they first started. They have been trying to make a big condenser and can't make it. They have started the old St. Lawrence shop with some of the old country moulders who refused to work with Ersig, the NFA foreman up in the new shop. Jas Gillmore and Fred McGill is instruction [sic] them but ain't doing any better.[83]

Iron moulders then, unlike coopers, maintained a high degree of workplace control on into the twentieth century. This was primarily due to their strong organization but was also partially contingent on the slowness with which technology replaced their skill. Machines for moulding were experimented with in the mid-1880s but were an extremely expensive failure.[84] Massey imported its first machines in 1889.[85] Thus, unlike the coopers and shoemakers, the moulders had time to perfect their organization before their major contest with machinery.

Moulders also developed an early understanding of the need for solidarity with their unskilled co-workers. Thus, when the Knights of Labor struck the huge Massey works in Toronto in 1886, moulders left the job in their support. Peterborough I.M.I.U. local no. 191 also co-operated with the Lindsay Knights of Labor.[86]

III

The workers' control enjoyed by Toronto moulders, and their struggle to retain it, was more than equalled by the experiences of Toronto printers. The printers' control of the shop floor demonstrates extremely well early union power. In the 1890s the President of the Toronto local of the I.T.U. insisted:

> The work of the composing room is our business. To no one else can we depute it. It is absolutely ours. The talk of running another man's business will not be hold. It is ours; we learned it and must control it. [87]

Unionism among the Toronto Printers owed much to the customs and traditions of the craft. Organized first in 1832 the Society lapsed in 1836 but was refounded in 1844 to resist a new Toronto employers departure from the "settled usages of the trade." [88] In 1845, when forced again to fight the initiatives taken by George Brown, the printers issued a circular to the Toronto public demanding only "to maintain that which is considered by all the respectable proprietors as a fair and just reward, for our labour and toil—'the labourer is worthy of his hire.'"[89] Here the tenacity of pre-industrial notions of traditional wages can be seen. Customary usage dictated wages—not any abstract notion of what the market might bear. Employers as well as workers had to learn the new rules of a market economy and the disruptions caused by the Browns' arrival in the Toronto printing trades in the 1840s, suggest that until then wages had been "largely a customary and not a market calculation." [90]

The printers possessed a strong tradition of craft pride and identification. In their 1845 statement to the Toronto public they resolved "to maintain by all legitimate means in their power their just rights and privileges as one of the most important and useful groups in the industrious community." [91]

Members of the "art preservative," they saw themselves as the main carriers of rationalism and the enlightenment. No trade dinner or ball, and these were frequent, was complete without a set of toasts to the printers' patron, Benjamin Franklin, and to Gutenberg and other famous printers. Franklin replaced the older European craft tradition of saints and his rationalism fitted very well with the printers' disdain for other societies who had recourse to secret signs and fiery oaths. The printers prided themselves on the fact that:

> initiation ceremonies melo-dramatic oaths, passwords, signs, grips, etc., though advocated by many worthy representatives and repeatedly considered by the national union, never found a place in the national or subordinate constitutions. [92]

The printers saw their craft as crucial in maintaining all that was best in the western literary tradition. As one printer toasted in an 1849 Anniversary Dinner: "To the art of printing—under whose powerful influence the mind of fallen and degraded man is raised from nature up to nature's God." [93] Thus printer's shop committees were "chapels" and the shop steward was "the father of the chapel." This pride in craft was manifested time and time again throughout the nineteenth century.

In 1869 the executive recommended the initiation of a reading room and library:

> where the members of the craft can have access in leisure hours for the enjoyment of study and mental recreation and where may be ever within

> their reach increasing facilities for the acquisition of whatever in our art it may be of advantage to know ... It is a laudable endeavour to support one's calling which two centuries age was deemed the most honourable of all professions ...[94]

The union seal depicted a printing press with light emanating from all around it. [95]

The Toronto printers had a strong sense of the history of their craft and their union. They were particularly proud of being the oldest Toronto union and parts of their frequent fetes were often spent on these themes. The 1888 picnic programme, for example, contained original histories of both the art of printing and of the Toronto Typographical Union. [96] All these traditions were put to use by the printers and they brought the craft lore together in stirring addresses involving custom in the struggle against oppression:

> Fellow-workingmen, knights of the stick and rule, preservers of "the art preservative,"—ye whose honourable calling is to make forever imperishable the noblest, truest and most sublime thoughts of the statesman, the philosopher, and the poet,—to you is committed the mightiest agent for good or ill which has yet been pressed into the service of humanity. The printing press, the power mightier than kings, more powerful than armies, armaments, or navies, which shall yet overthrow ignorance and oppression and emancipate labour, is your slave. Without your consent, without the untiring labour of your skillful fingers and busy brain, this mighty giant, with his million tongued voices speeding on wings of steam all over this broad earth of ours, would be dumb. Shorn of his strengths which your skill imparts, his throbbing sides and iron sinews might pant and strain in vain; no voice or cry of his or your oppressors could ever reach or be heard among men. Realizing this my friends it is easy to determine our proper station in the grand struggle that is now in progress all over the civilized world, the effort of the masses to throw off oppression's yoke .... We belong in the front rank, at the head of this column. Since the discovery of printing humanity has made great progress and already we see the dawn of the coming day when light and knowledge shall illuminate all lands and men shall no longer oppress his fellowman. [97]

Central to the power of the International Typographical Union was the extent to which each local maintained its control over production. The composing room was the preserve of the printer. Management's only representative there, the foreman, was a union member and subject to the discipline of his brothers. This was true in Toronto from the inception of the T.T.U. and was very important because the union also demanded that all hiring be done through the foreman. [98] In 1858 the I.T.U. convention had ruled that:

> The foreman of an office is the proper person to whom application should be made for employment; and that it is enjoined upon subordinate unions that they disapprove of any other mode of application. [99]

The new I.T.U. constitution of 1867 fined members who applied for jobs to anyone other than the foreman. Four years later this control was reasserted but foremen were also warned:

> It is the opinion of your humble servant that the foreman of an office belongs to the union under which he works and the union does not belong to the foreman ... and that no foreman has the right to discharge a regular hand ... on any other ground than that of shortness of work or willful neglect of duty ... [100]

In an extraordinary 1873 case the I.T.U. ruled that the Ottawa local was correct to strike against J. C. Boyce, the proprietor of *The Citizen*, when he took over operation of his own composing room. Only if Boyce submitted a clear card from the London (Eng.) Trades Society would he "be allowed to work under the jurisdiction of the Ottawa Union." [101]

This effective union control of the hiring practice was augmented by the role the foreman played in enforcing the printer's right to divide work. In newspaper offices each regular employee had a "sit" and with this place came the right to choose a replacement any time the regular wanted time off. Although not technically employed by the regular printer that was actually what the practice amounted to. In Toronto the *Mail* paid the money to the regular who then paid the subs from his salary. [102] When bosses tried to regulate this custom by utilizing "sublists" which delineated the substitutes from whom regulars were forced to choose, the International roundly condemned the practice and refused to allow locals to cooperate with it. [103] The union claimed ever more interest in the hiring process. In 1888 a resolution was introduced at the I.T.U. convention "that would have placed the regulation of hiring and discharging of employees entirely in the hands of the local unions." [104] In 1890 "the priority law" was passed by which the grounds upon which foremen could discharge were even more tightly circumscribed. Only incompetency, violation of rules, neglect of duty or decrease of labour force were acceptable causes for firing and on discharge a member was entitled to a written statement of cause. In addition the final part of the law ruled that "subs" in an office had priority when positions became available. [105] The power of the union then, in controlling the selection of printers, was almost total.

The union also retained a strong position in bargaining. The union would first arrive at an approved scale of prices unilaterally and would then take it to the employers. [106] Some negotiation was possible but much of the scale was regarded as non-negotiable. For example after the strike of 1872 for the nine hour day never again were hours subject to consideration; having been won once they were off limits for further discussion. [107] The scale was a complex document divided into three major sections: time work; piece work, news and magazines; and piece work, books. Time work was not the traditional method of payment in the printing industry but throughout the late nineteenth century more and more job shops adopted it. However the time rate was closely tied to the piece rate. In Toronto where the piece rate was 33 1/3 cents per 1,000 ems, the time rate was 33 1/3 cents an hour the general assumption being that a hand compositor averaged 1,000 ems an hour. In newspaper offices the usual method of payment was by the piece, which in the compositor's case was measured by the area of type that he composed and expressed in "ems." Printers were thus paid per 1,000 ems of matter. There were a number of areas of conflict implicit in this type of payment. Rates were set for the newspaper as a whole but special rates were set for material classified as difficult such as foreign languages or tables or even for illegible copy. [108] As the century progressed more and more newspaper work consisted of advertising which contained far more blank space than regular material. This copy became known as "fat" matter and was the most lucrative for the printer. The printers insisted that rates were set for the paper as a whole thus retaining the higher rate for fat matter as well. The traditional way of distributing the material was that all copy was hung on the "hook" as it arrived in the composing room and the compositors picked it up in order thus insuring an even distribution of the "fat." Bosses began to object to this and tried to create "departments" by which specific printers did the special composing. This the union resisted strenuously and forbade locals from accepting "departments." They offered, as a compromise, to allow members to bid for the "fat" matter. The successful bidder who gained the ads then paid back the union the amount of his bid, usually a percent of his earnings, which was then used to buy things in common for all the printers, to hire a person to clean everybody's type, or was distributed equally among the members. [109] The Toronto local however resisted all employer incursions in this area. Toronto employers certainly tried. In 1882 the *Mail* offered its printers an advance but in return demanded the return of the ads. Instead the new scale of 1883 reiterated that "where weekly and piece hands are employed the piece hands shall have their proportionate share of 'fat' matter." [110] Seven years later another new scale still insisted that "compositors on newspapers were entitled to equal distribution of any 'phat.'" [111] The complexity of the Toronto printer's scale is suggested by the 39 sections of the 1883 and 35 sections of the 1890 contracts. [112] All this led one managerial strategist named DeVinne, who was later to play a major role in the United Typothetae, to moan that "It is the composition room that is the great sink-hole. It is in type and the wages of compositors that the profits of the house are lost." [113]

So far we have spoken entirely of only one branch of printing—the compositors. Until the middle of the century in the cities and until much later in small shops, a printer ran the press as well as composing. With the rise of power presses, the pressman's role became more and more complex and increasingly the old time printer who did both jobs disappeared and new specialists took over. By 1869 the Toronto local had special piece rates for pressmen and the job definition of the compositor prevented him from performing press work. The pressmen's new consciousness led the I.T.U. to begin to charter Pressmen's locals separately in 1873 and ten years later the Toronto Pressmen set up their own local. Disputes with Local 91 however led them to join the new International Printing Pressmen's Union in 1889. This splintering of the printing crafts caused many problems but the pressmen as an equally skilled group carried with them the traditions of printers' unionism. Time was spent at meetings, for example, in designing outfits for the various marches and parades that were so much a part of working class life in Toronto in the 1880s." [114]

Although the major focus of this paper is the skilled worker's power on the job one cannot discuss the Toronto printers without alluding also to their political strength in the city, in provincial and even in national politics. They provided the Toronto working class community and movement with important leadership. It was natural for these literate, working class intellectuals to play key political roles but the extent of their dominance is striking nevertheless. Although not the initiators of the Toronto Trades Assembly (this honour belongs to John Hewitt of the Coopers International Union) they did play an important part in this organization and in the Canadian Labour Union. In the 1880s they helped found the Toronto Trades and Labor Council after the meeting of the I.T.U. in Toronto in 1881 and later were quite active in the meetings of the Trades and Labour Congress. Moreover of the six labour papers published in Toronto between 1872 and 1892 three of them were published and edited by printers— *The Ontario Workman* under J. S. Williams, J. C. MacMillan, and David Sleeth, all prominent members of Local 91; *The Trade Union Advocate/Wage Worker* of Eugene Donavon; and D. J. O'Donoghue's *Labour Record*. Other members of Local 91 also enjoyed prominent careers in labour reform—John Armstrong, a former International President of the I.T.U. (1878-9) was appointed to Macdonald's Royal Commission on the Relations of Labour and Capital in 1886; D. J. O'Donoghue, prominent as an MPP, leading Canadian Knight of Labor and later collector of labour statistics for the Ontario Bureau of Industries; E. F. Clarke, arrested in 1872 and later Mayor of Toronto, MPP and MP; and W. B. Prescott, International President of the I.T.U. from 1891-1898. This was just one generation of Local 91's membership: the next was to include two mayors of Toronto and a senator. [115]

Local 91's political role stemmed from its union activities. Toronto printers, for example, had little use for George Brown's brand of Liberalism. As early as 1845 they had noted the irony implicit in his labour relations policies:

> A person from the neighbouring Republic commenced business here and has ever since been unremitting in his Liberal endeavour to reduce as low as possible that justly considered fair and equitable rate of remuneration due to the humble operatives. [116]

His "Liberal" endeavours were to lead him into conflict with the printers time and time again, culminating in the Printer's Strike for the nine hour day in 1872. [117] Brown's use of antiquated British laws against combination to arrest the leaders of the I.T.U. was turned against him by Macdonald's passage of the Trade Union Act. The Tories controlled Toronto working class politics for a number of years following until D. J. O'Donoghue, the Knights of

Labor, and the legislative responsiveness of the Mowat Ontario government started a swing towards the Liberals.

The political expertise of the printers had of course grown throughout their various struggles and the tactics perfected in 1872 were used again in the 1880s. Thus when John Ross Robertson's *Telegram* came under union attack in 1882 the union first turned to the boycott to bring pressure on the owner. They decided that in this way they could expose

> the treatment which union printers have received at the hands of JRR for many years past, and the manner in which that gentleman (?) invariably casts aspersions upon the union mechanics of this city generally through the columns of his vasculating [sic] paper. [118]

John Armstrong and D. J. O'Donoghue were appointed to visit the merchants who advertised in the *Telegram* and convince them to place their ads elsewhere. The next year when I.T.U. No. 91 passed a new scale of prices they struck the *Telegram* pulling most of the compositors out on strike. They then received the endorsement of the whole Toronto Trades and Labor Council for the boycott and late in March held a mass meeting at which speeches were delivered by most of the prominent Toronto labour leaders pledging support for Local 91. [119]

The strikes the following year against the *Mail* and the *Globe* were even more eventful and suggestive of the printers' political acumen. The papers united with other Toronto publishers and print shops to demand a 10% reduction in the printers' wages and gave only a week for consideration. The printers refused and struck. The union was successful in forcing job offices and smaller papers to withdraw the reduction but the *Globe* and the *Mail* held out. The *Globe* insisted that it had never become a union shop because "the boss needed absolute control in a newspaper office." [120] The morning papers after a hard fight won the reduction to 30 cents per 1,000 ems down from 33 1/3 cents but their victory was short lived. In 1885 the *Globe* reversed its position of a year before and the political game of the 1870s by becoming a union shop for the first time. This left only the Tory *Mail* holding out against the typos. The *Mail* succumbed in February of 1886 and became a union shop, withdrawing the iron-clad contract that it had adopted after the troubles in 1884.

What tactics had the I.T.U. used to win these long-range victories after their apparent defeat in 1884? The printers had employed their usual measures against the papers. They first withdrew all their members from the shops and when they failed to prevent the shops' filling up with the much despised "country-mice," nonunion printers from small towns, they turned to the boycott and mass demonstrations of workingmen. [121] But this time they also requested all workingmen to boycott any candidates supported by the *Mail* in the municipal election campaigns of the winter of 1885-6. [122] Local 91 passed a resolution: "That this union will oppose to its utmost any candidate for municipal honours who may be supported by the Mail newspaper." [123] The following weeks saw union after union endorse the I.T.U. motion and also saw a number of Tory ward heelers running for cover and abandoning the *Mail*. The union issued a circular exposing its dealings with the *Mail* since 1872 and then placed advertisements in the Toronto papers in January of 1886 strongly attacking Manning, the *Mail's* candidate for Mayor:

> Resolved that this union consider Mr. Manning a nominee of the Mail, he having advertised in that paper ... and having been editorially supported by it, particularly so on Saturday morning January 2; and therefore we call on all workingmen and those in sympathy with organized labour to VOTE AGAINST MANNING, THE NOMINEE OF THE MAIL. [124]

The same Local 91 meeting also decided to blacklist aldermanic candidates who had not broken with the *Mail* and decided to issue 10,000 circulars denouncing Manning and these candidates. After Howland's stunning election as mayor, widely regarded as a working class victory, the I.T.U. issued this statement:

> To the Trades and Labour organizations of Toronto—Fellow unionists: Toronto Typographical Union No. 91 takes this opportunity of thanking the labour organizations of this city and their friends who so nobly supported us at the polls in our effort to defeat the Mail. To the workingmen of Toronto who have had the honour and manhood to rise above party ties in the cause of the labour, the heartiest thanks of the 300 members of the TTU are due .... At a time when we needed your assistance you have shown that the mottoe of our union 'United to support not combined to injure' is the guiding stone of the honest toiler everywhere. [125]

This electoral defeat led to the *Mail's* total reversal in February, 1886 when it surrendered to the Union. Local 91 had had to prove its strength at the polls however for as early as 1884 leading Tory printers had warned Macdonald of the possible repercussions of the *Mail's* adventure. J. S. Williams had written in August, 1884:

> Not only will the matter complained of [Mail lock-out] alienate a very large proportion of the working men who have hitherto nobly supported the party, but it places a barrier in the way of any prominent or representative workingman actively working or speaking in the future.

Moreover he predicted that the *Mail's* reactionary policies could cost the Tories two to three seats in Toronto and perhaps seats in other urban centres as well. E. F. Clarke, a prominent politician and member of Local 91, wrote to the same effect:

> A reduction of wages at a week's notice and a refusal of the Mail to leave the settlement of the question to arbitration will alienate the sympathies

> of a large number of workingmen who have hitherto supported the Conservative cause, and will weaken the influence of the journal with the masses ....

A non-working class Tory politico wrote that the labour friends of the party were now in an impossible position since they "cannot support the party that treats them so shabbily" and expressed the fear that the loss of the whole Toronto Trades and Labor Council might result in electoral defeat in the City.[126] Nevertheless these warnings were ignored until the humiliating defeats of January 1886. Then the party rushed in to settle the matter once and for all. Harry Piper, a Tory ward heeler, wrote to Macdonald in February to inform him that the I.T.U.- *Mail* fight "had of late assumed a very serious aspect" since a number of old party workers had clearly transferred their allegiance in the election. As a result he arranged a meeting with John Armstrong, a Tory leader of Local 91 who had lost his own job at the *Mail* during the strike. Piper convinced Armstrong that "the Union was *killing our Party* and the Grits were reaping the benefit of the trouble and using our own friends." Armstrong promised to help if the iron-clad was removed. Piper then arranged with the manager and directors of the *Mail* that the document be ceremoniously burned before the printers and Armstrong agreed to have the union lift the boycott.[127] Thus the seeming defeat of the summer of 1884 had been translated by political means into a striking victory for Local 91. Neither the *Globe* nor the *Mail* were to cause the union difficulty again in the late nineteenth century.

Similar tactics were employed successfully against J. H. Maclean of the *World* in 1888 when he tried to defeat the union's control of "fat" matter. The struggle was precipitated by a fight over the price to be paid for an advertisement that was inserted twice. The union rule was that if the advertisement was run in an identical manner then the compositor was only paid once but that if any changes were made the compositor was paid again for the whole advertisement. The foreman supported the printers' case but the Macleans, after paying the money owed, locked out the union. The I.T.U. then reiterated its position on "fat" matter:

> Only by the getting of the advertisements and other "fat" matter are the men able to make anything like living wages, and this fact is recognized by all fair-minded employers as well as the men.[128]

In late July after filling his shop with "country-mice" Maclean sought an injunction against the I.T.U.'s boycott of the *World*. It was granted on an interim basis and then made permanent in mid-August.[129] The injunction did not solve Maclean's problems:

> The World is in sore straights as a result of the law compelling union men not to buy it or patronize merchants who advertise therein. Internal storms are of such common occurrence that a couple of weeks ago the vermin employed there went out on strike even but returned to the nest again.[130]

A few months later Maclean again sought to make his paper a union shop. Again the political dimensions of the settlement are clear. W. B. Prescott, the President of Local 91, wrote John A. Macdonald and sought his intervention with Maclean to insure that the *World* came around. Prescott pointed out that "the cheap labour policies of the *World* antagonized organized labour."[131] Perhaps one reason that Maclean and the *World* felt the pressure was the Local had quickly found a way to circumvent the injunction by promoting union papers rather than naming those boycotted. They continued to use this technique especially in a political context. In the municipal campaigns of 1891-2, for example, they issued the following circular:

> Having been informed that you are seeking municipal honours, we desire to call your attention to the fact that there are a few printing and publishing houses in this city who do not employ union labour, and we, believing it would be to your advantage to patronize only those who do employ such, request you to place your patronage and advertising in union offices only, as we can assure you that from past experience, your chances of election are greater by so doing.[132]

The circular then listed the dailies that were union shops which by 1891 included all but the *Telegram*, which was shortly to enter the fold. In March, 1892 the T.T.U. also began the use of the union label.[133] Thus the power of the Toronto printers continued to grow throughout the late nineteenth century and a larger proportion of Toronto printers were unionised in the early 1890s than had been at any previous date.[134]

The initial encounter with mechanization served to strengthen their position. Until the invention of linotype and monotype machines in the late 1880s, typesetting had remained unchanged from the sixteenth century.[135] In Toronto the *News* introduced the Rogers typograph machine in 1892 and offered the printer operators 14 cents/1,000 ems. The I.T.U. had recommended in 1888 "that subordinate unions ... take speedy action looking to their [linotype machines] recognition and regulation, endeavouring everywhere to secure their operation by union men upon a scale of wages which shall secure compensation equal to that paid hand compositors."[136] This was amended in 1889[137] to demand that in all union offices only practical printers could run the machines and that the rates on the machines would be governed by the local unions.[138] In Toronto the union's right to control the operation of the machine was not challenged initially and their *Typographical Journal* correspondent reported in March of 1892 "that so far we have not suffered from their use." However that summer the *News*, appealing to the craft custom of piece rates, refused to pay operators by the day. After a seven week strike the union won its demand that the printers be paid by time. They were to receive $12.00 a week for six weeks while learning the machine operation and then $14.00 after they demonstrated their competency, which was set at 2,000 ems per hour or 100,000 ems per week. This settlement brought the union not only control of the machine and the wage style it sought but also implicitly recognized the printers' right to limit production since the rate of competency set was far below the actual capabilities of the machine which were estimated to be anywhere from 3-8 times as fast as hand composition. [139] The International was also concerned to prevent any proliferation of speed-ups with the new machine and ruled that "no member shall be allowed to accept work ... where a task, stint, or deadline is imposed by the employer on operators of typesetting devices." [140] The union later successfully resisted any attempts by employers to speed up work totals. The victory over the *News* and the union's previous success with Robertson's *Telegraph* also brought Local 91 control of all Toronto newspapers for the first time in its history. [141] The printers had learned their lessons well. They left the century not only with their traditions intact but also with their power actually augmented. They had met the machine and triumphed. [142]

IV

What ramifications did shop floor power have in terms of how workers thought about their society, how it was changing and their own role in it? David Montgomery has argued that the major impact of this early workers' control was the skilled workers' growing awareness that the key institution for the transformation of society was the trade union. [143] From their understanding that they, through their unions, controlled production, it was a relatively easy step to the belief that all the capitalist brought to the process was capital. Thus an alternative source of capital would transform the society ending the inequities of capitalist production and creating the producer's society that they all dreamed of. This ideology looked to co-operation administered through the trade union as the major agent of change. All the unions we have discussed favoured co-operation.

John Monteith, President of Toronto I.M.I.U. Local 28, wrote *Fincher's Trades Review* in 1863 to describe the work of Canada West members in discussing and investigating co-operation. A union moulders' committee had contacted Rochdale and now recommended both producers and consumers co-ops to their local unions. They sought co-operation because "our present organization does not accomplish what we want. That is to take us from under the hand of our employers and place us on an equal footing." [144] Co-operation of course would accomplish this very end. Five years later another Toronto moulder complained that "We are but little better off than our forefathers who were serfs to the feudal barons. We are serfs to the capitalists of the present day ...." His solution:

> Let the next conviction create a co-op fund to be devoted entirely to co-operation .... We have been co-operating all our lives, but it has been to make someone else rich. We have been the busy bees in the hives while the drones have run away with the honey and left us to slave in the day of adversity .... Day after day the wealth of the land is concentrating in the hands of a few persons. The little streams of wealth created and put in

> motion by the hard hands of labour gravitate into one vast reservoir, out of which but a few individuals drink from golden cups; while labour, poor, degraded and despised labour, must live in unhealthy hovels and feed upon scanty, unhealthy food from rusty dishes .... [145]

The I.M.I.U. founded as many as twenty co-operative foundries in the 1860s. [146]

Toronto printers started three co-operative newspapers. At the height of the nine hour struggle in 1872 *The Ontario Workman* was started as a co-operative venture as was D. J. O Donoghue's *Labor Record* of 1886. In 1892 during the strike at the *News* a group of printers banded together and founded the *Star*.[147] *The Ontario World* operated as a co-op paper for only six months and the *Labor Record* and the *Star* each lasted about a year. Capital for the *Star* was raised from the T.T.U. and T.T.L.C. They initially used the presses of the *World* since W. F. Maclean offered them his facilities in return for 51% of the operation. This "Paper for the People" enjoyed quick success in winning the readership of the *News* which had from its inception in 1882 posed as the paper for Toronto workers. [148] Riordan, the owner of the *News* attempted to buy the operation and Maclean tried to merge it with the *World* but the printers refused both offers and instead bought a press. However they failed to make a go of it and the paper suspended publication in June of 1893. It was continued after its purchase as a pro-labour paper but control had passed out of the printers hands. [149]

Machinists and blacksmiths in Toronto organized a co-operative foundry early in 1872 after losing a strike at the Soho works. [150] Six years later Toronto cigar makers established The Toronto Co-operative Cigar Manufactory Association. Here, as with the moulders in the 1860s, the push for co-operation came as a logical extension of their knowledge of the trade and their refusal to accept management's reduction of wages. Alf Jury, a Toronto tailor and labour reformer, denounced "the wage system as a modified form of slavery" and demonstrated that there could be "no fraternal feeling between capital and labour" at a cigar makers' strike meeting that year. Jury then cited production statistics to repudiate the employers' claims that the reduction was necessary. A number of bosses who had agreed to pay union rates supported this assertion. Jury's logical solution was the great aim of working class struggle: "to do away with the capitalists while using the capital ourselves"—the establishment of a co-operative factory.[151] An association was founded, shares were issued, a charter was obtained and the factory opened for business in March 1879. About a year later the Toronto local of the C.M.I.U. reported that the co-operative was "progressing finely" and "doing a good trade." [152] Stratford cigar makers also founded a co-operative factory in 1886 which was owned by the Knights of Labor and run under C.M.I.U. rules. It employed between 20 and 30 men and produced a brand known as "The Little Knight." [153] Toronto Bakers Assembly LA 3499 also set up a cooperative bakery which lasted about two years in the mid-1880s. [154]

The successes or failures of these co-operative ventures are of less importance than the ideological assumptions on which they were based. Often originated only in crisis situations, they, nevertheless, flowed directly from the shop floor experience of skilled workers and the practices of their unions in struggling to control production. It was a relatively easy step from there to envisioning a system that was free of the boss who did so very little. A Chatham moulder wrote in 1864:

> This then shows both classes in their just relations towards each other—the capitalist and the mechanic; the one, the mechanic is the moving power—the capitalist bearing about the same relation to him that the cart does to the horse which draws it—differing in this respect, that the mechanic makes the capitalist and the horse does not make the cart; the capitalist without the mechanic being about as useful as the cart without the horse. The capitalist no doubt at times increases the sphere of usefulness of the mechanic; so does the cart that of the horse, and enables him to do more for his owner than otherwise he could do; but deprive him of it, and there is little that he can do with it that he could not accomplish without it. In short the workingman is the cause the capitalist the effect. [155]

The syntax may be confused but the moulder's meaning comes through clearly. In 1882 at the time of a Toronto carpenters' strike, during discussion of a co-operative planing mill, a reporter asked union leader Thomas Moor if the carpenters had the requisite skills. Moor's response was simple but profound: "If the men can manage a mill and make it a success for their employers, surely they can do the same thing for an institution in which they have an interest."[156]

Co-operation was one extension of workers' control, socialism was to be another. [157] Capital, however, also began to respond to the challenges raised by the growing tradition of workers' control. F. W. Taylor, capital's main work place ideologue, understood very well the power of the "autonomous workman":

> Now, in the best of the ordinary types of management, the managers recognize the fact that the 500 or 1,000 workmen, included in the 20 or 30 trades, who are under them, possess this mass of traditional knowledge, a large part of which is not in the possession of management .... The foremen and superintendents know, better than anyone else, that their own knowledge and personal skill falls far short of the combined knowledge and dexterity of all the workingmen under them. [158]

Taylor also reminisced at length about his first job experience in a machine shop of the Midvale Steel Company in the late 1870s:

> As was usual then, and in fact as is still usual in most of the shops in this country [1912], the shop was really run by the workmen, and not by the

> bosses. The workmen together had carefully planned just how fast each job should be done, and they had set a pace for each machine throughout the shop, which was limited to about one third of a good day's work. Every new workman who came into the shop was told at once by the other men exactly how much of each kind of work he was to do, and unless he obeyed these instructions he was sure before long to be driven out of the place by the men.[159]

After his appointment as foreman Taylor set out to increase production. He fired some of the men, lowered others' wages, hired "green" hands, lowered the piece rate—in general engaged in what he described as a "war." His limited success in this "bitter struggle" he attributed to not being of working class origin. His middle class status enabled him to convince management that worker sabotage, not the speed-up, was responsible for a sudden rash of machine breakdowns.[160]

The new popularity of Taylor and the other proponents of "scientific management" in the early twentieth century was indicative of capital's new attempt to rationalize production.[161] This, combined with the rise of the large corporation, the rapid growth of multi-plant firms, and the ever-increasing extension of labour-saving machinery, challenged directly not only workers' control traditions but also the very existence of the labour movement.

Toronto workers, who had struggled throughout the late nineteenth century for shop floor control, were about to face new, more virulent battles. The custom of workers' control, widely regarded as a right, had become deeply embedded in working class culture. The fight, initially to maintain and later to extend this control, became the major focus of class struggle in the opening decade of the twentieth century.

Thus even in the cases where craft unions abandoned the traditional practices of the "autonomous workman" in return for concessions or out of weakness, the leadership could not always assure management that the membership would follow union dictates. As one investigator noted about the foundry business:

> The customs of the trade ... do not always vanish with the omission of any recognition of "the standard day's work" in wage agreements. Nor can it be expected that the entire membership of an organization will at once respond to the removal of limitations on output by a national convention of that organization. Trade customs, shop practices grow; they become as much a part of the man as his skill as a moulder ...[162]

Written in 1904 these cautions were as true of other skilled workers as they were of moulders. Customs of control, established by struggle, would not vanish; they had to be vanquished by persistent management assault.

Excerpts from "Working Class Experience"

KNIGHTS AND WORKMEN

The most vibrant institutional development in the history of nineteenth-century North American workers-began in Philadelphia in 1869 when a small group of garment workers came together under the leadership of Uriah Stephens. They created a secret society, bound by oaths, elaborate ritual, and a commitment to the unity of all workers. More than a trade union, the resulting body, which they dubbed the Noble and Holy Order of the Knights of Labor, combined aspects of a religious brotherhood, a political reform society, a fraternal order, and a pure and simple unionism. Expanding into Pennsylvania coal mines, Pittsburgh shops, and New York factories, the Noble and Holy Order grew slowly in the 1870s, and Stephens was succeeded by Terence V. Powderly, uncharitably described by one historian as a vain and disingenuous rabble-rouser. But under Powderly the Order threw off the cloak of secrecy and, in the 1880s, captured the support of the American working man and woman as had no other labour reform organization.

The Knights drew workers into their ranks through a relatively simple procedure and institutional apparatus. Individual members joined local assemblies, either in mixed assemblies (according to diverse occupational affiliations) or trade assemblies (adhering more rigidly to specific craft categories). For a local assembly to be formally organized, a minimum of ten members was required. Once established, LAs were known to swell in membership to over 1,000. Initiation fees were set by the local, but the minimum fee was one dollar for men and fifty cents for women. Local dues, again, were controlled by individual assemblies, but they were to be not less than ten cents per month. Members were also expected to contribute to the co-operative fund, men paying ten cents monthly, women less. If a specific geographical region or trade contained five or more assemblies, a district assembly could be formed. The Order, then, was a highly centralized body, with a well-defined hierarchy and structure; yet it was also relatively egalitarian, and the local assemblies had a large measure of autonomy, with their own courts to prosecute those who transgressed the disciplines and regulations of knighthood.

Although strongest in the rapidly expanding industrial cities of Ontario such as Toronto and Hamilton, the Knights also penetrated the province's towns, villages, and tiny hamlets. Throughout the 1880s and into its declining years that stretched out to 1907, Ontario's Knights of Labor organized locals in eighty-three towns from Amherstburg in the west to Cornwall in the east, from Port Colborne in the south to Sudbury in the north. A total of 252 locals formed ten district assemblies. The province's five largest cities contained almost half of all local assemblies, but if a town had a minimum population of 3,000 or was anything of a railway centre it was almost certain to have Knights organized within it. Trade assemblies dominated in the large industrial cities where all occupations had sufficient strength to organize LAs; mixed assemblies were much more popular in smaller towns and villages where few crafts and diverse labouring sectors had the sheer numbers to stand on their own.

How many workers were drawn into the Order? This is difficult to determine. Membership peaked at different moments in different regions, and the bookkeeping of the Knights was never all that precise. Across south-central Ontario, membership in the Knights of Labor climbed to its highest point in 1886 and then declined, rapidly in some areas, more slowly in others. Towns near the American border (Brockville and Hamilton, for instance) seemed to experience the Order's impact earliest. But in north-western Ontario and in the timber country of the Muskoka region the prominence of the Knights came later, as it did in some eastern Ontario towns such as Kingston, where the Knights were said to have 1,500 supporters in 1887. In Ottawa, the Order's successes came, not in the 1880s, but in 1891. This conflicting pattern of growth is further complicated by the fact that even *within* industrial cities like Toronto and Hamilton, which followed the classic pattern of cresting in 1886, there were some working-class groups – letter carriers, longshoremen, and unskilled labourers – that joined the Knights even after the organization was in obvious retreat.

A count of peak membership at any static point in time is thus a poor measure of the Order's capacity to draw workers into its halls. Adding up

peak memberships across Ontario, for specific points in time, reveals that the Knights organized a minimum of 21,800 workers. A figure double, perhaps triple, this tally is likely a more accurate reflection of the number of workers that passed through the Order. Considering the expansion of the trade unions at the same time, it is apparent that organized labour as a percentage of the Ontario work force was reaching significant levels for the first time in the nineteenth century. In large industrial cities, manufacturing towns, and railway centres, it is entirely possible that the Knights drew 20-40 per cent of all employed workers, and in some locales the figure may well have been much higher.

In Quebec the organizational centre of the movement was in Montreal, where sixty-four local assemblies were formed between 1882 and 1902. Unlike the case in Ontario's metropolitan centres, Montreal's upsurge of the Knights continued throughout the 1890s, with a period of significant expansion in 1893-94. Approximately 2,500 workers were enrolled in Montreal's Order in 1887, and local assemblies in 1886 averaged almost 200 members. A secondary district was that of Quebec City, where at least a dozen LAs were formed. Across the province of Quebec a total of 100 or more assemblies existed, bringing French- and English-speaking workers into the same body and providing the first working-class organization for many *canadiens* in smaller towns.

To the west, the Knights of Labor quickly established themselves in the expanding railway towns and industrial enclaves of the prairie provinces. Telegraph operatives, railway workers, tailors, and carpenters led the way in Winnipeg, where as many as six local assemblies were probably established by 1887. Organization drifted west with migrant workers, and in Calgary an assembly was set up by itinerants from Owen Sound and Winnipeg. But in British Columbia, where the industrial frontier was starkest in the railway camps and mining towns, the Knights of Labor found their most receptive western Canadian audience.

Vancouver Island-based miners battled Robert Dunsmuir's coal empire throughout the 1870s, facing a stern Scot who tolerated no unionist assault on his arrogant and uncompromising rule. Politically and economically omnipotent, Dunsmuir drove his workers to clandestine organization, and they created a Miners' Mutual Protective Association that surfaced in periodic clashes between capital and labour in the years 1877-83. Class conflict in the Vancouver Island mines was always confused by the issue of race and the consciously constructed notions of "white work" versus "Oriental labour." Chinese workers had, since the 1860s, been employed in the mines, where they were relegated to the lowliest labouring job, hauling coal, often on the surface. White workers, in contrast, worked the seams underground and cultivated a sense of themselves as skilled and privileged miners. When the Chinese tried to better their lot through collective action and even early strike activity, they received little support from their white co-workers. As mine managers concentrated on increasing production, some white miners were convinced to allow the Chinese underground with them, where they could be used to do the rough work required if white miners were to up their output. The result was something of a class bargain between white labour and white capital, in which the Chinese were virtually used as beasts of burden while the miners increased their pay packets, being paid by the ton mined, and the owners saw productivity soar.

"White" and "yellow" work was thus rigidly separated, the working class irrevocably divided. As class conflict erupted in the mines in the later 1870s, the Chinese, now underground and having for years observed their white counterparts, were a ready force of strikebreakers. Popular white working-class mythology held that they had been brought into the mines as blacklegs. The truth was somewhat different, but no less destructive of working-class solidarity: white capital and white labour had, in alliance, forced the Chinese workers into a context in which their only recourse was to scab on those who had scabbed on them.

This was the unfortunate background to the labour struggles of the 1880s in British Columbia, in which the Knights of Labor would figure centrally. As Dunsmuir exploited white racism and Chinese need, bringing in more and more Orientals in the face of work stoppages, miners and other white workers formed the Workmen's Protective Association in 1878 to combat "the great influx of Chinese." Building on such precedents, the Knights of Labor entered British Columbia in 1883, establishing six local assemblies in Vancouver, two in Wellington, and one each in Nanaimo, New Westminster, Victoria, Yale, Kamloops, and Rossland. These LAs gained prominence in the mid-1880s and rallied the west coast's white working class in opposition to the Chinese, recently thrust even more prominently into the labour market with the termination of their exploitation on the construction gangs of the Canadian Pacific Railway. In Victoria, the Knights of Labor upheaval coincided with the emergence of John Duval's *Industrial News* and the rise of the Anti-Chinese Union.

The Knights of Labor history on the west coast is thus interwoven with a racist working-class attack on Oriental workers. This attack was sustained as the Knights of Labor constructed an image of the Chinese worker as "the Other," that which was the very opposition of the "manly" mechanic. In a Knights of Labor statement to an 1885 Royal Commission, Oriental labour was denounced as "low, degraded, and servile." Being "without family ties," this sub-species of workers was not only able to work for wages far below those demanded by white labour but to "grow rich" on this inferior pay. Products of "humble submission to a most oppressive system of government," the Chinese were, in the eyes of the Knights of Labor, "willing tools whereby grasping and tyrannical employers grind down all labor to the lowest living point."

The conjuncture of working-class upheaval and organization associated with west coast Knights of Labor and the explosion of an intense anti-Oriental working-class agitation skewed the content of class conflict in British Columbia (and elsewhere) in the 1880s. But the exclusion of the Chinese, however nefarious as a plank in labour's program, was far from the only cause promoted by the Order. Shorter hours, antagonism to monopoly, condemnation of political corruption, organization of workers, and resistance at the workplace were also all critically important, if understudied, aspects of the Knights of Labor presence on the west coast.

On the east coast, the Knights of Labor also secured a foothold, albeit a weak one. Local assemblies existed in Moncton, Saint John, Halifax, Amherst, North Sydney, New Glasgow, Campbellton, and Truro, although they never extended into the working class in any significant way, being almost entirely restricted to the telegraph operatives whose defeat in a momentous 1883 international conflict seemed to seal the fate of the Order in the Maritime provinces. A number of LAs arrived in the late 1890s among the coal miners of Cape Breton, organized in District Assembly 35 at Glace Bay, but this minor organizational growth was but a pale reflection of the east coast's more entrenched and previously established regional labour movement, based on a body that opposed the Knights of Labor at the same time as it seemed strikingly similar.

As workers in central Canada flocked to the Knights of Labor in the 1880s, east coast labourers in the mines, on the docks, and in the shops cast their lot with Robert Drummond's Provincial Workmen's Association (PWA). Originally formed in the woods adjacent to the Springhill Mining Company, the PWA established its pioneer lodge in late August, 1879, and first bore the name of the Provincial Miners' Association (PMA). But like the Noble and Holy Order of the Knights of Labor (also formed by workers of a particular occupation), it soon tried to extend its organizational focus as well as its name, and took as its slogan the words, "Strength lies in unity."

Never as successful as the Knights in broadening its appeal beyond a specific group of workers, the PMA was led by the miners of Springhill, Stellarton, Westville, and Thorburn. It organized loaders, check weightmen, trappers, labourers, and miners in the mainland coal fields of Nova Scotia, and by October, 1879, enrolled almost 650 in its ranks. Wharfmen at Granton, engaged in loading coal on the ships, formed a lodge soon afterward, and following the October, 1880, meeting of the organization in Truro the five-lodge body changed its name to the Provincial Workmen's Association. Drummond was encouraged to bring the Cape Breton miners, previously unorganized, into the cause. Nine lodges were soon established, and the PWA claimed a membership of 1,200 in Cape Breton (probably an exaggeration since there were only 1,725 miners on the island, and they did not attain closed-shop status during this period). Glass and foundry workers in New Glasgow and Pictou County also joined, and throughout the 1880s the PWA expanded; in 1884 it had 1,860 members in good standing. In

Amherst, boot and shoe workers once associated with the Knights of Labor LA 2209) founded Concord Lodge of the PWA in 1891 after their employer fired a number of the Order's activists.

By 1897 the PWA claimed to be "the strongest single labour organization in Canada," but it was already on the verge of an internal crisis as Robert Drummond followed an increasingly conciliatory policy of refusing to oppose the "pluck-me" stores of the Dominion Coal Company in return for the company's willingness to collect union dues regularly. This collaboration angered Drummond's members, who gravitated to the more militant tactics of the Knights of Labor in the years after 1898. By 1899, the number of PWA lodges had declined from sixteen to three, and membership dropped to 1,000. Surviving into the twentieth century (and outlasting the Knights), the PWA, abandoned by Drummond, would continue to follow a moderate stance in its dealings with employers and would be used later as a force to keep the United Mine Workers of America (UMWA) out of the region's coal fields. Its powerlessness apparent by 1904, the Provincial Workmen's Association eventually succumbed to the larger international union; the body dissolved in 1917.

Where the Knights of Labor failed, the UMWA would succeed, and in 1918, 98 per cent of the PWA's former membership voted to affiliate with District 26 of the international union. Ultimately liquidated by its own rank and file, the early PWA was nevertheless, as Sharon Reilly has argued, and as an 1886 statement claimed, "a response to the wishes of men who had been subjected to indignities, who had suffered loss, who were well trodden down, and yet who had in them a sturdy spirit of independence." Like the Knights of Labor (which it resembled in its attachment to ritual and fraternity, as well as its message of solidarity), the PWA was an initial announcement of the consolidation of working-class opposition in the 1880s.

The form of that opposition was obviously different in the Maritimes than it was in central Canada, as Ian McKay has recently suggested. The PWA shared a good deal with the Knights of Labor, but it also evolved in ways that reflected the contrasting material experiences of workers in Canada's regions. In Ontario the Knights of Labor reached into virtually every community and drew on a continental labour-reform vision; the Provincial Workmen's Association was a more limited body. Yet in its limitations lay a good part of its potency: militant lodges, few in number but powerful in their influence and impact, had a greater longevity than the more volatile local assemblies of the Knights; ethnic and occupational homogeneity secured the PWA in the world of the Scottish collier in ways that were unlikely if not impossible in the more economically diversified and culturally heterogeneous industrial heartland of Ontario's Noble and Holy Order; and Drummond's orchestration of a political alliance with the Nova Scotia Liberal Party, rooted in the vital importance of coal mining to the region's political economy, allowed labour a legislative impact that may well have

been greater than anywhere else in Canada. All of this rested on the PWA's commitment to working-class independence. This was never an easy end to achieve, but it was at the heart of the coal miner's conception of himself, was negotiated with employers in complex ways that played on the coal community's paternalist ethos, and was regularly fought out in strikes. As McKay notes, the Provincial Workmen's Association was "the critical force of dissent in the Maritimes," its seventy-two strikes in the 1879-1900 years being the "major nineteenth-century response in the region to the coming of industrial capitalism."

Knights and Workmen, then, dramatically expanded the institutions of the workers' movement in the 1880s, providing the organizational focus of a labour upsurge. Different but similar, these oppositional movements mark a new stage in the development of workers within Canada's regions. The preceding discussion has provided a cursory introduction to this process, a brief listing of some achievements. Workers in the 1880s attained their greatest accomplishments as the ambiguous, fractured, and unfocused raw material of working-class life was moulded into a movement culture of opposition and alternative, a process of working-class self-activity that took the collectivist impulses of labouring experience and shaped them into a reform mobilization.

A MOVEMENT CULTURE

This movement culture was most visible in the Ontario experience of the Knights of Labor, where ritual and procession, symbolism and soirée, combined to proclaim the unity of all labour, an undertaking of opposition and challenge that distinguished the 1880s from previous decades of labouring people's experience. The Order's effectiveness stemmed from its ability to build on the mundane class distinctions of daily life and to construct out of this a movement that attempted to unite all workers to oppose the oppression and exploitation that they lived through both on and off the job. On the one hand, the Knights of Labor developed out of a social, cultural, political, and economic context in which class differentiation had been developing over decades; on the other, they pushed all of this forward, posing alternatives, striking a posture of opposition. Much of this also happened in other regions and among workers unaffiliated with the Noble and Holy Order, particularly among the militant and large colliers' lodges of the Provincial Workmen's Association. But the Knights of Labor present perhaps the clearest expression of this process, providing insight into how the closing decades of the nineteenth century elevated the "labour question" to a previously unanticipated importance.

The men and women of the new movement entered their local assembly halls with deeply held convictions. In the symbolism and richly suggestive ritual of the Order, both the strengths of the past and the purposes of the present were revealed, introducing us, as well, to the class values upon which the Knights constructed their alternative vision and the movement culture that sought to transform the very nature of Victorian Canada.

Indeed, each Knight of Labor entered the Order through a ritualistic procedure that cemented him or her in specific traditions, pledging eternal secrecy, strict obedience, and scrupulous charity toward new brothers and sisters. Every initiate vowed to defend the interest and reputation of all true members of the Knights of Labor – employed or unemployed, fortunate or distressed – and was instructed that "to rescue the toiler from the grasp of the selfish is a work worthy of the noblest and best of our race." The Order endeavoured to "secure the just rewards" of honest work and to prevent the trampling of "poor humanity in the dust." Secret signs, oaths, passwords, and grips further consolidated the attachment to collective principles and protected labouring people from the hostility of anti-Knights of Labor employers. Reverberating throughout this ritualistic and symbolic content of the Knights of Labor was the centrality of class pride, the awareness of the worth of the working man and woman. This, above all else, drew adherents to the cause.

Festivals, dinners, and workers' balls gave cultural force to this developing opposition, "cementing together the bonds of unity," as one early labour newspaper reported in 1873. Picnics and dinners came to assume an importance beyond mere recreation, uniting workers and making them more "competent to fight the Monster (Capital)." Across central Canada in the 1880s – in Hamilton, Toronto, London, Montreal, Oshawa, Gananoque, Belleville, and Ingersoll – workers affiliated with the Knights of Labor mounted huge labour parades and demonstrations drawing thousands to the public proclamation of labour reform. French and English came together in a series of labour demonstrations, picnics, and excursions in Montreal that took place during the 1880s and culminated in a grand Labour Day parade held in September, 1891. Such events, like the earlier trade processions in Saint John, were visible reminders of labour's strength. But unlike the community-based events of 1840 and 1853 in Saint John, the parades of the 1880s linked towns and cities. If the district assemblies of Toronto and Montreal drew 10,000 or more to their gala events, no less impressive were the thousands the Order could attract to manufacturing hamlets like Ingersoll and Gananoque.

Challenged by such public displays of worker unity, segments of the dominant culture were driven to adapt to the new realities of industrial-capitalist society and its class polarization. There is evidence that in some communities established religion suffered setbacks and that the Knights of Labor usurped the traditional role of the church. Montreal labour activist William Darlington claimed: "The Knights preach more Christianity than the churches." Church sources bemoaned "the gradual falling away of those whom the respectability of the middle classes does not see and the dignity of the rich . . . ignores," and were distressed by the "lapsed masses." Historians have long recognized the class tensions inherent in church-labour movement relations, and from the pulpit came many hostile commentaries on strikes and working-class activism. The labour leadership gave as good as it got. A Hamilton leader, using the pen name "Vox Populi," expressed what must have been a widespread critique in labour circles of city pastors and their houses of worship: "You love Jesus Christ, you love to preach about him and do his will, I too with my Br. Knights love his doctrine, and strive to carry out his will, also to obey his command, love one another . . . it is not Christ I find fault with, but the inconsistent doctrines taught in or favored by the church."

Among some sectors of established religion – Methodists and Presbyterians, especially – these words found a hearing, and there were condemnations of "selfish capitalists" and admissions that "upon our land lies a dark reproach. By those in high places the poor are repressed." One Kingston minister proclaimed that "Labor was squeezed and enslaved by monopolies . . . because of this enslavement production was slackened just as land was schackled also, the same effect was produced." Religion, then, was often confronted by labour's upsurge. If it could bare its teeth in class hostility and condemnation of worker activism, it was also on occasion forced to adopt a stance and a language of recognition if not appeasement. Few workers lost totally their conceptions of Christian behaviour, but many reconstructed their religious views in ways that attended more directly to class grievance and need. The movement culture had not so much defeated religious institutions, but Christian practice – both in its organizational sense and in terms of its working-class constituency – might be modified in the face of it.

As Doris O'Dell shows in a unique study of the class character of church participation in Belleville, there were all kinds of ways in which class distinctions, supposedly absent in religious life, were reinforced within congregations. Seating arrangements, uneven financial contributions, styles of worship, differences between evening and morning services, and contrasts between neighbourhood churches of the same denomination all reflected the presence of class within religious life. O'Dell establishes that workers involved themselves in this life at the same time as they filtered its messages and forms through their own class-informed conceptions of the world.

The extent to which enthusiastic religious movements alternative to the established churches, such as the Salvation Army, might attract working-class men and women also reinforces the point that class was, by the 1880s, an unmistakable factor within the spiritual milieu of Victorian Canada. The raucous services of the Sally Ann, its rowdy parades, all-night meetings, and circus-like performers appealed to the unskilled and working-class women who, for a time in the 1880s, flocked to the Hallelujah Army. Lynne Marks has provided an invaluable look at the class content of Salvation Army experience in small-town Ontario of the 1880s, tantalizingly suggesting that the experiences of the Knights of Labor and the Sally Ann overlapped. There is little proof of this since comparable membership lists are simply not available, but a sensitive and sympathetic reading of Marks's excellent research suggests the potency of class identifications in the 1880s as well as the extent to which the Knights of Labor employed religious rhetoric and evangelical language to convey its message and draw workers to its ranks. The Salvation Army was often strong in precisely those communities where the Knights of Labor set up local assemblies, and Marks hints at connections between the working-class soldiers of the Army and the workplace presence of the Knights, noting that Kingston labourers held noon-day prayer meetings in the midst of an 1883 Salvation Army campaign and then, four years later, joined the Knights of Labor and went out on strike. In the same year, there is evidence that Belleville's iron worker Knights attended Salvation Army meetings.

So much was clearly in turmoil in the 1880s and class identification was central to what must have been a turbulent period in the formation of working-class identities. One reading of Marks's exploration of the Salvation Army is that it galvanized class-based religiosity at the very point that mainstream churches were occasionally failing to address adequately working-class realities. This process may have actually pre-dated the mass upsurge of the Knights of Labor, helping to condition a climate in which workers would be drawn to the Order in later years. Many interpretive questions remain, but Marks's detailed examination of the working-class content of the Salvation Army in the 1880s reminds us of the importance of religion within class formation. Like O'Dell, she is suggesting strongly that attempts to see religious experience as only a denial or suppression of working-class needs and aspirations are misplaced. Obviously, the conjuncture of class and religion in the 1880s had many sides, and the experience is not easily collapsed into specific interpretive containers, one receptive to class, the other antagonistic.

Even in Catholic-dominated Quebec, where Church opposition to the Knights of Labor in particular and labour militancy in general probably exceeded that found elsewhere, circular letters from Archbishop Taschereau (February 2, 1885) and all bishops (June 20, 1886) prohibiting membership in this "cosmopolitant" "occult-led" secret society failed to drive the Order from the province. Although the membership did indeed decline after this antagonistic intervention, the Vatican overrode Taschereau, and Richard J. Kerrigan, a Montreal workers' advocate, recalled the "dynamic year of 1886" as one in which the Knights defended themselves against the Archbishop's attack:

> The Knights of Labor grew to alarming proportions in the country, and the Province of Quebec, always the political storm centre of Canada, had to get drastic treatment if it were to be kept safe and sane for law and order. Bishop Taschereau of Quebec launched his famous excommunication decree against the Knights of Labor.... This did not hurt the Knights much.... This high-handed action of this over-officious servant of God had the effect of driving the bulk of the intelligent French-speaking proletariat away from the "faith of their fathers" and when the edict was spoken of among the French militant Knights of Labor it was agreed that ... "Of this we will not die."

Across Canada, the bishops' opposition produced only minor problems, and even in Montreal, where one would expect the edicts to have their most far-reaching consequences, twenty-three new local assemblies were organized in 1886. While the ecclesiastical furore may have led to the disappearance of some Montreal assemblies and of a few others at Richmond and Upper Bedford, those throughout the rest of the province survived, and by 1887 the Order in Quebec was approaching its peak strength.

Other aspects of the dominant culture also seem to have undergone change in response to the rise of the Knights of Labor. Temperance, an early plank in industrial-capitalist work discipline, became a mark of working-class independence, a cause for all Knights of Labor to champion vocally and practically. Instead of relying totally on dime novels and popular religious tracts, which were always capable of being produced and read with a content of class differentiation in mind, workers turned as well to works of social criticism and tracts of labour reform. The cumulative effect of these and other developments altered the nature of social relationships in hundreds of Canadian communities.

The most vital contribution of this movement culture was the message of labour solidarity. Long-standing points of division within working-class life – skilled versus unskilled; male versus female; Protestant versus Catholic – were opposed by the Order's conscious and persistent attempt to construct an alternative vision of the possibility of solidarity. In their call for all workers to unite, the Knights of Labor struggled to create a national working class committed to the internationalism of the labour movement. One Hamilton Knight wrote of this in 1887:

> When we entered the Order we were taught that in the home of labor there would be no distinctions of Country, Creed & Color because all were of the Earth and with equal rights to Earth, when we understood this great truth that all men are brothers we rejoiced, and we solemnly resolved that we would do all in our power to strengthen the bonds of unity between the workers of the world and we are still steadfast to our principles.

This promise of working-class unity was nowhere more apparent than in the attempts to integrate Irish workers into the labour movement, for in the process of overcoming ethnic and religious prejudice the traditional gulf separating skilled and unskilled was also bridged because many Irish lacked craft skills. The Knights of Labor hailed efforts to unite Orange and Green, declaring that "Sectarian bigotry is now the only weapon that capital has to wield, and . . . [the Order] is rendering it more and more harmless every day." A good part of the Noble and Holy Order's force lay in a radical alliance composed of one part support for Irish nationalism and another part endorsement of labour reform. Thus, Gordon Bishop, a Gananoque steel worker, recalled in the 1940s that the Knights were led "by members of the Irish race who fled the slavery of peonage in their own lands and who hated as fiercely the economic slavery of the New World."

Symbolic and ritualistic practice, coupled with public display and assaults on previously divisive forces therefore stood at the centre of the movement culture's experience throughout the 1880s. As the Knights of Labor swept across Canada, they forged a unity among labourers previously unattained and unanticipated. They found some of their strongest backers and promoters among working-class intellectuals and activists, and achieved new organizational strength by including women, uniting the particular oppression of sex with the cause of the exploited working class.

BRAINWORKERS

In April of 1886, J.L. Blain of Galt wrote to Knights of Labor leader T.V. Powderly, describing himself as a well-educated "rat from the sinking ship of aristocracy." He told of his efforts in the cause of labour reform, of the lectures he had given on "Capital and Labor," where he proposed remedies for the "present unjust state of society in which 50 percent of the products are absorbed by nonproducers." Blain was one of literally hundreds of intellectuals (called "brainworkers"), activists, editors, lecturers, people's poets, and organizers who "spread the light" during the 1880s and 1890s. As both products and producers of labour's upsurge, these working-class advocates emerged from the local assemblies of the Knights of Labor, lodges of the Provincial Workmen's Association, and the trade unions, mounted platforms in labour demonstrations where their talents as speakers were exploited to the full, and penned social criticism that attacked the inequities of the age.

The labour-reform newspaper was their most obvious vehicle for activism. In the pages of well-known Toronto-Hamilton journals, such as the *Labor Union*, *Palladium of Labor*, *Wage Worker*, *Trade Union Advocate*, *Canadian Labor Reformer*, *Labor Record*, and *Labor Advocate*, the movement culture of the 1880s and 1890s was at its most vibrant and visible. The

existence of other similar organs, from the Victoria-based *Industrial News* to the PWA's *Trades Journal*, demonstrated the scope of the working-class reform presence in these years. Always balanced delicately on the brink of financial ruin, such newspapers kept afloat during these years only by dint of extraordinary effort, personal perseverance, and occasional support from a long-established trade union. They had many differences, but all strove to "take a broader and more comprehensive view of the entire subject of Labor Reform than is embodied in mere unionism, and to grasp and apply those great underlying principles of equity and justice between men which alone can permanently and satisfactorily solve the issues between Labor and Capital." This was an important component of what Frank Watt has referred to as the "freely germinating radicalism" of the 1880s.

In this environment Canada's most significant late nineteenth-century labour reformer eventually came of age as a radical social critic. In the early 1860s, while working for the *St. Catharines Post*, Phillips Thompson started the intellectual odyssey that would take him from the humour columns of the daily press through the Knights of Labor to the post-1900 socialist movement. By the 1880s his writings consistently sought to elevate people's conception of their own sense of self, striking at deeply rooted feelings of inadequacy. For Thompson, as for so many other "brainworkers" in labour's cause, the industrial struggle was waged not just in the factories, mines, and shops but also in the realm of ideas. In his major work, *The Politics of Labor*, Thompson alerted Canadian workers to new ways of viewing history, political economy, and literature, launching a trenchant critique of bourgeois culture. Always suitable for mass consumption, his message represented something of the "high" side of the movement culture's agitational prose: its sophisticated and radical scrutiny focused with rigour on monopoly in the economic sphere and the privileged snobbery of the "uppertendom" in areas of social relations and the arts. Quietly assimilated if not loudly endorsed by local reformers, Thompson's arguments found an echo in the "low" realms of the movement culture, appearing in anonymous lines of verse that chronicled class grievances:

> Oh! ye toilers have ye felt cold and hunger,
> And been warned with poverty's breath?
> Have your hearts been soaked with your sorrow?
> Have you slept in the shadow of death?

or offered words of encouragement:

> 'Tis the foremost thing to do –
> Spread the Light!
> Till the world is made anew –
> Spread the Light!

It is darkness that enslaves,
Those who dwell in dens and caves,
Knowledge strengthens – knowledge saves –
Spread the Light!

This kind of exhortation to activism was at the centre of the recruiting drive that brought the Knights of Labor to prominence and pushed and promoted the ideas and activities of other labour bodies across Canada.

Those cities in which Thompson figured centrally – Toronto and Hamilton – produced labour spokesmen whose impact would be felt across the province: A.W. Wright, Alfred Jury, Charles March, William H. Rowe, George Collis, William Vale, Thomas Towers, Edward Williams, and D.J. O'Donoghue (who had moved from Ottawa to Toronto). In Montreal, activists such as A.T. Lépine and future socialists William Darlington and Richard Kerrigan were prominent, while in the Maritimes the PWA's Robert Drummond and Martin Butler, editor of his own Fredericton-based *Journal*, championed the workers' cause in the 1880s and 1890s. The latter was an exemplar of nineteenth-century radicalism, proclaiming his religion as "universal brotherhood" and determining, in 1893-94, to "abolish the false economic system that makes one man rich out of the blood and sweat of a thousand of his fellow men."

Butler, who lost an arm to a machine while working in an American tannery at the age of eighteen, eked out a living as a pedlar, poet, and journalist, all the while sowing the seeds of labour reform. By the turn of the century his radicalism was tempered by the unpopularity of his anti-Boer War views. In 1900 he noted, "The democratic tree has been pulled up by the roots and the ground seeded down with the seeds of imperialism and aristocracy." Like Thompson, he left behind the nineteenth century to enter the twentieth, where, he told his readers, "One star only shines on the horizon, and that is Socialism, the doctrine that all men are brothers, have the same rights of opportunity, education and enjoyment and the product of their hands, wrung from the bountiful mother earth, created by the Father of all for the equal use of his children." This was a language that indicated how much the developing "progressive" ideas of the epoch were cast in older, familiar vocabularies of religion and masculinist power, but it was also, in its embrace of socialism, an expression of political movement.

What was in part unique about the 1880s, then, was that the decade produced a stratum of bona fide working-class leaders, some drawn from the ranks of labour, others attracted from the outside. These "brainworkers" served, as G.H. Allaby has argued in a study of New Brunswick reformers around 1900, as "prophets of radicalism." In the 1860s there had been only a handful of such types, and they had little continuous, stable presence in the ranks of the working class. Moreover, they often embraced activities and rhetoric that were thoroughly compromised. This had

changed by the 1880s. Working-class intellectuals and activists were a significant social force, a dispersed collection of dissidents with a movement at their back and institutions and vehicles at hand to help propagate their ideas. They helped to cultivate, in Phillips Thompson's words, a vision of an alternative society in which universal democracy and co-operation could triumph over war and monopoly. The "beautiful ideal" of the brainworkers was born in the 1880s, when the possibilities of labour reform seemed boundless. This ability to "dream of what might be" if "the world's workers were only educated and organized" was deepened and complemented by significant achievements in drawing an important and previously excluded segment of the working class into the movement culture.

WOMEN

Women had become a vital component of the labour force across North America by the 1880s, representing approximately 15 per cent of the gainfully employed and numbering almost 3 million. Shunned by most labour associations, women were even excluded by the Knights of Labor until, in 1881, Mary Stirling and her co-workers in Philadelphia's Mundell & Company's shoe works defied their employer in a strike and spontaneously organized the Garfield Assembly, named in honour of the recently assassinated president. With the aid of some male Knights, Stirling and her sisters persuaded delegates at the 1881 General Assembly to open the Order's doors officially to women. From that point on, women became a force in the Knights of Labor, and by 1886 almost 200 women's local assemblies had been organized in the United States.

In Canada, especially in the Ontario stronghold of the Order, women became an important presence in the Knights of Labor. By 1891, one wage labourer in eight was a woman, and female workers comprised a low-paid group that the Royal Commission on the Relations of Labor and Capital in Canada (1889) reported could be "counted on to work for small wages, to submit to exasperating exactions, and to work uncomplainingly for long hours." Concentrated in cotton textiles, shoe factories, and domestic service (by far the largest category), women also worked in the sweated trades of garment production and the tobacco industry, and were scattered across a wide array of other employments. Their wages, on average, were approximately one-third those of their male counterparts.

This material divergence had long formed the basis of a profound separation between male and female workers, and the introduction of women into the mass struggles and organizational upsurge of the 1880s began to overcome decades of complacency. While the Order as a whole failed to address decisively the particular oppression of sex, often being inhibited by a confining adherence to the consensual norms of Victorian morality and conventional gender relations, it nevertheless raised the question of the role of women within working-class circles with a seriousness that was unprecedented. In examining the fragmentary historical evidence of the relationship of the Knights of Labor to female workers, it becomes obvious once again that the Order contributed to an alternative vision of social relations, edging the consolidating working-class opposition on to entirely new ground. For if the Knights of Labor remained inhibited by the cultural norms of a society that circumscribed woman's role and established the usual "proper sphere," it did defy those norms in its attempts to build a movement encompassing all workers – male and female. And in this it appears to have gone beyond much of the practice of other working-class organizations, such as the PWA and many of the trade unions, an advance not unrelated to the ways in which gender, skill, and occupation came together in the coal fields or the trades as compared to the more heterogeneous manufacturing milieu the Knights entered into in Ontario in the 1880s.

Hamilton's *Palladium of Labor* reflected the Order's refusal to ignore the plight of the woman worker at the same time that it echoed the confinements of the age. It argued, on the one hand, that women came into the Knights of Labor as the peers of men, equal to them and deserving of the same pay in the workplace and the same recognition in the political and social spheres. There was apparently no position within the movement that a woman could not hold, and women such as Leonora M. Barry became organizers, while others, such as Amherstburg's Rose Le May, became district master workmen. This practice of equality, however, was occasionally undermined by conventionality, and some women's LAs petitioned Powderly to allow them to invite men to chair their proceedings, so reluctant were many women to occupy public posts of authority. Moreover, a commitment to women's advance was often tarnished within the Order by a retreat into the domestic ideology of the times and a chivalrous deference to femininity: "Upon motherhood we base brotherhood, and in our family circle we pledge ourselves to defend the fair name and reputation of an innocent sister even with our lives," declared the *Palladium*. "If there is any preeminence given either sex in our Order," continued the paper, "it is given to women."

The flip side of this "elevation" of woman was, of course, the rights of male protectors, which could run amuck in familial authoritarianism and traditional assertions of patriarchal power. The Knights of Labor thus defied convention by opening assembly halls to women workers at the same time that they extended this invitation to organize with a hand gloved in the traditionalism of gender difference. When Canadian women were won to the cause of labour reform, it was seldom through the strike, the mass campaign, the boycott, or the demonstration. Rather, for the "fair sex," the ticket into the Order was often stamped at the soirée, the hop, or the social,

and it was possible for editors like Hamilton's William H. Rowe to contrast the "pining and wasp-waisted, doll-dressed, consumption-mortgaged, music murdering, novel-devouring, daughters of fashion and idleness" to "the real lady" who could "darn a stocking and mend her own dress . . . a girl that young men are in quest of for a wife." Passages like this spoke simultaneously of the Knights of Labor attempt to address class and gender *and* the limitations of that effort.

Rowe's crude moralizing and constricted view of women's place did not deter workers like Katie McVicar, Hamilton's pioneer woman organizer, from posing the issue of central concern to working women in a more realistic manner: "Our employers are organized for the purpose of keeping the selling prices up and the manufacturing prices down, and we ought certainly to accept the assistance and invitation of our gentlemen Knights and organize; remain no longer strangers to each other, but combine and protect ourselves to some purpose." In the years after 1884, McVicar's line of argument would be pursued by others, albeit often anonymously. But women also came out openly for reform, and a few, like Belleville poet Marie Joussaye and Picton social critic and writer Elizabeth Johnson, joined the ranks of central Canadian "brainworkers." These developments helped to instill a sense of sisterhood among working women, but one that was class bound. An open letter to the "working girls" of Canada in 1885 closed on the note that female workers must not look to the law, the church, or "the high-born sister women for help." "Sisters," concluded this address, "by our dignity, co-operation, and organization, we must protect ourselves." As the movement grew and more women became attached to the cause of labour, gains were made, and in the consequent expansion of understanding the restrictions of women's place were cut back and eroded.

Out of this emerged demands for women's suffrage, a recognition of the vitally important place of unpaid domestic labour, attempts to organize previously unorganized women workers, and calls for equal pay for equal work. The act of drawing women into the labour movement – women who had before been isolated on the margins of trade union, workplace, or political struggles – was critical in many Canadian communities, an initial step in the process of overcoming gender subordination within the working class. Over the course of the 1880s approximately 10 per cent, or twenty-five out of 250, of the Ontario local assemblies contained women. Most of these female members of the Order were employed in cotton mills, shoe factories, and the garment industry; isolated domestics and clerks were less responsive, understandably, to the lure of the Knights of Labor. Throughout this recruitment, the Order's defence of "the right of women to be regarded in all matters of citizenship and all relations between the government and the people as the equal of men" was paramount. This, according to Phillips Thompson, could "hardly be denied by any clear-sighted and consistent Labor Reformer." American land reform and single tax advocate Henry

George put the matter in a similar light when he argued before a Hamilton audience that "The women have a right to come into your organizations. . . . The women are the best men we have."

In late nineteenth-century Knights of Labor strongholds like Belleville, Brantford, Hamilton, Montreal, Stratford, Thorold, and Toronto, then, women joined the Order in assemblies named "Hope" and "Advance" with the intention of realizing parts of the possibility of women's emancipation. From today's standpoint, attendance at musical and literary entertainments as "Goddesses of Liberty" or membership in a local assembly named "Excelsior" (which expressed elevated status) might point less to liberation than to an innately sexist idolization of femininity. Yet in the challenge of the 1880s, such honorifics were an articulation of dignity and worth felt to be the birthright of all individuals, including labouring women. To acknowledge the place of working women within the general human condition represented a great advance over past practice and played a not inconsiderable role in changing male workers' views of women and female workers' views of themselves. The possibility, in the end, was far from realized; but it nevertheless existed. The Knights of Labour, and the movement culture of the 1880s, had begun the process whereby the questions of class and gender could be considered as one.

POLITICS

The movement culture of the 1880s shifted parts of the existing terms of class relations, drawing unskilled workers, women, and the Irish from the periphery into the very centre of late nineteenth-century labour-reform agitation. In this attempt to construct a wider-ranging solidarity, workers glimpsed the potential of working-class unity that could change the world in which they lived.

Labour leaders knew that party attachments were strong among workingmen (women, too, had their loyalties, but they could not vote) and many who espoused reform were actually committed to one of the established political bodies, Grit or Tory. But politics of this sort was often regarded as a dirty corner, crowded with manipulators, "wire-pullers," and con artists. There was money to be had from the conventional parties, and many in the labour-reform milieu saw the need to overcome the consequent compromising character of traditional political involvement and influence-peddling. Some opted for simply pressuring the established parties to behave more honestly and operate in the interests of workers, but the more unique and lasting accomplishment of the decade was the initiation of independent political action. Sir John A. Macdonald, leader of the federally entrenched Tories and long adept at turning working-class discontent to his own party's good fortune, worried in the 1880s that he was losing his grip on the political workingman. In his view there were dangerous "rocks ahead," threatening the Conservative ship. Among them were the Knights of Labor.

From the moment of its entrance into Canada, the Order engaged in politics actively. As early as 1882 pro-labour aldermen were elected in Hamilton, and in the 1883 Ontario provincial election labour reformers launched independent campaigns to seat working-class candidates. In some cities Labor Political Associations were formed. Much of this political work was engineered by leading Knights of Labor, who were also involved heavily in the influential Toronto Trades and Labor Council and the recently founded Trades and Labor Congress of Canada, which first met in 1883. They played a key role in the election of W.H. Howland, an unambiguous reformer, as mayor in Toronto in 1885. Such gains drew concessions from the Ottawa-ensconced Tories and spurred labour reformers on to new political efforts.

Both the December, 1886, Ontario election and the February, 1887, federal election saw strong working-class efforts to vote labour spokesmen into the respective legislative bodies. In the provincial contest, seven working-class candidates took the field. One ran for the Grits (Reform/Liberal) and two ran for the Tories (Conservatives), but their labour affiliations were made more important than those of previous working-class candidates in that they billed themselves as "Liberal-Labour" and "Labour-Conservative." Four candidates ran as independents, shunning the established political parties. They would all lose, but often such independents took a major share of the vote. London Knight of Labor Samuel Peddle, for instance, gave Tory opposition leader W.R. Meredith a run for his money in the provincial election. Meredith had won his seat by easy acclamation in the previous contest. Two of the labour candidates who campaigned on traditional tickets actually won provincial seats: St. Thomas Tory brakeman and Knight of Labor Andy Ingram in West Elgin, and Lib-Lab candidate William Garson in Lincoln-St. Catharines. The February federal election, however, saw working-class candidates shut out. In this context of minor victories the Knights of Labor stepped up their lobbying efforts, establishing a legislative committee in the late 1880s. But the most accessible political lever was still that of the municipal council, and combined Knights of Labor-trade union forces won a number of impressive political battles in this area: Brantford, Chatham, Brockville, and Ottawa were all sites of municipal victories.

In Quebec, labour's political voice was heard most clearly in the Knights of Labor stronghold of Montreal. Described in detail by Fernand Harvey and in unpublished studies by Victor Chan and Robert Cox, labour became especially active in politics in 1886, when the Order supported three candidates in the provincial election. Another workers' candidate, Charles Champagne, ran in the industrial district of Hochelaga. All were backed by the working-class community, all were affiliated with the Knights of Labor, and all would refuse to compromise their independence by running for the established Grit and Tory parties. However, none of these labour candidates won. As in the case of Scots saddler William W. Robertson, defeat was partly attributable to principled political stands against national chauvinism. Robertson refused to placate English-speaking prejudices against French Canadians and no doubt paid the price in Anglophone votes. "Make the labour candidates custodians of the country's morality and integrity," he shouted from one podium, raising the movement culture's banner of an alternative to partyism and corruption. When one French-speaking candidate was wooed by the Liberals, led by nationalist Francophone Honoré Mercier, he declined the bait of easy identification with a party headed by a Québécois. "I will not put the labour question in second place," he replied. Although defeated, the labour trio gained 6,000 of the 18,000 votes cast in the three Montreal districts. William Keys, an Irish machinist employed in various Griffintown shops, took his failure at the polls in stride, assessing his campaign positively: "I consider my candidature to be a triumph as it has shown the wealthier classes what workingmen can do."

This entry into the political fray necessarily moved the established powers in the direction of concession. Defeats conditioned a more tolerant view within labour-reform ranks of those who would combine class interests with traditional party politics, and in an 1888 federal election a Tory workingman and Knights of Labor organizer, A.T. Lépine, won a seat in Montreal East. As in Ontario, however, the most influential victories may well have taken place at the municipal level. The Order elected an alderman and a councillor in Quebec City in 1892, and the mayor and nine of twelve aldermen in Hull in 1894.

Miners on the east and west coasts also took their first strides into the political field in these years. The *Trades Journal*, voice of the Provincial Workmen's Association, declared in 1885 that the "ballot must be the means to secure our just desires, maintain our rights, put good men in power, and hurl tyrants out." PWA candidates ran in the Nova Scotia provincial election of 1886, Robert Drummond as an independent Liberal in Pictou County and James Wilson as a straight workers' candidate in Cumberland. Both lost, but in the process the PWA, Drummond, and Liberal Premier W.S. Fielding began to negotiate a complex alliance that would result, according to Ian McKay, in the PWA securing "the most impressive series of reforms wrung by a Canadian trade union from a nineteenth-century government." Over the course of the late 1880s regulatory legislation did much to establish a regime of industrial legality in the coal fields, key features of which were the introduction of compulsory arbitration as an alternative to strikes and certification procedures for colliery officials. When Fielding, in 1889, extended the franchise to miners

living in company housing it appeared that Drummond had indeed secured for the coal miners "the badge of citizenship." This had not so much been won at the polls as it had been accomplished through a mutually beneficial set of parallel understandings on the part of Drummond and Fielding. The personalized icing on this political cake was Drummond's appointment to the Legislative Council in 1891, a posting that would gradually degenerate from one of misguided good intentions to overt enjoyment of the pleasures of office.

There would be other problems with this statist panacea, but the PWA had shown how much of a political presence labour could be in a province in the midst of economic transformation. Tensions between Drummond and Fielding, as well as between Drummond and militants within his ranks, were never easily resolved. When employers consolidated and expanded their operations in the 1890s and increasingly demanded labour acquiescence, Drummond was less and less capable of either directing the PWA response or containing it. In the midst of an 1895-96 strike fought against a wage reduction, one PWA lodge disregarded Drummond's instructions, armed its militants, barricaded 200 miners inside its hall, and used considerable physical force to discourage scabs. The political turn was stopped dead in its tracks; its regime of early industrial legality in the coal fields was over.

In the West, workers raised their objections to the importation of Chinese labour and protested the land-grant system that gave concentrated economic authority to coal baron Robert Dunsmuir. Although not solely the creation of the Knights of Labor, west coast political action was greatly influenced by the Order. Occupationally, the political agenda often seemed set by the influential miners. As Paul Phillips notes, the four worker candidates nominated in 1886 were unmistakably linked with the cause of the Knights of Labor. In Victoria, one candidate, John Duval, was a reform editor whose newspaper, the *Industrial News*, was endorsed by British Columbia's Knights of Labor. S.H. Myers, candidate in Nanaimo, was a coal-miner member of the Order who would later die in a mine disaster. The platform of the Workingmen's Party called for mine safety laws, land reform, and exclusion of the Chinese. It signalled the first political expression in British Columbia of "a basic divergence of interest between the 'toiling masses' and the 'wealthier part of the community'." Municipal politics also became a focus of activity in Vancouver, while in Winnipeg political action seemed restricted to the provincial election of 1886.

These diverse and unco-ordinated labour efforts stand as evidence of an underlying similarity in working-class experience that, in spite of many variations and diversities, fed into the rise of a movement culture of working-class opposition and resistance. Advanced most emphatically by Knights and Workmen, the ideals of this culture were tested in the politics of the 1880s and 1890s, when the first concerted attempts to decrease worker dependence on old-line political parties were made. This often led to a sense of independence within sectors of the working class. Few independent labour candidates won seats, but the gains registered in consciousness and political recognition of class needs extended beyond the failures of the polls. And at the local level tangible victories were being secured: early closing, union wages and jobs in corporation work, just assessment rates, opposition to bonusing capital's consolidation, and responsible public transit were just a few of the issues that were, on occasion, resolved in favour of labour.

In the national sphere, significant concessions were won as both Liberals and Conservatives courted a growing working-class political constituency increasingly aware of its own potential as a "spoiler" in electoral battles. Oliver Mowat, Premier of Ontario, and, to a lesser degree, Macdonald in Ottawa responded to this new development of the 1880s with factory acts, bureaus of labour statistics, arbitration measures, suffrage extension, employers' liability acts, improved mechanics' lien laws, and royal commissions, just as Fielding in Nova Scotia reacted to the miners' tug at his political arm. Hence, the political struggles of this period cannot be cavalierly dismissed as failures. But independent labour politics was still far from a realization in the 1880s and 1890s. The established parties proved sophisticated opponents of this emerging working-class autonomy, and through patronage and concession, power and force, they managed to contain much of the working-class opposition. But in the workplace, where class relations often unfolded in their sharpest, least mediated manner, a growing divergence of labour and capital was becoming apparent.

STRIKES

One expression of the rift between labour and capital that emerged in the 1880s was the rising number of strikes. This willingness to resort to the strike pointed to an increase in working-class grievances that grew out of the movement culture, indicating that labour was beginning to see alternatives to accommodation. To be sure, many of the conflicts of the 1880s were mundane confrontations over wages, but workers also made attempts to retain control over work processes that seemed to be drifting into others' hands as capital consolidated its authority.

The increase in strike activity in this period is indisputable, and this alone accounts for a good deal of the public recognition of a working-class presence in politics, in the pages of the daily newspapers, and between the covers of late nineteenth-century popular novels such as Albert Carman's *The Preparation of Ryerson Embury* and Agnes Maule Machar's *Roland Graeme: Knight*. In Hamelin, Larocque, and Rouillard's *Répertoire des Grèves dans la Province de Québec* (a useful source that nevertheless understates significantly the number of strikes) there are references to 102 strikes between 1880 and 1895, compared to a mere sixty-one conflicts in the entire period from 1843 to 1879. Kealey's *Toronto Workers Respond to Industrial Capitalism, 1867-1892* indicates that 112, or over 70 per cent, of the 156 strikes fought in Ontario's largest city in the post-Confederation period occurred in the years after 1880. As we have already noted, the PWA fought more than seventy strikes between 1879 and 1900. More than 430 labour-capital conflicts erupted across Canada over the course of the 1880s. Compared to the 1870s this represented a rough doubling of the number of strikes and lockouts; if the 1880s are set against earlier decades – the 1850s or 1860s – such figures signal a sixfold increase in conflict. Individual craft unions led the majority of these struggles, but relations between Knights and unionists were so close prior to 1886 that it is often difficult to distinguish the role of trade unions from that of the local assemblies.

Even where craft unions and Knights of Labor were relatively weak or virtually non-existent, as in Halifax, there are indications that the 1880s marked a new period of class conflict. An unpublished study by Ian McKay contends that there were as many strikes conducted in Halifax in the 1880s (fifteen) as there were in the preceding two decades. Communities previously uninterrupted by the upheavals of class conflict, like Milltown, New Brunswick, first witnessed strikes and labour organization in 1886. The 1880s were thus a time of heightened workplace militancy, symbolized by the Halifax Carpenters' Union, which marched on Labour Day in 1888. It displayed the Stars and Stripes, indicative of the internationalism of labour, and for the first time brought before the public a handsome silk craft banner, made in London in 1864 at a cost of $250. Bearing a Latin inscription, "By diligence and perseverance we overcome all things," the carpenters' 1888 unveiling of their union's motto did indeed indicate that finally, after a quarter of a century, their craft pride and organization had moved beyond fear of hostile reception. But lest others miss this message, the carpenters of the 1880s introduced yet another symbolic piece, expressive of the new social climate: an enormous mallet they claimed would be employed to level scabs. As McKay notes, in the conjuncture of the symbols of old and new, workmanship and militancy, lay a part of labour's new perception of itself.

The Knights of Labor epitomized this new self-perception: it grew because it was willing to organize class forces larger than itself, marshalling numerous trade sectors or industrial groupings for particular struggles. Thus, in Toronto the Knights of Labor contributed to the formation of a coalition of forces knit together by experienced labour reformers and trade union militants who all found common cause in the need to support striking women boot and shoe operatives in the spring of 1882. This was apparent again in the summer of 1883 when District Assembly 45 (Brotherhood of Telegraphers) engaged in a continent-wide strike against the monopolistic telegraph companies that united operatives in Canada from Sydney in the East to Winnipeg in the West.

The ultimate failure of the telegraphers' strike and its bitter aftermath, which saw DA 45 withdraw from the Knights of Labor, appeared less important, in 1883, than the solidarity expressed in its course. Workers struggled to obtain abolition of Sunday work, the eight-hour day and the seven-hour night, equal pay for members of both sexes, and a universal wage increase of 15 per cent. They posed the moral authority of what the Knights liked to call "modern chivalry" against the "tyranny and unjust treatment of a soulless corporation." And when they lost this battle it was not defeat they remembered but the importance of labour unity and the necessity of continuing the struggle. "The telegraphers' strike is over," declared Hamilton's *Palladium of Labor*. "The People's Strike is now in Order."

The "People's Strike" took many forms in the years to come. At its most dramatic it involved mass strikes that crippled whole industries or polarized entire communities. Examples of struggles of this magnitude included the two Toronto street railway strikes of the spring and summer of 1886, cotton mill strikes in Merritton in 1886 and 1889, in Cornwall (1887, 1888, and 1889), and in Milltown in 1886. The great lumber workers' strikes in Gravenhurst in 1888 and in Ottawa-Hull in 1891 were also part of this wave. Each of these strikes unified working communities, increased the level of class struggle to previously unmatched heights, and involved workers long excluded from labour action in a wide-reaching solidarity that linked men and women, skilled and unskilled, French and English, in a bond of unity. For the most part these labour upheavals, waged to secure organizational recognition, humane conditions, and better wages, had few parallels in the history of labour before 1880. The only previous strikes comparable in sheer numbers were the canallers' battles, which lacked the level of solidarity achieved in the strikes after 1880, and the ship labourers' conflicts in Saint John and Quebec City, which failed to draw other workers to the cause with the same force.

Beyond these epic battles, Knights of Labor often formed alliances with long-established craft unions to mount smaller struggles aimed at the preservation of particular forms of worker autonomy or limited job control. The Order provided an institutional backing for literally thousands of workers who sought to maintain wage standards in the face of prosperity's inflation and the wage cuts of more depressed years. One of the most massive confrontations occurred in January, 1887, when more than 1,000 primary metal workers led by the Knights of Labor walked out of the Montreal Rolling Mills and two other companies in opposition to a 10 per cent wage reduction.

Among Canadian moulders, perhaps the most conflict-ridden trade in the 1880s and early 1890s, Knights and unionists fought classic battles that turned on the issue of work autonomy and managerial prerogatives. Organized throughout Ontario and Quebec, and to some extent in the Maritimes, moulders were concentrated in agricultural implements shops and stove foundries. Employer opposition to unions, workers' rejections of wage cuts, moulder demands for limited numbers of apprentices, union attacks on employer use of helpers, known as "berkshires" or "bucks," revisions to the standard wage rate or shop book "prices," and antagonism to arbitrary authority all led to a series of worker-employer clashes in the 1880s.

But to discuss only strikes is undoubtedly to distort much of the character of productive relations, however much such conflicts contribute to our understanding of work relations in these years. The labour-capital relationship was a symbiotic one, based on give and take, in which workers appropriated some of the power of decision-making at the workplace, establishing procedures and controlling limited aspects of the production process. This is revealed dramatically in an exciting study of workers' control among the Springhill miners by Ian McKay.

Basing his study on rare papers and minutes of the Pioneer Lodge of the Provincial Workmen's Association, McKay argues that between 1882 and 1886 miners and proprietors existed within a structure of "organic control" in which pit democracy, worker autonomy, and a culture and ideology of independence thrived within the mining community. Workers enjoyed extensive powers over production, although long-term decisions regarding entrepreneurial strategy rested in the hands of the company. The PWA lodge minutes record almost 140 attempts to resolve working-class grievances through labour action in the mid-1880s. Almost 20 per cent of the cases involved discussion of a strike, but only four actual work stoppages occurred. Wages were the likeliest cause of discontent, but the miners discussed and debated matters of hiring and firing, management, and customary working-class rights. Collective bargaining obviously evolved within this particular structure of organic control and resembled a situation in which proprietors (one the owner of capital, the other, of labour) struck a bargain within well-defined relations of reciprocity. But that reciprocity was walled in, as all understood, by the ultimate power and threat of workers withdrawing their labour. Springhill's PWA launched perhaps the first 100 per cent strike in the history of Nova Scotia's collieries in 1890; as the mine began to flood and as politicians rushed to the scene, the company, fearful of the prospects of the destruction of its property, capitulated totally to the workers' demands.

Throughout the 1880s and early 1890s, then, a sense of working-class autonomy, often resulting in conflict, was never far from the surface of class relations. Whether it emerged visibly in a walkout of more than 2,000 lumber workers in Ottawa-Hull, in a riot against Toronto street railway magnate Frank Smith, in a defeated struggle to control the nature of production in a Brockville foundry, or in deliberate debate in the lodge room of Springhill's PWA, the strike was a forceful feature of social relations and everyday life. An elementary lesson was learned in these years, as a movement culture heightened worker awareness, challenged capital, and promoted the cause of labour militancy and unity.

ON THE MARGINS OF THE MOVEMENT

The movement culture of the 1880s touched many workers and, in its various expressions and promotions of collectivity, shifted the nature and meaning of working-class experience. To underestimate all of this would distort the past and be a disservice to those many workers who struggled to create a more just, humane world. But it is also nevertheless true that, however great its impact, the movement culture exercised its influence strongly in some areas, less decisively in others. It could not be expected to transform all of working-class life at one fell swoop, and it did not. In smaller towns and in realms of private life the movement culture may well have registered its presence more weakly than in the larger industrial-capitalist cities and in the more obvious class context of the workplace. A look at the underside of family life and the practice of male violence toward women exposes how resistant some sectors of the working class were to the message of the movement culture, a message that was itself not unproblematic.

As we have seen the Knights of Labor conceived of themselves as chivalrous protectors of women's virtue: they deplored the capitalist degradation of honest womanhood that resulted from exploiting women at the workplace; many took great offence at the coarse language, shared water closets (toilets), and intimate physical proximities that came with virtually all factory labour in Victorian Canada. Nor did the Order turn a blind eye to domestic violence and the ways in which men could take advantage of women sexually. Local assembly courts could try and convict members of the Knights of Labor for wife-beating, and the Ontario Order was a strong backer of the eventually successful campaign to enact seduction legislation.

Three points need making about the movement culture's conception of how best to address the conjuncture of class and sex. First, its very willingness to enter into this realm is a reflection of the undeniable advances the workers' movement was making in these years, reaching past the conventional concerns with wages and workplaces to try to reconstruct the meanings of life in a class society. That the Knights of Labor considered the question of sexuality primarily as a matter of libertine aristocratic philanderers and tyrannical, licentious bosses despoiling working-class womanhood was itself an expression of how much "the labour question" had expanded in the 1880s, of how much class had become a central reality in

people's lives. Second, however, as Karen Dubinsky and others have argued, the construction of the relation of sex and class in this way was, as we have seen earlier in this chapter, premised on highly traditional notions of gender in which a hierarchical opposition – man/woman – conveyed distinctions that were themselves antithetical to the project of equality and repressive in their undertones of male protectors, womanly virtues, female chastity, and the sanctities of the home. Third, because of this, the Knights of Labor could only campaign for the kind of seduction law and state intervention into the realm of sexuality that would prove less of a liberation for woman and more of a new, institutionalized regime of regulation. Within this concept of regulation women secured few victories, the working class little in the way of wins.

Research into the extent and nature of male violence against women in late nineteenth-century Canada is just beginning, but it is already apparent that it was considerable and that the law offered women little in the way of security. Judith Fingard's exploration of the dark side of life in Victorian Halifax reveals extensive family violence, with particular wife-beaters charged repeatedly over the course of a decade. Wife battery was often related to drinking and desertion, but in both cases the law was reluctant to challenge the husband's implicit proprietary rights over his wife's person and sexuality. The passage of the Ontario Deserted Wives Maintenance Act in the late 1880s notwithstanding, working-class women got little from the courts. As court cases studied by Annalee Golz suggest, male authoritarianism and brutality were features of family life some women endured for years. Worsened by alcohol abuse, occasionally triggered by unemployment and destitution, usually reflective of an ugly masculinist pride that refused any and all acts that would undermine, however gingerly, a husband's "rule" over his household, male violence was the underside of the mythologized male protector image cultivated by the labour movement, the courts, and the wife-beater himself. If this male violence led to litigation, women had an uphill battle in winning any substantial redress. Judges commonly asserted that wives must bear some indignities, and acts of violence perceived as "isolated" were never grounds for any kind of settlement. If a woman had committed adultery, that, in and of itself, usually nullified any case she might have. Women's characters were constantly assaulted and questioned. The state, clearly, was no better a protector than some husbands.

This was also evident in another expression of male violence, sexual assault. Dubinsky's examination of rape and other sexual crimes explores a number of cases from the 1880s to the 1920s. Her analysis underscores the extent to which the labour movement's early focus on the evils of the industrial-capitalist workplace and the construction of sexual assault/seduction as the activity of designing employers and aristocratic dandies shielded sexual crime's perpetrators when they were themselves from the working class and, in the case of voluntary sexual activity, denied young women any active agency in the making of their own erotic lives, regulating their sexuality in ways that protected the "rights" of their working-class fathers and families. Most sexual assault actually took place within those families, and when it was work-related the home, not the factory, was the most likely site of attack: domestic servants comprised the most common occupation to come up in the courts. Over half of all the seduction prosecutions involved ongoing and mutual relations between two lovers, not the Knights of Labor image of deceitful aristocrats luring young working-class maidens into the recesses of sexual depravity, promising them marriage, tempting them with sweets and carriage rides, and abandoning them "virtueless" after sating their lust.

This history of physical and sexual abuse, centred in the family, is a revealing reminder that however much the movement culture changed working-class life in the late nineteenth century there were some areas and many workers immune to its impact. The Knights of Labor, the trade unions, and the Provincial Workmen's Association, all of which saw themselves as fighting for working-class respectability and battling to secure the family, regarded male violence against women as distinctly unrespectable. Yet, for all of this, there were locales and personalities they could not influence; most of the cases we have of overt abuse seem to involve labourers on the margins of the movement, unaffiliated to labour organizations of any kind, likely to be living their lives in "cultures" other than that of the movement. Still, there must have been those within the labour movement who were guilty of abuse and assault. The movement culture, for all that it affected them, had not broken through all of the ugliness of particular extremes of male power. And even where, rhetorically, it challenged this ugliness, it did so in ways that sentimentalized gender relations rather than equalizing them. As a result, the movement culture at its best was caught in a web of limitation, a process evident in other spheres as well.

Editorials to "Palladium of Labor"

GOVERNMENT!

Social Organization the True Function of Administration

THE REAL RULERS

Are Not the Politicians but the Monopolists

THE MONEY POWER

And the Machinery of Production and Distribution Should Be Controlled by the Whole People

SIDE BY SIDE with the system of government, which has hitherto had its function limited to the preservation of order and the maintenance of national power and dignity, has grown the greater and infinitely more important system of commercial and industrial organization, touching the lives and interests of the people at a thousand points where government controls them at one. Of gradual and [insidious] development at first it has latterly grown with wonderful rapidity, owing to the strides of modern invention. It is no longer kings, emperors, aristocracies or congresses that sway the destinies of the nations. It may well be said that 'the kings reign but no longer govern.' The real rulers are not the puppet princes and jumping jack statesmen who strut their little hour upon the world's stage, but the money kings, railroad presidents, and great international speculators and adventurers who

CONTROL THE MONEY MARKET

and the highways of commerce. Where is the emperor or premier in Europe that has the power of the Rothschilds? What are American presidents and congresses but mere tools in the hands of Vanderbilt and Gould? Every war, every peace, every commercial treaty is dictated not by the men who do the stage business, and dazzle the unthinking mob by their displays of regal splendour and court ceremonials, but by a few shrewd, sharp, long-headed business men, who form the power behind the throne. All the diplomatic flummery and formalism, all the pomp and glitter of imperial state are so much empty sham, behind which the hand of the financier and the representative of huge corporate interests pulls the wires.

THE REAL GOVERNMENT

in our nineteenth century civilization is not the parliamentary or administrative bodies, in the name of which laws are promulgated. It is the industrial and commercial and social organization which governs, which regulates matters by its iron laws that need no popular assent and cannot – as matters now stand – be affected by the vote of those whom they press hardly. LAWS! What law, pray, that can be passed at *Ottawa* or *Toronto has such vital, all-absorbing interest for* Labor as the unwritten arbitrary law which says, 'you, wage-slave, have produced us, your master, so much wealth that we are in fact suffering from over-production. Therefore it is decreed that the factory is closed until further notice.' What 'law' duly assented to by the governor-general in full panoply of cocked hat, laced coat, knee breeches and sword is of one-tenth part the importance to the toiler as the silent, informal decrees of landlordism 'whereas the necessities of the public for accommodation have increased, therefore rents are henceforth increased twenty per cent.' Where is the law duly formulated on the statute book in good set terms and legal phraseology that affects the toiling masses like the machination of the speculators who put up the prices of coal and wheat and pork? What are the government taxes to the exactions continually

LEVIED ON INDUSTRY

by the usurer and the landlord and the profit monger and the capitalist?

Just now there is destitution and semi-starvation in the land because of the latest edict of the government – the real government of the monopolists, not the pretentious fraud that amuses itself with stage plays and solemn burlesque – which has decreed that Labor must stint and starve itself to 'restrict production' – which decrees that wages must be reduced and factories shut down and until the surplus stocks are worked off? Who voted for this measure? What political candidate stumped the country promising to support a general measure of 'restricting production' as a cure for the ills of

the body politic? Where, in short, does the idea of self-government and popular freedom come in if measures of such

LIFE AND DEATH CONSEQUENCE

to the masses of the people can be carried out, not merely without the people having a voice in them, but without any body even imagining that it is a matter upon which they have a right to be consulted? How utterly paltry and insignificant are the miserable party issues over which politicians fight and voters spend their time and breath compared with the questions of work and wages, and freedom to use the natural resources of the earth without being taxed to maintain a host of drones and leeches! Yet we are told that such measures as would secure to Labor its rights are 'unpractical.' The real objection is that they are a great deal too practical for the ex*ploiting classes who are quite willing that the people should amuse* themselves by playing at politics, over-turning and reconstructing sham governments, while they retain in their hands the real power.

THE SOLUTION OF THE PROBLEM

lies in the extension of the powers and functions of government to include the organization of industry. The people have in some countries political power, in others they are obtaining it. But what is the good of it, if it is to be confronted and hemmed in on every side by the non-political but organized power of monopolies, rings, corporations and the entire social machinery in the hands of landlordism and capitalism? Where is the benefit to the toiler of a free ballot if on all live practical bread-and-butter questions he is to be told 'hands off, this is not a political question. This must be left in the hands of private enterprise. Mustn't interfere with the sacred

RIGHT OF FREE CONTRACT!'

The growth of popular sovereignty should be so dictated as to breathe the breath of life into the decaying and hollow systems of government and substitute for their formal parade and ceremonial, a vital, active interest in matters now considered beyond the scope of legislative interference. Let government representatives of the whole people step in and instead of being controlled by the machinery of capitalism, control it through all its ramifications. In place of the monopolistic rule which really in the true sense of the word governs the people by prescribing whether they shall work or not, and how much they shall receive let us have representative popular recognized government conducted on business principles, doing the same thing not for the profit of a few, but with an eye to the benefit of all. Instead of the monopolist being 'free' to say 'you shall work on my terms or go idle, buy bread on my terms or starve, buy coal on my terms or freeze, rent homes on my terms or become a houseless vagrant,' the people should be

FREE TO ORGANIZE

all these departments of Labor and subsistence through their representatives. Until this freedom can be secured, liberty to the disinherited is a mockery and a delusion. This is the ideal government which Labor Reformers should keep steadily in view. It is only capable of gradual attainment, and may take generations to accomplish, but in the meantime, the legislation which tends to the increase of the sphere of government and the assumption by the state of the powers now in the hands of corporations should be welcomed as initial steps in the right direction.

ENJOLRAS

EDUCATION

Must Follow up and Secure the Results of Agitation

SOCIAL REVOLUTION

Impossible Until the People are Imbued with Labor Reform Principles

MEN WHO ENVY CAPITALISTS

Are not Fit Material to Found a Better Social State

THE CRYING, URGENT NEED of the Labor Reform movement is the education of the masses who are being drawn into sympathy with it. The work of organization is proceeding as fast as we could wish. Men and women are entering our ranks by tens of thousands. The popular mind everywhere is receptive to our teachings. The oppressions of capitalism are compelling those who never before thought of uniting to protect themselves from its encroachments, to join Labor organizations. The utter futility of strikes, as a means of settling the question of the remuneration of Labor, upon a permanent and equitable basis, is realized as it has never been before, and the workers are asking themselves what better weapons can be furnished from the armory of combination.

THE PHENOMENAL GROWTH

of the Order of the Knights of Labor is attracting many to its ranks by the sheer prestige of success. It is gathering in recruits on every side and the contagion of enthusiasm daily widens the circles of those who sympathize with the efforts to advance the cause of Labor Reform. There is abundance of zeal -- we must take care that it is not zeal without knowledge.

Power and ignorance do not go well together. All that has really been done so far is to break ground to obtain a hearing, to get the

Reform that they are prepared to receive new ideas. Admitting a man into a Labor organization no more makes a Labor Reformer of him than enlisting a recruit into the army and putting a red coat on his back and a rifle in his hand makes him a soldier. The instruction in the one case – the drill and discipline in the other – are necessary to produce the trained man who can be depended upon in an emergency. To thoroughly assimilate and indoctrinate with sound ideas the numbers who are now pressing to join the standard of Labor Reform is the most imperative and essential work for some years to come. The world is not yet ripe for

A SOCIAL REVOLUTION.

Were such a general upheaval as would utterly prostrate the power of monopoly and put capital under our feet to come now, it would come too soon, because it would find us unprepared. It is very difficult, in view of the outrages perpetrated by organized capital, the murderous assaults by its hirelings upon workingmen – the brutal and ferocious expressions of its subsidized press, the lavish ostentation and riotous waste of the millionaire, and the penury and starvation of the pale and haggard victims of their greed – it is difficult, I say, in view of these wrongs and shames and outrages, to help sympathizing with the anarchists and dynamiters of the John Most and Justice Schwab type, who would solve the whole question by an uprising of the people against their oppressors. If ever a revolution was justifiable, the wage-slaves who have been robbed, not only of their natural rights, but of those solemnly guaranteed them by the constitution which purports to hold

ALL MEN 'FREE AND EQUAL,'

would be perfectly justified in reclaiming those rights by force. But suppose they did so. Suppose that in the present condition of public opinion the wage-workers throughout this continent rose as one man, overcame the police, the military, the Pinkerton murderers, hung every monopolist to the nearest tree or lamp-post, sent their palaces up in smoke and confiscated their stolen goods to the public use, what, so far as the condition of Labor is concerned, would be the result? Why, simply that a few years later all the evils and abuses which had provoked the outbreak would again be in full blast. We should have a new set of millionaires and monopolists created out of the dominant working class, by the operation of the same conditions

and influences which evolved the existing task masters, and the masses would be no better off than before. The people are not yet sufficiently educated to change the conditions and overthrow the system which breeds monopolists. If the monopolists as a class are worse men than their victims it is the fault of a system under which

THE BASER QUALITIES

of human nature conduce to prosperity while the nobler traits of humanity are often obstacles to success in life. The individuals who have climbed to the pinnacle of fortune over the heads of their fellows, careless of whom they crushed, bleeding to earth, may deserve all that a bloody revolution would bring upon them. But their fate would not of itself alter the conditions and other greedy and unscrupulous men would soon step on over prostrate humanity into their places.

With too many workingmen the millionaire is an object of envy. The only reason they have for hating the system, is because they do not happen to have drawn prizes in the lottery of life. – They desire nothing so much as to be monopolists themselves. 'I only wish I were

AS RICH AS VANDERBILT.'

'Ah, if somebody would die now and leave me a million dollars,' and such expressions which we hear every day from men who profess to be in favor of Labor Reform, show how deeply the virus of Mammon worship has tainted the community.

So long as the great bulk of the people wish and long to be privileged loafers – so long as envy of the fortunate condition of the millionaire rather than hatred of the infernal system which enabled him to become such, inspires the masses we cannot hope for any material gain by either a [peaceable] or a forcible revolution.

Now men are not individually to blame for wishing they were in Vanderbilt's shoes. It is the fault of wrong education – not school education merely, but the teaching of the press and the platform and the whole circle of influences which go towards the formation of opinion.

THE ACQUISITION OF WEALTH

and position at the expense of others has been held up before us all from boyhood as a perfectly natural and laudable ambition. There is all the more necessity therefore for true teachings on the subject, for the inculcation of right sentiments regarding the matter to counteract the false education which sets up the millionaire as a man to be admired and envied. We have to create a revolution in public opinion before we can hope to revolutionize the system. – We have to change not only men's formally expressed beliefs, but their aspirations and desires – to eradicate the deeprooted selfishness begotten of competition and instill in its place a love for humanity and a

STRONG SENSE OF JUSTICE.

It is an education of the heart as much as the head that is needed. There are countless prejudices to be overcome, the lessons taught by centuries of false education and embodied in a misdirected public opinion are to be unlearned, and the grand principles of human freedom and equality in the broadest sense – including the equal right of every man to natural opportunities and resources and his own earnings – to be inculcated. Not until this work now just begun is accomplished, can the old order of things give place to the new.

ENJOLRAS

WHAT MIGHT BE.

If the World's Workers were Only Educated and Organized

SOCIAL REORGANIZATION

Universal Democracy and Co-operation – No Wars or Monopolies

A BEAUTIFUL IDEAL
Which Can Never be Realized While Labor is uneducated, Apathetic and Divided

AN AIM TO WORK FOR

By Doing Our Part in Spreading the Light

IT IS PRETTY GENERALLY UNDERSTOOD by this time among those who are interested in Labor Reform that it is a much wider and more comprehensive question than the mere matter of wages or hours – that it includes everything relating to the mental, moral and physical advancement of the worker, and implies a war to the death against every influence which tends to depress the condition of Labor. Yet there are still many whose sympathies are with us to a certain extent who do not realize to the full the ideal which ought steadily to be kept in view – amid temporary defeats and discouragements as the ultimate end and aim of the movement. Just let us think for a while what the effect upon government and society would be supposing the great majority of workingmen everywhere were thoroughly educated in the principles of Labor Reform, and determined at any sacrifice to carry them into effect. Let us picture to ourselves

THE SOCIAL CONDITION

that would result were our ideals realized by the resolute determination of the masses in all civilized lands to use their power for the good of the whole people, instead of letting the selfish few play upon their prejudices and passions, and rule them for the benefit of the upper class.

In the first place we should have a universal Democracy – kings and queens, statesmen and aristocracies, and every form of restriction upon the power of the people in government would disappear. And with them would go all the useless ceremonials of government, all the pomp and parade of state affairs, all the fooleries and frivolities of courts and parliaments and embassies. The host of titled and untitled idlers, lords in waiting, ushers of the Black Rock [sic!], and kindred functionaries who receive life pensions for imaginary services would be turned out to hustle for an honest living.

THE ENORMOUS EXPENSE

attaching to personal government would be saved, and one source of taxation cut off. More than this, however, the necessary and legitimate work of administration and legislation would be immensely cheapened and simplified, by being put upon a business basis. The governing body of the nation, parliament, congress or whatever it might be called, would meet without any more nonsense or formality, than a county council and settle right down to the public business. Annual elections would bring the members into closer relations with their constituents than at present, and any want of fidelity to the public interest would be promptly punished. All wars between civilized nations would of course cease. As it is always the working class who are called on to do the fighting and bear the expense of war, and the wealthy and aristocratic class who get all the benefit, educated Labor would soon put an end to the military system. Such international disputes as might arise would be settled by arbitration. Standing armies would no longer be necessary, and the principal cause of heavy taxes and national debts would be got rid of.

MONOPOLIES WOULD GO,

one and all of them. Railroads, telegraphs, steamship lines, insurance and the issuing of currency would all be in the hands of the government. – Having no military establishment, no court tomfooleries or red-tape formalities to occupy their attention, the administration could little by little increase its sphere of action and take out of the hands of private individuals the public trusts they have so badly abused. There would be no more waste from unnecessary competition and no more extortion from the public for the profit of the Vanderbilts, Goulds and Stephens. These enterprises would not be run to pay, but to accommodate the public as the Post Office is now. The [employees] would receive good living wages, and both industry and commerce would prosper by the change.

ON THE SAME PRINCIPLE

the gas supply, street railways, ferries, telephones and other local enterprises would be run by the municipalities. – No individual would be permitted to grow wealthy out of public undertakings. Land monopoly would also cease. The right of the whole people in the land would be recognized, and such a tax would be levied on the occupancy of the soil as would make speculation impossible and render it improfitable [sic] for any one to hold more land than [he] could actually use. The proper housing of the poor would be one of the first questions to be considered.

There would be no abject poverty. It would be recognized as part of the legitimate business of the state to see that every man who was able and willing to work, should have employment at good wages. The land tax would place the government in possession of an ample revenue without any other taxes being necessary – with this parks, public libraries, colleges, museums, picture galleries, magnificent public buildings for every purpose of research and recreation could be constructed.

PAUPERISM WOULD BE UNKNOWN.

Those who were by disease, accident or old age unable to work would be pensioned not as a charity, but as a right – as their share of the returns from the common inheritance – the earth. All industry would be co-operative The interest of the workingmen and women in the great enterprises of industry and commerce would be recognized by law – and while organizing capacity, and brain work received its just return, it would not be permitted as now, to treat Labor as a mere commodity. And Labor would get the benefit of all the wonderful discoveries and inventions, such as steam, electricity and Labor saving machinery in a shortening of the hours of toil by abolishing much of the useless work caused by the competition and the waste of war. The really necessary Labor of the world, all men being workers, could probably be done in three or four hours a day.

By this time, no doubt, the readers who have followed me so far are ready to exclaim 'utopian!' 'visionary!' 'Altogether wild and impracticable!' I know it. Look back a little and you will see that I based the whole picture on the supposition that the great majority of

THE WORLD'S WORKERS

were educated as to their true interests and resolute in carrying out their purposes. Nobody can say that the state of things I have endeavoured to outline would not be to the best advantage of Labor – that we should not gladly welcome such a condition of society were it possible. Why then is it 'utopian?' – why is it the dream of a visionary? If it would be for the benefit of the immense majority of mankind, why cannot it be realized? Why? Simply because the people who do the world's work, and physically at least have the immense advantage over all opposing forces

ARE NOT EDUCATED,

– are not self-reliant – are not ready to make sacrifices. There you have the whole thing in a nutshell. The picture is merely a faint presentation of what might be – what cannot be at present solely because of the blindness, ignorance and want of union among workingmen – but what I trust yet will be when the scales of error, of misleading education and of temporary self-interest have fallen from their eyes – so they can see the light.

ENJOLRAS

CHAPTER 1

European Immigrant Workers and the Canadian Economy, 1896-1914

Between 1896 and 1914 Canada experienced unprecedented economic growth: railway mileage doubled, mining production tripled, and wheat and lumber production increased tenfold. This economic expansion was accompanied by dramatic population growth; in the decade 1901-11 the nation's population increased by a remarkable 34 per cent. Much of this increase was attributed to immigration; in 1914, it was estimated that three million people had entered the country since 1896. Although a substantial number of these newcomers settled on the land, the vast majority derived some portion of their annual income from the wage employment offered by the booming agricultural and industrial sectors of the economy whose demand for labour, both skilled and unskilled, seemed insatiable.

Led by the spokesmen for labour-intensive industries, including agriculture, Canadian public opinion came to favour an immigration policy that went beyond the traditional open-door approach to the systematic recruitment abroad of men and women who could meet the challenge of a nation freshly embarked upon great enterprise. This opinion found expression in the immigration policies of successive Dominion governments. Although the official pronouncements of the Immigration Branch in this period stressed that only farmers, farm labourers, and domestics would be recruited, exceptions were frequently made to accommodate the needs of businessmen in the expanding sectors of the economy. That Canada's search for immigrant agriculturalists was largely in the hands of steamship agents in search of bonuses further qualified official policy;

many who entered the country as farmers and farm labourers quickly found their way into construction camps, mines, and factories.[1]

Ironically, agricultural immigrants were also turned toward wage employment by a settlement policy that tended to give priority to a central European peasantry too poor to establish itself directly on the land. For many who entered the country during these years the life of a yeoman farmer was either irrelevant or but a distant ideal that could be realized only through the slow accumulation of capital by wage labour. As W.F. McCreary, the Winnipeg commissioner of immigration, put it in 1897: "We have a long and wearisome task before us if we expect to settle this country with . . . men with even modest means. The settlement, if it comes at all rapidly, must come from men without means, who will earn in this territory itself the capital to enable them to homestead."[2] It was therefore assumed by both immigration officials and employers that many agricultural immigrants would initially, at any rate, provide a source of cheap seasonal labour. Industries such as commercial agriculture, railroad construction, mining, and lumbering all experienced peak annual work periods; their needs and the needs of the immigrants could be harmonized – or so it appeared at the turn of the century. In the event, this arrangement was not entirely satisfactory to either party. The immigrant workers were exposed to a labour market both highly unstable and fraught with physical difficulties. The ideal of the Canadian developmental capitalists of this era was the sort of labour market H.C. Pentland has described, where "the capitalistic labour market represents a pooling of the labour supplies and labour needs of many employers, so that all may benefit by economizing on labour reserves."[3]

Faced with the demands of projects such as the building of two new transcontinental railways, Canada's captains of industry required a work force that was both inexpensive and at their beck and call. To them the agricultural ideal at the root of Canadian immigration policy increasingly appeared obsolete. Supply and demand should be the new governing principle of immigration policy. The best immigrants would be those willing to roam the country to take up whatever work was available. This view ran against the deep-seated Canadian myth of the primacy of the land but it nevertheless prevailed. By 1914 it was obvious, even to immigration officials, that Canada had joined the United States as part of a transatlantic market.[4]

Immigration Trends

Statistics on the ethnic composition of this immigration and the regional concentrations of immigrants (settlers and resource workers), as well as their distribution within the occupational structure, bring to the surface the contours of what could be called "the specificity of the Canadian experience." In 1891, at an early stage in Canada's industrialization, the foreign-born population accounted for 13.3 per cent of the total population, a figure roughly comparable to that for the United States. However, this foreign population came overwhelmingly from British sources, as 76 per cent were British-born. During the following thirty years British immigrants continued to constitute the majority among the foreign-born population; but there was also a dramatic increase in the number of foreign-born coming from other European areas, most notably eastern and southern Europe. By 1921, these new trends were clearly reflected in the population statistics. The proportion of all foreign-born within the total Canadian population had jumped to 22.2 per cent (about 7 percentage points higher than that of the U.S.), while the foreign-born other than British now accounted for 46 per cent of all the foreign-born population.[5] The large-scale arrival of southern and eastern Europeans into Canada occurred significantly later than the massive movement into the United States. As well, despite their numbers, European immigrants were still overshadowed by the volume of immigrants of British origin. Indeed, it is important to remember that English Canadians often had to reconcile their status as nationalists and imperialists, given Canada's important role in the British Empire prior to 1920.[6]

Another factor was the spatial distribution of the foreign-born population during this period of major industrialization and economic growth. In 1901, for example, Ontario, the country's largest province, accounted for 46.3 per cent of all foreign-born; during the following two decades this share declined to 32.8 per cent. In contrast, the surge of immigrants into western Canada greatly changed the demographic character of these four provinces. In 1901 they had 31.5 per cent of all foreign-born in the country; in 1921 they had 54 per cent. Thus, despite the importance of industrial growth in central Canada, these population trends reflect the significant place that land settlement occupied in Canada's economic growth. The significance of these trends is confirmed when one adopts a rural/urban classification system to analyse the residential choice of immigrants. Compared to the ratio of the Canadian-born population (52 per cent rural and 48 per cent urban in 1921), the non-British foreign-born were 54 per cent rural and 46 per cent urban, while 65 per cent of British immigrants were attracted to the cities.[7]

Immigrant workers had a different impact on the various Canadian regions. The Maritime provinces, for example, received relatively few of the immigrants and sojourners who crossed the Atlantic between 1890 and 1930. The few that did come were primarily hived in the coal and steel complex on Cape Breton Island.[8] In Quebec quite a different situation existed. During the latter part of the nineteenth century there was a large-scale movement of French-Canadian workers to the expanding mining and lumbering communities of the Canadian Shield, a migration strongly encouraged by the province's Roman Catholic hierarchy. Although some immigrant workers found jobs elsewhere in Quebec, the majority gravitated to the Montreal metropolitan region, which soon became conspicuous for the complexity of its occupational structure and the cultural heterogeneity of its work force.[9]

Many of the same characteristics were evident in the experience of immigrant workers in the resource industries of northern Ontario and western Canada. In one year an immigrant worker might find himself in many roles: in February a lumber worker in northern Ontario; in June a railroad navvy along the Canadian Pacific mainline in British Columbia; in August a harvester in Saskatchewan; in November, a miner in northern Quebec. Significantly, this pattern of work coincided with the needs of the labour-intensive resource industries and transportation companies that largely determined Canadian immigration policies in these years.[10]

Immigration Policy and Resource Industries

Until World War One Canadian immigration policy had two determinants: the willingness of the Dominion government to give businessmen a free hand in the recruitment of the immigrants they needed for national economic development; and the determination of the Immigration Branch to recruit agriculturalists, particularly for the settlement of western Canada. The tendency to equate population growth through immigration with national prosperity was especially pronounced during the years 1896-1914. The Immigration Branch in these years was under the direction of men who reflected the expansionist outlook of western Canada: Clifford Sifton (1896-1905), Frank Oliver (1905-11), Robert Rogers (1911-12), and Dr. W.J. Roche (1912-14). In many ways Clifford Sifton established the pattern followed by his successors. The operational budget was expanded from a modest $120,100 in 1896 to a remarkable $900,000 in 1905, Sifton's last year as Minister of the Interior.[11] This increase was accompanied by personnel changes that saw many of Sifton's business and political associates assume key positions. Men such as James A. Smart (deputy minister of the interior), Frank Pedley (superintendent of immigration), W.F. McCreary (Winnipeg commissioner), and W.T.R. Preston (commissioner in London, England) shared Sifton's faith that the key to Canadian prosperity was the settlement of western Canada through expanded immigration and railroad construction. These men also accepted the notion that government officials and businessmen should work closely together to promote the opening of new agricultural regions and the development of resource industries such as lumbering and mining.[12]

Sifton and his hand-picked civil servants saw immigration in the most pragmatic terms; it didn't matter where immigrants came from as long as they could be made to fit Canada's economic priorities. Racial and cultural factors could not be ignored, but above all immigrants should be selected according to their ability to adjust to the environmental and occupational demands of the Canadian frontier. Sifton also stressed the advantages of the family model of immigration, both for economic and social purposes. Anglo-Canadians might resent the influx of Poles, Russians, and Ukrainians with their vastly different ways, but his utilitarian approach guaranteed their entry. Sifton's attitude was summed up in one remark: "I think a stalwart peasant in a sheep-skin coat, born on the soil, whose forbearers have been farmers for ten generations, with a stout wife and half-a-dozen children, is good quality."[13] By this standard British immigrants were a doubtful quantity. Many of them not only refused to go on the land, they also refused "heavy-handed work." In 1907, Dr. P.H. Bryce, the chief medical officer of the Immigration Branch, suggested that a high percentage of British immigrants were poor physical specimens, especially those from "classes which have been for several generations factory operatives and dwellers in the congested centres of large industrial populations."[14] Immigrants from the British Isles, the ancient homeland of so many English-speaking Canadians, continued to flow into the country. But for the Immigration Branch the "peasant in a sheep-skin coat" chiefly had to be found elsewhere. Under Sifton's direction Canadian immigration policy acquired a vigorous continental European dimension.

Between 1896 and 1914 approximately a million immigrant farmers were found for Canada's burgeoning agricultural economy. Immigration officials were particularly anxious to maintain a steady supply of farm workers since agriculture in Canada was labour-intensive and large numbers of men were required during both spring seeding and fall harvest. The demand for seasonal labour was most pronounced in the grain belt of western Canada and in the sugar-beet and fruit-farming regions of Ontario, Alberta, and British Columbia. The declining number of native-born family farm workers increased the demand for immigrant farm labourers.[15] This desperate shortage of agricultural workers was vividly described by one Alberta farmer in 1907: "The government is trying to bring settlers or farmers into the west all the time. What is needed is men to work for the farmers that are already here, or those who are here will have to go out of business. . . . I hired a man from the Salvation Army. . . . He is with me yet, but . . . he knows he could get $3.00 a day if he were free, and reminds me of that fact quite often. He is the boss and I am the roust about, or chore boy."[16]

In its attempts to meet the mounting needs of Canadian farmers the Immigration Branch employed a variety of methods. The most common and traditional of these was the payment of a bonus to steamship agents and colonization organizations for each agricultural immigrant brought into the country.[17] Unfortunately, there was no way to guarantee that particular immigrants were agriculturalists or that, once in the country, they would be available for farm work. Many steamship agents assumed no responsibility beyond the bonus.[18]

In 1899 an attempt was made to provide a more systematic and responsible system for the recruitment of continental European agriculturalists, particularly from Germany, the Austro-Hungarian Empire, and the Scandinavian countries. This took the form of a clandestine agreement between the Canadian government and the North Atlantic Trading Company. By 1906, when the Dominion government backed out of the arrangement, the company had directed over 70,000 immigrants to Canada, most of them from the Austrian provinces of Galicia and Bukovina, and had been paid $367,245.[19] The elimination of the company signalled a return of chaotic market conditions in the immigrant industry, though the Dominion government continued to pay bonuses to a variety of organizations and agents to bring farm workers to Canada. One of the most controversial of these emigration organizations was the Salvation Army. In 1903 the "Army next to God" had created a Department of Migration and Settlement for the transportation and placement of the "deserving" poor of Great Britain. The Salvation Army was able to persuade the Dominion authorities to include it in the bonus scheme for bringing agriculturalists to the country. Bonus payments to the Army rose dramatically from $500 in 1903 to $9,052 in 1907 and $25,000 in 1914, despite continual charges from the Trades and Labour Congress of Canada that most of these "agriculturalists" soon became industrial workers.[20]

Organized labour was even more hostile toward the schemes of commercial emigration companies. One of these had at its head James A. Smart, Sifton's first deputy minister. In 1905 Smart was able to convince immigration officials to support a prepaid passage scheme whereby his agency would act simultaneously as immigrant bank, steamship agency, and labour bureau. Immigrants resident in Canada would purchase steamship and rail tickets for friends or relatives overseas through one of Smart's local offices. Those recruited in this fashion were then brought to Canada and placed in agricultural jobs by the Smart labour agency. For its efforts the company would receive both a commission on steamship tickets sold and a bonus from the Dominion government.[21]

In 1907, the Immigration Branch itself became directly involved in the recruitment and placement of British agricultural labourers in the provinces of Ontario and Quebec. Approximately 100 government agents were appointed, each of whom received a two-dollar bonus for every farm labourer placed. W.D. Scott, the superintendent of immigration, explained the new system in these terms: "Each agent is supposed to correspond with the [3,000] British booking agents pointing out the needs of his individual locality, the rate of wages there and to request the booking agent to direct suitable farm labourers to him. When the booking agent has succeeded in selling a ticket to an emigrant . . . he immediately mails an advice form to the agent interested . . . and delivers to the emigrant in question a card of introduction."[22]

In many ways this placement scheme was an attempt to attract a higher percentage of British agriculturalists to Canada. Conditions in Great Britain did not favour the emigration of such persons since agricultural wages and working conditions were often better than in Canada. Indeed, British farm labourers had little incentive to leave for a harsh new land where irregular employment, low wages, and poor accommodations were commonplace. Nor did Canadian farmers show themselves particularly willing to make the prospect of immigration more attractive for British labourers. In 1907, the Winnipeg commissioner of immigration became so annoyed with the outlook of Prairie farmers that he suggested a reduction in the efforts being made to recruit farm labour for spring seeding.[23]

His suggestion was neither economically expedient nor politically wise. In fact the opposite occurred. Pressure from the railway companies and Prairie farmers and businessmen led the Immigration Branch into further involvement in the farm labour market in conjunction with private labour bureaus such as the Canadian Pacific Employment Agency, the Grand Trunk Pacific Employment Agency, the Canadian Northern Employment Agency, Allons Employment Agency, and Hislop Employment Agency. The phenomenal increases occurring in wheat production ensured that business interests recruiting farm labour would have the active co-operation of the Immigration Branch. In 1901, 20,000 harvesters had to be induced into the fields; by 1914 the number had jumped to 50,000. The movement of seasonal workers on this scale required resources that only the Dominion government and the large railway companies could supply. Immigration officials and railway agents worked together to obtain the necessary manpower. On the government side a careful estimate was made each spring of the requirements of the following harvest. The major contribution of the railway companies was the harvest excursion rates by both rail and sea. In 1907, the CPR reduced its rates for British harvesters to such an extent that it incurred the wrath of the North Atlantic Shipping Convention.[24]

Yet from the point of view of both Canadian farmers and immigration officials the British harvesters left much to be desired. A common complaint of western farmers was large numbers of them "had no skill with the pitchfork, but great enthusiasm for the dinner fork," and that they soon abandoned farm work for easier jobs in urban centres. This in turn led to problems between organized labour and the Immigration Branch. In 1904, Arthur Puttee, the labour member of Parliament for Winnipeg, charged that urban wage earners were being required "to bear the whole brunt of carrying labour on a labour market for nine months in order that farmers may use it for two or three months."[25]

Continental European immigrants proved much more malleable. Work in the grain fields of more affluent Anglo-Canadian farmers provided these men with necessary subsistence and offered farmers the means to expand existing land holdings. One survey of rural settlement in western Canada revealed that 50 per cent of the 832 families interviewed had no money on arrival in Canada; another 42 per cent had less than $500. As a result, it was necessary for the Ukrainian settler to seek temporary employment in farm labour, railroad construction, lumbering, or mining. The initial years of adaptation of one Ukrainian family in the Vonda district of Saskatchewan were typical of the experience of many continental European immigrants:

> When they arrived at Rosthern, Saskatchewan, they had not a cent left. Her husband could not get work on account of a strike of section labourers [July, 1901]. Later he managed to obtain farm work for 3 months from a German farmer near Rosthern. The money thus earned was their means of living for a whole year. They lived after this fashion for three years until they were settled on their own homestead.[26]

Steamship and railway companies assumed a central role in the recruitment and distribution of agricultural immigrants. By 1900, the British and European companies had thousands of agents and sub-agents circulating throughout the British Isles and continental Europe advertising economic opportunities in North America and the advantages of travelling with their company.[27] At European ports such as Rotterdam, Hamburg, and Trieste steamships received their human cargo for the still difficult transatlantic crossing. Upon arrival at Halifax or Quebec City the European peasants then boarded primitive railway coaches for their journey to the Golden West. At Winnipeg and other regional centres they set out for government homesteads, or to railway land, spread throughout the Prairies.[28] In *The Sowing* Emerson Hough offered this vivid account of the arrival of immigrant trains in Winnipeg:

> There is no more picturesque, albeit no more pathetic spectacle in the world than that afforded by the Canadian Pacific Railway Station in Winnipeg where most of the European immigrants make the first stop in their long journey to their chosen land. . . . In this gathering ground there are to be seen Swedes, Norwegians, Germans . . . numbers of Hungarians, Galicians, and others . . . their striking and bright-coloured costumes of silks and skin, their strange embroidered boots and bright head coverings. . . . A babel of tongues arises. Here wanders a helpless soul, with no record of any recent meal visible in his gaunt form or features, and no understandable human speech by which he may set himself right with the world.[29]

The attitude of the CPR toward immigration was typified in a comment made to Thomas Shaughnessy by Archer Baker, the European emigration manager in 1907: "We have done more in the last two years with reference to encouraging the immigration along intelligent lines from the United States, Great Britain and Europe than the whole Dominion Department of Immigration. . . ."[30] The company had many reasons for this level of involvement. The sale of its land was a major consideration; between 1896 and 1913 sales expanded from $216,081 to

$5,795,977. The CPR saw advantages in an arrangement whereby European immigrants would be directed by the Immigration Branch into the construction of colonization railways in the underdeveloped regions of western Canada. Here the immigrants would satisfy several needs: they would serve as a source of cheap labour in the construction of CPR branch lines; their crops would bring further business to the company; and, ultimately, they could be directed into complementary resource industries like lumbering and mining. From the point of view of immigration policy, work on railroad construction gangs would be a means of initiation whereby the newcomers could adapt to Canadian society. In 1900 the Winnipeg commissioner of immigration suggested that the presidents of the CPR and Canadian Northern should be informed that it was "their duty to employ all immigrants who have taken up land, whether they be English-speaking or foreign, in preference to importing labour of any kind."[31]

The initial response of the railway companies was favourable; settler-labourers seemed to meet their needs admirably in that they were "obedient and industrious." Docility was a virtue highly prized by both the railway companies and the Immigration Branch. In 1900, James A. Smart, deputy minister of the interior, made it clear to his subordinates that Slavic navvies should be actively discouraged from any attempt at collective bargaining: "They should be told when they need work they had better take the wages they are offered."[32] Consideration was also given in the Immigration Branch to a system whereby time spent on railroad construction work would count toward securing a land patent.[33]

In northern Ontario immigrants were distributed throughout the Clay Belt both by private railway companies and by the provincially owned Temiskaming and Northern Ontario Railway. Here, when the railway construction season ended, the immigrants often found work in logging camps and sawmills. Boards of trade and municipal governments in northern Ontario pressed continually for more immigrants who would adapt to the seasonal job market of the region. In 1901, for example, the Port Arthur Board of Trade made the following appeal to the Minister of the Interior: "So many pulp and paper mills have been building in the northern country, which by reason of its unlimited supply of spruce timber and paper trade, that labour is becoming very scarce, and we need immigrants who, whilst making pulp wood in clearing their farms, will also help to work the mills." The arrival of Finnish and Scandinavian "agriculturalists" experienced in "wood cutting and timber floating" and the cultivation of marginal lands soon provided an abundant source of manpower. Some of these immigrants also found their way in the winter months to the mining camps at Sudbury, Cobalt, and Timmins; others drifted west and joined with homesteaders and farm labourers from the Prairies in seeking employment in a rapidly expanding Rocky Mountain coal-mining industry.[34]

Recruiting Industrial Workers

By the turn of the century it was quite clear that a large percentage of the peasant farmers and farm labourers recruited by the Dominion government were not becoming full-time agriculturalists. Neither seasonal employment in farm labour nor subsistence agriculture was enough to sustain life; other means had to be found and the numerous railroad construction, lumbering, and mining camps scattered across the country provided the necessary outlets. But this adaptation of the immigrant to the Canadian environment had produced many dislocations. Commercial farmers bitterly complained about the lack of help during periods of peak production. Spokesmen for labour-intensive industries voiced a similar complaint. Occupational specialization rather than occupational pluralism was what both the established farmers and captains of industry required of the immigrant worker.[35]

The railway companies were loud in their demand that the priorities of the marketplace take precedence over those of immigrant adaptation. By 1900, the CPR had apparently decided that certain groups of immigrants made poor construction workers. British immigrants were especially suspect; not only were they unwilling to tolerate low wages and primitive working conditions, but they could use the English-language press to focus public attention on their grievances. In 1897, for example, the CPR was charged with gross mistreatment of Welsh and other British immigrants recruited for work on the Crow's Nest Pass Railway. The report of Justice R.C. Clute on the matter generally confirmed the accusations, particularly those with respect to sanitary conditions in the camps.[36] The CPR did not, however, meekly accept blame for the harsh working conditions. Instead, CPR president Shaughnessy claimed the type of worker, rather than the company, was at the root of the problem:

> Men who seek employment on railway construction are, as a rule, a class accustomed to roughing it. They know when they go to the work that they must put up with the most primitive kind of camp accommodation. . . . I feel very strongly that it would be a huge mistake to send out any more of these men from Wales, Scotland or England. . . . it is only prejudicial to the cause of immigration to import men who come here expecting to get high wages, a feather bed and a bath tub.[37]

Slavic and Scandinavian settler-labourers also became unpopular with the railway companies; their temporary commitment to railroad construction created an unstable labour market. Many of these men were available to the companies only during the late spring and earlier part of the summer; in August they quit their jobs to harvest their crops. Moreover, large numbers of them were gradually able to accumulate their money and to establish themselves full-time on the land. Ironically, in 1903 James A. Smart complimented the CPR on its generosity "to foreigners coming to this country, to such an extent that hundreds and perhaps thousands of them today are living in their own homes and are practically independent."[38] But the company was not to be denied. During the 1901 maintenance-of-way employees' strike, the CPR had imported hundreds of itinerant Italian navvies from the United States, despite anguished protests from immigration officials that these workers were undesirable racially and were taking jobs from "labourers who have taken homesteads." On this occasion, Mackenzie King, deputy minister of labour, had informed the CPR president that the private employment agencies that had recruited the Italian navvies had apparently violated the Canadian Alien Labour Law. Yet no action was taken against either the agencies or the CPR itself; quite clearly the Laurier government had accepted the advice of former Winnipeg commissioner W.F. McCreary that strained relations with the CPR "would be disastrous for Canadian immigration ventures."[39]

After 1901 the CPR systematically increased the proportion of Italian workers in its construction crews; many of these were supplied by Montreal-based labour agents such as Antonio Cordasco.[40] Between 1901 and 1904 Cordasco had a virtual monopoly in supplying labourers to the company; for his efforts the CPR paid him a salary of five dollars a day and expenses. He was also given the right to provision the Italian rail gangs. On this particular concession Cordasco made between 60 per cent and 150 per cent profit on each item sold. What Cordasco offered the CPR was not only a regular supply of unskilled workers, but men who could be controlled either by his interpreters or by Italian foremen. The outlook of Italian navvies was greatly appreciated by CPR officials. As George Burns, the company's employment agent, put it: "Italians are the only class of labour we can employ who can live for a year on the wages they earn in six months . . . if we have the Italians . . . there is no danger of their jumping their jobs and leaving us in the lurch."[41]

Pressure for the recruitment of "industrial" immigrant navvies mounted after 1907 when the Canadian Pacific, Grand Trunk Pacific, and Canadian Northern were all engaged in immense construction projects. During the next seven years between 50,000 and 70,000 railroad workers were engaged annually in completing the two new transcontinental railways, in double-tracking the CPR main line, and in building numerous colonization lines. In their insatiable demand for cheap unskilled labour all three companies pressured the Immigration Branch to facilitate the entry of immigrant navvies "irrespective of nationality." A survey of the labour demands of railroad contractors in 1909 revealed that the most popular immigrant workers were "non-preferred" southern European immigrants; these, it was claimed, "were peculiarly suited for the work." Wheaton Bros. of Grand Falls, New Brunswick, reported that it "would not employ Englishmen"; the Toronto Construction Company announced that it was entirely dependent "upon Italians, Bulgarians, and that class of labour"; while the Munro Company

of La Turque, Quebec, expressed a preference for foreigners – "Polacks, Bulgarians, Italians."[42]

There were also several schemes to import large numbers of immigrant workers from Russia. In 1907, as a mark of his goodwill toward the Canadian government, Doukhobor leader Peter Veregin announced that he would recruit 10,000 Russian labourers for the building of the Grand Trunk Pacific. Nothing came of this plan, but Russian workers were brought into the country in 1909 and 1913 from Vladivostok.[43]

Dismayed at the growing percentage of "non-preferred" industrial immigrants entering the country, immigration officials embarked on a spirited defence of the settler-navvy. In 1908 they claimed that Slavic settlers were superior construction workers since they "could be had at more reasonable figures than many others who are either in large cities or who have had past experience in railway construction work and rates of wages." This line of argument appealed to the self-interest of railroad entrepreneurs. Wages had increased appreciably from the $1.75 daily wage of 1900. By 1907 they had risen to $3, and by 1913 some contractors were paying as much as $5. But for the railway companies a return to the older settler-labourer employment pattern did not offer a realistic solution to this problem. In fact, their answer represented a further retreat from the agricultural ideal that inspired official immigration policy. What they now demanded as a solution to their problem was the flooding of the labour market with itinerant workers who would be hired cheaply and thus keep costs down. In short, the railway companies became the outstanding spokesmen for an open-door immigration policy.[44]

This position was opposed both by organized labour, for economic reasons, and by nativist elements, for social and cultural reasons. Many of these immigrant navvies, it was charged, were nothing more than "professional vagrants" whose habits and attitudes were "repugnant to Canadian ideals." They were, in short, people who tended "to lower the Canadian standard of living." Gradually the Immigration Branch was forced into a position of reconciling the opposing demands of the railway companies and the advocates of a more selective immigration policy. The labour and nativist point of view was reflected in the introduction between 1908 and 1910 of new standards for admission to the country. Immigrants were now required to make a continuous journey to Canada and to pass a means test that required them to have an amount of money varying from $25 to $200, depending on place of origin.

Politically, the Dominion government had no choice but to acknowledge the strength of nativist opinion.[45] But on balance it came down on the side of the railway companies. This was clearly revealed in 1910 when Duncan Ross, the lobbyist for the powerful construction company of Foley, Welch & Stewart, convinced Prime Minister Laurier to reverse the decision of the Minister of the Interior and his immigration officials to stiffen the immigrant means test. The extent of the railway victory could be seen in a circular letter sent to all immigration border inspectors in July, 1910; this letter placed "railway labourers in practically the same position as farm labourers." Moreover, railroad navvies were defined as "those who are physically able to [endure] strenuous labour and [who] . . . must be able to handle a pick and shovel."[46]

The coming to power of the Conservatives in 1911 did not significantly disrupt the government-contractor relationship; indeed, the ability of the business lobby to influence immigration policy decisions was again clearly revealed in 1912. In that year immigration officials once again attempted to limit access to the country in response to a public outcry that immigrants from southern Europe "constituted a serious menace to the community." This time they were overruled by Robert Rogers, a politician whose corporate connections were myriad.[47]

By 1913 immigration officials were concerned that Canada was becoming increasingly committed to a guest-worker form of immigration. But the influx of itinerant immigrant workers continued. Indeed, in the spring of 1913 arrangements were made to bring immigrant workers from eastern Russia on short-term contracts that gave them a semi-indentured status. In fact, to prevent desertions both the Canadian Pacific and the Grand Trunk Pacific transported these workers from Vancouver to the Prairies in closed boxcars and with armed escorts.[48]

The mining and lumbering companies aided and abetted the efforts of the railway companies in seeking to keep the immigration door open. Corporate unity on this issue reflected economic interdependence; the transcontinental railway touched all segments of the developing resource-based industries of the "new" West and their point of view was widely shared. The movement of lumber and firewood, especially from British Columbia, provided the railways with a source of revenue that grew dramatically during this period. In 1896 the CPR moved 636,128,374 feet of lumber and 166,831 cords of firewood; by 1914 these figures were 2,953,125,699 and 287,910 respectively.[49] The rapidly developing metalliferous and coal mines of the Kootenays and Crow's Nest Pass provided an important new market for lumber. In 1910 a report of the Department of the Interior estimated that the coal mines in the Crow's Nest Pass alone were using "three million lineal feet of mining props and two and one-half million feet of board measure of lumber and dimension timber." The report also claimed that within five years this quantity would probably double, thereby requiring the product of 66,000 acres of forest. Thus the railway and mining companies had a common interest in seeing that the British Columbia forest industry had an ample supply of cheap reliable labour. The railway entrepreneur was, therefore, often the spokesman for a region whose views would be ignored by politicians at their peril.[50]

A particular concern of the transcontinental railway companies – the Canadian Pacific, Grand Trunk Pacific, and Canadian Northern – was that there should be no serious work stoppages in the mining industry of the West. Coal

was an indispensable source of energy; lignite coal was an essential fuel in the harsh Prairie winter; coke was a necessary ingredient in smelting; and bituminous or steam coal gave motive power to the railways themselves. Hence the determination with which the railway companies attempted to guarantee a reliable mining operation and to meet their seasonal demands for coal. They did this in two ways, by effecting a secure corporate link with the coal producers and by going into mining themselves.[51] In 1908 the CPR opened its own mine at Hosmer, Alberta; in 1911, Canadian Northern acquired the extensive Dunsmuir holdings on Vancouver Island. The Hosmer mine was acquired by the CPR not only to ensure coal for its locomotives during the peak harvest season, but to provide additional coke for the silver-lead-zinc smelters at Nelson, Greenwood, and Trail, British Columbia. Indeed, the previous year the company had acquired the economic leadership in this region through the formation of the Consolidated Mining and Smelting Company. Not surprisingly, these corporate changes were accompanied by an intensification of the demand for an open-door immigration policy.[52]

Mining promoters welcomed this initiative as the labour traditions of the Canadian mining industry were well suited to the outlook of the railway companies. During the boom years from 1896 to 1914 mining companies became even more active in the recruitment of immigrant workers. One mining authority gave the estimate of the industry's labour situation: "Canadians won't work in the mines. They are quite willing to boss the job but they are not going to do the rough work themselves. . . . What we want is brawn and muscle, and we get it." The *Canadian Mining Journal*, the voice of the industry, continually maintained that the number of immigrant miners entering the country was insufficient. In 1907, the *Journal* argued that it was "quite feasible not only to select the proper class of workers across the ocean, but to place them where they are needed."[53] Although the Dominion government did not undertake the systematic recruitment of miners, it placed few obstacles in the way of the recruitment efforts of the mining companies themselves, even when strike-breaking was involved. By 1911 over 57 per cent of mine workers in Canada were immigrants; in British Columbia and Alberta the equivalent figures were 84 and 88 per cent. In Ontario, only 48 per cent of the mine workers were foreign-born. But these workers were concentrated in the northern part of the province; their presence gave that region a destructively "non-Canadian–non-British" character.[54]

The Rocky Mountain coal-mining region of western Canada was equally polyglot. In most of the mining communities those of British stock constituted less than 50 per cent of the population; Slavic and Italian workers were in the majority. A study prepared by the Royal Commission on Coal provided the information given in Table 2 below.

In their frantic search for immigrant unskilled labour the mining companies, in keeping with the traditions of Canadian big business, turned to private

Table 2
Ethnic Distribution in Alberta Mines: A Percentage Breakdown

	Crow's Nest	*Lethbridge*	*Drumheller Park*	*Mountain*	*Brazeau*	*Edmonton*
British	44	40	61	41.5	44.5	60
American	1	2	2	1	2	1
Slavic	25	32	26	36	17.5	19
French and Belgian	7	–	–	–	5.5	–
Italian	14.5	15	3	17.5	25.5	–
Others:						
European	8.5	8	7	4	5	18
Finnish	–	–	1	–	–	–
Oriental	–	3	–	–	–	–
	100	100	100	100	100	100

SOURCE: *Report of the Alberta Coal Commission, 1925* (Edmonton, 1926), 181.

employment agencies. In 1904 there were about 100 agencies in operation in the country; by 1913 the number had grown to over 300. Of these, Ontario had the largest number (97), followed by British Columbia (45), Manitoba (36), Alberta (32), and Quebec (26). Together the agencies were placing over 200,000 workers a year, most of whom were immigrants. These agencies recruited workers not only in Europe but in the United States, where they worked closely with similar labour bureaus.[55]

Agents supplying large industrial concerns often specialized in a particular ethnic group. Thus, the Dominion Coal Company of Nova Scotia was supplied with Italian workers by the Cordasco agency of Montreal, and with Armenian and Syrian workers from agencies operating in Constantinople. The approach of one of the Constantinople agencies was explained in a leading Armenian newspaper in these terms:

> The Dominion Company Ltd. of Sidney, Canada, North America, undertakes to furnish employment, which will pay you from $2.00 to $5.00 per day. Emigrants would have to go via Trieste (Austria) and there sign contracts concerning their future employment and wages. The steamship fare is $50.00 paid in advance. . . . Come, without losing time, to our office, American Travellers' Company, No. 2, Custom House, Galata, Constantinople, which is the greatest and most important of such organizations.[56]

Many of the immigrant workers who came by this route were transported first to St. John's, Newfoundland, where there was no immigration inspection; from there they travelled on the iron-ore carriers of the Dominion Coal & Steel Company to the company's piers at Sydney.[57]

During periods of industrial conflict the Dominion Coal Company and other mining concerns looked to the labour agencies for relief. Strike-breakers were frequently imported into the country despite the Alien Labour Act of 1897, which made it unlawful "for any person, company, partnership or corporation, in any manner to pre-pay the transportation of, or in any other way to assist or solicit the importation or immigration of any alien or foreigner into Canada under contract or agreement . . . to perform labour or service of any kind in Canada."[58] During the ferocious strikes in the metalliferous regions of British Columbia between 1899 and 1901 the mining companies blatantly imported Italian and Slavic strike-breakers through labour agencies in Fernie, Spokane, and Seattle. Organized labour strongly resented the recruitment of these "foreign scabs." In July, 1899, for example, the secretary of the Sandon (British Columbia) Miners' Union appealed to Prime Minister Laurier to enforce the Alien Labour Act: "1000 Canadian miners of the Slocan, with their wives and families, are being driven out of Canada by the importation of labour from the United States. . . . As British subjects we naturally resent the circumstances which are driving us from our native land. Will you, as First Minister of the Crown, secure for us the protection which the Alien Labour Law provides?"[59]

The degree of support the miners received from labour organizations across the country eventually forced the Dominion government to establish a royal commission under Justice R.C. Clute of the British Columbia Supreme Court to investigate the situation. But violations of the Alien Labour Act remained a feature of life in the region. In 1901, the mining companies expanded their recruitment of alien strike-breakers, most of whom were Italians. The blunt comment of Edmund Kirby, the manager of the War Eagle Mine, showed the importance of these new industrial recruits to the position of local capital: "How to head off a strike of muckers or labourers for higher wages without the aid of Italian labour I do not know." Nor were the companies deterred either by the protests of organized labour or by warnings from Mackenzie King, the deputy minister of labour, that the Alien Labour Act would be enforced "to prevent wholesale importation of labour." Despite two convictions under the Act the mining companies achieved their goal: sufficient strike-breakers were secured to re-open the mines and crush the offending union.[60]

The events of 1901 in British Columbia revealed much about the power politics of Canadian immigration. When large industrial concerns, possessing appreciable political power, were determined to import workers, even for the purpose of strike-breaking, they would usually get their way. This principle would be demonstrated on many occasions, most notably in the metal-miners' strike in Cobalt in 1907, the CPR machinist strike in 1908, the coalminers' strike in Nova Scotia in 1909, the dockworkers' strike in Port Arthur in 1910, the coalminers' strike in Crow's Nest Pass in 1911, the railroad navvy strike in British Columbia in 1912, and the coalminers' strike on Vancouver Island in 1913.[61]

Immigrant Recruitment and Work Camps: The Critique

The most comprehensive contemporary examination of the impact of immigration on North American society was the U.S. Senate *Report of the Immigration Commission* of 1911, better known as the Dillingham Commission Report. After a three-year study of North American and European conditions, this Commission concluded that most new immigrants were not coming to the United States to settle on the land but to sell their labour in "a more favourable market." It also claimed that large numbers of immigrant workers were essentially sojourners who regarded their stay in North America as temporary and who used their wages to effect an elevation in their own social status when they returned to Europe. According to the Commission one of the most important influences on this transatlantic labour market was the activity of shipping and labour agents who made excessive profits at all stages of the immigration process.[62] They received commissions from steamship companies, kickbacks from money-lenders in Europe, labour agency fees from immigrant workers themselves and from the American companies for whom they acted, and interest from ethnic bankers for handling remittances and pre-paid tickets. In order to deal with these "human traffickers," the Commission recommended state laws regulating both employment agencies and immigrant banks. It further recommended that the Bureau of Immigration and Naturalization monitor more effectively the Alien Labor Act.[63]

The report of the Dillingham Commission had a decided impact on those advocating reform of Canadian immigration laws and practices. Under the Canadian Immigration Act of 1869 and subsequent amendments, various types of undesirables were excluded from the country. These included paupers, criminals, and the diseased. The immigration of Chinese, East Indians, and Japanese was also controlled.[64] These restrictions were enforced by immigration officials employed at the major ports and border crossings. At the request of municipalities, immigrants who became public charges could be deported. There was also the Alien Labour Act of 1897. In the long run, however, this legislation proved to be a great disappointment to Canadian trade unionists concerned about the problem of cheap labour. There were two reasons for this: the Act only applied to workers coming from the United States; and the Dominion government failed to establish effective administrative machinery for the enforcement even of this limited arrangement.

The anger of Canadian unionists over the foreign labour problem was clearly

revealed during the 1901 strike of the maintenance-of-way employees of the Canadian Pacific Railway. On this occasion the Brotherhood of Railway Trackmen complained to Dominion authorities that the CPR practice of recruiting Italian navvies constituted a blatant violation of the Alien Labour Act. This view was strongly endorsed by the Winnipeg Trades and Labour Council; indeed, in Winnipeg pitched battles occurred between resident workmen and Italian scabs. Yet the Dominion government did nothing more than protest to the CPR president. In CPR tradition, this protest was politely ignored.[65]

The controversy also focused attention on the role of the private employment agency, which could mobilize from its urban base a pool of unskilled labour in both Canada and the United States. The growth of these agencies was noted in the *Labour Gazette* of 1904. According to this source about 100 agencies in operation in the country could be divided into three groups: those placing female domestics; those placing skilled workers; and those placing unskilled workers.[66].

The search for immigrant domestic servants was an important activity for charitable and patriotic organizations such as the Salvation Army and the British Women's Emigration Association (BWEA). By 1911 over one-third of domestic servants in Ontario, and a whopping three-quarters in the West, were immigrants. The vast majority of these were of British working-class background, who viewed domestic service as "the main bridge to Canada for women of limited funds." Dominion authorities were impressed with the consensus that existed between rural and urban residents: both wanted a steady supply of cheap and respectable homecare workers. As a result, generous bonuses were paid by the government to steamship and labour agencies for recruiting immigrant domestics; as well, subsidies were given to the Salvation Army and to BWEA reception homes. In turn, these reception centres "segregated domestics from other immigrants so they would not acquire notions about better opportunities in other kinds of work."[67]

Between 1905 and 1908 there were a number of incidents involving the importation of skilled immigrant workers.[68] The 1905 amendments to the Alien Labour Act relating to misrepresentation applied only to agencies located in Canada, and this became a source of difficulty in itself. British employment agencies such as Grahaeme Hunter of Glasgow and Louis Leopold of London were outside Canadian jurisdiction.[69] This was remedied somewhat when William Lyon Mackenzie King was sent by the Laurier government to negotiate an agreement with imperial authorities that brought British agents into line.[70]

Another important change in 1906 was the removal of W.T.R. Preston from his position as Superintendent of Emigration in Great Britain. Preston had held this position since 1899, and had become the *bête noire* of organized labour in Canada. Specifically, he had become discredited in the eyes of Canadian unionists because of his connection with Louis Leopold's Canadian Labour Bureau.

Not only was Preston's office next door to that of the Canadian Labour Bureau, but he and Leopold shared the same telephone, thereby bringing to a new height of perfection the network that existed between Canadian businessmen and civil servants.[71] Once this became public knowledge, Prime Minister Laurier was deluged with petitions from Canadian trade unions demanding that Preston be fired. Even the backing of the Canadian Manufacturers' Association (CMA) and the Montreal Builders' Exchange was not enough to save Preston's hide; he was discreetly transferred to Hong Kong as the representative of the Department of Trade and Commerce.[72]

The Canadian Labour Bureau, however, survived Preston's decline. In fact, in 1907 Leopold was placed in charge of the newly opened London labour office of the CMA; the president of the Association, C.M. Murray, even went so far as to suggest to the Minister of the Interior that Canadian immigration officials "refer potential emigrants to Mr. Leopold."[73] The direct involvement of the CMA in overseas labour recruitment was short-lived, partly because of the recession of 1907-08 and partly because of a campaign against it by the Canadian Trades and Labour Congress.[74] Nevertheless, skilled workers continued to be readily available for Canadian employers even during strikes.[75]

While the recruitment of immigrant domestics and British skilled workers periodically embarrassed federal authorities, the most serious problem was the treatment of unskilled alien workers by Canadian labour agencies and railroad, lumber, and mining companies. For its part the Dominion government seemed prepared to allow the companies a free hand in the industrial use of immigrant workers, particularly in the railway camps. The rapid completion of the Grand Trunk Pacific and Canadian Northern was regarded by both the Laurier and Borden governments as a crucial economic and political priority. So great was the commitment of the government in this regard that Dominion authorities rarely questioned the characterization given by employment agencies of life in the railway work camps. In April, 1910, this description of working conditions in the Grand Trunk Pacific camps appeared in the British newspaper *Answers*.

> Life in the camps is strictly teetotal. . . . But the feeding provided is not only unstinted, but of the best obtainable, and on a scale undreamed of by the navvy in this country . . . there is an unlimited choice . . . of fresh meat, fresh vegetables, groceries, butter, eggs, milk, bread and fruit. . . . After work, the men amuse themselves to good purpose, with sing-songs in the shorter days of spring and autumn, and with games and sports, fishing and shooting during the long summer.[76]

The reality of immigrant life in Canada was rather different. Foreign workers were frequently cheated out of their wages and subjected to harsh and dangerous working conditions. In the spring of 1904 the evils associated with the immigrant traffic were dramatically revealed when the Italian labour agencies of

Antonio Cordasco and Alberto Dini, vying for steamship and employment commissions, lured thousands of Italian labourers to Montreal. These men soon faced unemployment and destitution; in time, their condition became so desperate that both the municipal and Dominion authorities were forced to intervene. Although a royal commission appointed to investigate this episode documented the many problems with unregulated labour agencies, and legislation was passed providing severe penalties for anyone "inducing people to come to Canada by false representations," the abuses continued.[77]

In 1907, the Austrian consul-general in Ottawa registered an official complaint about the treatment of Austrian nationals in Canada by Ukrainian and Bulgarian labour agencies operating out of Montreal and by foremen in various railway camps. What had happened, he asserted, was so cruel and exploitative "as to make my blood curdle and . . . bring shame and dishonour upon your country." His specific charge related to the recruitment by the Davis & Nagel agency of Montreal of hundreds of Ukrainian, Polish, and Hungarian immigrants for work on the construction of the Temiskaming and Northern Ontario Railway. Some of these workers had been engaged by the bureau after they had landed in Montreal; others had been sent to Montreal by labour agents in the United States. Before leaving Montreal for the construction camps in northern Ontario these immigrant workers had signed contracts with the Davis & Nagel Company.[78]

By the time they had reached the job site many of the men had already spent all their money on labour agency fees, rail fares, and hotel accommodation. The cost of these latter two items had been grossly inflated by kickbacks to labour agents. The situation of the workers had been made worse by the fact that Davis & Nagel had misled them into believing that they would receive a refund for their transportation costs from the McRae, Chandler & McNeil Construction Company. No such refund was ever forthcoming. In addition, the construction company and the labour agency had conspired to prevent the workers from leaving the campsites. Many of the foremen and sub-contractors had used firearms to intimidate recalcitrant workers, and most of these camps had jails where "unruly" workers had been confined after kangaroo court proceedings. Workers who had managed to escape from camp had often been tracked down by special constables and detectives engaged by their employers. These "specials" were often assisted by local police and justices of the peace. The police state tactics used in the construction of the railway had been clearly revealed in June, 1907, when a group of thirty Slavic workers had been seized for violation of their labour contracts. One of the captured men described his experience as follows:

> On the 20-th inst [*sic*] at night, 12 men who represented themselves as policemen came again to our place and began to make a wholesale arrest, firing revolvers at the Immigrants. . . . 35 men of us were arrested and packed into a fright [*sic*] car, for a whole long night with no water and no place to

> rest or even sit upon. In the morning, as they made preparations to take us away, we began shouting, whereupon said policemen entered the car and putting the muzzles of their guns to our mouths, threatened to shoot if we continued our alarm. A number of us have been beaten with sticks . . . we have obtained our release, but only after . . . binding ourselves to pay each $17 for transportation and $35 for the policemen who had beaten and fired at us.[79]

The investigation conducted by the Immigration Branch provided evidence substantiating much that the Austrian consul-general had alleged. It was shown that Davis & Nagel had indeed been guilty of misrepresentation and that their agents had been guilty of physical intimidation. The quasi-judicial activities of McRae, Chandler & McNeil were also censured. Yet no attempt was made to prosecute either the labour agency or the construction company. Both Dominion and provincial officials argued that it was the responsibility of the victimized immigrant workers themselves to take legal action. This, of course, was impossible: the men were virtually without money and were scattered across the country.[80]

The coercive measures employed against immigrant navvies were characteristic of their harsh and dangerous lives.[81] The accident rate at "the end of steel" was particularly shocking. Between 1904 and 1911, for example, out of a total of 9,340 fatal industrial accidents in Canada, 23 per cent were related to the railway industry. But even these statistics do not tell the whole story. It was not until 1912 that the Dominion government required contractors receiving public funds to register fatalities occurring in their camps. Yet even this provision did not produce accurate statistics: "Oh, some Russian is buried there" was the passing remark that commonly designated an unkempt plot in the vicinity of an erstwhile camp.[82]

There were also numerous complaints about the level of wages and the accommodation in the construction camps. Although there was an obligation on the part of the head contractor who accepted Dominion funds to grant wages that were consistent with local standards, to maintain a reasonable level of sanitation, and to provide medical facilities, it was difficult to enforce these measures.[83] Labour alleged that government inspectors visited the camps only infrequently and rarely came into contact with immigrant navvies. The foreign worker was particularly vulnerable to this type of exploitation. He was often unable to communicate in English, was frequently manipulated by an "ethnic straw boss," and often had a basic mistrust of state officials. For the navvies, the government inspector simply did not offer a viable channel of protest.[84]

Immigrant mine workers faced similar problems. This was especially true of the smaller mines, the so-called "gopher holes." In these, in addition to irregular

employment, it was not uncommon for the companies to declare bankruptcy and forfeit on wages. Within the mines the power of hiring and allocating contract places usually rested with the foremen and shift bosses. There were numerous allegations that these men exploited their positions and extracted bribes from desperate workers. These conditions were compounded by the danger of the workplace. The reports of the Ontario, Alberta, and British Columbia mining inspectors throughout the period 1896-1914 were generally critical of the prevailing high accident rates, especially among the foreign workers. This criticism was most effectively stated in a 1914 report of the Ontario mining inspector:

> Anyone looking over the list of mining statistics . . . cannot but be struck by the large percentage of names of foreign origin. . . . In part this may be due to unfamiliarity with the English language and the difficulty of comprehending quickly spoken orders in an emergency. Mental traits have also to be reckoned with, and the fact that few of these men were miners before coming to this country. . . .

The report neglected to state that many mine managers were reluctant to maintain costly safety regulations. The apparent lack of solidarity among the mine employees because of ethnic differences reinforced this callous approach.[85]

The lumber companies also employed large numbers of immigrant workers, especially Scandinavians, Finns, and Slavs, most of whom were recruited by labour agencies in Vancouver, Victoria, Winnipeg, Port Arthur, Ottawa, Montreal, and Sault Ste. Marie. There were numerous complaints about the working and living conditions, especially in the "long timber" industry of British Columbia. In 1918 the *British Columbia Federationist* gave this description of a typical camp: "muzzle loading bunks . . . pigs, lice and other vermin all over the place . . . the stench of drying clothes and dirty socks . . . enough to knock a man down."[86]

Conclusion

Between 1896 and 1914 Canadian immigration policy served, above all else, the dictates of the capitalist labour market. Under the banner of economic growth thousands of immigrant workers were encouraged to enter the country to meet the labour needs of commercial agriculture, railroad construction, lumbering, mining, and other labour-intensive industries. Increasingly, the long-standing goal of bringing into the country only the settler-labourer type of immigrant was displaced by a policy of importing an industrial proletariat. Immigration statistics reveal that the percentage of unskilled labourers entering Canada increased from 31 per cent of total immigration in 1907 to 43 per cent in 1913-14, while the percentage of agriculturalists decreased from 38 per cent to 28 per cent. This change from settler to worker immigrants was accompanied by a change in ethnic composition. In 1907, 20 per cent of the immigrants were from central and southern Europe; by 1913, when 400,000 men and women entered the country, this figure had advanced to 48 per cent.[87]

In the minds of many Anglo-Canadians the arrival of these "hordes" of foreigners stirred deep suspicion. The immigrants seemed to present a serious challenge to Canadian institutions, particularly in the rapidly growing urban centres of western Canada and northern Ontario.

DAVID GOUTOR

Constructing the 'Great Menace': Canadian Labour's Opposition to Asian Immigration, 1880 – 1914

ABSTRACT *Canadian labour's agitation against Asian immigration in the late nineteenth and early twentieth centuries has received a considerable amount of scholarly attention. Many historians have highlighted labour's concerns about Asian competition in the labour market, while others have explored the pervasiveness of anti-Asian racism in most segments of Canadian, and especially British Columbian, society. But these factors – while important – do not sufficiently explain labour's antipathy to Asians. They particularly fail to account for the unity against Asian immigration between unionists in different regions, the influence of campaigns for exclusion in other countries, and the class content of labour's anti-Asian rhetoric. Another under-explored issue is whether unionists approached Asians in the same way as other immigrants, minorities, and oppressed groups.*

Drawing on the growing literature on racialization, and focusing primarily on the 1880s, when labour's views on Asian immigration became well established, this article shows how Asians were set apart from any groups with whom labour might have sympathy or common cause. Asians were associated with oppressive forces, particularly of the emerging industrial capitalist system. This association can be seen in many of labour's stereotypes of Asians as industrial slaves, ruthless competitors in the economy, and threats to white women. These stereotypes also set Asians up as polar opposites to the basic class, race, and gender identity that labour leaders sought to foster.

L'agitation parmi les travailleurs canadiens devant l'immigration asiatique à la fin du XIXe *et au début du XX*[e] *siècles a fait l'objet de maintes études. De nombreux historiens ont fait ressortir les inquiétudes qu'avait ressenties la main-d'oeuvre canadienne devant la perspective de la concurrence asiatique sur le marché du travail, tandis que d'autres ont examiné l'étendue du racisme anti-asiatique dans la majorité des segments de la société canadienne, tout particulièrement en Colombie-Britannique. Bien qu'ils soient importants, ces facteurs ne suffisent pas, cependant, à expliquer l'aversion de la main-d'oeuvre canadienne pour les Asiatiques. En particulier, il n'est pas tenu compte, dans ces explications, de la solidarité qui a uni les syndicats de diverses régions dans leur opposition à l'immigration asiatique, ni de l'influence des campagnes d'exclusion des Asiatiques qui ont été menées dans*

The Canadian Historical Review 88, 4, December 2007

doi: 10.3138/chr.88.4.549

d'autres pays, ni du contenu du discours anti-asiatique de la main-d'oeuvre canadienne. On a également rarement examiné si les syndicats avaient eu le même type d'échanges avec les Asiatiques qu'ils ont eus avec les immigrants d'autres origines, les minorités ou les groupes opprimés.

À partir de la littérature de plus en plus abondante sur la question de la racialisation et en se concentrant essentiellement sur les années 1880, époque où le point de vue de la main-d'oeuvre concernant l'immigration asiatique s'est implanté, cet article illustre de quelle manière les Asiatiques ont été tenus à l'écart par rapport à tous les autres groupes avec lesquels la main-d'oeuvre aurait pu partager des affinités ou une cause commune. En effet, les Asiatiques ont été associés à des forces d'oppression et, tout particulièrement, au système industriel capitaliste émergent. Cette association se reconnaît à nombre de stéréotypes des Asiatiques, considérés comme esclaves industriels, concurrents économiques impitoyables, et comme une menace pour les femmes blanches. Ces stéréotypes ont placé les Asiatiques aux antipodes de la classe, de la race et de la politique des sexes que les dirigeants de la main-d'oeuvre s'efforçaient de favoriser.

In the late nineteenth and early twentieth centuries, one of the top priorities for Canadian labour leaders was demanding the exclusion of Asian immigrants. At the inaugural convention in 1883 of the labour central that would become Canada's largest, the Trades and Labor Congress, the first resolution adopted read: 'the future welfare of the working people of this country requires the prohibition of further importation of Chinese labor.' During the debate of the motion, a series of speakers assailed Chinese immigrants as 'uncivilized,' 'unassimilable' into Canadian society, 'immoral,' 'unsanitary,' 'criminal,' 'idolatrous,' 'nothing less than slaves,' and, above all, as 'forcing the working people out of industries ... [by the] cheapness of their labor.'[1]

Another demonstration of this priority came when the congress received delegates from British Columbia for the first time in 1890, and slowly expanded its regional scope throughout the decade. The primary goal of the first delegation from the Pacific West was to enlist the support of central Canadian unions in the campaign against the Chinese, and through the 1890s official correspondences from British Columbian organizations were dominated by the 'Oriental labor question.'[2] Moreover, labour leaders frequently identified Asian

1 *1883 Canadian Labor Congress Proceedings*, 12; Eugene Forsey, *Trade Unions in Canada, 1812–1902* (Toronto: University of Toronto Press, 1982), 437.

2 *1890 Trades and Labor Congress Proceedings* (hereafter referred to as *TLC Proceedings*), 25–6; 'Communication from Vancouver TLC,' *TLC Proceedings*, 1891, 11; 'Communication from the Vancouver TLC,' *TLC Proceedings*, 1893,18–19; 'BC Executive Report, *TLC Proceedings*, 1896, 10–14.

immigration as the most pressing issue facing Canadian workers. In his opening address to the 1895 congress, TLC president Patrick Jobin declared immigration to be foremost among 'the questions that will be presented,' and especially urged strong action against the 'unmitigated curse' of Chinese immigration.[3]

In 1898, when the congress set its 'Platform of Principles,' delegates unanimously adopted 'Principle No.9 – Exclusion of Chinese.' This 'Principle' was expanded in 1909 to become 'Exclusion of Orientals,' so as to cover the Japanese, and again in 1911, becoming 'Exclusion of Asiatics,' to cover South Asians.[4] The congress's platform should put to rest any doubts about whether Asian exclusion was a fundamental goal of mainstream Canadian labour or not.

Historians have explored many aspects of labour's antipathy to Asians. Peter Ward has presented anti-Asian racism as the product of the 'social psychology of race relations.'[5] Others, including a number of labour historians, have explored labour leaders' protests against 'unfair competition' from Asians in the job market. They emphasize that union leaders in the Pacific West viewed exclusion as crucial to the economic interests of Canadian workers.[6] Gillian Creese's study of anti-Asian agitation by Vancouver unionists stands as the most successful effort to develop an analysis that integrates economic and ideological factors. She shows the extent to which labour leaders saw race as both a criterion for membership in the working class and a dividing line in the workplace and the wider community.[7] Other studies have situated labour's views in the broader pattern of

3 'President's Address,' *TLC Proceedings*, 1895, 5.

4 *TLC Proceedings*, 1898, 1 and 31; *TLC Proceedings*, 1909; *TLC Proceedings*, 1911, 90.

5 Peter Ward, *White Canada Forever – Popular Attitudes and Public Policy Toward Orientals in British Columbia* (Montreal and Kingston: McGill-Queen's University Press, 1978).

6 See, for instance, Paul Phillips, *No Power Greater: A Century of Labour in British Columbia* (Vancouver: BC Federation of Labour/Boag Foundation, 1967); A. Ross McCormack, *Reformers, Rebels, and Revolutionaries: The Western Canadian Radical Labour Movement, 1899–1919* (Toronto: University of Toronto Press, 1977); David Bercuson, 'Labour Radicalism and the Western Frontier: 1897–1919,' *Canadian Historical Review* 58, no. 2 (1977), 154–75; Robert Wynne, *Reactions to the Chinese in the Pacific Northwest and British Columbia* (New York: Arno Press, 1978); Carlos Schwantes, *Radical Heritage: Labor, Socialism, and Reform in Washington and British Columbia, 1885–1917* (Seattle: University of Washington Press, 1979); Rennie Warburton, 'Race and Class in British Columbia: A Comment,' *BC Studies* 49 (Spring 1981), 79–85.

7 Gillian Creese, 'Exclusion or Solidarity? Vancouver Workers Confront the "Oriental Problem,"' *BC Studies* 80 (Winter 1988–89), 24–5.

anti-Asian racism, mostly in British Columbia. They have highlighted, in particular, how anti-Asian agitation was joined by groups representing different classes and interests, an array of media sources, and politicians of various parties and at municipal, provincial, and federal levels.[8]

This article builds upon themes that have been emphasized in the existing literature, but it also contends that key aspects of labour's anti-Asian agitation have not been sufficiently appreciated or explored. In particular, an interpretation based solely on job competition fails to account for many of the specific stereotypes foisted upon Asians (such as their alleged moral and social habits), the vast differences in labour's attitudes towards Asians and other immigrant groups, and the strong agitation for exclusionary policies in cases where the number of Asians was minimal. Moreover, the prevalence of racist attitudes in Canada does not explain why labour leaders assailed Asians but often expressed sympathy with other marginalized peoples such as Aboriginals and blacks, or why labour's anti-Asian rhetoric was often plainly different from that of other interest groups.

Undeniably, unionists portrayed Asian immigration as a threat to the general welfare of Canadian communities, but they saw the issue as linked to the particular struggles of Canadian workers. There was an unmistakable class component to labour leaders' agitation for Asian exclusion, and much of their anti-Asian rhetoric fit neatly with their rhetoric against employers and political elites. The links were also manifested in labour's stereotypes of Asian migrants. The portrayal of Asians as 'degraded' and 'docile' reflected labour's fears about the impacts of a fully developed industrial system of labour exploitation on Canadian workers. Labour's images of Asian workers as misers, ruthless schemers, parasites, 'drug fiends,' and hyper-sexualized menaces to white women were connected to the social and moral impact labour expected from capitalist development gone out of control. These stereotypes made Asians into Others, in contrast to which labour leaders often defined their movement as one of white working men. The strength of anti-Asian agitation in other countries strengthened unionists' convictions about the need to take action against the supposed 'Oriental menace.'

8 Patricia Roy, *A White Man's Province: British Columbia Politicians and Japanese Immigrants, 1858–1914* (Vancouver: UBC Press, 1989); Kay Anderson, *Vancouver's Chinatown: Racial Discourse in Canada, 1875–1980* (Toronto: McClelland and Stewart, 1995); David Cheuyan Lai, *Chinatowns: Towns Within Cities in Canada* (Vancouver: UBC Press, 1995).

By engaging with the recent work of anti-racist and post-colonial scholars on the construction of racist ideologies and the formation of racial identities, this article expands upon attempts to explore how particular minority stereotypes were, in part, projections of the anxieties, beliefs, and agendas of different segments of dominant white societies.[9] By doing so, it adds to the growing literature showing how Asians were not necessarily 'racialized' in the same ways as other minorities or immigrant groups, and how the white, working-class male identity formed in contrast to Asians similarly had many distinct characteristics.[10]

It proceeds from the position that the construction of Asians as a 'great menace' became firmly established during the 1880s and then endured in the minds of labour leaders up to the First World War. Space does not allow for a complete exploration of the continuity in labour's approach, which this author has done elsewhere, showing how unionists were not swayed from their basic views of Asians by changes in the economy, the political context, or the structure and composition of the labour movement itself. The Chinese were the first group of Asians to come to Canada and face hostility, and although groups that arrived later – the Japanese and South Asians – were not portrayed in precisely the same manner, they were mostly lumped together into an undifferentiated 'horde' allegedly

9 David Roediger, *Wages of Whiteness* (New York: Verso, 1991); David Roediger, *Colored White: Transcending the Racial Past* (Berkeley and Los Angeles: University of California Press, 2002); Alexander Saxton, *The Rise and Fall of the American Republic: Class Politics and Mass Culture in Nineteenth Century America* (New York: Verso, 1990); Theodore Allen, *The Invention of the White Race*, vol. 2, *The Origins of Racial Oppression in Anglo-America* (New York: Verso, 1997); Charles Mills, *The Racial Contract* (Ithaca, NY: Cornell University Press, 1997); Constance Backhouse, *Colour Coded: A Legal History of Racism in Canada, 1900–1950* (Toronto: University of Toronto Press, 1999); Timothy Stanley, 'Bringing Anti-Racist Theory into Historical Explanation: The Victoria Chinese Student Strike of 1922–3 Revisited,' *Journal of the Canadian Historical Association* 13 (2003), 141–66.

10 Thomas Almaguer, *Racial Fault-lines: The Historical Origins of White Supremacy in California* (Berkeley and Los Angeles: University of California Press, 1994); Matthew Frye Jacobson, *Whiteness of a Different Color: European Immigrants and the Alchemy of Race* (Cambridge, MA: Harvard University Press, 1998); Karen Dubinsky and Adam Givertz, 'It Was Only a Matter of Passion: Masculinity and Sexual Danger,' in *Gendered Pasts: Historical Essays in Femininity and Masculinity*, ed. Kathryn McPherson, Cecelia Morgan, and Nancy Forestell (Toronto: Oxford University Press, 1999); Ronald Takaki, *Iron Cages: Race and Culture in 19th-Century America*, 2nd ed. (New York: Oxford University Press, 2000).

waiting at Canada's gates.[11] Hence, the focus is primarily, although far from exclusively, on the 1880s, when organized labour began to view Asian immigration as a serious concern.

Before launching into the main arguments, however, the scope of this article should be delineated. The focus here is on organizations that were associated with Canada's largest national labour central from the 1880s to 1914, the Trades and Labor Congress (TLC). The key sources are the labour press, and proceedings and other reports from national congresses. The central figures are leaders of craft unions and the Knights of Labor up to 1902, when the Knights and other 'independent' unionists were expelled from the TLC at the Berlin convention and the international craft unions and American Federation of Labor asserted their power over the Canadian labour movement. In the particularly important decade of the 1880s, craft unions grew in strength and the Knights of Labor enjoyed a stunning expansion before starting a sharp decline around 1887. Not covered in this discussion are independent labour groups in Quebec, the Provincial Workingman's Association in Nova Scotia, the Industrial Workers of the World, and the Knights of Labour after 1902.

AN ECONOMIC AND SOCIAL 'MENACE'

The primary focus of anti-Asian agitation was economic, and on competition in the labour market in particular. There was a consensus among labour sources that white labour simply could not compete with 'Orientals.' Unionists complained constantly that Asian workers 'accepted' low wages and 'degraded' working conditions that white workers would not tolerate. Hence, Asian immigration was perceived as undercutting the standards of living of Canadian workers, or 'driving them out' of industries altogether. Exclusion of Asians, therefore, was presented as essential for the protection of the white working class.

While such economic concerns were crucial, they should not be viewed as the sole reason for labour's hostility towards Asians. Indeed, a solely economic analysis has a number of deficiencies. First, as Gillian Creese has noted, labour leaders assumed that Asian workers were impossible to organize, and therefore felt they had no choice but

11 See David Goutor, *Guarding the Gates: The Canadian Labour Movement and Immigration* (Vancouver: UBC Press, 2007), chapter 4, which also traces the signs of increased solidarity with Asians among a minority of unionists during the First World War, and a few signs of the moderating of anti-Asian sentiment during the late 1920s and early 1930s.

to demand exclusionary policies. Creese shows that unionists simply ignored instances in British Columbia of Asian 'involvement in labour militancy,' and continued to insist that exclusion was the only means of protecting the jobs of 'native' workers.[12]

Another problem is that labour leaders' complaints about competition from Asian workers rested on much more than straightforward comparisons of prevailing pay rates. Rather, they rested on an elaborate construction of Asians as 'inferior races.' The lower standard of living of Asians was one manifestation of their allegedly 'less civilized state.'[13] Canadian labour leaders went to great lengths in describing the 'inherent' standards of Asians, standards that Canadian workers could never bear. They provided graphic descriptions of 'Mongolians' as 'sunk in unspeakable degradation,' trained to 'live on garbage,' sleeping 'packed like sardines,' and 'herd[ed] like cattle.'[14] For labour leaders, these 'habits' and living standards were so deeply ingrained in the character of different races that it was physically impossible for whites to live at the 'level' of 'Asiatics.' The Victoria Knights asserted that whites would actually starve on the 'fare' the Chinese 'lived on.'[15] Similarly, 'Ah-Sin,' the pseudonym of the author of a notorious series of anti-Chinese letters to the *Palladium of Labor* argued, 'we cannot possibly feed and clothe ourselves for forty or fifty cents a week and they can.'[16]

Moreover, a number of the key characteristics of labour leaders' anti-Asian discourse contradict the interpretation that their attitudes were based solely on economic competition. Labour's arguments against Asian immigration went far beyond job competition and beyond economic concerns in general, and many labour leaders saw themselves not only as advocates of the economic interests of workers, but as guardians of Canada's moral and social fabric.[17] A number of

12 Creese, 'Exclusion or Solidarity?' 24–5.

13 Lawrence Glickman, 'Inventing the "American Standard of Living": Gender, Race and Working Class Identity, 1880–1925,' *Labor History* 34 (Spring-Summer 1993), 232; Lawrence Glickman, *A Living Wage: American Workers and the Making of Consumer Society* (Ithaca, NY: Cornell University Press, 1997).

14 *Palladium of Labor*, 27 Sept. 1884; *Toronto Daily News*, 16 Jan. 1884.

15 *Victoria Industrial News*, 23 Jan. 1886, 14 Aug. 1886.

16 *Palladium of Labor*, 24 May 1884.

17 See, for instance, Gregory S. Kealey and Bryan D. Palmer, *Dreaming of What Might Be: The Knights of Labor In Ontario* (New York: Cambridge University Press, 1982); Christina Burr, *Spreading the Light: Work and Labour Reform in Late-Nineteenth-Century Toronto* (Toronto: University of Toronto Press, 1999); Lynne Marks, *Revivals and Roller Rinks: Religion, Leisure, and Identity in Late*

scholars have highlighted different ways in which Asians were portrayed as major threats to this fabric, and were constructed as extraordinarily ruthless, hyper-competitive, and willing to abandon basic standards of civility in order to get ahead. The Japanese in particular were portrayed as 'frauds' and clever 'imposters,' who would give the appearance of assimilating into Canadian society only to 'get a footing in the country and, consequently, wedge out rivals ever loyal to the Crown.'[18]

Labour leaders also contributed to the image of Chinatowns as rife with drug use, gambling, and prostitution.[19] The Chinese were also regularly portrayed as sexual predators who sought to take advantage of white women. In the early twentieth century, unionists were key parts of successful efforts to lobby the provincial governments of Saskatchewan, Manitoba, and Ontario to enact laws prohibiting 'Orientals' from employing white women. A resolution passed unanimously by the 1911 TLC convention claimed that the legislation was necessary because 'Orientals employing white girls have . . . seduce[d] and destroy[ed] all sense of morality by the use of drugs and other means, bringing them down to the lowest depths of humanity.'[20] As James Walker has observed, labour leaders demanded these laws even though they would serve to increase job competition by damaging Chinese businesses and thereby pushing Chinese migrants back into the job market.[21]

As with standards of living, labour leaders were adamant that the alleged moral character of Asians was not the result of particular conditions, but part of the intrinsic character of the race. They not only rejected the notion that Asian 'habits' could be improved, but they furiously attacked anyone who raised the possibility. One of the best examples of these attacks is labour's assault on the Presbyterian Church when it became a vocal supporter of welcoming and

Nineteenth Century Small-Town Ontario (Toronto: University of Toronto Press, 1996).

18 *Independent*, 12 May 1900. See also 'Communication from the Vancouver TLC,' *TLC Proceedings*, 1893, 21–2; 'BC Executive Report,' *TLC Proceedings*, 1896, 12–13; *TLC Proceedings*, 1901, 10.

19 Kay Anderson, Vancouver's Chinatown: Racial Discourse in Canada, 1875–1980 (Toronto: McClelland and Stewart, 1995).

20 *TLC Proceedings*, 1912, 107. See also *TLC Proceedings*, 1914, 119; *Industrial Banner*, 6 Feb. 1913; *Voice*, 13 Feb. 1913; Constance Backhouse, *Colour Coded*, 132–46.

21 Walker, 'A Case for Morality: The Quong Wing Files,' in *On the Case: Explorations in Social History*, ed. Franca Iacovetta and Wendy Mitchinson (Toronto: University of Toronto Press, 1998), 206.

'Christianizing' the Chinese. TLC President Patrick Jobin accused the church of putting 'the dollar before the man,' while the Toronto Trades and Labor Council submitted a lengthy petition to the governor general denouncing the church's leaders.[22]

A further problem with viewing labour market concerns as the overriding source of anti-Asian sentiment is that they hardly treated all immigrant competitors equally. Although space does not allow for a detailed treatment of how labour leaders constructed a hierarchy of immigrant groups, certain key patterns can be identified. Labour leaders vigorously denounced the immigration of workers from British Isles, and especially from continental Europe. In particular, unionists argued that immigration from the 'Old Countries' also served to lower the wage rates and overall standards of living of 'native' workers, and to stress the social and moral vitality of Canadian communities.

But while they opposed immigration coming across the Atlantic, unionists often avoided vilifying the immigrants. In fact, labour leaders often expressed sympathy and solidarity with people coming from the 'Old Countries,' even while assailing the policies that brought them to Canada. Labour leaders often portrayed many British workers as 'honest' and 'worthy' people who had been duped into coming to Canada and thus 'forced' to compete with 'native' workers.[23] They displayed considerable ambivalence toward paupers and impoverished children, dismissing them as 'offscouring' and 'street arabs' from London, but also denouncing the 'unjust system' in Britain that had created their poverty.[24]

22 'President's Address,' *TLC Proceedings*, 1895, 5; RG 20, vol. 20, file 2955, 4, NAC. John S. Moir, *Enduring Witness: A History of the Presbyterian Church in Canada* (Toronto: Bryant Press, 1975), 150–2 and 167; Ruth Brouwer, *New Women For God: Canadian Presbyterian Women and India Missions, 1876–1914* (Toronto: University of Toronto Press, 1990), 6, 30.

23 See, for instance, *Palladium of Labor*, 24 Nov. 1883, 29 Sept. 1884; *Voice*, 11 Feb. 1898, 13 Jan. 1905, 16 Nov. 1906; *Industrial Banner*, January 1904, July 1906, July 1907; *TLC Proceedings*, 1924, 132.

24 See, for instance, *Toronto Daily News*, 8 Aug. 1885, 24 Aug. 1885; *Palladium of Labor*, 19 Jul. 1884, 26 Jul. 1884, 16 Aug. 1884; Canadian Labor Reformer, 24 Jul. 1886; *Voice*, 21 Mar. 1896; *Toiler*, 10 Jul. 1903; *Industrial Banner*, July 1906, March 1907, August 1908, April 1912; *Voice*, 2 Mar. 1906; *BC Federationist*, 5 Apr. 1912; Susan Houston, 'Waifs and Strays,' in *Childhood and Family in Canadian History*, ed. Joy Parr (Toronto: McClelland and Stewart, 1982), 129–42; Joy Parr, *Labouring Children: British Immigrant Apprentices to Canada, 1869–1924* (Montreal and Kingston: McGill-Queen's University Press, 1980), 53–6.

When it came to these types of immigration, the anger of labour leaders was directed primarily at the agents and promoters who treated migrants as 'so much filthy lucre' and often used 'bribery' or 'misrepresentation of the most heartless kind' to 'induce' people into coming to Canada.[25] Although there was undeniably a self-serving aspect to this approach, labour leaders devoted an impressive amount of energy and resources to campaigning against immigration agents. For instance, the TLC sent its own agent to Britain from 1907 to 1909 to expose cases of misrepresentation by agents and to combat 'myths' about Canada spread by promotional literature.[26]

Canadian labour was extremely hostile toward immigrants from southern and eastern Europe, calling them 'foreigners' who undermined Canadian living and working standards. Unionists often lumped these Europeans together with Asians into one large group as a 'menace' to Canada. However, eastern and southern European immigrants were not perceived as 'menaces' of the same magnitude as Asians, and the *extent* of the racialization of these migrants was much more limited. Labour committed much less energy to portraying Italians, Hungarians, or Poles as dangerous sexual predators, drug fiends, or transmitters of deadly diseases – although some of these characteristics were doubtless implied when they were likened to Asians.

Labour leaders often displayed an ambiguity regarding European 'foreigners' that was notably lacking in their approach to Asians. For instance, unionists sometimes applied to Europeans the narratives of the 'honest' immigrant 'duped' out of a good situation into becoming 'heartlessly exploited' in Canada.[27] Another difference with labour's treatment of 'Orientals' was that labour leaders did not have an unshakeable belief that eastern and southern Europeans could not be organized. TLC unionists were hardly vigorous in pursuing this option, but even at the highest points of their anger over European immigration, they did not dismiss it as a possibility.[28] In 1911, for example, as the influx of immigrants into Canada was setting new records, the TLC convention supported a request from the Amalgamated Carpenters to have some union material translated into 'Ruthenian' and Polish.[29]

25 Quotations from *Industrial Banner*, March 1908.
26 Goutor, *Guarding the Gates*, chap. 6.
27 See, for instance, *Voice*, 10 Aug. 1906, 6 Jun. 1908, 6 Jun. 1913, 23 Jan. 1914; *Industrial Banner*, September 1909, 17 Jul. 1914; *Toiler*, 19 Jun. 1903.
28 See for instance, 'Executive Report,' *TLC Proceedings*, 1907, 9; *Industrial Banner*, September 1909; Avery, Reluctant Host, 69.
29 *TLC Proceedings*, 1911, 86.

Probably the clearest articulation of the distinction in labour's view of Asians and any group of European immigrants came in the report of the Immigration Committee at the 1906 congress. This report organized the TLC's policies into a neat package that was reissued in subsequent years, and the third plank of its policy was a general demand for exclusiveness based on ethnicity and character. It demanded 'the exclusion of certain nationalities and classes of people who, either by temperament, non-assimilative qualifications, habits, customs or want of any permanent good their coming brings to us are not a desirable acquisition to our citizenship.' But its fourth plank singled out 'Chinamen, Hindus and all other Asiatic peoples' to be 'among the classes that are not desirable.' The fifth supported the Chinese Head Tax and insisted that 'Hindus' 'should be altogether excluded.' The committee did not make any specific request for the exclusion or even restriction of European immigrants – an especially instructive omission, given the massive influx from Europe and the relatively small influx from Asia in this period.[30] Even at times when other immigrant groups were creating far more economic competition, labour leaders still identified Asians as a particular menace.

Another problem with the position that labour's hostility towards Asians was grounded mainly in concerns about the economic security of white workers is that unionists whose members faced little or no competition from Asians were nevertheless adamant proponents of exclusion. Of course, anti-Asian agitation was strongest in British Columbia, where the Asian population was the largest, most established, and most familiar to labour activists. However, a number of scholars have shown that general interaction between whites and Asians in British Columbia had pronounced limits due to the extent of social and occupational segregation.[31]

Labour leaders east of the Rockies consistently expressed similar convictions about Asian migrants, although they may have felt them less forcefully. Even though many acknowledged they had never met an Asian worker, labour leaders in these regions had no doubt that any influx of Asians would have disastrous consequences. Labour leaders in central Canada and the Prairies were acutely aware that the Asian presence in their regions was miniscule – and they were determined to

30 'Report of the Immigration Committee,' *TLC Proceedings*, 1906, 80.
31 Roy, *Province*, 38–9; Anderson, *Vancouver's Chinatown*. Alexander Saxton makes a similar argument about the agitation in California in *The Indispensable Enemy: Labor and the Anti-Chinese Movement in California* (Berkeley and Los Angeles: University of California Press, 1971), 260–71.

keep it that way.[32] They continually pledged support for unionists in British Columbia, endorsed and reprinted their anti-Asian material, promoted similar constructions of the alleged menace, and sought to spur all workers in the Dominion to greater activism on the issue. 'The moan of white Labor in Vancouver, and all along the Pacific Slope is pitiful to hear,' stated the *Palladium*. 'Brothers, is there no help?'[33]

Unionists in central Canada and the Prairies were also convinced that their regions were vulnerable to a 'flood' of Asians. As President Carey put it to the 1897 TLC convention, 'the continued importation of these people to British Columbia will be felt in the Eastern Provinces, and if not stamped out at once our country will be honey-combed with [them]'[34] These fears proved remarkably resilient through the late nineteenth and early twentieth centuries, and became particularly evident when there was any perceived encroachment by the 'Oriental' hordes. For instance, the *Industrial Banner* went into an uproar in late 1905 in response to the opening of a few more Chinese laundries and the first Chinese-run restaurant in the paper's hometown of London, Ontario. The paper declared that the city might as well 'make preparations for a Chinese mayor' unless local workers took swift action against the growing 'menace.'[35]

'A UNIQUE CONCERN' FOR LABOUR

Labour leaders, of course, were far from alone in agitating against Asian immigration. The pervasiveness of anti-Asian racism in this period had a profound impact on the view of Canadian unionists. Labour leaders not only drew ideas and inspiration from anti-Asian agitation by mainstream politicians, the popular press, and other interest groups, but sometimes entered into broader alliances against the supposed Asian hordes. For instance, labour activists played roles in Asiatic Exclusion Leagues, and some labour leaders, such as Ralph

32 For examples, see *Toronto Daily News*, 16 Jan. 1884; *1883 Proceedings*, 13; *Voice*, 23 Jun. 1894, 9 Jan. 1897; *Industrial Banner*, February 1906.

33 *Palladium of Labor*, 6 Jun. 1886. See also *Wage Worker*, 5 Apr. 1883; *Palladium*, 12 Apr. 1884, 27 Sept. 1884, 12 Oct. 1884, 28 Feb. 1885, 26 Apr. 1884; *Toronto Daily News*, 9 Oct. 1884, 20 Sept. 1884, 9 Jun. 1885.

34 'Presidential Address,' *TLC Proceedings*, 1897, 7; 'Presidential Address,' *TLC Proceedings*, 1895, 5; *Voice*, 23 Jun. 1894, 1 May 1897, 11 Mar. 1898, 23 Sept. 1898.

35 *Industrial Banner*, November 1905. See also 'Communication from Moose Jaw TLC,' *TLC Proceedings*, 1906, 74; *Voice*, 17 Jul. 1906, 5 Oct. 1906, 4 Jan. 1907; *Labor's Realm*, 1 Oct. 1909; *Industrial Banner*, November 1905, March 1909, May 1911.

Smith, raised their public profiles substantially by participating in anti-Asian campaigns. One of the most brazen instances of labour seeking the support of other classes against Asian immigration was when the Victoria Knights of Labor welcomed to its ranks 'substantial business-men and property owners as well as workingmen' in the late 1880s. It is, therefore, not surprising that scholars such as Patricia Roy have concluded that anti-Asian sentiment 'transcended' class boundaries.[36]

As with the labour competition argument, however, there are several serious problems with viewing the pervasiveness of racism as a sufficient cause of labour's agitation. First, labour leaders, especially during the era of the Knights of Labor, believed that it was their mission to challenge the hegemonic culture. Gregory Kealey and Bryan Palmer have shown that, in Ontario, the Knights were both insightful critics of prevailing social norms and effective proponents of alternative values, such as cooperation.[37] For historians unwilling to dismiss the commitment of Ontario Knights and other labour leaders to challenging the economic and social order, their embrace of virulent anti-Asian racism requires specific explanation.

This is an especially serious consideration because labour leaders believed that a central part of their assault on the hegemonic culture was breaking down divisions it created among the masses on the basis of 'race, color, or creed.' Canada's most articulate labour reformer, Phillips Thompson, was particularly determined to show workers that forging a 'world-wide fraternity' was the only adequate response to a capitalist system that 'has no patriotism and no prejudices . . . [and] will levy its tribute from black or white, European and American, Protestant or Catholic with indiscriminating impartiality.'[38]

The desire for a wider movement and a broader sense of solidarity among all victims of the ruling elites can be seen in labour leaders' views of a number of marginalized peoples. In the labour press, one can find powerful condemnations of the 'unrighteous wars' in Africa and Asia waged by European imperial powers.[39] Labour leaders also expressed sympathy with the plight of Aboriginals in Canada.

36 Roy, *A White Man's Province*, xiii, 61, 93–5, 111–12.

37 Kealey and Palmer, *Dreaming of What Might Be*, passim.

38 Phillips Thompson, *The Politics of Labor* (New York: Bedford, Clarke and Co. Publishers, 1887),176–8; *Palladium of Labor*, 17 Jan. 1885. See also Hann, 'Brainworkers,' 35–5; Christina Burr, *Spreading the Light: Work and Labour Reform in Late-Nineteenth-Century Toronto* (Toronto: University of Toronto Press, 1999), 32–55.

39 *Palladium of Labor*, 14 Feb. 1885. See also *Palladium*, 3 Jan 1885, *Industrial Banner*, July 1899; *BC Federationist*, 24 Jul. 1914.

For instance, at the 1906 convention, the TLC made it a special order of business to welcome a new union local composed of Cowichan native people from Vancouver Island. The congress pledged its support to the efforts of the Cowichan people to gain land rights and a government-funded education system.[40]

Labour leaders' approach to blacks provides the most striking contrast to their approach to Asians. Labour leaders often declared that they wanted no part in the widespread racism against blacks in Canada. Unlike those faced by Asians, the hardships and discrimination blacks faced were not seen as a product of their 'uncivilized' character. In fact, labour leaders frequently supported blacks' efforts to make both Canada and the United States adhere to their often-stated principle that 'all are supposed to be equal before the law.'[41]

Labour leaders claimed to have common cause with people fighting against 'unrighteous' imperialist wars, Canadian aboriginals, and blacks. In particular, Canadian labour often identified these peoples as victims of the same 'monopolisitic' forces that oppressed workers in the Dominion. Labour papers denounced military campaigns in Africa as mostly for the benefit of 'usurers, speculators and bond thieves.'[42] They also put the blame for the Riel uprising in the North West on 'the Ottawa government and their ring of greedy, dishonest officials and land-grabbers, who have stolen themselves rich at the expense of the natives of the soil.'[43] Moreover, important lessons for workers in Canada were drawn from the plight of colonized people and Aboriginals. Labour papers suggested that Canadian workers might soon 'take a leaf out of Riel's book' and mount their own revolt.[44] According to the *Palladium*, 'Hindoos and Egyptians' had to recognize that 'unitedly [sic] they would be stronger than their

40 *TLC Proceedings*, 1906, 53–4.

41 *Toronto Daily News*, 17 Jan. 1884. See also *Toronto Daily News*, 18 Oct. 1883, 1 Feb. 1884; Palladium, 4 Oct. 1884; *Toiler*, 24 Jun. 1904; *BC Federationist*, 25 Apr. 1913; David Goutor, 'Drawing Different Lines of Colour: The Mainstream English Canadian Labour Movement's Approach to Blacks and the Chinese,' *Labor: Studies in Working Class History of the Americas* 2, no. 1 (Spring 2005), 63–4.

42 *Palladium of Labor*, 24 Jan. 1885. See also *Toronto Daily News*, 6 Feb 1885; *Palladium*, 14 Feb. 1885.

43 *Palladium of Labor*, 11 Apr. 1885, 8 Aug. 1885; *Toronto Daily News*, 1 May, 4 May, 8 May 1885.

44 *Palladium of Labor*, 18 Apr. 1885, 11 Jul. 1885; *Toronto Daily News*, 24 Mar. 1885.

conquerors . . . And just so, as regards the grip of monopoly on the resources of industry [in Canada], the toilers united would have everything in their power.'[45]

The strongest sense of connection for labour leaders was with the struggles of blacks. Especially during the era of the Knights, labour leaders claimed their campaign to free workers from the 'shackles' of industrial capitalism was following the same path as the effort to free blacks from chattel slavery. They insisted the 'corporate bondage' of the industrial era and the 'slave systems' of the Caribbean and, especially, the American South, were essentially the same: In both people were made to work 'for a bare existence [so] that others may reap the benefit of their toil.'[46] Labour leaders believed they would eventually be seen as heroes, much like abolitionists were, because 'just as surely as chattel slavery passes away, the industrial serfdom of the supply-and-demand system will vanish from the earth.'[47]

Canadian unionists were far from consistent in giving support to colonized people, natives, and blacks, although a more elaborate treatment of labour's views of these groups is not possible here.[48] Many labour leaders were supporters of the British Empire, and even the sources most committed to building the 'common bonds of humanity,' such as the *Palladium of Labor*, sometimes promoted stereotypes of blacks and aboriginals.[49] Moreover, with the decline of the Knights of Labor and the increased influence of more conservative craft organizations, unionists did not remain as engaged as they had once in the effort to create a broader solidarity. Labour generally became more narrowly focused on 'bread and butter' issues, although a significant

45 *Palladium of Labor*, 26 Apr. 1884.

46 *Palladium of Labor*, 2 Aug. 1884.

47 *Palladium of Labor*, 2 Feb. 1884, 19 Jul. 1884, 25 Sept. 1886; *Canadian Labor Reformer*, 5 Mar. 1887; *BC Federationist*, 25 Apr. 1913; Goutor, 'Drawing Different Lines of Colour,' 55–76. On the complex relationship between American labour and the plight of black slaves, see David Montgomery, *Fall of the House of Labor: The Workplace, the State, and American Labor Activism* (Cambridge, UK: Cambridge University Press, 1987); David Montgomery, *Beyond Equality: Labor and the Radical Republicans, 1862–1872* (New York: Knopf, 1967); Eric Foner, *The Story of American Freedom* (New York: W.W. Norton, 1998).

48 For a more detailed treatment of labour's approach to these groups, see Goutor, *Guarding the Gates*, chap. 3 and 4.

49 See, for instance, *Victoria Industrial News*, 19 Jun. 1886 (the paper's editor, J.M. Duval, was a noted imperialist), *Palladium of Labor*, 16 Jan. 1884, 9 May 1885.

number of leaders and papers continued to denounce 'our Glorious Empire' and draw parallels with abolitionists.[50]

Nevertheless, labour leaders' attitudes towards some other marginalized and oppressed groups provide an instructive contrast to their attitudes towards Asians. There were several international factors that encouraged Canadian labour leaders to set Asian migrants apart as a particular threat, and labour leaders were heavily influenced by hostility toward Asians in other countries. Since their own knowledge of Asians was limited, many Canadian labour leaders used 'the experience of other communities to guide us [in] the matter,' as the *Daily News* forthrightly stated.[51] Although unionists in British Columbia had the most 'exposure' to Asians, they were often the most aware of events elsewhere. The Canadian source that reprinted the most anti-Asian material from other countries was the *Victoria Industrial News*.[52]

Canadian unionists drew upon developments in an impressive array of locations. They contended that the experiences of Protestant missionaries and British officials in China provided further evidence that the allegedly 'degraded' standards of the Chinese could not be changed.[53] Labour papers reported on friction between Asians and resident populations in England, Hawaii, and the West Indies. They were especially attuned to anti-Asian agitations in other British dominions in the New World, particularly in New Zealand, Australia, and later, South Africa.[54]

As the dominant organizations in the Canadian movement – the Knights of Labor and the international craft unions – were American-based, the influence of anti-Asian agitation in the United States was especially important. The Canadian labour movement emerged mostly

50 *Labor Advocate*, 16 Jan. 1891, 10 Jul. 1891; *Independent*, 12 Apr. 1901; *Voice*, 30 Aug. 1901, 2 Nov. 1906; *Industrial Banner*, July 1899, September 1907; *BC Federationist*, 29 Jun. 1912, 25 Apr. 1913, 24 Jul. 1914.

51 *Toronto Daily News*, 16 Jan. 1884.

52 Some examples are 'The Sin of Cheapness,' *Victoria Industrial News*, 26 Dec. 1885, and 'Anti-Chinese Movement,' *Victoria Industrial News*, 20 Feb. 1886, which were taken from the *San Francisco Bulletin*; 'Christmas Without the Chinese,' *Victoria Industrial News*, 16 Jan. 1886, which was taken from Tacoma, Washington; and 'Chinese Invasion,' *Victoria Industrial News*, 3 Apr. 1886, which was taken from a rally in Washington State.

53 See, for instance, *Trades Union Advocate*, 18 May 1882; *1883 Proceedings*, 12–13; *Victoria Industrial News*, 2 Jan. 1886, 13 Feb. 1886.

54 *Toronto Daily News*, 4 Apr. 1884; *Palladium of Labor*, 26 Jul. 1884; *Voice*, 28 Mar. 1896, 21 Apr. 1899; *Industrial Banner*, May 1899, December 1905, February 1906; *Independent*, 21 Apr. 1900, 23 Jun. 1900; Resolution No. 23, *TLC Proceedings*, 1907, 65.

in the period after the Civil War, when American labour's sense of solidarity with blacks was especially strong. To be sure, racism hardly vanished in this period, and the image of blacks as inherently degraded labour endured. However, many unionists, including leaders of the AFL, showed new interest in organizing workers across 'the color line.'[55] The Knights of Labor in America were particularly committed to this cause, bringing in more than 90,000 black members by 1887.[56]

In contrast, anti-Chinese sentiment was becoming generally and firmly entrenched in American labour circles in the postbellum period. Key leaders of the American Knights of Labor, such as General Master Workman Terrence Powderly, and of the American Federation of Labor, such as Adolph Strasser and President Samuel Gompers, were fierce opponents of Chinese immigration. One of the thinkers who had the most influence on the Knights, Henry George, was also a vocal advocate of Chinese exclusion.[57] In short, the Canadian movement was establishing itself during a period when the American movement's antipathy toward the Chinese was surging and its antipathy to blacks was significantly tempered.

For Canadian unionists, developments in America and other settings not only 'proved' that Asians were a particular 'menace,' but also supplied models of the exclusionary laws they wanted the government to replicate without delay. Ottawa's inaction relative to other governments was viewed as magnifying the threat of a flood of Asian migrants. Labour papers fumed that other areas protected themselves while Canada 'is supposed to stand still with folded arms and calmly tolerate this menacing invasion.'[58]

55 Glickman, 'American Standard,' 232–3; Roediger, *Colored White*, 195–9; Saxton, *The Indispensable Enemy*, 260–71; Eric Arnesen, 'Specter of the Black Strikebreaker: Race, Employment, and Labor Activism in the Industrial Era,' *Labor History* 44, no.3 (Aug. 2003), 319–35.

56 Total membership of the American Knights peaked at over 750,000 in 1886. See Robert Weir, *Beyond Labor's Veil: The Culture of the Knights of Labor* (University Park: Pennsylvania State University Press, 1996), 7–8, 12; Kim Voss, *The Making of American Exceptionalism: The Knights of Labor and Class Formation in the Nineteenth Century* (Ithaca, NY: Cornell University Press, 1993), 81.

57 Takaki, *Iron Cages*, 240–8; Saxton, *The Indispensable Enemy*, 271; Henry George, 'Chinese Immigration,' in *Cyclopedia of Political Science, Political Economy, and the Political History of the United States by the Best American and European Writers*, ed. John Lalor (New York: Maynard and Mill, 1881), vol. 2, sect. 213 – 46; Stanford Lyman, 'The 'Chinese Question' and American Labor Historians,' *New Politics* 7, no. 4 (Winter 2000), 113–48.

58 *Industrial Banner*, November 1907. See also Roy, *White Man's Province*, 38; *Trades Union Advocate*, 18 May 1882; 'Victoria TLC,' *TLC Proceedings*, 1890, 21;

Canadian labour leaders were also inspired by the strength and influence that their 'brothers' in places like California, Australia, and South Africa achieved, particularly by using anti-Asian rhetoric as 'a powerful organizing tool.'[59] For instance, they saw a clear connection between San Francisco's position as one of the cities most affected by Asian immigration and as 'perhaps the greatest labour stronghold on the American continent.'[60] Unionists thus sought to use opposition to Asian immigration as a rallying point for Canadian workers, sometimes in ways that made the separation between Asians and other groups shockingly obvious. For instance, when the *Palladium of Labor* presented the Riel rebellion as an example to be emulated, it particularly urged white British Columbians to mount their own revolt to force the exclusion of Chinese immigrants.[61]

THE RACE STRUGGLE AND THE CLASS STRUGGLE

The rousing tone of pronouncements like these highlight a further problem with viewing labour's campaigns for exclusion as consistent with broader patterns of racism in Canada: that key parts of the anti-Asian discourse by labour leaders were plainly distinct from the discourses produced by other social groups. Indeed, unionists furiously attacked other social groups, particularly employers and business leaders, as being responsible for the influx of Asians. Labour leaders viewed the racist campaign to exclude Asians as inextricable from their fight against Canadian employers. This was put most plainly by the petition from a Victoria workingman's rally: 'The struggle against the further admission of Chinese to this province is a struggle of labor against capital.'[62]

The association between Asians and industrial capitalism can be detected in a number of aspects of labour leaders' agitation. While they continually vilified Asian migrants, labour leaders put the ultimate responsibility for their presence mostly on Canada's policy makers and the capitalists who were said to be controlling them. The links were

TLC Proceedings, 1893, 19; *Voice*, 23 Sept. 1898, 12 Sept. 1902; *Independent*, 21 Apr. 1900.

59 Quotation from Alexander Saxton, *The Indispensable Enemy*, 261–2.

60 *Industrial Banner*, May 1906. See also *Trades Union Advocate*, 18 May 1882, 29 Jun. 1882, 1 Feb. 1883.

61 *Palladium of Labor*, 18 Apr. 1885. See also *Labor Union*, 17 Mar. 1883; *Voice*, 23 Aug. 1901; *Industrial Banner*, February 1906.

62 The petition was reprinted as 'An Appeal – from Victoria,' *Toronto Daily News*, 8 Jun. 1885 – henceforth referred to as 'Victoria petition.'

especially clear between the Knights' anti-Chinese agitation and their growing challenge to the capitalist system in the 1880s. Stopping what the *Palladium of Labor* called 'the capitalist in his devilish scheme for forcing down wages by the aid of hordes of barbarians' was seen as a crucial front line in the struggle.[63]

The anti-Chinese campaign served to bolster many of the Knights' critiques of the ruling elite, and provided a basis for their calls to action against the 'monopolists.' In the political realm, the government's encouragement of Chinese immigration was seen as proof that Ottawa 'only cares for monopolists and capitalists and nothing for the working class,' as the Victoria *News* put it.[64] Kealey and Palmer observe that, in Ontario during the 1880s, anti-Chinese agitation served to 'further independent working class political action.'[65] An assessment of labour leaders' anti-Chinese agitation allows us to develop their argument. The issue of Chinese immigration was a favourite means of showing the corruption and fundamentally undemocratic nature of Canadian politics, and a favourite launching pad for calls for workers to vote 'their own' into power.[66] Some editorials that opened as considerations of Chinese immigration would slide into indictments of established politicians. For instance, in the final third of one of the *Palladium of Labor*'s most scathing diatribes on the subject, the Chinese were mentioned only once – their immigration had became the platform for an impressive rhetorical flourish against Canada's politicians: 'Appealing to Sir John and his venal gang of corruptionists or Blake and his windy incapables to stand by the rights of Labour . . . is a good deal like suing the devil and having the case tried in hell.'[67]

The moral and social attacks against Asians also translated into criticisms of the Dominion's elites. The willingness of Canadian employers to 'inflict the Mongolians' – and all the problems alleged to come with them – on the Dominion was upheld as a premier illustration of the 'inhumanity, greed and heartlessness of monopolist

63 *Palladium of Labor*, 12 Apr. 1884, 13 Jun. 1885; Nanaimo Knights of Labor submission to the 1884 Royal Commission on Chinese immigration, 'Nanaimo Knights of Labor – British Columbia,' *Palladium of Labor*, 27 Sept. 1884 – henceforth referred to as 'Nanaimo Knights.'

64 *Victoria Industrial News*, 1 May 1886.

65 Kealey and Palmer, *Dreaming of What Might Be*, 150–1.

66 See, for instance, *Trades Union Advocate*, 18 May 1882; *Palladium of Labor*, 4 Oct. 1884, 8 Nov. 1884, 27 Jun. 1885, 6 Jun. 1886; *Industrial Banner*, October 1907, December 1907.

67 *Palladium of Labor*, 13 Jun. 1885.

miscreants.'[68] For pursuing his 'devilish scheme,' the capitalist was portrayed as an enemy of all that dignified workers should hold dear. According to the Nanaimo Knights, capitalists were traitors to the Dominion because they were 'resolved to heap together a great fortune regardless of how the country prospers.'[69] The capitalists were also portrayed as traitors to their fellow whites, willing to 'debase and degrade their own race and blight the hopes of future civilization . . . in order to enrich themselves.'[70] They were presented as gender criminals, willing to strip away both masculine and feminine dignity for the sake of greater profits. As the *Palladium* put it, employers were undeterred by 'the prospect that tens of thousands of industrious workingmen may become tramps . . . and the streets of our cities be filled with harlots who might have been decent wives and mothers but for the ruinous competition of Mongolian slave labor.'[71]

Labour leaders not only indicted capitalists for bringing Asians to Canada, but sought at times to 'Mongolize' the ruling class, putting the elites at the same level as the 'barbarians.' For instance, after Ottawa disallowed one of British Columbia's anti-Chinese laws, the *Daily News* assailed the 'sniveling gang of corrupt legislators . . . [who] have no more principle or self-respect than the keeper of a Chinese opium joint.'[72] Similarly, when Senator Gilmour of New Brunswick opined that the Chinese were 'more moral' than whites, the *Canadian Labor Reformer* responded that 'if we are willing to accept [Gilmour's] testimony as between himself and the denizens of the slums of Chinatown, we insist that he must not presume to speak for Canadian workingmen.'[73]

This association of Asians and the ruling elite could also work in the other direction. In the minds of labour reformers, Asian immigrants were also 'capitalized.' Indeed, many of the particular stereotypes of Asian immigrants were heavily influenced by labour leaders' visions of the damage they expected from the unrestrained development of industrial capitalism. This is not to say that labour reformers neatly repackaged each part of their platform into their construction of Asians. Racialization was not a sensible process whereby different parts of the dominant society formed stereotypes through thoughtful calculation and careful observation of minority groups. Rather, various interest groups made racialized minorities into embodiments of their

68 *Palladium of Labor*, 27 Sept. 1884.
69 'Nanaimo Knights.'
70 *Palladium of Labor*, 27 Sept. 1884.
71 *Palladium of Labor*, 13 Jun. 1885.
72 *Toronto Daily News*, 21 Oct. 1884, 3 Mar. 1885.
73 *Canadian Labor Reformer*, 15 May 1886.

fears, their desires, and the personal characteristics they hated most. The results were jumbles of contradictory stereotypes that were attached to a racialized group.

For instance, there is an unmistakable link between Asian immigration and labour's fears about the impact of industrial economies on working people. Asian immigrants were portrayed as the docile and degraded labour that was ideal for industrial capitalist exploitation. Some of the aspects that were explored above of Canadian labour's economic arguments against Asians immigration are especially instructive here. Note the extent to which it seemed hopeless for whites to compete with Asians. Labour writers continually reiterated their view that against Asians, 'Caucasian labour has no chance' or even 'need not bother competing.'[74] Similarly, observe the degree of control that Asian immigration was expected to have over white labour. In the competitive labour market, Asian migrants would change, or even 'regulate,' the standards and conditions of white workers.[75] This was critical to labour's claims that white workers would be 'brought down' to Asian standards. 'What does this kind of competition mean to whites?' asked the *Canadian Labor Reformer*. 'Simply that they will live on rice, wear the least expensive clothing, give up their families and homes and pig together in dens. In a word, become the ignorant barbarians their competitors are.'[76]

It should not be surprising, then, that labour leaders connected Asians to their rhetoric about the emerging industrial order essentially being 'the slave system under another name.'[77] They regularly identified Asians as models of industrial slaves, highly coerced and disciplined, 'without manhood, without ambition, and without self-respect.'[78] Indeed, Canadian labour leaders probably used the terms 'slave,' 'virtual slave,' or 'slave labor' in reference to Asian immigration more than any other subject.[79] Unionists also drew Asians into their

74 *Labor Union*, 17 Mar. 1883.
75 *Labor Union*, 27 Jan. 1883.
76 Glickman, 'American Standard of Living,' 225–31; *Reformer*, 5 Jun. 1886; *Palladium of Labor*, 24 May 1884, 27 Sept. 1884, 4 Oct. 1884; *Toronto Daily News*, 9 Jun. 1885.
77 *Canadian Labor Reformer*, 10 Jul. 1886. See also *Labor Union*, 20 Jan. 1883; *Palladium of Labor*, 8 Nov. 1884, 25 Sept. 1886.
78 *Toronto Daily News*, 2 Oct. 1884.
79 For some examples, see *Labor Union*, 20 Jan. 1883, 17 Mar. 1883; *Wage Worker*, 19 Apr. 1883; *Palladium of Labor*, 2 Feb. 1884, 4 May 1884, 4 Oct. 1884, 28 Mar. 1885; 'Nanaimo Knights'; *Toronto Daily News*, 2 Oct. 1884, 8 Jun. 1885; *Victoria Industrial News*, 6 Sept. 1886; 'BC Executive Report,' *TLC Proceedings*, 1896, 11; *Industrial Banner*, December 1905, March 1912; *Voice*, 17 Aug. 1906.

argument that industrial servitude would become even more severe than plantation slavery. They argued that in the 'old' slave system, plantation owners, at least, would provide enough for the upkeep of their human property, but industrial masters seemed willing to let their slaves 'starve,' and to 'drive the girls into prostitution.'[80] As an illustration – and in one of the only cases in which they displayed any sympathy toward Asians – unionists pointed to how Chinese workers were 'turned loose' on British Columbia towns 'to starve or secure a living by improper means' after the completion of the Pacific Railway.[81]

Canadian labour's social and moral arguments against Asian immigration also reflected concerns about capitalism. The criminal activity ascribed to Asians noted above, such as drugs, gambling, and prostitution, was also among the chief problems that unionists said would increasingly afflict modern industrial urban centres. Regarding the portrayal of the Chinese sexual 'menace,' Karen Dubinsky and Adam Givertz argue that the particular characteristics attributed to the Chinese reflected the Knights of Labor's broader effort to present 'lascivious behaviour as one symptom of the disease of capitalism.' They contend that labour's portrayal of '"Chineseness" [as] a threat to young girls,' was heavily influenced by images of ruling class villains such as the 'aristocratic libertine.'[82]

Another pillar of labour reformers' critique of capitalism, especially during the era of the Knights, was that its basic values were formed by 'the gospel of greed and grab.' They contended that basic standards of morality in Canada were breaking down as capitalist values of materialism, selfishness, and ruthless hyper-competitiveness gained ascendancy. Phillips Thompson argued that 'in the modern industrial and commercial world . . . the man who is sordid and penurious in his habits, unscrupulous in his transactions, but shrewd enough to keep within the law,' would reap unprecedented fortunes at the expense of the exemplar of 'true manhood . . . who is generous

80 *Palladium of Labor*, 25 Sept. 1886. See also *Canadian Labor Reformer*, 8 Jan. 1887; *Palladium*, 8 Nov. 1884, 4 Apr. 1885, 15 Aug. 1885. On similar claims by US labour leaders, see Glickman, *Living Wage*, 17–20; Foner, 'Workers and Slavery'; Roediger, *Wages of Whiteness*, 76–7.

81 *Victoria Industrial News*, 23 Jan. 1886. See also *Victoria Industrial News*, 6 Jan. 1886.

82 Karen Dubinsky and Adam Givertz, 'It Was Only a Matter of Passion,' 70–2; *Palladium of Labor*, 3 Oct. 1885.

and humane, who would scorn to take unfair advantage of a competitor.'[83]

Naturally, unionists identified capitalists themselves as the primary carriers of these social problems, but Asians were also made into manifestations of the most anti-social characteristics bred by capitalism. Unionists' portrayal of the 'Oriental' character as cheap and ruthless to the point of having 'no regard for human life' is particularly important in this regard. The *Trades Union Advocate* claimed that the Chinese would 'murder' their own baby girls 'wholesale' simply because they did not want the expense of raising them.[84] We have also seen that Asians were described as using their 'cunning,' and 'deviousness' to gain any advantage against 'loyal' Canadians.

Given this construction of Asians as ideally suited to the degraded working conditions and the 'heartless competitiveness' of capitalism, it is not surprising that labour leaders also believed that Asians possessed extraordinary powers in the emerging industrial order. They were portrayed as 'miserable slaves' who could thrive in their servitude, who could 'horde' money and even 'grow rich' and 'live luxuriously' at the same time as they 'accepted' low wages and the most 'unwholesome' conditions.[85] The Japanese in particular were described as 'resourceful beggars,' who quickly adapted to new surroundings while 'living on almost nothing and laboring for the merest pittance.'[86] On one level, these twin images appear hopelessly untenable, but by making Asians into caricatures of fully dehumanized 'tools of capitalism,' labour leaders could find them credible.

In fact, this 'racial reasoning' was so compelling to unionists that they were convinced Asian 'slaves' could achieve dominance in a capitalist Canada. Unionists constantly claimed that Asians had 'taken over' certain industries, and were on the verge of taking over more sectors of the economy. For instance, the 'Chinaman' appeared as a

83 Thompson, *Politics of Labor*, 159. See also *Labor Union*, 3 Feb. 1883; Kealey and Palmer, *Dreaming of What Might Be*, chap. 4; Burr, *Spreading the Light*, chap. 3; Dubinsky and Givertz, 'It Was Only a Matter of Passion,' 71–2.

84 *Trades Union Advocate*, 18 May 1882; See also 'Victoria petition'; *Victoria Industrial News*, 23 Jan. 1886; *Independent*, 12 May 1900, 'Communication from the Vancouver TLC,' *TLC Proceedings*, 1893, 21–2; 'BC Executive Report,' *TLC Proceedings*, 1896, 12–3; *TLC Proceedings*, 1901, 10.

85 'Nanaimo Knights'; *Toronto Daily News*, 29 Sept. 1884; 'Ah Sin' letter, *Labor Union*, 17 Mar. 1883.

86 Independent, 12 May 1900.

giant in labour cartoons, towering over white workers, Canadian unions, and even the prime minister himself.[87]

These particular stereotypes were particularly important in making Asians into enemies against whom labour leaders tried to rally white workers. The *Palladium*'s call for British Columbians to follow Riel's example was just one example of how Asian immigration sparked incendiary labour rhetoric against the ruling classes. Labour sources issued a number of warnings of a 'popular uprising' by white workers who were being 'crushed to the earth under a curse that can readily be lifted by the Government.' A speaker at a meeting of the Anti-Chinese Union in Victoria vowed: 'We will shed blood before we become slaves.'[88]

Implied in most of the specific characteristics thrust upon Asian migrants were contrasting virtues of white workers. Against the 'Mongolian' who 'accepted' 'degraded standards' was the white worker who demanded 'civilized standards' of living. For instance, the *Palladium* issued a welcome to 'the men of the races akin to us and willing to preserve the same standard of civilization.'[89] Against Asian 'slave labor' stood free white labour that commanded respect in the workplace. 'White men demand the treatment of rational beings, while Chinese are willing to be treated as beasts of burden,' declared the Nanaimo Knights of Labor.[90] As we have seen, against Asian hording and miserliness stood the generous consumption of the white worker. Against Asian parasites and frauds stood the white working-class citizen dedicated to keeping his country democratic and to resisting the schemes of monopolists. 'An intelligent population is the best safeguard against the tyranny of capitalism,' stated the Victoria *News*. 'This is why monopolists and syndicates are endeavoring to force servile Chinese coolie labor on this community.'[91]

This process of the formation of a white labour identity meant Asians often served as a reference point in general discussions of labour's struggles. A prime example is the *Industrial Banner*'s 1904 editorial entitled 'Trade Unionism Stands For A High Type of Civilization.' The first half of the editorial credited workers'

87 See for instance Burr, *Spreading the Light*, 75; *Labor Union*, 10 Mar. 1883; 'Nanaimo Knights.'
88 *Palladium of Labor*, 27 Sept. 1884; *Victoria Industrial News*, 23 Jan. 1886. See also *Palladium*, 8 Aug. 1885; *Toronto Daily News*, 24 Sept. 1885; *Independent*, 21 Apr. 1900; *Industrial Banner*, December 1905.
89 *Palladium of Labor*, 27 Sept. 1884.
90 'Nanaimo Knights.'
91 *Victoria Industrial News*, 6 Mar. 1886.

organizations for allowing Britain, the United States, and Canada, 'to stand at the highest in the scale of civilization.' To illustrate the difference unions could make, the paper claimed that 'there is an immense gulf fixed between the status of the Canadian workman and the Chinese coolie. The Chinese coolie accepts his lot and is content with his position. He has no aspirations; he is an animal . . . The trade union has developed the Canadian workman. . . . He has higher aims and more manly aspirations than the Oriental.'[92]

While the white/anti-Asian racial consciousness served as a rallying point for labour leaders, it also created deep contradictions and problems in Canadian labour's worldview. Not only were even the faintest gestures of support and solidarity with Asians ruled out of the question, but aggression against them – even though they were one of the most exploited and vulnerable segments of the labour force – was often sanctioned as a valid form of working-class self-action. Canadian labour defended violence against 'uncivilized' immigrants by claiming the right of white workers to protect their livelihoods. Although capitalist oppression was blamed for the violence, labour papers usually accepted that immigrants, rather than the bosses, were the primary targets.[93]

In particular, belligerence against the Asian (particularly Chinese) 'menace' to the Canadian family was constructed as the duty of the white workingman. Indeed, against the Asian 'moral offal' stood the manly white worker who understood his patriarchal role as protector of his home, his family, and the morality of his community. Calls to action against Asian immigration often appealed to this sense of gender duty. 'Workingmen!' pleaded the *Trades Union Advocate*, 'if you love your wives and little ones, and want to keep a roof over their heads, then agitate at once for the abolition of Chinese immigration.'[94] Dubinsky and Givertz have shown that perceived threats to young white women from Chinese sexual 'villains' elicited a fierce response. In 1884, the *Palladium* alleged that white teenage girls 'noticed' in Chinese laundries had been 'plied with opium and taken advantage of.' The paper issued 'a note to parents of girls "to stay away from

92 *Industrial Banner*, May 1904.
93 See for examples, Thompson, *Politics of Labor*, 80; *Palladium of Labor*, 4 Jan. 1884, 3 Oct. 1885; *Toronto Daily News*, 24 Sept. 1885; Saxton, *The Indispensable Enemy*, 258–9.
94 *Trades Union Advocate*, 18 May 1882. On the connections between the Ontario Knights' anti-Chinese agitation and their sense of chivalry, see Kealey and Palmer, *Dreaming of What Might Be*, 151; Dubinsky and Givertz, 'It Was Only a Matter of Passion,' 70–2.

John Chinaman" ' and 'a not-so-subtle threat to "Wah Lee" to "give up coaxing little girls" or else.'[95]

Of course, exclusion was not one of labour's ultimate goals, and not a 'finality' as Phillips Thompson put it. Thompson reminded labour reformers that campaigns such as the one for Asian exclusion could 'give labor a chance to hold its own,' but were helpless when it came to the 'gigantic wrongs' of the 'spoilation' and 'robbery' brought by the monopolists.[96] Although labour leaders in British Columbia were most absorbed in anti-Asian agitation, they also asserted that ownership of the province's resources was the most important factor in entrenching 'a few individuals' in a position of power 'beyond the reach' of the rest of the population. Subjecting white workers to the 'killing competition' of Asian migrants was identified as the next – and the secondary – measure that 'dispossessed' the labouring classes of any means of resistance.[97]

On the other hand, complete defeat on the issue appeared certain to entail the end of the Canadian labour movement. Labour leaders were certain that they would lose all hope if the 'Mongolian swarm' was allowed to overrun the Dominion. They particularly feared that white workers would have to abandon the Dominion or else join Asians in the ranks of industrial slaves. 'Unless the plague be speedily stopped,' declared the Nanaimo Knights, 'in a very few years there will only remain a few immensely wealthy men, and a servile, slavish people, chiefly Chinese.'[98] Stopping Asian immigration, therefore, was viewed as a necessary precondition for the realization of the goals of Canadian labour leaders.

CONCLUSION

Altogether, labour leaders portrayed Asians as a 'great menace' to Canada, and to its working class in particular. Anxiety about competition in the labour market accounts for much of labour's hostility, but unionists hardly limited their complaints to wage levels as they continually depicted Asians as irretrievably degraded workers, and put a major emphasis on social and moral issues. Moreover, the

95 Dubinsky and Givertz, 'It Was Only a Matter of Passion,' 71; *Palladium of Labor*, 23 Aug. 1884.

96 *Palladium of Labor*, 12 Oct. 1884.

97 *Palladium of Labor*, 27 Sept. 1884; 12 Oct. 1884; *Victoria Industrial News*, 15 Mar. 1886.

98 'Nanaimo Knights.' See also *Canadian Labor Reformer*, 6 Jun. 1886; *Voice*, 26 Oct. 1906; *BC Federationist*, 31 Oct. 1913.

support for exclusionary measures in areas where the number of Asians was minimal, and the dramatically different approach taken to other groups of immigrant workers, show that more than a rational assessment of workers' economic interests informed labour leaders' agitation.

The widespread racism against Asians in Canada, and especially in British Columbia, was another crucial reason why labour leaders demanded exclusion. However, key aspects of labour's anti-Asian rhetoric, particularly its anti-capitalist component, were plainly different from the rhetoric of other social classes. Law enforcement officials, medical professionals, and middle- and upper-class commentators, did not continually describe the Asians as 'tools of the capitalists,' and use their immigration as proof of the 'inhumanity and greed' of Canadian employers.

Moreover, labour leaders in this period were hardly uncritical adherents of prevailing social norms, and particularly of prevailing views of many minorities or marginalized groups. But while some groups were associated with admirable struggles against oppression in earlier time periods or distant lands, Asians were seen as a new threat that arose largely with advance of industrial capitalism. Events elsewhere in the British Empire and the United States played a vital role in strengthening this view of Asians.

Indeed, far from showing interest in forging solidarity across this particular racial line, labour leaders saw their campaign against the Asian 'menace' as an important part of their broader struggle against capitalism. As a result, the agitation for exclusion could appear whenever labour leaders contemplated their political, social, and economic agenda. For example, a large proportion of the statements in Knights of Labor newspapers about Chinese immigration – most of them brief references – appear in general reports on labour's priorities, or in broad assessments of the state of the Dominion.[99]

However, the racist campaign for exclusion put major limits on hopes for the creation of a broader working-class movement. Canadian unionists may have used constructions of the Asian 'menace' to bolster

99 Some examples are in *Trades Union Advocate*, 26 Oct. 1882, 11 Jan. 1883; *Wage Worker*, 19 Apr. 1883, 25 Aug. 1883; *Palladium of Labor*, 6 December 1884, 16 May 1885; *Toronto Daily News*, 19 Jul. 1884, 8 Aug. 1885; *Victoria Industrial News*, 29 May 1886. Particularly because of the frequency of references such as these to Chinese immigration, I would argue that Bryan Palmer underestimates both the number and the importance of anti-Chinese comments in the *Palladium of Labor*. See Palmer, 'Historiographic Hassles,' *Social History/Histoire Sociale* 33, no. 65 (May 2000), 120–1.

their rhetoric against political and economic elites, their calls on the rank-and-file to get active, and even their identity as leaders of a movement of white working men, but these constructions and the identities formed in opposition to them were fundamentally antagonistic toward many of Canada's, and many more of the world's, working people.

HISTORY

OF

WINNIPEG GENERAL STRIKE

1919

SYNOPSIS OF EVENTS

Leading up to the **Walker Theatre meeting**, the **Calgary Convention**, the **Formation of the O. B. U.**, the **Winnipeg General Strike** — May and June, 1919 — and the prosecutions arising out of the same.

Eight men, Russell, Johns, Pritchard, Armstrong, Heaps, Queen, Bray, and Ivens, are now before the Assize Court of Manitoba, charged by the Government with seditious conspiracy to overthrow the state, etc.*

These men were arrested, together with five non-English speaking men, on June 17th, last, when the general strike was at its height. The real purpose of the arrests was to smash the strike then in existence.

The **Crown alleges** that they were arrested because they were seditiously planning a revolution and that the strike was an attempt to establish a soviet form of government.

The Crown is **attempting to prove** that meetings held in Winnipeg in December, 1918, to protest against orders in council, to demand the withdrawal of troops from Russia, and the release of political prisoners; the various meetings of the Labor Church in Winnipeg; a meeting planned by the Socialist Party of Canada — but prevented by rioting soldiers; a convention of representatives from the Trades Unions of Western Canada, held in Calgary in March, 1919; the Winnipeg general sympathetic strike of May and June, 1919, and the formation of an industrial organization in place of the craft organizations, under the name of the One Big Union, are all connected parts of one big conspiracy.

The facts are that the Labor Church was formed by the Rev. W. Ivens, M.A. B.D., when he was denied, or driven from the pulpit of the Methodist Church, because of his pacifist views. The Walker Theatre meeting was planned because the workers realized that the Trades Congress officers were impotent in the matter of securing from the Government redress of the grievances complained of, and were

*The actual trials, which were held before the Court of King's Bench, began at the end of November 1919 and were concluded in April 1920. This reference would indicate that although this book appeared after the trials, much of it consisted of material written or published earlier.

determined that the voice of protest should be heard. The Majestic Theatre meeting was one of a series planned by the Socialist Party to propagate their views. The Western Convention, held in Calgary, March, 1919, was arranged to form some plan of organization that would free Western Canada from the control of a Trades Congress machine which the Western workers claimed defeated their every plan and proposal. The plan of industrial organization was launched at that convention and was accelerated by the active and persistent opposition of international officers to the Winnipeg strike. The strike itself grew spontaneously out of the refusal of the "iron masters" — owners of the contract metal shops — to recognize the unions or the Metal Trades Council, and the refusal of the Builders' Exchange to recognize the Building Trades Council or to pay the men engaged in all branches of the building industry a living wage.

The idea of a conspiracy is preposterous. The contention of the Crown that these activities were part of an attempt to set up a soviet and to bring about a revolution, is a **pretext** by which they hope to **railroad active leaders of the working class to jail**, and an excuse for them to carry on an active propaganda against "Reds," "Revolutionists," "Left Wingers," "Radicals," "Progressives," or whatever they may be called. "Bolshevists" is, of course, the most telling expression from their standpoint.

If they are successful in this endeavor it is quite clear that **the Government will pass legislation, or, more orders-in-council, suppressing every organization, and imprisoning every person** who in any way seeks to better the general condition of the workers.

That **this is no mere suspicion** on our part is proven by the fact that, while the strike was in progress, the **Immigration Act** was re-introduced into the Federal Parliament. It had already been amended and signed by the Governor-General, not more than a couple of days previously. When **re-introduced it was re-amended purposely to destroy the right of trial by jury for all British born citizens**, and also make it possible to deport the strike leaders, without legal trial.* This act was re-introduced into the Ottawa Parliament, and amended within the short space of time of twenty minutes. It was next rushed

*The Immigration Act was amended on June 6, 1919, to permit the deportation without trial of persons of British birth accused of sedition. The act had already been amended to permit this to happen to persons who came from other countries, but when it was discovered that most of the strike leaders came from Britain, this new amendment was rushed through the House of Commons and Senate in forty minutes. Years later, Meighen defended this action by saying: "All that was done in 1919 was to add another class to those who were not entitled to jury trial. The class we added were those who came from the Old Country and were anarchists. In a word we added anarchists to prostitutes and beggars." (House of Commons *Debates*, June 2, 1926, vol. 4, page 3996.)

through the Senate, then to the Governor-General for signature. From first to last the time taken for the whole process was less than 45 minutes. There is not a parallel for this stampede legislation in the whole of British history.

Shortly after this amendment was passed the accused were **arrested, rushed to the penitentiary**, and, on the third day, brought before the **Board of Enquiry**, so that they **might have a secret hearing and then be deported**. That this plan was not carried out was due, we believe, wholly to the **storm of protest** raised in all parts of Canada against the outrage.

The fact that they were unable under the re-amended Immigration Act, at that time, to accomplish their designs, halted them for the moment, but it also accentuated their determination to crush the whole progressive working class movement.

This means that a publicity campaign such as that secured by these long drawn out trials, where their side of the case is published in the daily press down to the slightest detail, while we have no such means of setting forth our side of the case, will, they hope, create an atmosphere where not only the conditions of the Immigration Act — which are still intact — may be enforced, but also **such additional legislation** as shall accomplish their designs.

Because of these facts it is necessary that at this time we should present to the entire Labor Movement a complete statement of the various events mentioned in the charges, and the causes leading up to the same, so that it will be able to form an intelligent, complete and accurate opinion of the whole matter, assist us in protecting labor's right to organize, and work out its own emancipation.

We therefore set forth in order the progress of events as follows: —

1. The reason for calling the Walker Theatre meeting and a report of the same.
2. The Majestic Theatre meeting as planned.
3. The formation and aims of the Labor Church.
4. The calling of, and report of, the Calgary Convention.*
5. The calling of, reasons for, and progress of, the General Strike.
6. The Arrests, etc.
7. The prosecutions and progress of the Trial.

*The crown in its indictment linked these first four events with the general strike, alleging that the accused had "conspired" and "plotted" at these meetings to call an unlawful general strike and to overthrow the government by revolutionary means. These events are therefore included here by the strikers to give their side of the story, and to show how ludicrous was the charge of a "conspiracy" being "plotted" at open public meetings.

Pages 6-19 have been omitted.

the Canadian Government for fear of being landed in jail, but he proceeded to read an editorial from the Winnipeg Tribune, wherein it characterized the politicians of Canada as tricksters and pirates.

Dealing with the question of reconstruction, the speaker then stated that when you reconstruct a building you do not do it on an old foundation, as, if you did, the plaster would crack and the shingles fall off, and you would find yourself in the same position you were in before. They tell you that we are going to have prosperity, but let me tell you that capitalist prosperity means poverty for the working class.

He showed that in the United States, in the year 1917 — the most prosperous year in its history — poverty had increased eight per cent. In conclusion he called upon the returned soldiers, farmers, and workers, to unite and overthrow the capitalist system.

At this meeting it was announced that another meeting would take place the following Sunday, in the same place, to discuss the causes of the German Revolution. During the week the management of the theatre were warned that this meeting, if held, would be broken up by returned soldiers. In order to avoid trouble, the Socialist Party immediately cancelled the meeting. It was later discovered that one of the members of the party had, on his own responsibility, announced the meeting for the following Sunday to take place on Market Square.

When the Sunday arrived some 2,000 returned soldiers arrived on the Market Square and started a demonstration. This was followed by the raiding of the Socialist Party headquarters, and developed into two days of rioting and demonstrations against foreigners, and ended by the soldiers marching in a body to various industrial establishments, demanding that Alien employees be dismissed and returned soldiers be employed in their places.

Very little need be said concerning the Labor Church.

It was organized July, 1918, by the Rev. W. Ivens, who was up to that time pastor of a Methodist Church in the city.

He had taken a Pacifist position throughout the war, and was compelled to vacate that particular church on that account. He then started a church for the workers in the Labor Temple.*

The platform was open. Subjects pertaining to the fundamental problems of the day were discussed. This, naturally, placed emphasis on both international and economic questions, and brought the church under suspicion of the Government.

From the first it has been a popular movement with the workers, and they have now ten branches in Winnipeg, alone. Other cities are

*For more on the interesting Labour Church movement, see R. Allen, *The Social Passion* (Toronto, 1971).

also forming similar organizations.

It stands entirely on its own feet. It has no connection with any other organization. But, being composed of workers, it is keenly alive to their interests.

During the strike it was held in the open air and was attended on Sunday nights by tens of thousands. All its finances were given to the strike funds.

Section 4

THE CALGARY CONVENTION

The Western Convention met in Calgary in March, 1919. It was not a hastily called affair, nor was it the work of a few hot-heads. It was the culmination of a long line of suggestions growing out of deep and long continued discontent of the Western workers. This discontent was largely caused by the fact that the Canadian Convention was always held in the East. Each local had to pay the travelling expenses of its delegates and the vast distances the Western delegates had to travel under this arrangement, deprived them of their proper representation. Many attempts were made to have the convention held at a more central point, but without success.

No better case of this unfairness and the grounds whereon it rested can be found than the conduct of the Trades Congress which met in Quebec in October, 1918.

This Congress defeated all the resolutions sent from the West, with two exceptions. Furthermore, the East succeeded, for the most part, in defeating the candidates for office who were favored by the West, and elected those to whom the West was bitterly opposed.

The result was strong protest which resulted in a series of meetings of the Western delegates while at Congress; the appointment of a **provisional executive for the calling of a Western Convention**, and suggestions as to date and place of meeting for same.

On the return of the Western Delegates, the Winnipeg Trades and Labor Council endorsed the stand of its representatives at the Congress, and the executive of the Council on January 10th, 1919, made the following recommendations re Western Conference:*—

Western Conference

In the matter of a special Western Convention the following action was taken: —

*Although the Western Conference represented most of the Western locals of unions affiliated to the Trades and Labor Congress, the top officials of the TLC and the heads of international unions were opposed to it, because they saw in it a breakaway from the main body of the trade-union movement.

The importance of making the coming Inter-Provincial Convention an expression of Labor in the West cannot be over emphasized.

To accomplish this end at least two things are necessary:

1. The necessity for every organization to be represented if possible.

2. A policy to be well thought out and discussed before being adopted by the Council to be sent to the Convention.

We recommend that a committee be appointed to wait upon the unions that have not expressed approval of the Conference, to stimulate their enthusiasm and to get the closest co-operation. A committee of three together with the executive (incoming) to draft a policy to lay before the Council, and the affiliated organizations for approval.

Organizations to be asked to send suggestions along this line to the Council Secretary so that they may receive due consideration.

Respectfully submitted,

E. ROBINSON, Secretary.

Official Call for Calgary Convention

Early in February the following **official "call"** was sent out from V. R. Midgely, of Vancouver: —

Call for Western Conference

A letter from V. R. Midgley was read calling the Western Labor Conference to meet at Calgary on Tuesday, March 13th, at 10 a.m. Del. Russell supported the Conference, especially in view of the present unrest. He moved that a committee be struck to visit every local to get delegates appointed.

Call for Convention

"To all Labor Organizations in the West: Greeting.

"The Western Inter-Provincial Convention will convene in the Labor Temple, Calgary, Alta., on Thursday, March 13th, 1919, at 10 a.m.

"Last November a circular letter was sent out from this office advising the membership throughout the four Western Provinces that arrangements were being made for a Western Conference. The arrangements necessary for a successful Convention have been completed, and every organization should make an effort to be represented by at least one delegate.

Representation

"Representation at the Conference will be based as follows: — **One delegate for one hundred members or less and one additional**

delegate for each additional hundred members or major fraction thereof. Central Labor Councils will be entitled to two delegates each.

"The election of delegates to the Western Conference does not entail the payment of any per capita tax.

"Write the delegates' credentials on the letterhead of your organization and send them to this office, room 210 Labor Temple, Vancouver, B.C., or the delegates can present them to the Secretary of the Conference at Calgary."

Del. Logan moved that the council appoint its full quota of delegates at the next meeting. Del. Flye moved in amendment that the delegates be now appointed. The motion carried.

Council Appoints and Instructs Delegates.

The Trades Council, on February 11th, appointed R. J. Johns and R. B. Russell as its two representatives to this Convention.

At a meeting held on February 18th it was suggested that **special meetings should be held to discuss a programme for the Western Convention. It was further suggested that the delegates to the Conference from all unions should meet for discussion as soon as possible.**

On March 7th the delegates met as suggested. Then, on Sunday, March 9th, a special meeting of the Trades Council was called to decide the policy of its delegates at the Convention.

Calls for "Industrial Unionism," "Thirty-Hour Week"; Opposes "Industrial Commissions" and "Liquor Traffic"

The special meeting of the Trades and Labor Council, held on Sunday evening, March 9th, to discuss matters pertaining to the Western Convention, was a "humdinger." Every seat was filled, and every person was keen. Everything suggests that this Convention will be a land-mark in the history of Canadian Labor.

The following resolutions were adopted: —

Industrial Unionism

The first resolution was on industrial unionism: —

Whereas the capitalist class of this country has in the past used every means at its disposal to defeat the workers in their attempt to ameliorate the conditions under which they live; and

Whereas, to successfully conduct a strike, all crafts in an industry must act together; and

Whereas, the present craft union organization which makes it necessary for each craft to secure sanction from its international tends to defeat this object;

Therefore be it resolved that a referendum vote be taken of all affiliated crafts on the following questions: —

"Are you in favor of scientifically reorganizing the workers of Canada upon the basis of industrial organization instead of craft unionism?"

Carried unanimously.

Industrial Committee

In order to more effectively work out the plan of the sympathetic strike in Western Canada, the matter of the appointment of a Central Industrial Committee was introduced. Following is the resolution adopted: —

We recommend; "the appointment of a Central Industrial Committee to function in any dispute that may take place in the West, with a view to united action, and that representatives be elected according to industries."

Delegates Lovatt, Durwood, Johns, Anderson, Flye, Higley, Hammond, Barlow, and Robinson spoke to this resolution. Carried.

30-Hour Week

The shorter work day again was to the fore. The immediate cure for unemployment is shorter hours even though profits are thereby reduced. The following resolution was passed:

"Whereas the cessation of hostilities has, because of the demobilization of troops and the shutting down of munition factories, caused a state of chaos in the labor market through unemployment; and

"Whereas no provision has been made for such a crisis;

"Therefore, be it resolved, that the Western Convention at Calgary take cognizance of such an emergency and immediately take steps to promulgate a six-hour day, and a five-day week for all labor in this Dominion, so as to assist in absorbing the surplus labor and safeguard against unemployment."

Because of the importance attached by the Crown to the resolutions passed by that Convention, we append **the report of these delegates**, back to the Council, in full.

Delegates Johns and Russell Report Western Convention

Before starting our report as delegates to the Western Conference, it has come to our notice since arriving in the city last night, that the local press have been attempting to raise a propaganda to disrupt the work accomplished at the Western Conference by unanimous voice; and for the information of the delegates attending here tonight, let us say, **that the reports of the Convention in the Calgary**

papers were exactly what transpired and are fairly accurate and were sent to all newspapers in Canada by the Associated Press (as they appeared in the Calgary papers) **and yet, on arriving here we find the Convention proceedings are all misconstrued.** However, a verbatim report was taken and will be published shortly, which will clear away any room for doubt — but to proceed with our report: —

At 10 a.m. on Thursday, March 13th, R. J. Tallon, President of the Railway Shopmen Organization (known as Division No. 4) called the Western Conference to order. In his opening remarks he reminded the delegates that, while the Conference was brought about by the differences in the viewpoints of the workers in the East from those in the West, that the Eastern movement was rapidly waking up — and he trusted the Conference would result in a definite policy being laid down for Labor.

He then called upon David Rees, Vice-President of the Dominion Trades Congress, to take the gavel and open the Convention. Bro. Rees, in his opening remarks, stated that he was pleased to act as temporary chairman, pointing out that the Conference had not been called for the self-aggrandizement of any individual, but in the interests of Labor — he referred to the work the committee had done since the Quebec Convention, to bring about this meeting, and hoped the Conference would at least be as good as the one just finished by the B.C. Federation.

The Credential Committee then reported and recommended the seating of **237 delegates**, made up as follows: B.C., 85; Alberta, 89; Saskatchewan, 17; Manitoba, 45; after which a committee on resolutions was appointed, with J. Kavanagh, of Vancouver, as chairman; and also a committee on ways and means, with Bro. Miller, of Winnipeg, as Chairman, after which the resolutions in the hands of the Secretary were read and handed over to the Resolutions Committee.

On reconvening Thursday afternoon, Bro. Tallon was elected Chairman of the Convention (by unanimous vote) after which the Resolutions Committee reported they were prepared to give their first report.

At this time it was decided to wire to Fernie, B.C., for a stenographer — it being impossible to secure one in Calgary, everyone being so busy they could not undertake the work.

Chairman Kavanagh, of the Resolutions Committee, then stated that the committee desired to offer a resolution as to the general policy of the Conference, so that the delegates would be able to deal intelligently with the matters that were brought before them. **The resolution was as follows: —**

"Realizing that the aims and objects of the Labor movement

should be the improving of the Social and Economic conditions of Society and the Working Class in particular; and

Whereas, the present system of production for profit and the institutions resulting therefrom prevent this being achieved;

***Be it therefore resolved*, that the aims of Labor as represented by this Convention are the abolition of the present system of production for profit and the substitution therefor of production for use, and that a system of propaganda to this end be carried out."**

A lengthy discussion followed the presentment of this resolution, and on the vote taken **the resolution carried without a dissenting voice, amid prolonged cheers.**

The Resolutions Committee then presented the following resolution, as a substitute for the many resolutions presented on Industrial Organization: —

"Resolved, that this Convention recommend to Organized Labor in this Dominion, the severance of the present affiliation with the International Organizations, and that steps be taken for an Industrial Organization of all workers; and that a circular letter, outlining the proposed plan of organization be sent out to the various organizations; and that a referendum on the question be taken at the same time; the votes east of Port Arthur to be compiled separately from those of the West."

This resolution caused considerable debate, but in the main it centered around the question of what form of organization it would be, and seemed to draw out ideas as to the details of the form of organization, in order to provide for a further discussion of the details of the organization. **A Policy Committee of representatives of the five provinces was appointed**, with Bro. Johns representing Manitoba. After a lengthy discussion, the resolution was finally passed without a dissenting vote, amid ringing cheers from the entire Convention.

The debate on the above resolution will be found in the Labor News, next issue, provision having been made for same.

During the debate on the above resolution, Vice-President Rees, of the Trades Congress, took the floor — stating he was not going to speak on the resolution, but was rising to a point of privilege, and then proceeded to state that there might be a number of Police Spotters and Secret Service men in their midst; and that one man, William Gosden, alias Smith, alias Brown, well known in Calgary Labor circles, as an "Enemy" was in the Balcony of the hall. Every head turned in the direction of Mr. Rees' fingers as he pointed to the figure of a man who sat in the balcony of the hall.

"That man," Mr. Rees stated, "was well known to Labor men as Smith. He went to Fernie, B.C., and tried to make strife there. Some time later he made a visit to Hillcrest. Thinking it would be better for his plans, he changed his name to Brown, and succeeded in getting in on the Miners' Committee, and secured credentials to come to this Convention as a Miners' delegate. On the night he was to have left Hillcrest, he was put under arrest by the police, and the Miners, thinking it was an innocent Labor man that was being put under arrest, stoned the policeman who made the arrest."

A Vancouver delegate stated Gosden came to Vancouver at the time of the Island strife and tried to create sabotage.

Another delegate suggested that Gosden be hailed into the front of the hall so all and sundry could get a look at him. The suggestion was greeted with shouts of laughter.

Friday morning session brought forth the report of the Policy Committee, as follows: —

1. We recommend the name of the proposed organization to be "The One Big Union."

2. We recommend the Conference elect a committee of five, irrespective of geographical location, for the purpose of carrying out the necessary propaganda to make the referendum a success.

3. We further recommend that delegates from each province meet and elect a committee of five to work in conjunction with the Central Committee in carrying on the necessary propaganda to accomplish the wishes of the Convention.

4. We recommend the drafting and issuing of the referendum be left to the "Central Committee," also receiving and publishing returns of the vote.

5. In the opinion of the committee it will be necessary in establishing an industrial form of organization to work through the existing Trades Councils and District Boards, and no definite plan of organization be submitted until after the referendum has been taken.

6. The committee further recommends that after the return of the vote is received the Central Committee call a Conference of Representatives of Trades Councils and District Boards to perfect the plans of organization; basis of referendum of affiliated membership of 5,000 or less to be one delegate; over 5,000, two delegates; over 10,000, three delegates.

7. We recommend that an appeal be made to the Trades Councils and District Boards for the payment of two cents per member affiliated to finance the educational campaign for the inauguration of "The One Big Union."

The seven resolutions covering policy were taken up separately, and after a lengthy discussion on each, were passed without a negative vote.

At this time a Telegram was received from the Seaman's Union of America, complimenting the Western Conference in sounding the death-knell of Gomperism, which was handed to the Resolutions Committee to deal with.

Free Press, Free Speech, Political Prisoners

The Resolutions Committee then reported on a number of resolutions, the most important of which were demand **Free Speech, lifting of the Ban from Literature,** and **the Release of Political Prisoners and the delegates were demanding that a General Strike vote be taken on the question; and after a lengthy discussion, wherein it was pointed out that the resolution calling for the six-hour day, five days per week, for a general strike to go into effect on June 1st, if same was not granted — and it was decided to couple the whole lot of resolutions together, and if not granted, let us call the general strike at the one time.**

After a further discussion, it was decided to **send a wire to Ottawa, demanding the immediate release of all Political Prisoners, and the repeal of Orders-in-Council, restraining the liberties of the workers — and demanding a reply before the Convention adjourned.**

Endorse Self-Determination

The next two resolutions read, were passed without a dissenting vote, and were as follows:

Whereas, holding the belief in the ultimate supremacy of the Working Class in matters economic and political, and that the light of modern developments have proved that the legitimate aspirations of the Labor movement are repeatedly obstructed by the existing political forms, clearly show the capitalistic nature of the parliamentary machinery, this Convention expresses its open conviction that the system of Industrial Soviet Control by selecting of representatives from industries is more efficient and of greater political value than the present form of Government;

Be it resolved, that this Conference places itself on record as being in full accord and sympathy with the aims and purposes of the Russian Bolshevik and German Spartacan Revolutions, and, be it further resolved, that we demand immediate withdrawal of all Allied troops from Russia; and further, that this Conference is in favor of a general strike on June 1st should the Allies persist in their attempt to withdraw the Soviet administration in Russia or Germany, and that a system of propaganda be carried out and that a referendum vote be taken.

Another recommendation of the committee which was unanimously adopted and without debate read: —

Proletariat Dictatorship

That this Convention declares its full acceptance of the principle of "Proletariat Dictatorship" as being absolute and efficient for the transformation of capitalistic private property to communal wealth, and that fraternal greetings be sent to the Russian Soviet Government, the Spartacans in Germany, and all definite working class movements in Europe and the world, recognizing they have won first place in the history of the class struggle.

Yet another resolution, on which there was no discussion, and which was adopted, read: —

That the interests of all members of the working class being identical, that this body of workers recognize no alien but the capitalist; also that we are opposed to any wholesale immigration of workers from various parts of the world and who would be brought here at the request of the ruling class.

Six-Hour Day Resolution

The resolution that was adopted at the Convention of the British Columbia Federation of Labor, demanding a six-hour day; five days a week, to come into effect on June 1st, this year, was adopted by the Congress with acclamation.

The following resolution was then taken up, which changes the attitude of Labor towards Legislation: —

Whereas, great and drastic changes have taken place in the industrial world; and

Whereas, in the past the policy of the organized workers of this country in sending their Provincial and Dominion Executives to the Legislative Assemblies pleading for the passage of legislation which is rarely passed, and which would be futile if it were, is now obsolete;

Therefore be it resolved, that this Conference of Western workers lay down as its policy the building up of an organization of workers on industrial lines for the purpose of enforcing, by virtue of their industrial strength, such demands as such organizations may at any time consider necessary for their continued maintenance and well-being, and shall not be, as here-to-fore, sending Executive officers to plead before Legislatures for the passing of legal palliatives which do not palliate.

After a lengthy discussion, wherein it was shown that the time had come for Labor to take a definite position — **the resolution was carried unanimously.**

The election of the Central Committee to carry on the propaganda necessary for the establishing of the One Big Union was then taken and after an interesting election, the following were declared elected

Pritchard, of Vancouver.
Johns, of Winnipeg.
Knight, of Edmonton.
Midgley, of Vancouver.
Naylor, of Cumberland, B.C.

The meeting then adjourned to allow the provinces to elect five men from each to carry out the propaganda, and the following were elected to represent Manitoba: —

Russell, Winnipeg.
Lovatt, Winnipeg.
Scoble, Winnipeg.
Roberts, Winnipeg.
Baker, Brandon.

After which a number of resolutions, calling for the formation; also Joint Councils of Soldiers and Labor were carried; also resolution condemning Gompers and Draper, for refusing to participate in Labor Conference was passed and numerous others of less importance. The Convention was declared adjourned to allow the Central and Provincial Committees to get together and start their work.

In closing let us say that our reason for only reporting the most important features at this time was in view of the fact that we have made arrangements to have the proceedings of the Convention published verbatim in the B.C. Federationist and the Western Labor News and also in pamphlet form later.

Thanking the Council for the opportunity of being present at the most important Convention ever held in the North American Continent.

R. B. RUSSELL,
R. J. JOHNS.

The above report completely explodes the theory of any "Conspiracy." It was a gathering of trades unionists, and was dominated by the spirit of working class solidarity.

Resolutions similar in spirit and content have been passed in every part of the empire, but it remains for the Canadian Government alone to use them as part of a seditious conspiracy.

Causes and Development of General Sympathetic Strike. Was the Strike a Revolution?

The Crown alleges that the strike was an attempted revolution. We must, therefore, now describe the issues involved in the calling of the general sympathetic strike, on May 15th, 1919.

The two issues of the strike were: —

1. The recognition of the principle of collective bargaining.
2. A living wage.

After the general strike was called a third demand was added; namely, the reinstatement of all workers on strike.

The general strike did not take place until May 15th, after the metal workers and the building trades workers had been on strike for two weeks.

An Ordinary Strike at First, on May 1, 1919

It was in the month of February that the Building Trades Council got into negotiations with the Builders' Exchange upon a new schedule, based upon recognition of the Council as representative of the workers in the industry, and embodying a new scale of wages.

The only objection to the former was the recognition of the laborers. So far as the wages were concerned, representatives of the Builders' Exchange admitted the reasonableness of the claims to the men, but gave as the reason for their inability to grant the increase, that the bankers refused to do business upon the new basis.

A counter proposition was submitted by the employers seeking to divide one craft from another, which was refused by the men, and a deadlock ensued, as a result of which the men went on strike on May 1st.

We reproduce from the Western Labor News of May 2nd, the statement re the Building Trades' strike, as it affected, at that time some 1,400 workers: —

> Wages only 18 per cent higher than in 1914 — cost of living up 80 per cent — Bosses say demands of men reasonable and necessary to maintain standard of citizenship, but others must take responsibility for increase men demand. — Blanket increase of 20 cents an hour.
>
> All workers, including the Building Trades' Council, went on strike on Thursday morning, May 1st, after holding in the convention hall of the Industrial Bureau, the greatest meeting in the history of the Building Trades Council. The vote was 1,199 for strike to 74 against.
>
> A. E. Godsmark, Secretary of the Building Trades Association states that "the firms have reached the limit of their ability to pay with the proposal they had submitted to the men." The following figures do not bear out his contention. The fact is, that, while building expenses have increased 35 to 40 per cent during the war, the wages of the men have increased on the average of all trades involved, only 18 per cent. An increase of only 18 per cent in wages while the cost of living has increased 80 per cent, proves both the justice of the present demands of the men and their lack of responsibility

for the added cost of building construction.

The average increase offered by the master builders is 15 1-3 per cent, while the men are determined on a flat increase of 20 cents per hour, or approximately 32 per cent on present prices. This still leaves them considerably worse off than before the war. This is the reason *the bosses themselves admit that the claims of the men are reasonable* and justified. But, they say, other persons than the builders must bear the responsibility of increasing the cost of construction. The defence of the worker is that he is worthy of his hire and he must have a living wage.

Here is the schedule of wages now paid, the offer of the bosses, and the demands of the workers:

NAME	Present Rate	Rate Offered
Bricklayers and Masons	.80	.90
Painters and Decorators	.55	.65
Plasterers	.70	.80
Sheet Metal Workers	.58½	.68½
Structural Iron Workers	.75	.85
Asbestos Workers	.60	.70
Steamfitters	.70	.75
Plumbers	.65	.75
Mill Hands — Class A1	.55	.65
Mill Hands — Class A2	.50	.57½
Mill Hands — Class B2	.47½	.55
Mill Hands — Class C3	.40	.45
Stone Cutters	.75	.80
Stone Carvers	.87½	.92½
Planermen	.60	.70
Hoisting Engineers — A	.75	.85
Hoisting Engineers — B	.70	.80
Hoisting Engineers — C		.70
Firemen	.42½	.60
Carpenters	.60	.75

Strikers demanded an increase of 20 cents per hour on present rates of pay.

Master Builders Say Demands Are Reasonable. The Figures Speak for Themselves

And the master builders openly acknowledge the reasonableness of the demands.

The fight in this case, therefore, is not on because the men are unreasonable, but that the employers say that a further rise in wages will make building prohibitive.

Here is the crux of the whole thing, so far as they are concerned. The master builders say, your demands are reasonable, you cannot *live on less than you demand, yet we cannot pay the increase. The reply of the worker was a perfectly natural one. He said, well, if* I work I must have a living wage. I cannot live on less than a living wage. His only resource and his only alternatives were work and starve, or strike for a high enough wage to live. And now let us say once more, the bosses themselves agreed that his demands were reasonable.

Demands of Strikers Exceeded When Strike Smashed

It is a fact not generally known, that, when the strike was smashed, and, after the Government had railroaded the workers into jail and penitentiary, the employers actually agreed to pay wages in excess of the schedule demanded by the Building Trades Council. In the case of the plasterers, as an example, the demand was for an increase of 20 cents per hour, while the wages actually agreed upon was an increase of 30 cents per hour.

The Bankers and Financial Magnates Dictate

There has never been any misunderstanding on the part of Labor as to the real merits of the case, or as to the real source of the denial of a living wage to them. There has not been written a single line of vituperation concerning individual employers in the various building trades. There was no need for this. They were not the impossible ones, but **the persons who were responsible for the refusal of a living wage were the men who control the finances of this city; bankers and brokers and the big interests.**

These are the very same men who are directly responsible for the high cost of living. They controlled the markets — the workers did not have a say as to the increase in the cost of living. Their part was to pay the higher price as it was demanded at the store. The storekeeper charged higher prices because the wholesales charged higher. The wholesales raised the prices because they and the bankers, etc., were in absolute control. Full proof of this contention is supplied by the parliamentary committee that investigated the High Cost of Living.

Prices of Living Go Up, Up, Up!

Flour jumped in price over night. Bacon did the same. So did butter and eggs. So did shoes, and clothing and beef, and coal, etc. The only salvation for the workers was to ask more wages, and when this was denied his only way of enforcing a higher wage was through organization.

Then, when he presents his schedule, the boss says his demands are fair and reasonable, but he cannot pay the increase. This has been so with a vengeance for five years. The result is that the financial magnates have heaped up wealth as never before, while the struggle for the workers has steadily become harder and more impossible, till at last they have reached the point where it is impossible to live on the wages offered. Then when they ask for a further raise of pay they are told that the limit has been reached. That is why the crisis has been reached at this time. That is why Labor as a whole is standing behind the men.

Cost of Living as Submitted to Mathers' Industrial Commission.

We take a set of figures presented to the Mathers' Commission while in Winnipeg in May, 1919, on the amount that an average working family must spend to maintain life and decency. The figures are not exaggerations, nor are they the absolutely irreducible minimum, but they are based on an actual statement as taken from the books of the person who presented same.

We were informed that the second column was the amount this family actually spent, and the first column is his deduction therefrom as to where some slight reductions could be made in his monthly budget.

Cost of Living at Winnipeg, Monthly, During the Year 1918, for a Family of Five, Including Three Children of School Age

	Minimum Healthful	Comfort Reasonable
Groceries	$25.00	$27.00
Meats	9.00	9.00
Bread	4.50	4.50
Milk	6.00	6.00
Fruit and vegetables	6.00	6.00
Total Food	**$50.00**	**$52.50**
Clothing for children	$10.00	$10.00
Clothing for husband	5.00	7.50
Clothing for wife	5.00	7.50
Total Clothing	**$20.00**	**$25.00**
Rent	$25.00	$35.00
Fuel	8.00	11.00
Water and Light	1.00	2.50
Total Shelter	**$34.00**	**$48.50**
Help and Laundry	$ 9.00	$ 9.00
Medical	5.00	11.50
Replacements	5.00	5.00
Gifts	2.00	4.00
Total Sundries	**$21.00**	**$29.50**
Recreation	$ 2.00	$6.50
Education	1.00	7.00
Car Fares and Lunches	3.00	9.50
Subscriptions, Telephones, Church, etc.	2.00	9.50
Health Insurance, Lodge Dues	3.00	8.00
Total Extras	**$11.00**	**$40.50**

Recapitulation

Total Food	$50.50	$52.50
Total Clothing	20.00	25.00
Total Shelter	34.00	48.50
Total Sundries	21.00	29.50
Total Extras	11.00	40.50
Grand Total before providing for Life Insurance	**$136.00**	**$196.00**

Let anyone compare this budget with the schedules demanded by the building workers and it will be seen that they are not asking that their wages reach these figures. That is why their demands are said by the Master Builders to be reasonable.

National Contours: Solidarity and Fragmentation

CRAIG HERON

The great appear great to us because we are on our knees. Let us rise!
W.A. Pritchard[1]

Rarely in the history of capitalist society do workers stand poised to overthrow the social system in which they live and work. More limited hopes and horizons generally frame their lives. Workers may harbour an intense sense of injustice but feel powerless to achieve redress. They may grumble fatalistically. They may have come to believe that as workers they have no right to expect more from their society. Or they may channel their anger and aspirations into daily trench warfare over terrain marked by more immediate, and more modest, objectives. It takes a major rupture in the material underpinnings of their daily experience and in their understanding of the way the world works – their 'common sense' – to fashion a new and shared conviction that their subordinate status within capitalist society must and can change. Then masses of workers may suddenly rise boldly to assert a new place for themselves within transformed relations of production, politics, and social life generally. Capitalists, politicians, and others in positions of authority cannot ignore them. It then takes a grinding destruction of the bases of working-class strength in everyday life and an erosion of that heady new ideological openness to force workers back into compliance and resignation to their subordinate fate.

In the four years after 1916, workers in Canada developed a remarkably assertive sense of purpose and power – their society could be different and their actions could transform it. The war launched Canadian

workers on a trajectory of escalating demands and expectations. By the mid-1920s, however, labour's upsurge had been snuffed out across the country. The rise and fall of the workers' revolt followed a distinctive rhythm in each region, but there were key features that emerged in all major industrial centres. We have already seen the common conditions of wartime society that were confronting most Canadian workers. The purpose of this essay is to examine country-wide patterns in the revolt and its defeat.

The Workers' Challenge, 1917–1920

The most visible manifestation of the emerging workers' revolt was the wave of strikes that began after 1916 – a clear indication that the more individualistic drifting and shifting of the preceding two years was moving towards more collective responses and longer-range concerns about post-war society. As the research of Douglas Cruikshank and Gregory Kealey indicates,[2] the 218 strikes recorded for 1917 involved more than fifty thousand workers, twice the previous year's total and far more than in any single year since the turn of the century. Moreover, militancy paid off. Aside from those in the coalfields, most of the few big confrontations of 1916 had resulted in failure, but the following year strikers were successful in an unprecedented 40 per cent of their strikes and settled for compromises in another 20 per cent; employers got clear victories in only 19 per cent of strikes.[3] Strikers were also more regularly jumping the gun on the slow procedures of the Industrial Disputes Investigation Act by engaging in illegal strikes.[4] The annual total of strikers had doubled by 1919, when nearly 150,000 workers marched out in 427 strikes. In 1920 the number of strikes peaked at 457, though the number of strikers dropped by half. Over the four-year period 350,000 wage earners participated in strikes in Canada, distributed remarkably evenly across the country: 17 per cent in the Maritimes; a fifth in each of Quebec, the Prairies, and British Columbia; and a quarter in Ontario. More than a third of strikes were in manufacturing and a quarter in mining; three out of five strikers in this period were in these two sectors. Within manufacturing, the metal trades, shipbuilding, and clothing and textiles were flashpoints; together they constituted 44 per cent of strikes and more than half the strikers in that sector. In all parts of the country but the Maritimes, the peak of this strike wave was in mid-1919; however, the rate of militancy's decline varied across regions. In particular, after the crushing of the Winnipeg General Strike, workers on the Prairies retreated from the picket lines much more quickly than elsewhere in the country.

Workers were not simply striking; they were also rapidly banding together into unions. There can be no doubt that the various workers' organizations that appeared across the country between 1917 and 1925 constituted a mass popular movement of wage earners throughout most of urban Canada. At the end of 1915 union membership reported to the federal Department of Labour bottomed out at just over 140,000, and during the next year rose to only 160,000, still below the totals for 1913 and 1914. By the end of 1917, however, it was just shy of 205,000 and then leaped to almost 250,000 in 1918. Yet the most spectacular increase was recorded in 1919, when total reported union membership in Canada reached 378,000, the highest to that point in Canadian history. That high-water mark held through 1920, when only five thousand members were lost from the total union rolls.[5] These official figures for 1919–20 amount to just under 18 per cent of the non-agricultural workforce counted in the 1921 census, a historic peak in union membership up to that point. Yet, as the labour department admitted, these totals are undoubtedly low since many unions did not submit membership statistics and the reporting was at the end of the year, well after the great defeats in the spring and summer of 1919. A reasonable estimate is that at least one worker in five took out a union card. Probably well more than one in four passed through a union in these years, a level comparable to that of the mid-1940s. The dramatic increase in membership after 1918 and the many demands for union recognition in the industrial battles of this period point to the change in working-class consciousness that had set in by the end of the war. Workers were not simply trying to win immediate demands; they were turning to unions to solidify wartime gains and to prevent a return to the insecurity and indignity of the pre-war era. 'If we don't do something we will get our heads taken off after this great war is over,' a Gananoque unionist warned.[6]

Initially, the growth in union membership primarily revived pre-war patterns of organization. The first to put their unions back on their feet were craft unionists, especially the metalworkers in the munitions plants and shipbuilding yards, and coal miners in the East and West. Union locals then began to appear among the less skilled workers who also had a record of organizing – street railwaymen, teamsters, longshoremen, and the like. By 1918, however, workers who had never before shown much interest in unions were signing up. Among the new union members were factory workers in resource processing plants in British Columbia and mass-production plants in southern Ontario, Quebec, and Nova Scotia; loggers in the West and northern Ontario; unskilled workers of various kinds; clerical workers in several cities; and public-sector workers at all three levels of government, including municipal labourers, policemen (in ten cities), firemen, teachers, and letter carriers.[8] In fact, public-sector strikes were often the most controversial and menacing to dominant social relations.[9] Wage earners in all parts of the country, in large cities and small towns, were entering the house of labour. Women were found in growing numbers among the unionized and even on union executives, although in a role subordinate to that of men.[10] There was also more ethnic diversity in many of these unions, especially those in the mass-production and resource industries, from Sydney steel mills to Thetford asbestos mines to Toronto meat-packing factories to Trail smelters. A number of unions were organized primarily along ethnic or racial lines – for example, the Chinese Shingle Weavers' Union and Japanese Camp and Mill Workers' Union in British Columbia, the Finnish loggers in northern Ontario, the Jewish clothing workers in Montreal and Toronto, the black sleeping-car porters on the CPR, and the Italian construction labourers in several cities.[11] Some of these workers were inspired by the Russian Revolution; many more rode a wave of ethnic self-consciousness and assertiveness as political change convulsed their homelands.[12] Whatever their inspirations, all these workers were eager to confront the oppression and exploitation they experienced as wage earners in Canada.

Joining a union in this period was no passive process under the manipulative control of union bureaucrats. The established labour leaders were overwhelmed by the flood of new members who eagerly signed their union cards with little prompting and by the restlessness and combativeness of rank-and-file unionists in all parts of the country. Labour officials tried frantically to cool this ardour as it reached the boiling point in many workplaces. Often the workers ignored their leaders completely and pressed on with bold demands and direct action. 'At the foundation of all this agitation is the general restlessness and dissatisfaction,' the national government's security chief warned. 'The greater number of labour men, and probably the community as a whole, are in an uncertain, apprehensive, nervous and irritable temper. Perhaps these agitators are but the foam on the wave.'[13] Montreal machinist J.O. Houston captured both the spirit and trajectory of working-class mobilization: 'More and more each worker is doing his own thinking, is becoming his own intellectual, and to the extent that this is so he is placing less and less trust in labour leaders. He is looking for neither a Moses nor a Saviour. All the Sammy Gompers are doomed. His new representative will be an instrument to perform a specific act decided upon by the rank and file of an industrial organization.'[14]

Rank-and-file activism and solidarity soon forged a qualitatively different labour movement. More than ever before, divisions between workers seemed to be giving way to a remarkable spirit of working-class unity and class consciousness. As we have seen, organizational structures became more flexible in devising imaginative experiments readily adapted to immediate needs and conditions. In addition to less exclusivist craft unionism and more widespread industrial unionism, there was an innovative, all–inclusive 'community unionism' that touched many centres with weak or non-existent union traditions, and in some cases, a small, diverse local workforce close to primary production. Across the country the objective was the same: to mobilize greater numbers in common cause. Before the middle of 1919, the great majority of these new unions were affiliated with international organizations headquartered in the United States. At the same time, Canadian branches everywhere found new ways to work together with other union locals while maintaining considerable independence from their American parents. District councils linked up locals of some of the larger unions, and many locals federated across occupational lines into more cooperative local, district, and provincial bodies. For the most part, it was the local trades and labour council or district miners' organization that played the active coordinating role of drawing together and speaking for the local wage-earning population. In many cities trades councils sponsored, directly or indirectly, local labour newspapers that were produced independently of the international union publications, and that grew in number from four in 1914 to seventeen by 1919 and became important forums of information on local issues, international labour news, and debate about evolving strategies.[15] Some radicals even began to envisage the trades councils as the new base of the labour movement.[16] Whatever their political cast, the councils reflected the decentralized, community-based focus of most of the workers' movements in these years.

The new spirit of solidarity and working-class consciousness was evident in action as well as organization. The best-known example, the general sympathy strike, was widely discussed and began to appear in many parts of the country in 1918. It had mass popular support when it got its first major tests in Winnipeg and Amherst, Nova Scotia, in May

1919. As sympathy strikes spread across the West in response to the repression of the Winnipeg strikers, the radical leadership could do no more than place itself at the head of a burst of solidarity and militancy that was largely beyond its control.[17]

In this context of militancy and confrontation, the thousands of new unionists quickly grew impatient with some of their more cautious leaders.[18] Although most of the existing labour leaders held on to their old power bases, they had to face an emergent cadre of feistier, more radical leaders in the new union locals: Pictou County's Clifford Dane, Cape Breton's J.B. McLachlan, Montreal's Tom Cassidy, Gananoque's Gordon Bishop, Toronto's Jack MacDonald, Hamilton's Fred Flatman, Winnipeg's R.B. Russell, Regina's Joseph Sambrook, Calgary's R.J. Tallon, Edmonton's Joe Knight, the Crows Nest Pass's Phillip Christophers, and Vancouver's Jack Kavanagh.[19] Among the best-known female militants were Helena Gutteridge in Vancouver, Amelia Turner in Calgary, Sarah Johnston-Knight in Edmonton, Helen Armstrong in Winnipeg, Mary McNab in Hamilton, and Rose Henderson in Montreal.[20] These were the men and women who chaired meetings, helped organize new unions, led strikes, edited labour newspapers, and generally tried to awaken workers to wider visions of a reconstructed society after the war. Many were local socialists who after years of conflict with the existing labour leadership had found a receptive ear among the increasingly militant workers. They were more popular partly because, as socialists, they had reassessed their long-standing reservations about industrial action and were undertaking, among themselves, an ideological renewal that reflected lessons learned from the massive militancy of Canadian workers in the period.[21] Ironically, the socialist parties to which they belonged made fewer adjustments in their formal programs and continued their narrow emphasis on socialist education and propaganda.

The workers' movements that took shape in the 1917–20 period were rooted first and foremost in industrial action. They followed in the long Anglo-American tradition of struggling for their goals primarily (though not exclusively) in the workplace, as opposed to the European tradition of forging a broader assault on an illiberal, authoritarian state through some kind of socialist party. It was powerful unions and tough bargaining with employers that held out the most promise for shoring up the male breadwinner's family wage and guaranteeing his dignity and relative independence in the workplace. Many radicals in this period put special emphasis on organizing the working class for confrontations at the point of production. Yet, apart from some voices in the

West Coast logging camps,[22] few were espousing genuine 'syndicalism' – that European brand of radicalism that rejected radical social change through electoral politics in favour of the revolutionary potential of direct action on the picket line. Canadian historians have too often applied the label loosely to cover various forms of radical rhetoric in favour of tough-minded industrial unionism.[23] Even in western Canada, the One Big Union was led by socialists who saw the value of solid industrial organization in mobilizing the working class but never imagined a general strike as anything more than the most militant form of exerting working-class power for immediate goals, whether in workplace negotiations or in confronting the government over specific grievances.[24] Despite the hysterical claims at the time, the general strikes in eastern and western Canada never involved any attempted seizure of state power. And there was no 'return to politics' after some kind of sydicalist interlude. In fact, as we have seen, the class solidarity of the picket line and the union hall started overflowing into Canadian politics in industrial centres across the country as early as 1917. Immediate issues had become so politicized in any case that the distinction between the two spheres of activity must have seemed increasingly obscure.

In a period of great experimentation and fluidity of working-class organization, the precise form of independent working-class politics could have been an open question. In 1917 James Simpson, the socialist vice-president of the Trades and Labor Congress, proposed that the labour movement respond to the introduction of conscription by organizing workers' and soldiers' councils similar to Russian soviets (and to some new organizations in Britain at that time, as Simpson must have learned during his three-month visit that year).[25] But before the middle of 1919, outside some limited socialist circles (especially the eastern European radicals who were inspired by the Russian Revolution),[26] that idea generally fell on deaf ears. Anglophone and francophone labour leaders of all stripes were thoroughly constitutionalist in their political orientation, and the vehicle chosen in working-class communities across the country was the independent labour party. Well before the Trades and Labor Congress of Canada put out its call for a Canadian Labor Party in the fall of 1917, many union leaders had taken the initiative in organizing such a party in their own communities. These local labour parties, which always remained completely separate from their union structures, soon began to federate into loosely structured provincial political organizations, though never into an official national labour party. By organizing speakers' bureaus, distributing literature, and generally acting as a clearing house for debate and strategizing, the provincial parties provided important coordination of political organizing and education. The political wing of the workers' movements in this period nonetheless remained highly decentralized, with the local city-based parties retaining the power to nominate their own candidates and run their own campaigns.[27]

The 1917 federal election marked the first major foray of independent labourism, but, under the heavy torrents of Unionist jingoistic hysteria, most of the thirty-five labour candidates lost their deposits (even though the Laurier Liberals stepped aside for thirteen of them).[28] More successful were efforts at the municipal level in several industrial centres. Handfuls of labour representatives were also elected to provincial legislatures in 1919–20 – two each in New Brunswick and Quebec, three in British Columbia, four in Nova Scotia, eleven in Manitoba, and the same number in Ontario, where they entered the country's first Farmer-Labour government.[29] That coalition was only the most visible of its kind. In an electoral system in which wage earners were outnumbered by independent commodity producers, the independent labour parties were motivated to look for political allies among the organized farmers. In some constituencies containing smaller urban centres, fusion candidates had the support of both groups, but generally the workers and farmers kept their own distinct organizations.[30] The other group that labour parties had to learn to work with were the returned soldiers, who were being pulled in different political directions as they pursued a better deal for themselves and their families. While officers tried to direct their men's anger against the new radicalism of the period, in some parts of the country a more proletarian, left-of-centre faction responded favourably to labourist proposals of electoral cooperation, one example of which was the Canadian Union of Ex-Servicemen, known as CNUX.[31] The labour parties themselves also began to attract disaffected middle-class citizens, including the famous 'social gospellers' J.S. Woodsworth, William Ivens, William Irvine, and A.E. Smith.[32] Yet, unlike the situation in the British Labour Party in this period and the Co-operative Commonwealth Federation in the 1930s, no radicalized middle-class intelligentsia moved into key roles in the parties.[33] On the whole, the leadership and membership of the various independent labour parties across Canada remained predominantly working-class.

The local labour parties became remarkably lively, relatively non-sectarian forums for discussion and debate about pressing concerns in working-class life and the most appropriate strategies for organizing.

Until the middle of 1919 a rare ideological openness, fluidity, and tolerance prevailed among the labourists, single-taxers, socialists, and sundry freethinkers who joined the parties. Each local branch tended to have a slightly different ideological emphasis that fell somewhere between the old pre-war working-class liberalism known as 'labourism' and unadulterated Marxist socialism.[34] Generally, these organizations had shifted considerably further to the left than their pre-war counterparts – a shift owing largely to the presence of committed socialists or a regular dialogue with members of the main socialist parties (especially the Social Democrats, who had now carved out a primarily educational role for themselves within the political wing of the workers' movements). Across the country the labourist–socialist alliance expressed itself through more visionary rhetoric and more ambitious programs aimed at, in the words of the Cape Breton ILP, 'the working class ownership and democratic management of all the social means of wealth dis-tri-bution at the earliest possible date,' or, at least, in the words of the Ontario and Quebec labour parties, 'the industrial freedom of those who toil and the political liberation of those who for so long have been denied justice.'[35]

As the federal government's Royal Commission on Industrial Relations (the Mathers Commission) discovered on its cross-country trek in the spring of 1919, many workers shared in the search for a new vision.[36] In the words of Calgary postal worker Clifford Nichols, 'the worker has gotten enormous ideals and he is determined to work them out.'[37] The 'common sense' that had guided most workers' lives for so long had been shattered in the wartime crucible. As they looked to a future in which things would be different, workers across the country were receptive to a variety of voices that called for more working-class dignity, independence, and material well-being, and that proposed more power for them to influence decisions that affected their lives on the job, as citizens, and in society more generally. For some, these demands were part of a revolutionary project that would sweep away capitalist society and replace it with a democratically managed workers' republic; for others, they were the harbingers of social reforms that would democratize government and soften the impact of market forces. But the distinction between reform and revolution was frequently blurred in the millennial rhetoric of the period (how many hopes and dreams were hung on, for example, the oft-repeated slogans 'production for use' and 'New Democracy'?). Political distinctions were also blurred by the commitment of virtually all political factions to orderly

social change through some combination of mass industrial action and parliamentarism.

At all points along the political continuum, the new vision was about workers' power. It was a revolt against the kind of subordination that workers had hitherto known in Canadian capitalist society, against the elitist, authoritarian, and paternalistic ways in which business and the state had grown accustomed to ruling in Canada. It was an affirmation of working-class pride in their role as producers and a deep sense of natural justice captured in the constitutional preamble of Toronto's Domestic Workers' Association (chartered as Local 599 of the Hotel and Restaurant Employees International Alliance), which proclaimed its belief in 'the natural right of those who toil to enjoy to the fullest extent the wealth created by their labor, realizing that under the changing conditions of our times it is impossible for us to obtain the full reward of our labor except by united action.'[38] If the whole social system was not to be replaced, it would have to be drastically democratized. 'Democracy' meant reforms to guarantee that political institutions were not in the tight, exclusive grasp of other classes. Political platforms bristled with long-sought-after reforms: the abolition of property qualifications and election deposits for candidates; the scrapping of the Senate and its provincial equivalents; proportional representation in legislatures; and popular democracy through referendums, initiative, and recall. Privilege should be removed from the economy by placing railways, public utilities, banks, and natural resources under public ownership and democratic management. The state should also intervene to soften the effects of an unrestrained market on workers, in the form of mothers' allowances, old-age and veterans pensions, and health and unemployment insurance. In contrast to later versions of social democracy, there was no call for state bureaucracies and rule by experts. Working-class redress was not to be achieved by proxy. Fundamentally, the workers' revolt was a movement rooted in notions of rank-and-file mobilization, autonomy, and democracy. In place of the traditional authority of bosses, politicians, and even union officials, working-class organization and action would be the surest safeguard of Canadian labour's interests.

In large part what was at stake was the contested meaning of democratic citizenship as workers strove to articulate their own sense of citizenship and nationhood within the British political and cultural heritage. As they invoked the traditions of British rights and justice, for which they believed the war had been fought and the peace treaty signed, they could more easily make common cause with returned soldiers and challenge both the undemocratic examples of 'Kaiserism' and the post-war capitalist efforts to define citizenship more narrowly as a matter of 'loyalism.' 'We, brought up under British laws, thought that the fight for political freedom had been fought and won ... [but] the fight is on!' the *Western Labor News* announced in the midst of the Winnipeg General Strike. For these workers, democratic citizenship brought broad entitlements within the body politic. The Union Jack itself became a contested symbol. For Peterborough's Labour Day parade in 1919, the moulders decorated their float with 'a bull dog in a setting of Union Jacks' and a sign announcing, 'What We Have We'll Hold.'[39]

At the same time, the 'industrial democracy' so often demanded would mean much more working-class power on the job. Organized wage earners used their unions to confront their employers with demands not only for immediate changes in the terms of their employment (especially higher wages) but also for a formalization of the union–management relationship that would give them greater decision-making authority in the workplace.[40] A huge proportion of the strikes in the period that did not formally include the demand for union recognition resulted from employers' refusal to deal with union leaders and the demands they carried from their members. By the end of the war many union leaders, confident of workers' labour-market leverage, were turning to the state for support and demanding that the once-despised Industrial Disputes Investigation Act (which now covered all munitions work) be used to compel their bosses to pay attention to their concerns. Union requests for boards of conciliation poured into the federal Department of Labour, as did demands for royal commissions to investigate various industries.[41] The department's Fair Wages Officers became roving conciliators sent into scenes of simmering industrial conflict. This state involvement, along with the urgent labour shortages and the unflinching determination of unionized workers, convinced reluctant employers in several sectors and all regions to agree to some kind of regular collective bargaining arrangement. In steel, meat packing, rubber, textiles, and pulp and paper, the agreements were generally informal and tenuous.[42] Workers and their employers on the railways, in urban construction and printing, in Nova Scotia and Alberta coal mining, and in the Toronto and Montreal clothing industries devised more elaborate agreements, with signed contracts and grievance and arbitration structures.[43] 'Industrial legality' became one concrete mechanism sought by many local union leaders in their campaign for 'industrial democracy.'

Determining the most appropriate negotiating structures provoked considerable debate and ideological disagreement. Many union leaders, including the Trades and Labor Congress executive, supported the single-enterprise industrial councils proposed by the British government's Whitley Committee – a model involving equal numbers of management and union representatives. This notion of collective bargaining was challenged on two fronts. Employers preferred the so-called Colorado Plan (developed for the Rockefellers by William Lyon Mackenzie King) because it involved no unions from outside the enterprise.[44] Radicals, for their part advocated a soviet-style council, described by a Victoria printer as an agreement in which 'the employer does not appear, he is pitched overboard, and the people themselves take control of the industry.'[45] Cape Breton's workers had some of the country's most elaborate plans for workers' self-management presented to them in their local labour paper in the early 1920s.[46] Visions of some kind of workers' control of production began to assume a mass resonance.

The strike weapon, and especially the sympathy strike, could also be used to advance political goals. Radical propaganda promoted the general strike as an effective response to both the challenge of post-war reconstruction and for such political outrages as the repressive orders-in-council of 1918, the brutal crushing of the Winnipeg General Strike the following spring, the arrogance of Montreal's unelected city administration in 1920, and the heavy-handed use of troops against Sydney steelworkers in 1923.[47] The mass general strike and the increasing interest in strikes as political weapons set this working-class upsurge dramatically apart from most of its predecessors in Canada.

The single demand that probably rolled up most of the aspirations of the workers' movements in this period was for a shorter workday. In 1919 a quarter of strikes incorporated this issue, far more than ever before or since.[48] The One Big Union was prepared to launch a general strike across the West over the issue.[49] Labour leaders raised it in every forum of discussion – especially the Mathers Commission and the National Industrial Conference in September 1919 – and labour representatives carried it into the provincial legislatures.[50] Most often the demand was for an eight-hour day, though the western labour movement and radicals elsewhere in the country wanted only six hours. The demand for a shorter workday served many functions: it encapsulated the desire for greater independence from the rigours of intensified work in mines and mills of Canadian industry; it held out the promise of minimizing unemployment by spreading around available work; it raised the possibility of a fuller social, recreational, and political life for wage earners, a prospect first introduced in the shorter-hours campaigns of the 1870s and 1880s; and it could touch a responsive chord among middle-class sympathizers. By 1919 several groups of workers had convinced their employers to shorten their hours of work, though no legislature would yet touch the issue.[51]

Overall, then, workers were united in the search for greater economic security, on-the-job independence and power, political influence, and overall dignity for the working class. In that sense, the vision of a different kind of society at the heart of the workers' revolt was greater than the sum of its individual parts. The democratizing vision behind all these demands nonetheless incorporated important distinctions within the working class itself. This imaginative vision was conceived primarily by white, English-speaking men (especially married men) whose manhood was deeply enmeshed in their status as breadwinners for their families. Throughout the language of the workers' revolt their notion of entitlement assumed male dominance of public life and the dependence of women and children on their men. Most working-class leaders continued to believe that the best place for women was tending the home fires while their menfolk earned the family's wages. Yet these same leaders gave more help to women who wanted to unionize than had ever been extended before, allowed a few into leadership roles, and welcomed small bands of committed working-class housewives into a special supportive relationship within the workers' movements with their own Women's Labor Leagues and Women's Independent Labor Parties. Female activists used this separate space provided for them, along with the greater public receptiveness to gender equality that had flowed from the granting of voting rights to women during the war, to push for a wider social and political role – one that recognized their participation in both the men's world of production and the domestic realm of reproduction. The main thrust of their activities nonetheless remained a working-class variant of what has become known as 'maternal feminism,' in this case a central concern with family and community needs.[52] Similarly, labour leaders carried an image of the typical worker as not only male but also white and English-speaking. Yet while they still suspected the European newcomers as a potential threat to their 'skilled' status in the workplace and to their expectations of a 'British' standard of living, they willingly gave them union membership cards.[53] Distinctions and prejudices did not disappear during the workers' revolt, but they were certainly eroded.

By 1919 most Canadians of any class would have been aware that something profoundly different was afoot in working-class Canada. They could even see it from their windows. The new assertive class-consciousness brought a new use of urban space. The 'constitutionalism' of the revolt included the rights to free speech and association and to open assembly. Instead of keeping to the confined paths of their individual daily lives, workers used the public spaces of their towns and cities for parades, mass picnics and sporting events, huge educational forums featuring guest speakers, and spontaneous gatherings for particular protests. Since their towns and cities had few facilities built to hold large numbers, they took control of streets, parks, theatres, and churches. In reasonably compact urban centres where most workers still got around by foot or on streetcars, the working-class crowd was an aggressive force to be reckoned with. Strikes would become massive community events as working-class families extended their long-standing patterns of mutual support out of their neighbourhoods and into picket-line support, collective action against strike-breakers, or sympathy strikes. Workers thus became a much more publicly visible force in Canada's urban centres.[54]

The Workers' Defeat, 1919–1925

The workers' revolt had emerged in full form by the spring of 1919, and maintained much of its momentum across the country for at least another year. (In the eastern and western coalfields, the buoyancy lasted through 1922.) Yet, as early as the spring of 1919, the severe limitations on the workers' movements were becoming evident. From that point onward, workers were on the defensive. By 1922 most of their gains had been lost almost everywhere outside the coalfields. Strikes were defeated, union locals lost members and often disintegrated, provincial federations collapsed, independent labour parties expired, and the spirit of hope and determination drained away. The decline and fall of such a major social force was a complex process. In part, as so many Canadian historians have argued, the momentum of the revolt was sapped by ideological disagreements between a right and a left that had serious consequences for the strategic direction of the movements. To a much greater extent, however, the workers' revolt foundered on the hard, inhospitable rocks of the Canadian economy, class formation, and state.

Workers never get to choose the terrain on which they confront capital or the state. By 1919 a variety of capitalists had already made some decisions about the location and structure of their enterprises and the kind of workforce they would need. At the same time, the larger market forces continued to set constaints on what kind of working-class resistance would be possible. In Canada the industrial capitalist economy was fragmented into a myriad of widely separated projects in capital accumulation that followed quite different rhythms of development and crisis. The many isolated parts of the resource economy struggled to secure a space in highly competitive markets, the manufacturers cowered behind their tariff walls, and the transportation industries tried to survive on the success of the others. After the war each of these sectors, and their many subsectors, faced its own agonizing readjustment. Every capitalist economy contains this diversity, but Canada seemed to be an exaggerated version, not least because of the vast distances that separated industrial activity but even more because of the various sectors' disarticulated links to the larger international economy that were unconnected to each other. Here was a good part of the explanation for the regionalism that ran through the workers' movements, as it did through the rest of Canadian society. Yet none of the regions itself had a single industrial pattern. So, despite their efforts at solidarity, wage earners found themselves divided by the fragmented, uneven structure of the Canadian economy and drawn into the ideological framework of regional politicians and businessmen who had their own agendas for coping.

Reinforcing those divisions was the unevenness of working-class power within the production processes of the various industries. While this different leverage was partly a matter of the skill content of jobs and workplace independence of wage earners, skilled workers usually had the additional advantage of ethnic and sexual homogeneity. Once again, these were for the most part structural characteristics of particular occupations that emerged from that process of capitalist planning and organizing. But, by World War I, occupational identities of skilled, white, English-speaking (and many French-speaking) male wage earners bore the stamp of long-standing fights to preserve their shop-floor power, independence, and self-esteem. The occupational groups at the forefront of the workers' revolt – coal miners, metal trades workers, and 'frontier labourers' – had each fashioned a version of the distinctive muscular, masculine working-class culture that was idealized in the visual arts of the period, whether art nouveau or socialist realism.[55] This reservoir of resistance was not available to wage earners made vulnerable by their

limited skills or by their gender or ethnic identity. The weaker participation of factory workers in the workers' revolt is not surprising given that skills had been drastically reduced or eliminated in many factories, while the skills that survived were industry-specific and tied closely to occupational mobility inside individual firms. This was also where female and non-Anglo-Celtic labour had often been integrated into the least skilled jobs and lacked the social sanctions enjoyed by the skilled male breadwinners. These were also workers with little accumulated history of mobilization in their own defence. What is remarkable about the working-class revolt in this period is the extent to which these vulnerable workers participated aggressively, and to which the better-placed workers often reached out to offer them support. However, occupational and ethnic differences, in combination with the industrial fragmentation of the country, made holding together a broad-based revolt a formidable task.

However much workers in all parts of the country shared common aspirations and similar patterns of organizing in the 1917–25 period, the various working-class movements that emerged faced very different opportunities and obstacles. The consciously decentralized nature of the movement made coordination of these distinct struggles extremely problematic. Canada had an archipelago of isolated industrial centres between which it was difficult to maintain regular, informed communication among the various workers' movements. The failure of western radicals to make common cause with their comrades east of the Lakehead was one of the best indicators. National labour institutions in Canada were weak, and national debate and the bonds of national solidarity were never fully developed.

Differences based on gender and ethnicity further divided Candian workers. The white, anglophone and francophone male wage earners who marched in the front ranks of the workers' revolt remained ambivalent about the role of women in the workforce and labour movement. 'There is no doubt that the women are being exploited by the manufacturers,' wrote a machinists' union official in 1917, 'and their use in the munitions factories has been the cause of reducing the wages of men shell operators.'[56] Despite women's enhanced role in working-class organizing, the patriarchal mould of the working-class family had certainly not been broken. On the contrary, a central goal of the workers' revolt of 1917–25 was to defend the household economy that had been the bedrock of working-class life in Canada for more than half a century and of the husband-father's role as chief breadwinner.[57] Working men took their families on labour picnics and welcomed them onto mass picket lines, yet the vast sea of men's faces that fill up photographs of labour meetings taken during the Winnipeg General Strike suggest how thoroughly male the public life of the workers' movements still was.[58] Even the radical left had a heavily male-centred, productionist focus that left little room on its agenda for the female half of the working class.[59]

Not all men were welcome, however. Anglo-Canadian wage earners had often been highly suspicious of capitalists' use of non-Anglo-Celtic and non-white immigrants as cheap labour in many industries and feared a direct threat to their status and earnings within the rapidly changing capitalist labour process. As a result, Anglo-Canadian and other workers eyed each other cautiously and often resentfully in ways that suggested that the elements that employers had drawn together into a workforce had not yet congealed into a full community of working-class solidarity, especially considering the continuing transiency of so many of the non-Anglo-Celtic 'sojourners.' Three vigorous counterpoints to the workers' revolt stood out in the 1917–20 period: the French Canadians' blistering anger over their forced participation in the 'English' war; rising Anglo-Canadian hysteria about European 'enemy aliens,' accompanied by demands (spearheaded by the veterans) for their expulsion from industry;[60] and the revival of anti-Asian agitation in British Columbia. The two exclusionary campaigns, which led to the immigration restrictions of 1920, must have sown deep bitterness in immigrant urban enclaves. Many labour leaders refused to be associated with such nativist activities and appealed for tolerance and working-class brotherhood. But the ethnic fissures did not disappear. The French kept their distance from the Jewish and English-Canadian radicals in Montreal.[61] Rarely were European immigrants as well integrated into the rising workers' movements as they would be in the CIO period. They were virtually never found within the ranks of the labour parties in this period (although left-wing elements in some eastern European communities maintained contact with radical socialists). The Asians, who were so numerous in West Coast industries, were completely shut out.[62] Not until the 1930s and 1940s, when the endless waves of sojourners and newcomers stopped and the working-class communities stabilized somewhat, would the ethnic divides start to close. In the meantime, the wage-earning members of many ethnic groups were drawn into rising cross-class nationalism within their own communities in Canada, especially in Quebec and in many European immigrant ghet-

toes in central and western Canada. These ethnic divisions had different dimensions in each region, and, aside from the West Coast anti-Asian animus, they may not have amounted to the same wall of hostility that rose up in the United States as hundreds of thousands of blacks moved north in this period.[63] But they did deflect some of the energy of the workers' revolt along paths that weakened class-conscious solidarity.

In addition to overcoming internal fragmentation and division, working classes in industrial capitalist societies sought to situate themselves within a larger configuration of classes. In most industrialized countries outside Britain, they found themselves in a minority, and the Canadian class structure was essentially no different. Unless the workers' movements opted for the Bolshevik model of seizing power and imposing the dictatorship of the proletariat, as few Canadian labour leaders suggested before 1920, they had to find political allies. In Canada labour leaders attracted, or maintained a friendly dialogue with, disaffected elements of the urban middle class whose influence could be great but whose numbers were not large. In fact, aside from such celebrated exceptions as J.S. Woodsworth, most of the middle class either stood uncomfortably aloof from the workers' revolt or participated in attempts to contain or repress it. The white-collar workers who organized their own unions, especially teachers and civil servants, generally kept their distance from the rest of the labour movement.[64] Even the country's most celebrated suffragist, Nellie McClung, nervously opposed the Winnipeg General Strike.[65] Most social gospellers began looking for some mechanisms for reconciling the warring camps of capital and labour.[66]

In most industrialized countries in the period, the largest other class was usually some version of independent commodity producers, whether peasants or commercial farmers. At the end of the war, farmers were still by far the largest and electorally most powerful element in Canada, at least east of the Rockies. They posed the same 'agrarian question' that perplexed working-class movements throughout the world. As we have seen, in their relationship with workers, farmers were, at best, ambivalent allies and, at worst, strong hindrances. They occasionally sniped at the militancy, showed limited concern about the mass working-class unemployment of the early 1920s, and refused to support labour's most prized legislative measures, most notably the eight-hour day.[67] But this rural population posed an even thornier problem. People in the rural world of early-twentieth-century Canada often shaded over from independent primary producer to wage earner, bringing far more uncertainty about their quasi-proletarian status and far less commitment to urban-based movements.[68] Much of the logging, fishing, and construction industries rested on their labour. Some undertook remarkable organizational campaigns on an unprecedented scale – the Fishermen's Protective Union of Newfoundland under William Coaker and the Lumber Workers' Industrial Union in British Columbia, in particular.[69] But most rural workers remained outside the workers' revolt or were only tangentially connected. The same point could be made about native peoples, especially on the West Coast.[70] Canadian capitalism would not be seriously challenged on this front.

Beyond calling for unity and solidarity, the leaders of Canadian workers' movements rarely reflected on the structural constraints of economic, regional, sexual, and ethnic fragmentation and isolation of Canadian workers. Probably pondering such dilemmas was a luxury the immediate organizational exigencies did not allow them. Whatever theorizing they did drew not from the specifics of the Canadian social formation but rather from the thinking of labourists or Marxists elsewhere. In this sense they were clearly disadvantaged in the face of corporate capital and the state in Canada, whose existence rested on their ability to overcome that kind of fragmentation and to integrate diverse parts of the social formation. By the end of World War I, workers confronted highly centralized corporations with national or continental networks of organization and a national state with a remarkably strong executive branch (much more aggressive as a result of its interventionist wartime experience). The workers' movements were thus overwhelmed by powerful forces that were better able to manoeuvre in the difficult Canadian setting. Whatever the structural constraints, the real crisis facing wage earners came from the aggressive resistance of employers who dug in their heels against workers' demands, and the state, which set out to undercut the radical potential of the workers' movements. Both employers and the state followed a course of crushing the militants and radicals and then appealing to 'safe and sane' wage earners and, if necessary, their leaders.

The surest indication of unprecedented class conflict in post-war Canada was the extent to which both capital and labour mobilized to assert their interests. The economic dislocations and instability rampant across Canada in the immediate aftermath of hostilities drove both to new extremes in attitude and organization. In 1919–20 the prospect of a renewed rivalry with both European and American industry (the return of 'competitive competition again,' in the telling redundancy of one BC

manufacturer)[71] convinced many Canadian employers that the viability of their operations was now at stake. Capitalists across the country worried that markets for the products of their vastly expanded productive apparatus were disappearing, that price inflation had made them uncompetitive (especially in terms of labour costs), that the creation of many new unions limited their ability to alter wages and labour processes (perish the thought of an eight-hour day!), and that the free-trade sentiments of the powerful new farmers' movements would threaten their tariff protection. At a more general level, they sensed that a large mass of the population had come out of the war with a cynical, if not openly hostile, view of corporate dominance over Canadian social and economic life. Capitalists had not only to secure the subordination of the working class but also to restore the legitimacy of their hegemony more generally.

After the Armistice employers launched a concerted offensive of union-busting and wage-cutting in an effort to reclaim ground conceded to labour under extraordinary wartime circumstances. Workers in virtually all the twenty-eight cities visited by the Royal Commission on Industrial Relations in the spring of 1919 complained of extensive firing and blacklisting of union supporters since the end of the war.[72] Many of the protracted (and ultimately defeated) strikes of the post-war era were marked as much by capitalist intransigence as by labour's militancy. In 1920 workers won less than one strike in five, and employers were clear winners in a third – a dramatic reversal of the strike outcomes in 1917–18. From 1921 to 1924 close to half these confrontations ended on employers' terms, to which could be added many of those strikes whose outcomes were classified as 'Indefinite' (27 per cent in 1920, 24 per cent in 1921, and 20 per cent in 1922).[73] The decisive defeats came at different points in each industry and region. The collapse of the Winnipeg General Strike and the various sympathy strikes marked the beginning of the end in urban centres across the West. The defeat of the prolonged metal trades strikes in several Canadian cities in 1919 was devastating, but for most manufacturing industries in Ontario, Quebec, and Nova Scotia the major symbolic defeats did not arrive until mid-1920. The shipyards strikes of that year were catastrophes for organized labour in several parts of central and eastern Canada. Even the solidly entrenched printers' unions were dealt a crippling blow in their unsuccessful struggle for the forty-four-hour week.[74] Sydney steelworkers did not meet their Waterloo until 1923, and coal miners in Cape Breton and Alberta held on for two more years.[75] The final confrontation of Cape Breton's miners and corporate bosses in 1925 was as bitter, brutal, and devastating as any in the whole period under study.

As the many studies of strikes in the period have revealed, a common pattern emerged almost everywhere. Companies forced a strike by refusing to negotiate and then frequently hired strike-breakers, often from professional strike-breaking operations such as the Pinkerton or Thiel detective agencies. As defeated workers drifted back, employers blacklisted local union militants to drive them out of town; some even installed spies on the shop floor to watch for potential troublemakers. Little of this activity was carried out under the defiant 'open shop' banner that American capitalists were unfurling at this time,[76] but the outcome was the same. Anti-union tactics became much easier to implement in the context of a rapidly declining economy. The 16.5 per cent unemployment rate among unionized workers in the spring of 1921 was destroying their leverage in the labour market.[77] Nearly universal wage cuts of 10–20 per cent in the early months of that year met with little resistance. By the end of 1922 the Department of Labour's statistics showed over 100,000 fewer union members than at the 1919 peak – a loss of 27 per cent.[78]

As workers were taught the lesson that militancy and unionism would not be tolerated, many corporations tried to sweeten the medicine with a package of welfare reforms for their employees to promote loyalty and dedication to the individual firm rather than to the working class. Out of corporate boardrooms cascaded safety plans, lunch rooms, company magazines, recreation programs, and pension and insurance plans. To workers who were once again facing economic insecurity, the pension and insurance plans were far more attractive than patronizing programs aimed at constructing a 'corporate family.' In a few large plants, corporations also responded to the call for 'industrial democracy' with industrial councils (made up of equal numbers of management and employee representatives) in which issues arising in the workplace could be addressed. Company executives quickly found they had to deflect their employees' attempts to discuss wages and hours, and the councils rapidly dissolved into toothless forums for debate on safety and recreation issues.[79] Probably only a small minority of Canadian wage earners ever enjoyed any crumbs from the table of welfare capitalism in any case.

At the same time, capitalists launched a campaign to relegitimize their dominant role in Canadian society. In addition to publicizing their corporate welfarism,[80] they sought a common enemy against which

workers and the broader population could be rallied. Industrialists contributed heavily to propaganda that tried to terrorize Canadians into believing that the democracy they had just fought for was endangered by blood-thirsty Bolshevists. Lurid, full-page advertisements informed newspaper readers of the 'alien' quality of the workers' revolt. A Canadian-made, employer-funded movie called *The Great Shadow* depicted Bolshevik subversion of labour struggles in a shipyard (several companies supplied free tickets for their employees).[81] Some capitalists even bought the support of conservative labour leaders by funnelling money to them secretly and by supporting such red-baiting newspapers as the Ottawa-based *Canadian Labor Press*.[82]

The various (mostly rural) forces threatening the tariff structure could be constructed as another common enemy. The most powerful corporate capitalists threw their support behind Sir John Willison's Canadian Reconstruction Association, the statesmanlike public face of capital that highlighted the benefits of corporate welfarism and built broader support for the tariff.[83] Eventually, the Tories held onto most of industrialized Ontario in the 1921 federal election, as they had in 1911, by exploiting working-class fears of job loss in a free-trade economy.[84] In Quebec the Catholic Church provided another successful alternative in the form of Catholic unionism, which preached worker–employer harmony (within a framework of Catholic values) and began to mushroom in size and influence in 1919. Quebec's employers were pleased.[85] Finally, in the East, local employers placed themselves at the head of a new Maritime Rights movement in the early 1920s.[86] In each case workers' anger and insecurity were deflected into class-collaborationist channels, though only once their industrial militancy had been crushed.

The Canadian state made no effort to curb the attacks on workers and their organizations. On the contrary, as we saw in the essay by Heron and Siemiatycki in this volume, politicians and state officials had moved decisively to repress and undermine working-class militancy and radicalism. They turned loose against radical leaders their secret-service spies, federal troops, and new criminal-law and immigration legislation, as well as their blandishments of more moderate leaders with a royal commission and a National Industrial Conference. The federal government offered no solid inducements or protection for working-class organization.

At this point the structure of Canadian federalism played its complicated role in mediating class relations. Workers' movements across the country had directed much of their political energy into provincial politics wherein resided many of the constitutional responsibilities for such worker concerns as the eight-hour day. That meant battling on nine different fronts. Provincial governments had been the first to respond to the general unrest in the population after 1916, and several administrations (especially those run by reform-minded Liberals) had used such measures as minimum-wage legislation and mothers' allowances to try to buy back some legitimacy for the social and political system.[87] Some provincial politicians, such as Ontario's Henry Cody, looked to longer-term means of restoring the legitimacy of the social order with increased schooling for adolescents to inculcate appropriate notions of 'citizenship,' as did the National Conference on 'Character Education' held in Winnipeg in October 1919.[88] Each of these moves by the provincial branches of the Canadian state reinforced the regional particularities in the timing and rhythms of the workers' revolt. Since no federal election was called until 1921, workers' movements were not able to confront the national Borden government directly on the hustings until after the revolt had lost most of its momentum.

It is against this agonizingly difficult backdrop of structural constraint and repressive counter-attack that we must assess the splits that had opened up within the labour leadership by the spring of 1919. Once again, they hit each region at different moments. Yet this was fundamentally a divergence between left and right, not East and West. In every region of the country labour leaders were engaging in heated debate about the appropriate industrial and political working-class response to the new resistance that the revolt was facing. While the left urged escalation, the right called for a retreat. The major points of disagreement concerned the most appropriate form of union organization, the link with the international unions centred in the American Federation of Labor, and the willingness of the workers' movements to show more aggressiveness in pursuit of their goals. Since the middle of the war, labour leaders had argued over these issues, and, as we saw, those who constituted the movements' national voice in the Trades and Labor Congress of Canada had always counselled and practised restraint. The confrontation came to a head at the 1918 Congress convention, where a minority report denouncing the executive's cozy relations with the government sparked a furious debate about the directions of the labour movement. A set of militant tactical resolutions was defeated and a more conservative slate, headed by carpenters' union organizer Tom Moore, was elected to the Congress executive. Moore had been a solid supporter of conscription and a central figure in the rapprochement with the Borden

government in 1918. The defeat for the left at the 1918 convention was not simply a matter of the East overpowering the West (fifty-one easterners joined twenty-nine westerners on the losing side, against a majority of three from the West and eighty-one from the East). It was quite significant, however, that the Western delegates constructed the defeat in regional terms. They chose to minimize the evidence of support for their position East of the Lakehead and to use a Western Labour Conference as a springboard for reconstruction of the whole labour movement. Then, in the early spring of 1919, they moved decisively towards secession with the creation of the One Big Union.[89]

That spring well-established craft union leaders in most major cities began to consider the risks associated with the widening solidarity and political radicalism. In the Western conferences leading up to the formation of the One Big Union, there were dissenting voices. J.H. McVety in Vancouver, David Rees in Fernie, Alfred Farmilo in Edmonton, Alex Ross in Calgary, and Ernie Robinson in Winnipeg all opposed withdrawing from the international unions to form the One Big Union. The Calgary labour movement was lukewarm about this new experiment, while the Edmonton trades council stayed out altogether.[90] In southern Ontario and Montreal the more entrenched craft union leaders were not prepared to see their organizations disrupted by surging notions of industrial unionism.[91] All these men were still looking to the state and capital for the legitimacy and recognition they believed caution and moderation would bring. Their strategy was to raise the threat of labour unrest and to present themselves as the restraining force that would curb militancy and radicalism. In an address to the Canadian Manufacturers' Association in February 1919, Tom Moore was reported to have advised his audience that 'the responsible, intelligent trades unionist was the capitalist's strongest bulwark, if only a friendly co-operation were extended to him, since the trade unionist, and indeed, the worker fully realized that the downfall of the capitalist, and the cessation of the work in the factory spelled his own idleness and possible starvation.'[92] (Moore later insisted that he had referred to unions as '*civilization's* strongest bulwark'; misquote or not, his message was clear.) The same concern with cementing an accord with the state and capital explains the enthusiastic participation of the craft union leadership in the National Industrial Conference.[93]

By the end of 1919, the fluidity of the previous two years had evaporated, and positions on the right and left were hardening. In the wake of the OBU breakaway, the Canadian branches of the international unions threw themselves into a campaign to win back the West and to prevent any further secessions. The more conservative craft union leaders steadily withdrew their support for the more experimental organizational forms and practices that had blossomed alongside the normal channels of international union procedure. They insisted on the honouring of contracts negotiated with individual employers. (This abiding faith in 'industrial legality' discouraged various groups of wage earners from joining larger struggles.)[94] They used the disciplinary power of their organizations to curb unauthorized sympathy or general strikes. In many cases they seriously undermined local struggles by curtailing solidarity actions by their members. By rejecting cooperation and amalgamation of crafts and rigourously defending individual craft jurisdiction and rights, these union officials undoubtedly robbed less skilled workers of leadership, resources, and negotiating strength. Over the next two years the leading figures in the craft union movement distanced themselves from the main currents of the workers' revolt. They also opened a rhetorical barrage against the left in general, using some of the existing labour newspapers as well as the new *Canadian Labor News*, the *Edmonton Free Press*, and, from the end of 1919, *New Democracy*. By 1921 the leaders of the Trades and Labor Congress even refused to endorse the independent labour candidates who were running in that year's federal election. These craft unionists settled solidly into the cautious, complacent, apolitical mould that had been developed in the Gompersite American Federation of Labor and would not wander far from those moorings until World War II.[95]

Facing these men across the increasingly bitter political battlefield were a variety of militants and radicals who, as we have seen, were spread across the country. Region does not help explain their location as much as industry, occupation, ethnicity, and the recent history of industrial relations in their respective communities. Some were based in the older male occupations with long traditions of workplace pride and independence and recent success in confronting their employers, especially the coal miners and the highly skilled railway shopcraft workers.[96] Others had a solid following in the newly organized unions of semi-skilled and unskilled workers, notably in mass production, resource processing, and water transport.[97] Also providing some ginger were clusters of European-born socialists who were found in logging, mining, and clothing production.[98] The radicals' success depended on the strength of the local unions in their respective industries and on the established power of the international craft union leadership in the local

labour movement. AFL-style craft unions were much weaker in the Maritimes and the West, where they had never put down as deep roots and had always had to coexist with bumptious industrial unions, usually most solidly based in mining.[99] They were also somewhat weaker in Quebec, where their insensitivity to francophones had limited their impact (the AFL finally appointed a bilingual organizer for the province in 1918).[100] Southern Ontario was the heartland of this cautious brand of unionism and the headquarters of a solid cadre of full-time labour officials – business agents, organizers, Canadian vice-presidents, and the leading officials of the Trades and Labor Congress of Canada – who were committed to the link with the AFL and industrial legality in collective bargaining. Their caution was more than a slavish mimicking of an American model; it was also the product of experience in a harshly anti-union climate that had kept unions out of Ontario's major industries since the turn of the century. The craft unionists' prominence and strength in the region's labour movement rested in large part on the lack of a substantial industrial union movement based in the province's many factories until the end of the war. Those industrial unions that eventually did emerge in cities like Toronto and Hamilton were latecomers and remained extremely fragile. The craft unionists greeted them with coolness and some apprehension.[101]

The divisions in the labour leadership went beyond the right–left tensions. The radicals themselves were divided on the issue of staying with the international unions. The great majority of westerners voted to leave and form the One Big Union. In central and eastern Canada, this strategy had its supporters.[102] (Because unions in these regions generally refused to hold referendums on secession, it is impossible to gauge the precise amount of support for the OBU.) However, most militant leaders in central and eastern Canada opted to remain within the international union movement. The left within the workers' movement was therefore divided at a crucial moment. By the end of 1919 the radicals' secessionist project in the West had foundered. East of the Lakehead those who remained in the mainstream labour movement became increasingly isolated. Only in the Maritimes did they maintain a leadership role, which persisted until 1923.

Beset by failures and a heavily repressive environment, many socialist militants began to gravitate towards the emerging Communist movement. The old Social Democratic Party had disintegrated soon after the state's iron heel came down on it late in 1918. Socialists from the party's right wing (notably James Simpson in Toronto) settled into independent labour party work. At the same time, feistier members of its left wing joined forces with a handful of revolutionary socialists and radical members of some Eastern European immigrant groups, some of whom had already begun clandestine propaganda early in 1919. In the heat of state repression and the general Red Scare, this new pro-Bolshevik left had both an underground life for theorizing and strategizing and a public forum for revolutionary education and unbridled attacks on the dominant labour leadership. Many of the militant sparkplugs from the workers' revolt – including Jack MacDonald in Toronto, Fred Flatman in Hamilton, Annie Buller in Montreal, and J.B. McLachlan in Cape Breton – were drawn to this emerging movement, as were many European-born socialists. In May 1921, at a secret meeting in a barn outside Guelph, the underground Communist Party of Canada was founded, uniting all these revolutionary socialists east of Manitoba. Its public face, the Workers' Party of Canada, emerged in February 1922. In the West the aging Socialist Party of Canada eventually disintegrated as branches left to join the Workers' Party. Branches of a few local labour parties in such places as Halifax and Fernie followed suit. Ironically, shortly after its founding the Communist Party, in line with the new direction of the Third International in Moscow, began to favour the politics of coalition over sectarian attacks on the established labour institutions and their leaders. The Workers' Party affiliated with the Canadian Labor Party, and individual Communists directed their energies back into locals of international unions, the trades councils, and the Trades and Labor Congress. However, the craft union leadership was unwelcoming, and by the late 1920s most Communists had been expelled from unions for their agitation.[103] The left, then, had also been unable to meet the challenge of the crisis facing workers after 1919. At that critical moment, the radicals' flamboyant sectarianism may have sometimes been unrealistic, but it was the divisive issue of secession from the mainstream international labour movement, combined with the ideological hardening that had taken place in the context of the well-orchestrated Red Scare, that deprived the radicals of the credibility and effectiveness that would have allowed them to take a larger role.

A substantial number of activists from the workers' revolt chose to embrace neither narrow craft unionism nor Communism. The minority of non-Communist socialists left behind after the splits in the old socialist parties continued to find common cause with the handfuls of still-committed labourists. Most of their political energy was devoted to maintaining the local labour parties. But the 1921 federal election, called in the depths of the post-war depression when most of the momentum of the workers' revolt had already been destroyed, was the final death knell for these socialists. They struggled on, but, with only two representatives in the House of Commons, without a majority in any provincial legislature, and thoroughly compromised in the Ontario Farmer-Labour government,[104] they had little to show for their efforts. Their constituency rapidly vanished. For several years in the mid-1920s they worked with the Communists in a revived Canadian Labor Party, but with no significant success. A handful of labour representatives would hang on in city councils, provincial legislatures, and Parliament, partly on the basis of personal popularity and probity, and a decade later would help to launch a new social democratic party, the Co-operative Commonwealth Federation.[105]

By the mid-1920s labour leaders from all these politial camps must have looked back in sober dismay at the opportunities that had been lost. In the years between 1917 and 1920 a massive number of Canadian workers had become part of a great collective groping for a new kind of society. With the limited resources available in working class neighbourhoods across the country, they had united in countless ways to show their determination to change the lot of workers in Canada. They had pursued their goals in a constitutionalist fashion through the existing institutions of society, especially unions and political parties, rather than armed insurrection, but their open-ended vision of working-class power had nonetheless carried radical dimensions and potential that did not escape the notice of bourgeois leaders. The workers had never been given the opportunity to carry their planning and dreaming far forward into the post-war era because Canadian capitalists would not consider the shift in power that even the mildest reforms implied, and because those in control of the state had shared this apprehension about a more powerful working class. When the crunch had come, the workers' revolt had failed to transcend the great diversity and structural weaknesses of the Canadian working class. Workers in every part of the country, in almost every occupational group, had participated in the revolt, but they had failed to coalesce (sometimes even at the local level) into an effective, coherent force able to withstand the crippling attacks of capital and the state and the enervating impact of unemployment. In this moment of crisis the leadership of the workers' movements had fragmented into three distinct currents according to their divergent readings of how to respond – cautious craft unionism, revolutionary Communism, and social democratic parliamentarism – none of which managed to capture the dynamism, mass mobilization, and ideological and strategic diversity of the early stages of the revolt.

Meanwhile, thousands of workers on the defensive by 1920 had begun to lose their optimism that working class movements could deliver the 'New Democracy.' The spirit of class solidarity had quietly faded away. Workers accepted what they could get from employers willing to hire them, abandoned their unions lest membership get them fired, and stopped voting for labour candidates (if they voted at all). Fearful caution and cynicism, if not fatalism, had settled in.

The long-term impact was devastating for the Canadian working class. For the next twenty years, despite some determined efforts in the 1930s, workers did not come close to regaining the collective power they had summoned up in 1917–20. Although unions did not disappear (total union membership by the mid-1920s had not, in fact, tumbled to the pre-war lows), they were for the most part marginal to Canadian industrial life. Most industrial corporations could confidently expect to operate in a 'union-free' environment. Canadian political life would take some time to recover from the various post-war crises, but in working-class communities voter absenteeism or traditional Liberalism and resurgent Toryism were predominant by 1925. The moment when the Canadian capitalist system faced one of its most serious challenges in the country's history had clearly passed.[106]

The legacy of the workers' revolt would nonetheless endure. The most negative part of this legacy concerned working-class organization. The lessons of the period had left labour activists of all political stripes sceptical about the ideological and organizational fluidity of the revolt. Craft unionists, social democrats, and Communists hardened permanently into their own increasingly rigid views of the most appropriate forms of working-class mobilization. The survivors of the revolt also shaped the options for the future. Rather than the imaginative organizational flexibility for uniting workers in 1917–20 period, the feeble torch that was passed on to the next generation of militants in the 1930s was two variants of cautious, rigid, bureaucratic organization – namely, the AFL's craft unionism and the narrower industrial unionism promoted by the United Mine Workers and the clothing unions. Both regarded challenges to capitalist property rights or its attendant industrial legality as anathema. Labour leaders would use their control of trade unionism to ensure that working-class aspirations were confined to issues of 'reconcilable class differences,' leaving industry controlled by capital and unions controlled by their officers.[107]

On a more positive note, the working class had undoubtedly carved out a somewhat larger place in Canadian public life. Canadian politicians could never again ignore the concerns of workers to the extent they had in the past. A small residue of social legislation remained on the statute books,[108] and a handful of labour parliamentarians at all three levels of the state would continue to voice workers' concerns. J.S. Woodsworth's success in extracting an old-age pension plan from Mackenzie King in 1926 was the most impressive example.[109] Moreover, in some parts of the country where the revolt was not buried beneath the suffocating blankets of Maritime Rights, francophone nationalism, or industrial protectionism, the struggles of 1917–20 were not forgotten and would be used to rally workers in future battles. It seems that the mass strikes (such as those in Winnipeg and Cape Breton) that had drawn workers into direct confrontation with the armed might of the state, rather than simply mobilization through the ballot box, had etched the deepest memories.

The working class in Canada would indeed rise up again a quarter-century later. The form of the new workers' movements would be as different as this one had been from its predecessors in the 1880s, but workers' renewed aspirations for economic security, independence, and dignity would make clear that they were not prepared to remain on their knees forever.

Notes

1 Quoted in Smith, *Let Us Rise!*, 1.

2 Cruikshank and Kealey, 'Canadian Strike Statistics'; and Gregory Kealey, 'Parameters of Class Conflict.' Their statistics provide the basis for the following discussion.

3 Bob Russell's analysis of wartime strikes assumes that a compromise was a loss for strikers, but in this period it was more likely that gaining any ground, even if less than they wanted, was a major accomplishment for workers. Russell, *Back to Work?*, 140–52.

4 Bob Russell calculates that nearly three-quarters of strikes in 1917–18 and two-thirds in 1920 were illegal. Russell, *Back to Work?*, 161–3.

5 Canada, Dept. of Labour, *Labour Organization in Canada*, 1914–20. A careful reading of these Labour Dept. reports makes clear that the totals were rough estimates and undoubtedly underestimated union membership. Tables that broke the statistics down by province reveal that generally about a third of the locals failed to report their membership. The dept. then filled in the holes 'from dept. records and other sources' (ibid., 1919, 243).

6 Quoted in Heron and De Zwaan, 'Industrial Unionism,' 167.

7 Siemiatycki, 'Munitions and Labour Militancy'; Marine Workers and Boilermakers Industrial Union, *History of Shipbuilding*, 10–20; Frank, 'Cape Breton Coal Miners'; Seager, 'Proletariat in Wild Rose Country'; Canada, Dept. of Labour, *Organization in Canada*, 1916–20.

8 Siemiatycki, 'Labour Contained'; Kealey, '1919'; Heron, *Working in Steel*; Naylor, *New Democracy*; Montague, 'Trade Unionism in the Canadian Meatpacking Industry'; Schonning, 'Union–Management Relations in the Pulp and Paper Industry'; Scott, 'Profusion of Issues'; Hak, 'British Columbia Loggers'; Radforth, *Bushworkers and Bosses*; Thomson, '"The Large and Generous View"'; McLean, *'Union amongst Government Employees'*; Marquis, 'Police Unionism' and 'History of Policing in the Maritimes,' 94; Doherty, *Slaves of the Lamp*; and the regional essays in this volume.

9 Gregory Kealey, 'Parameters of Class Conflict,' 225–6.

10 Linda Kealey, '"No Special Protection"' and 'Women's Labour Militancy'; Roome, 'Amelia Turner and Calgary Labour Women'; Bernard, 'Last Back' and *Long Distance Feeling*, 50–71; Horodyski, 'Women and the Winnipeg General Strike'; Campbell, 'Sexism in British Columbia Trade Unions; Smillie, 'Invisible Workforce'; Frager, 'No Proper Deal.'

11 Avery, *'Dangerous Foreigners'*; Creese, 'Class, Ethnicity, and Conflict'; Radforth, *Bushworkers and Bosses*, 110–19; Martynowych and Kazymyra, 'Political Activity in Western Canada'; Wickberg, ed., *From China to Canada*, 130; Rouillard, 'Les travailleurs juifs'; Frager, *Sweatshoop Strife*, 35–54; Calliste, 'Sleeping Car Porters.'

12 Burnet, *'Coming Canadians'*; Harney, *Italians*, 20–2; Zucchi, *Italians in Toronto*; Radeki, *Member of a Distinguished Family*; Montgomery, 'Immigrants, Industrial Unions, and Social Reconstruction.'

13 Quoted in Gregory Kealey, '1919,' 39.

14 International Association of Machinists, *Bulletin* (Winnipeg), August 1918.

15 In 1914 there were four labour papers: Vancouver's *BC Federationist*, Winnipeg's *Voice*, Hamilton's *Labor News*, and Toronto's *Industrial Banner*. By mid-1919 all but the *Voice* were flourishing and had been joined by the *Citizen* (Halifax), the *Eastern Federationist* (New Glasgow), *Workers' Weekly* (Stellarton), the *Union Worker* (Saint John), *Le Monde ouvrier* (Montreal), *l'Unioniste* (Quebec City), the *Canadian Labor Press* (Ottawa), the *Labor Leader* (Toronto), *New Democracy* (Hamilton), the *Herald* (London), the *Western Labor News* (Winnipeg), the *Confederate* (Brandon), the *Searchlight* (Calgary), and the *Edmonton Free Press*. Canada, Dept. of Labour, *Labour Organization in Canada*, 1919, 295.

16 At the famous 1918 convention of the Trades and Labor Congress of Canada, radicals failed to win majority support for their proposal that the officials at this level should be consulted by the government, not the officers of international unions. The One Big Union later made these bodies the centre of its organizational structure. Robin, *Radical Politics and Canadian Labour*, 161; Bercuson, *Fools and Wise Men*, 149.

17 Siemiatycki, 'Labour Contained,' 279–325; McCormack, *Reformers, Rebels, and Revolutionaries*, 145–6; Bercuson, *Confrontation at Winnipeg*; Reilly, 'General Strike in Amherst'; Friesen, '"Yours in Revolt."'

18 Among the discredited or ignored were Nova Scotian miners' leader John Moffatt, the aging Quebec Lib-Lab MP Alphonse Verville, prominent Hamilton labour journalist Sam Landers, Winnipeg's venerable Arthur Puttee, Alberta miners' leader David Rees, and Vancouver's J.H. McVety and W.R. Trotter. MacEwan, *Miners and Steelworkers*, 46; Ewen in this volume; Heron, 'Working-Class Hamilton'; McCormack, *Reformers, Rebels, and Revolutionaries*, 137–64; Bercuson, *Fools and Wise Men*, 65–7.

19 Heron, 'Great War and Nova Scotia Steelworkers'; Frank, 'Cape Breton Coal Miners'; Heron and De Zwaan, 'Industrial Unionism,' 170–1; Angus, *Canadian Bolsheviks*, 66–9; Heron, 'Working-Class Hamilton,' 251–9; Bercuson, *Fools and Wise Men*, 65–8; Akers, 'Rebel or Revolutionary?'

20 Wade, 'Helena Gutteridge'; Linda Kealey, '"No Special Protection"'; Roome, 'Amelia Turner and Calgary Labour Women'; Horodyski, 'Women and the Winnipeg General Strike'; Heron, 'Working-Class Hamilton,' 380–489.

21 Peterson, 'Revolutionary Socialism and Industrial Unrest'; Angus, *Canadian Bolsheviks*, 3–62; Friesen, '"Yours in Revolt."'

22 Hak, 'British Columbia Loggers.'

23 Robin, *Radical Politics and Canadian Labour*, 170–7; McCormack, *Reformers, Rebels, and Revolutionaries*, 143–5; Bercuson, *Fools and Wise Men*, 83 (but see also his rethinking of this subject in 'Syndicalism Sidetracked').

24 On this point the interpretations of the Western revolt by Gerald Friesen and Larry Peterson are more convincing; see Friesen, '"Yours in Revolt,"' 145–7; Peterson, 'One Big Union in International Perspective,' 53–8. See also Akers, 'Rebel or Revolutionary?' 19–20.

25 Robin, *Radical Politics and Canadian Labour*, 130; Coates, ed., *British Labour and the Russian Revolution*.

26 McCormack, *Reformers, Rebels, and Revolutionaries*, 142; Angus, *Canadian Bolsheviks*, 27–48; Krawchuk, *Ukrainian Socialist Movement*; Usiskin, 'Winnipeg Jewish Radical Community.'

27 Heron, 'Labourism and the Canadian Working Class,' 48–9.

28 Scarrow, *Canada Votes*, 28–9.

29 Canada, Dept. of Labour, *Labour Organization in Canada*, 1917–20.

30 MacKenzie, 'Farmer-Labour Party in Nova Scotia'; Watson, 'United Farmers of Ontario'; Naylor, 'Ontario Workers and the Decline of Labourism'; Mardiros, *William Irvine*.

31 Akers, 'Rebel or Revolutionary?' 24.

32 McNaught, *Prophet in Politics*; Allen, *Social Passion*; Mardiros, *William Irvine*; Petryshyn, 'From Clergyman to Communist'; Mitchell, 'From the Social Gospel to "The Plain Bread of Leninism."'

33 Horn, *League for Social Reconstruction*.

34 Labourism was a brand of working-class liberalism that challenged political privilege, undemocratic practices, economic monopoly, and the exclusion of workers from social and political power, but stopped short of a full-scale assault on the capitalist system. Heron, 'Labourism and the Canadian Working Class.'

35 Quoted in Frank, 'Cape Breton Coal Miners,' 304–5; and Canada, Dept. of Labour, *Labour Organization in Canada*, 1919, 57.

36 Gregory Kealey, '1919,' 11–15; Siemiatycki, 'Labour Contained,' 279–325.

37 Labour Canada Library, Royal Commission on Industrial Relations, Evidence, Calgary, 3 May 1919.

38 *Globe* (Toronto), 20 March 1919.

39 Reimer, 'War, Nationhood and Working-Class Entitlement' (quotation on 231); *Examiner* (Peterborough), 2 September 1919; Naylor, *New Democracy*; McKay and Morton, and Mitchell and Naylor in this volume.

40 Wages were an issue in 46 per cent of the strikes in 1917, 44 per cent in 1918, 39 per cent in 1919, and 45 per cent in 1920. Gregory Kealey, 'Parameters of Class Conflict,' 240.

41 Selekman, *Postponing Strikes*, 168–78. The device of the royal commission was used, for example, in the Toronto and Hamilton munitions industry and Cobalt silver mining in 1916, and the Nova Scotia coal and steel industries several times after 1916. Siemiatycki, 'Munitions and Labour Militancy'; Hogan, *Cobalt*; MacEwan, *Miners and Steelworkers*; Heron, 'Great War and Nova Scotia Steelworkers.'

42 Heron, *Working in Steel*, 141–2; Schonning, 'Union–Management Relations in the Pulp and Paper Industry'; Montague, 'Trade Unionism in the Canadian Meatpacking Industry'; Naylor, *New Democracy*, 51–3, 209–10.

43 Peitchinis, *Labour–Management Relations in the Railway Industry*, 104–12; Naylor, *New Democracy* ,185–8; Zerker, *Rise and Fall of the Toronto Typographical Union*, 178–204; McKay, *Craft Transformed*, 68–73, and 'Industry, Work, and Community'; Seager, 'Proletariat in Wild Rose Country'; Brecher, 'Patterns of Accommodation in the Men's Garment Industry.'

44 Scott, '"A Place in the Sun"'; Naylor, *New Democracy*, 159–88; Levant, *Capital and Labour: Partners?*, 9–36; McGregor, *Fall and Rise of Mackenzie King*.

45 Royal Commission on Industrial Relations, Evidence, Victoria, Phil Smith, 26 April 1919.

46 Frank, 'Contested Terrain,' 114–18.

47 McCormack, *Reformers, Rebels, and Revolutionaries*, 146, 165–6; essays by Ewen and Naylor in this volume; Macgillivray, 'Military Aid to the Civil Power.'

48 Gregory Kealey, 'Parameters of Class Conflict,' 40.

49 Bercuson, *Fools and Wise Men*, 85.

50 MacEwan, *Miners and Steelworkers*, 71–2; Naylor, *New Democracy*, 193–4.

51 See Palmer, *Culture in Conflict*; Gregory Kealey and Palmer, *Dreaming of What Might Be*. The issue of shorter hours within workers' movements has been the subject of much fascinating recent research. See Roediger and Foner, *Our Own Time*; Cross, *Quest for Time*; Cross, ed., *Worktime and Industrialization*; and Hunnicutt, *Work without End*.

52 Parr, *Gender of Breadwinners*, 149–52; Linda Kealey, '"No Special Protection"'; Roome, 'Amelia Turner and Calgary Labour Women'; Naylor, *New Democracy*, 129–55; Campbell, 'Sexism in British Columbia Trade Unions'; Lindstrom-Best, *Defiant Sisters*, 147–55; 'Finnish Socialist Women in Canada'; Lindstrom-Best and Seager, '*Toveritar* and Finnish Canadian Women'; Penfold, '"Have You No Manhood in You?"'

53 Scott, 'A Profusion of Issues'; Seager, 'Class, Ethnicity, and Politics'; Heron, *Working in Steel*, 135.

54 Bercuson, *Confrontation at Winnipeg*; Penner, ed., *Winnipeg 1919*; Horodyski, 'Women and the Winnipeg General Strike'; Morton, 'Labourism and Economic Action'; Naylor, *New Democracy*; Heron and De Zwaan, 'Industrial Unionism in Eastern Ontario'; Ewen in this volume.

55 See Donegan, 'Iconography of Labour.'

56 Quoted in Heron, 'Working-Class Hamilton,' 388–9.

57 Joy Parr has appropriately dubbed this collective defence of the family wage 'social fathering' and 'breadwinner unionism.' Parr, *Gender of Breadwinners*, 149–50.

58 See photos in Penner, ed., *Winnipeg 1919*, and Bumstead, *Winnipeg General Strike*. Even the large Central Strike Committee had only two female members.

59 McKay and Morton in this volume; Frager, 'Class and Ethnic Barriers' and *Sweatshop Strife*.

60 The 'Reconstruction Policy' of the Greater Toronto Labor Party called on the government to 'tax all Aliens and enemy aliens very heavily; immigration after the War to be of friendly Aliens only for a definite period.' *Canadian Annual Review* (Toronto), 1918; 343.

61 Ewen in this volume.

62 Seager and Roth in this volume.

63 See, for example, Tuttle, *Race Riot*.

64 The BC Provincial Service Association affiliated with the Trades and Labor Congress but refused to join the Victoria Trades and Labor Council. McLean, *'A Union amongst Government Employees,'* 5, 15. See also Thomson, '"The Large and Generous View"'; and Makahonuk, 'Masters and Servants.'
65 Savage, *Our Nell*, 142–3.
66 Allen, *Social Passion*, 104–96.
67 Naylor, 'Ontario Workers and the Decline of Labourism'; Yeo, 'Alliance Unrealized'; and 'Rural Manitoba'. On the general topic of rural workers, see Samson, ed., *Contested Countryside.*
68 This important feature of the Canadian social formation has had far too little attention from Canadian historians, especially in English Canada. For some discussion, see McKay and Morton and Ewen in this volume; Séguin, 'L'économie agro-forestière'; Hardy and Séguin, *Fôret et société*; Hughes, *French Canada in Transition*; Ramirez, *On the Move*; Igartua, 'Worker Persistence'; Radforth, *Bushworkers and Bosses*; Parr, 'Hired Men'; Thompson, 'Bringing in the Sheaves'; Avery, 'Canadian Immigration Policy'; Sandberg, 'Dependent Development'; Sacouman, 'Semi-Proletarianization and Rural Underdevelopment'; Johnson, 'Precapitalist Economic Formations'; Knight, *Stump Ranch Chronicles.*
69 McDonald, *'To Each His Own'*; Hak, 'British Columbia Loggers.'
70 Knight, *Indians at Work*; Ray, *Canadian Fur Trade.*
71 Royal Commission on Industrial Relations, Evidence, Vancouver, J.J. Coughlin, 29 April 1919.
72 Siemiatycki, 'Labour Contained,' 249.
73 Gregory Kealey, 'Parameters of Class Conflict,' 241.
74 Zerker, *Rise and Fall of the Toronto Typographical Union*, 178–204; Allen, *Social Passion*, 175–96.
75 Heron, 'Great War and Nova Scotia Steelworkers'; Seager, 'Proletariat in Wild Rose Country'; Frank, 'Cape Breton Coal Miners'; Macgillivray, 'Industrial Unrest'; MacEwan, *Miners and Steelworkers*; McKay and Morton in this volume.
76 Naylor, *New Democracy*, 188–214.
77 *Labour Gazette*, May 1921, 709; and June 1921, 817.
78 Two years later total reported union membership had fallen by a further 17,000 to 260,000. Canada, Dept. of Labour, *Labour Organization in Canada*, 1921, 257; and 1924, 10.
79 Scott, '"A Place in the Sun"'; Naylor, *New Democracy*, 188–214; Parr, *Gender of Breadwinners*, 39–49; Seager, 'New Era for Labour?'; Heron, *Working in Steel*, 98–111; McCallum, 'Corporate Welfarism.'
80 Heron, *Working in Steel*, 105.
81 Morris, *Embattled Shadows*, 67–9; Naylor, *New Democracy*, 199. The Red Scare deserves fuller research; see Avery, *'Dangerous Foreigners'* and *Reluctant Host*; Baxter, 'Selected Aspects of Canadian Public Opinion'; Samuels, 'Red Scare in Ontario'; Boudreau, 'Enemy Alien Problem'; Askin, 'Labour Unrest in Edmonton and District.' On the same campaign in the United States, see Murray, *Red Scare.*
82 Naylor, *New Democracy*, 199–201.
83 Ibid.; Naylor, 'Workers and the State'; Traves, *State and Enterprise*, 15–28.
84 Naylor, *New Democracy*; Heron, 'Working-Class Hamilton,' 522–59.
85 Rouillard, *Les syndicats nationaux*; Ewen in this volume.
86 Forbes, 'Rise and Fall of the Conservative Party' and *Maritimes Rights Movement*; McKay and Morton in this volume.
87 McCallum, 'Keeping Women in Their Place'; Linda Kealey, 'Women and Labour'; Campbell, 'Balance Wheel of the Industrial System'; Oliver, 'Sir William Hearst.'
88 Heron, 'High School and the Household Economy'; Mitchell, '"Manufacture of Souls of Good Quality."'
89 Siemiatycki, 'Labour Contained'; Robin, *Radical Politics and Canadian Labour*; Bercuson, *Fools and Wise Men*; Friesen, '"Yours in Revolt,"' 141. Gregory Kealey presents slightly different figures for the 1918 vote (a minority of fifty-eight easterners and thirty-two westerners versus a majority of three westerners and ninety-seven easterners) but notes that the pattern remains the same. The West sent only 45 of the 440 delegates to the 1918 convention, which was held in Quebec City. Kealey, '1919,' 36.
90 Bercuson, *Fools and Wise Men*; Bright, 'Bonds of Brotherhood?'; and '"We Are All Kin."'
91 Naylor, *New Democracy*; Ewen in this volume.
92 *Canadian Labor Press*, 1 March 1919.
93 Siemiatycki, 'Labour Contained.'
94 See Ewen and Naylor in this volume.
95 Robin, *Radical Politics and Canadian Labour*; Siemiatycki, 'Labour Contained'; Naylor, *New Democracy.*
96 Frank, 'Cape Breton Coal Miners'; Seager, 'Proletariat in Wild Rose Country'; Bercuson, *Confrontation at Winnipeg* and *Fools and Wise Men*; and the regional essays in this volume.
97 Naylor, *New Democracy*; Ewen in this volume; Heron, *Working in Steel.*
98 Radforth, *Bushworkers and Bosses*; Seager, 'Finnish Canadians' and 'Class, Ethnicity, and Politics'; Hogan, *Cobalt*; Rouillard, 'Les travailleurs juifs'; Frager, *Sweatshop Strife.*
99 McKay, *Craft Transformed*; Frank, 'Cape Breton Coal Miners'; MacEwan, *Miners and Steelworkers*; Heron, 'Great War and Nova Scotia Steelworkers.'

100 Ewen in this volume; Rouillard, *Histoire du syndicalisme québécois*, 134.
101 Heron and Palmer, 'Prism of the Strike'; Heron, 'Working-Class Hamilton'; Naylor, *New Democracy*.
102 In Amherst, Nova Scotia, the local labour movement affiliated with the OBU, as did its counterpart in Carleton Place, Ontario, and several northern Ontario miners' and loggers' organizations. In Montreal, Toronto, Hamilton, and a few smaller towns in southern Ontario, small groups of socialist militants set up local OBU units and set out to compete with the established local leadership for working-class support. Fred Flatman expanded the circulation of his Hamilton paper *New Democracy*, which became the eastern mouthpiece for the OBU. Reilly, 'General Strike in Amherst'; Bercuson, *Fools and Wise Men*; Naylor, *New Democracy*, 64–71.
103 Angus, *Canadian Bolsheviks*, 63–80; Rodney, *Soldiers of the International*; Avakumovic, *Communist Party*, 1–53; Buck, *Yours in the Struggle*, 89–140; Watson, *She Was Never Afraid*, 1–20; Vance, *Not by Gods*, 1–45; Avery, *'Dangerous Foreigners'*, 116–23; Frank, 'Working-Class Politics'; Akers, 'Rebel or Revolutionary?'; Campbell, '"Making Socialists"'; Manley, 'Preaching the Red Stuff'; Heron, 'Frederick J. Flatman.'
104 Naylor, 'Ontario Workers and the Decline of Labourism.'
105 McNaught, *Prophet in Politics*; Heaps, *Rebel in the House*; Steeves, *Compassionate Rebel*, 70–92; Mardiros, *William Irvine*, 109–204; Young, *Anatomy of a Party*, 2–37; Caplan, *Dilemma of Canadian Socialism*, 7–18; Avakumovic, *Socialism in Canada*, 11–70.
106 Palmer, *Working-Class Experience*, 214–67.
107 Ian McKay has developed this argument more fully in 'Industry, Work, and Community,' 800–28; *Craft Transformed*, 55–144; and (with Michael Earle), 'Introduction: Industrial Legality in Nova Scotia,' in Earle, ed., *Workers and the State*, 9–23.
108 Findlay, 'Protection of Workers in Industry.'
109 McNaught, *Prophet in Politics*, 215–20.

"In case you hadn't noticed!": Race, Ethnicity, and Women's Wage-Earning in a Depression-Era City

Katrina Srigley

ON ANY TYPICAL WORKDAY morning during the Depression, Toronto's wage-earning women emerged from their homes — flats in Kensington Market, bungalows in suburban Weston, or row houses in the East End — and headed to work where they earned wages as domestics, teachers, clerical staff, garment workers, and the like. Although Canadian histories of the Depression have not granted them a great deal of attention, these female breadwinners were major players in Toronto's labour market: in 1931 one in four wage-earners were women; by 1941, amid World War II, the proportion had risen to nearly one in three.[1] The growing presence of women in the workforce was not peculiar to Toronto, of course. In urban centres across North America industrial expansion, new forms of office administration, and altered labour processes had provided growing job opportunities for employed women. The widespread economic insecurity of the 1930s had also accelerated this trend. In a period when "men's" jobs in primary industry were particularly vulnerable, women, who had a much lower unemployment rate, occupied

[1] In Toronto between 1931 and 1941 the number of gainfully occupied woman 14 years of age and over rose from approximately 91,780 to 111,334. Canada, Bureau of the Census, *Occupations and Industries Vol. VII* (Ottawa 1941), 1,102. Many women who were doing piecework from their home, domestic work (inside and outside their home), and helped with the family business would have been overlooked as non workers. At this time Greater Toronto included the following communities: Etobicoke, Forest Hill, Leaside, Long Branch, Mimico, New Toronto, Scarborough, Swansea, Weston, York Township, York East Township, and York North Township. Canada, Bureau of the Census, *Monographs Vol. XIII* (Ottawa 1931), 470-1.

Katrina Srigley, "'In case you hadn't noticed!': Race, Ethnicity, and Women's Wage-Earning in a Depression-Era City," *Labour/Le Travail*, 55 (Spring 2005), 69-105.

increasingly central roles in their families as primary wage-earners.[2] In many more households than before, "the gender of breadwinners" was female, as women's wages fed, clothed, and provided shelter for their families.[3] While such factors pulled more women into the workplace, job availability and economic need were not the only determinants of a woman's access to (and desire for) employment in Toronto's labour market. Women's employment options were conditioned by race — by which I mean both whiteness and non-whiteness — ethnicity, marital status, gender, and class. In 1931, Toronto's population was roughly 631,200 and its 5 largest racial and ethnic groupings included 510,432 members of the "British Races," 13,015 Italians, 45,305 Hebrews, 10,869 French, and 9,343 Germans. Groups such as the Polish and the Dutch hovered between 9,000 and 5,000 people, while Blacks, Russians, Greeks, and Ukrainians registered between 5,000 and 1,000 in the decennial census for the 1930s.[4] As these numbers indicate, Toronto was largely a WASP city during the 1930s. Anglo-Celtic dominance created both privileges and disadvantages for female workers who received differing access to training and employment.[5] An analysis that pays particular attention to the importance of racial identities to women workers, while also acknowledging the multiple identities they held, uncovers critical and otherwise hidden aspects of working women's experiences in this 1930s labour market.[6]

The importance of a race critical analysis of Toronto's Depression-era women workers is particularly well illustrated by Claire Clarke's still painful memories of her work experiences. In our 2001 interview, Clarke, 88 and still living in her own home, related some of the challenges faced by wage-earners in 1930s Toronto. With obvious pride, she remembered how she had stood second in her graduating class at Central High School of Commerce in 1931, telling me "I graduated at the top of my class ... you know I received the Timothy Eaton scholarship medal. The Jewish girl received the gold medal and I received the silver medal." Equally evi-

[2]In 1931, roughly 18 per cent of Canada's male wage-earners were unemployed compared with 7 per cent of its female wage-earners. Canada, Bureau of the Census, *Unemployment Vol. VI* (Ottawa 1931), 94. This statistic must be viewed critically. First of all women were often not counted among the unemployed because of prevailing assumptions that women were dependents fulfilling their domestic role. There were certainly many more unemployed women than this statistic suggests.

[3]Joy Parr, *The Gender of Breadwinners: Women, Men, and Change in Two Industrial Towns 1880-1950* (Toronto 1990).

[4]Canada, Bureau of the Census, *Cross-Classifications Vol. IV* (Ottawa 1931), 912. Religious groupings also reflect important cultural divisions. In 1931, 68 per cent of the city worshipped at Anglican, Presbyterian, or United Churches. Canada, Bureau of the Census, *Cross-Classifications Vol. IV* (Ottawa 1931), 912-3.

[5]Joan W. Scott, *Gender and the Politics of History* (New York 1988).

[6]For more on this theme see: Nancy A. Hewitt, *Southern Discomfort: Women's Activism in Tampa, Florida, 1880-1920s* (Urbana 2001); Tera W. Hunter, *To 'joy my freedom: Southern Black Women's Lives and Labors after the Civil War* (Cambridge, Massachusetts 1997).

dent all these years later was her disappointment that despite her impressive academic achievement, "there was no [job] placement for me." That was "very unusual" she added, "because during all my years at the school in the summertime they would select girls and send them off to the parliament buildings to work. I was never selected."[7] Clarke expected, like other girls her age, to find employment in order to help her family who, in this case, were living in a newly purchased home in a downtown Toronto neighbourhood (near Bathurst and Queen Streets). With a smile, that broke into laughter she recalled: "I ended up making hats!"

> Well I would get up and go down to King Street you know and see if they needed any help. The proprietor was a Mr. Wise. I remember him to this day. He hired me to sit and make hats. And then all this time I was lobbying, writing civil service exams and, you know, keeping my (pause) qualifications up.[8]

In many respects, Clarke's work experiences confirm the findings of feminist historians who have examined how gender and class have shaped the employment of women workers in early twentieth-century Canada.[9] Wage-earners like Clarke faced sexist job segregation; indeed, an increased number of available jobs in Ontario's largest urban centre did not ensure women a position of choice. Of the women employed in Toronto in the early years of the Depression, 27 per cent of them worked in personal service, 28 per cent in clerical occupations, 17 per cent in manufacturing (primarily in the textile industry), and 11 per cent in professional service occupations such as teaching and nursing.[10] By 1941, despite the onset of the war and the movement of women into non-traditional occupations, little had changed. Eighty-four per cent of employed women were involved in these sectors of the labour market.[11] This ghettoization denied women access to skilled jobs in

[7]Claire Clarke, interview by Katrina Srigley, May 2001, October 2001, April 2002.
[8]Claire Clarke, interview.
[9]See for example: Nancy Christie, *Engendering the State: Family, Work and Welfare in Canada* (Toronto 2000); Parr, *The Gender of Breadwinners;* Joan Sangster, *Earning Respect: The Lives of Working Women in Small Town Ontario, 1920-1960* (Toronto 1995); Veronica Strong-Boag, *The New Day Recalled: Lives of Girls and Women in English Canada, 1919-1939* (Toronto 1988).
[10]Of the 79,120 women reported as employed in 1931, 21,263 worked in personal service, 21,959 in clerical occupations, 13,352 in manufacturing, and 9,172 in professional service. These broad areas of occupation were further divided into categories such as teaching, domestic service, and stenography. Canada, Bureau of the Census, *Occupations and Industries Vol. VII* (Ottawa 1931), 226-237.
[11]Canada, Bureau of the Census, *Occupations and Industries Vol. VII* (Ottawa 1941), 218-220. For a discussion of gender based job segregation in the American context see: Ruth Milkman, *Gender at Work: The Dynamics of Job Segregation by Sex during World War II* (Chicago 1987). In this important study of job segregation in the US electrical and auto industry, Milkman asserts that employment discrimination based on sex was a consequence of

the industrial sector and positions as administrators, principals, and doctors in offices and hospitals. It also legitimized lower earnings: women received on average one-third to one-half the earnings of men.[12] Hampered by these obstacles, Clarke was searching for work when the plight of the male breadwinner prompted widespread anti-feminist sentiment in the country's newspapers. Moreover, government sanctioned regulations allowed employers — particularly in occupations in the civil service, nursing, and teaching — to deny women employment after marriage. These discriminatory expectations about marital status and wage-earning ensured, as Veronica Strong-Boag puts it, that women were "defined and delimited, not so much by any lesser capacity for work or determination, or thought, but by patriarchal custom and male authority."[13] Clarke undeniably lived in a society that valued the labour of men over women. She could not find work despite her vocational education.[14] However, sexism alone does not adequately explain Clarke's labour force experiences. Significantly, when asked why she had difficulty securing employment Clarke did not mention issues related to gender or class; instead she exclaimed with great conviction, "I AM BLACK IN CASE YOU HADN'T NOTICED!"[15]

Clarke's story, and her explicit racial explanation of her failure to find work in her field, as well as the work memories of the other women — Anglo-Celtic, European and African Canadian – who are the subjects of this study, compel us to scrutinize more closely how race interacted with gender, class, and other variables to produce not only certain kinds of experiences — and women's memories of them — but also the complex identities that women workers forged in this period of economic stagnation. Certainly, high rates of male unemployment generated considerable insecurity about the position of male breadwinners within the family and the increasing rates of female employment did little to quell these fears; instead they expanded concerns that the Depression was diluting female domesticity as well. Such anxiety is well represented in the editorial pages of daily newspapers. In both

industrialization rather than a natural division based on family responsibility. Once established, she claims this division was intractable and did not respond to the jump in women's employment in 1930s and 1940s.

[12]In Ontario in 1931 women earned on average $636 per year, while men earned $1,005. By 1941 the situation was worse. Women earned on average $574 per year, while men earned $1,112, 49 per cent more. Canada, Bureau of the Census, *Summary Vol. I* (Ottawa 1941), 801.

[13]Strong-Boag, *The New Day Recalled*, 3.

[14]In 1931, 84 per cent of employed women in Toronto were single women. Canada, Bureau of the Census, *Unemployment Vol. VI* (Ottawa 1931), 1,172. For more on the employment of single women and the feminization of certain occupations see: Graham Lowe, *Women in the Administrative Revolution: The Feminization of Clerical Work* (Toronto 1987); Milkman, *Gender at Work*; Sangster, *Earning Respect*; Carolyn Strange, *Toronto's Girl Problem: The Perils and Pleasures of the City, 1880-1930* (Toronto 1995); Strong-Boag, *The New Day Recalled*.

[15]Claire Clarke, interview.

Canada and the United States, women and men took up their pens to challenge the position of women wage-earners, particularly those who were married. Their rhetoric, at times motherly, was more often venomous. One defeated (and particularly irrational) man claimed that "women ha[d] captured all the jobs except fatherhood!"[16] Such condemnations were quite frequent in the early years of the Depression and, not surprisingly, historians interested in issues of gender and work have paid considerable attention to these and other expressions of gender hostility and discrimination.

The 1993 *Gender & History* debate between US historian Alice Kessler-Harris and Canadian specialist Margaret Hobbs underscores some of the critical differences in how feminist historians have evaluated negative discourses of working women in the 1930s and offers a point of departure for addressing the relationship between the breadwinner's gender and identity formation.[17] While both historians agree that gender significantly influenced people's reactions to women's employment as well as workers' identity, perception, and behaviour, they ultimately provide different explanations of how gender as a social variable influenced those who challenged, rhetorically at least, the position of women workers.[18] In her reading of these attacks, Kessler-Harris suggests that in the context of a major depression economic need had a greater influence on these letter writers' perspectives than a desire to strengthen sexist notions of female domesticity. She thus challenges what she sees as the tendency of women's historians to give gender too much analytical weight.[19] She proposes instead that the dramatic changes in the labour market had created "a legitimate space for female breadwinners," particularly those who fulfilled the role of sole provider, such as single women, widows, and married women with husbands who were unable to work. In Kessler-Harris' interpretation, this legitimacy alters how we should understand sexism in the Depression context. For some female breadwinners identified "not only as women but as young people, family supporters, parents and dependents, they were vulnerable to any who threatened to undermine their family roles, whether such people were male or female."[20] Thus, Kessler-Harris concludes, basic issues of economic justice prevailed.

[16]Anonymous, "That's a Man's Job," *Business Woman, (*July 1930), 14.

[17]Alice Kessler-Harris, "Gender Ideology in Historical Reconstruction: A Case Study from the 1930s," *Gender & History,* 1, 1 (Spring 1989), 31-49; Margaret Hobbs, "Rethinking Antifeminism in the 1930s: Gender Crisis or Workplace Justice? A Response to Alice Kessler-Harris," *Gender & History,* 5, 1 (Spring 1993), 4-15; Alice Kessler-Harris, "Reply to Hobbs," *Gender & History,* 5, 1 (Spring 1993), 16-9.

[18]"A Man Talks to Women," *Toronto Daily Star,* 20 March 1939.

[19]Kessler-Harris, "Reply to Hobbs," 16.

[20]Kessler-Harris, "Gender Ideology in Historical Reconstruction," 40; Marcus Klee also has a good discussion of this in his dissertation. See Marcus Klee, "Between the Scylla and Charybdis of Anarchy and Despotism: The State, Capital and the Working Class in the Great Depression, Toronto, 1929- 1940," Ph.D. thesis, Queen's University, 1998, 233-4.

Like other feminist historians who have drawn connections between gender and class, Hobbs' reading of the Canadian material highlights the links between resistance to women's wage-earning and patriarchal assumptions about male breadwinning and female domesticity prevalent during the interwar years. And, in her debate with Kessler-Harris, she does not concede a less influential position to gender; while acknowledging that concerns about economic justice might have been influential, Hobbs insists that public cries for women to vacate the work force cannot and should not be "wrenched ... from the fundamentally gendered context, which spawned them."[21] In this debate and her national study of employment, unemployment, and social policy, Hobbs argues that such anti-feminist discourse reflects a labour market in which sexism kept women's earnings well below men's wages, limited their job options, and denied married women work even in periods of acute need. Thus, she concludes, gender was a central and important "ideological liability" for working women during the Depression.[22]

Whichever side of this debate historians may wish to position themselves, most would agree that gender matters a great deal. However, as Clarke's memories of racial discrimination, and the differing memories of the other women central to this study, suggest, we need to examine more closely how an individual's multiple identities influenced their lives in this particular time and place. For some women at least, gender was not the only, nor necessarily the most important, social factor shaping their work experiences; nor did they prioritize gender when remembering and trying to make sense of their past experiences. Thus, this paper, then, shifts the focus away from the debate over how much gender actually mattered and towards a more explicit discussion of how race and ethnicity, along with other variables, including gender and class, converged in various ways to shape women's lives and memories. In probing the individual stories of a diverse group of working women in Depression-era Toronto, I draw most explicitly on the scholarship of feminist historians whose important work on immigrant, ethnic, black, and other racialized working-class women in North America has well demonstrated the value of moving beyond static models of patriarchy that assume the primacy of gender as an explan-

[21]Hobbs, "Rethinking Antifeminism in the 1930s," 5-6.

[22]Margaret Hobbs, "Gendering Work and Welfare: Women's Relationship to Wage-Work and Social Policy in Canada During the Depression," Unpublished PhD, University of Toronto, 1995, 26; 71. Ruth Roach Pierson's well-documented study of the unemployment insurance debates during the Depression indicates that gender was central to insurance entitlement during the Depression. This left many female workers in untenable economic situations. Ruth Roach Pierson, "Gender and the Unemployment Insurance Debates in Canada," *Labour/Le Travail*, 25 (Spring 1990), 77-103. In the American context, Lois Scarf reaches similar conclusions with regards to the predominance of gender. See Lois Scarf, *To Work and To Wed: Female Employment, Feminism, and the Great Depression* (Connecticut 1980).

atory factor in historical experience.[23] While remaining attentive to gender and class, scholars such as Ruth Frager, Evelyn Brooks Higginbotham, Nancy Hewitt, and Franca Iacovetta have shown us that other social variables can be equally or in some cases more important than gender in structuring both the experiences of women in a given context and their memories of those events. Feminist historians who have examined women's lives and stories through the lens of ethnicity and race as well as gender, class, culture, age, lifecycle, and other social categories joined a rich literature on gender and class; they also offered new perspectives on women's wage-earning and activism that, for example, were particularly sensitive to immigrant women's different cultural understandings and expressions of femininity, waged work, resistance, and protest.[24] So doing, they also showed that these women's notions of their respectability and the ways in which they forged and articulated their identities as women, workers, foreigners, wives, and mothers differed significantly from both middle class and working-class Anglo-Celtic models of ideal womanhood and female respectability. Studies of supposedly unruly ethnic "female mobs," of Italian and other "Latin" women's direct action on the streets, and of neighbourhood and community-based mobilizations led by mothers and daughters remind us of the need to pay closer attention to European, Cuban, and other homeland strategies that women transplanted to North America, including

[23]Ruth Frager, *Sweatshop Strife: Class, Ethnicity, and Gender in the Jewish Labour Movement, 1900-1939* (Toronto 1992); Evelyn Brooks Higginbotham, "African American Women's History and the Metalanguage of Race," *Signs*, (1992), 251-74; Franca Iacovetta, *Such Hardworking People: Italian Immigrants in Postwar Toronto* (Montreal & Kingston 1992); Jacqueline Jones, "Race and Gender in Modern America," *Reviews in American History*, (March 1998), 220-38; Nancy Hewitt, "Beyond the Search for Sisterhood: American Women's History in the 1980s," *Social History*, 10 (October 1985), 299-322; Gerda Lerner, "Reconceptualizing Difference Among Women," *Journal of Women's History*, 1 (Winter 1990),106-122; Varpu Lindström, *Defiant Sisters: A Social History of Finnish Women in Canada* (Toronto 1988); Joy Parr, *The Gender of Breadwinners: Women, Men and Change in Two Industrial Towns, 1880-1950* (Toronto 1991); Elizabeth V. Spelman, *Inessential Woman: Problems of Exclusion in Feminist Thought* (Boston 1988); Carolyn Strange, "Dead Men and Wounded Womanhood: Trials of Clara Ford and Carrie Davies," in Franca Iacovetta and Marianna Valverde, eds., *Gender Conflicts: New Essays in Women's History* (Toronto 1992),149-88; Carolyn Strange, *Toronto's Girl Problem: The Perils and Pleasures of the City, 1880-1930* (Toronto 1995).

[24]See Julie Guard, "Authenticity on the Line: Women Workers, Native "Scabs," and the Multi-ethnic Politics of Identity in a Left-Led Strike in Cold War Canada," *Journal of Women's History*, 15, 4 (Winter 2004), 117-40; Franca Iacovetta, "Feminist Transnational Labour History and Rethinking Women's Activism and Female Militancy in Canadian Contexts: Lessons from an Internationalist Project," annual meeting of the Canadian Historical Association, Winnipeg, 3-5 June 2004; Donna Gabaccia, Franca Iacovetta and Fraser Ottanelli, "Labouring Across National Borders: Class, Gender and Militancy in the Proletarian Mass Migration," *International Labor and Working Class History*, 66 (Fall 2004), 57-77.

some important cultural tools such as women's stories of resistance that were told and retold at the kitchen table and in children's plays performed at the socialist hall.

For the Depression era, Frager's work on Jewish women workers in inter-war Toronto illustrates how the shifting influences of ethnicity, gender, and class shaped Jewish women's roles in family and workplace. Contrary to dominant Anglo-Protestant conceptions of womanhood, femininity for these women included a central, forceful, and sometimes highly aggressive role in protest — from housewives' bread strikes to union organizing — and workplace reform.[25] As with other studies of multi-racial or multi-ethnic communities on strike, Carmela Patrias' study of a strike that the multi-ethnic town of Crowland (Welland), Ontario waged against the provincial government for cutbacks on relief support, highlights the cross-ethnic class solidarities that developed among working-class residents. It also sheds light on ethnic women's role in the strike, especially their strategies involving children, and how their identities as workers (or the children of workers), foreigners (though many of them were Canadian-born), wives, and mothers were forged in a context of making common cause with others like themselves.[26] Québec historian Denyse Baillargeon uses ethnicity to define the parameters of her study of married working-class women in Depression-era Montréal. Taking us "into the very heart of the domestic sphere," she considers the living conditions, life cycle, and strategies used by housewives to combat economic instability and highlights the importance of domestic space for an understanding of working-class francophone Montréal during the Depression.[27]

With a few notable exceptions, Canadian feminist historians so far have paid significantly less attention to race than to gender as an analytical tool, particularly

[25]Other historians in Canada and the United States have reached similar conclusions when exploring the intersection of femininity and ethnicity. See Ardis Cameron, *Radicals of the Worst Sort: Laboring Women in Lawrence Massachusetts, 1860-1912* (Urbana 1993); Jennifer Gugliemo, "Italian Women's Proletarian Feminism in New York City Garment Trades, 1890s-1940," in Donna Gabbacia and Franca Iacovetta, eds., *Women, Gender and Transnational Lives: Italians Workers of the World* (Toronto 2002); Robert Ventresca, "Cowering Women and Combative Men?": Femininity, Masculinity and Ethnicity on Strike in Two Southern Ontario Towns, 1964-1966," *Labour/Le Travail,* 39 (Spring 1997), 125-58.

[26]Carmela Patrias, "Relief Strike: Immigrant Workers and the Great Depression in Crowland, Ontario, 1930-1935," in Franca Iacovetta, Paula Draper and Robert Ventresca, eds., *A Nation of Immigrants: Women, Workers, and Communities in Canadian History, 1840s-1960s* (Toronto 1998), 351.

[27]Denise Baillargeon, *Making Do: Women, Family and Home in Montréal during the Great Depression* Yvonne Klein trans., (Waterloo 1999), xi. Also see *Menagères au Temps de la Crise* (Montréal 1991); "If You Had No Money, You Had No Trouble, Did You?" Montréal Working-Class Housewives During the Great Depression," in Wendy Mitchinson *et al., Canadian Women: A Reader* (Toronto 1996), 251-68.

with regards to whiteness.[28] As Afua Cooper recently observed, "feminists, historians, and theorists alike have generally privileged gender oppression [over that of race] as the main cause of women's subordination" and thus have failed to understand the central role of both whiteness and blackness to Canadian women's and gender history.[29] For the Depression period in particular, the complex relationship between race, gender, and work experiences for women workers identities and memories deserves greater exploration. Dionne Brand's study of African Canadian women from 1920-1950 provides overwhelming evidence of the role of race and gender in structuring the labour market discrimination experienced by African Canadian women throughout the Depression, World War II, and post war period.[30] But Brand's work should represent the beginning, not the end, of exploration into as well as debate about race and gender in historical scholarship. Picking up the threads of race, gender, and citizenship in her recent study of women's employabil-

[28]See for example: Constance Backhouse, *Colour Coded: A legal history of racism in Canada, 1900-1950* (Toronto 1999); Carl E. James, *Seeing Ourselves: Exploring Ethnicity, Race and Culture* 3rd ed (1995; Toronto 2003); Carl E. James and Adrienne Shadd, eds., *Talking About Identity: Encounters in Race, Ethnicity, and Language* (Toronto 2001); Carl E. James, *Experiencing Difference* (Halifax 2000); Adele Perry, *On the Edge of Empire: Gender, Race, and the Making of British Columbia, 1849-1871* (Toronto 2001); Sherene Razack, *Looking White People in the Eye: Gender, Race, and Culture in Courtrooms and Classrooms* (Toronto 1998); Elizabeth Vibert, "Real Men Hunt Buffalo: Masculinity, Race and Class in British Fur Traders' Narratives," *Gender & History* (Great Britain), 8, 1 (1996), 4-21; Barrington Walker, "The Gavel and the Veil of Race: Blackness in Ontario's criminal courts, 1858-1958," Ph.D. thesis, University of Toronto, 2003. Though not generally using gender and race as categories of historical analysis, in the American context scholars have taken up the issue of African American women's work and the influence of race on labour force discrimination during the Depression era far more extensively. See: William Sundstrom, "Discouraging Times: The Labour Force Participation of Married Black Women, 1930-1940," *Explorations in Economic History*, 38, 1 (1998), 123-146; Robert Boyd, "Survivalist Entrepreneurship: A Test of the Disadvantage Theory of Business Enterprise," *Social Science Quarterly* 81 (2000), 972-984; Phyllis Palmer, "Black Domestics During the Depression: Workers, Organizers, Social Commentators," *Prologue*, 29, 2 (1997), 127-131; Yolanda Chavez Leyva, "Faithful Hard-Working Mexican Hands": Mexicana Workers During the Great Depression," *Perspectives in Mexican American Studies*, 5 (1995), 63-77.

[29]Afua Cooper, "Constructing Black Women's Historical Knowledge," *Atlantis*, 25 1 (2000), 39. Cooper's thoughts echo those of the following scholars: Kum-Kum Bhavnani, *Feminism and 'Race'* (Oxford 2001); Hazel V. Carby in "White Women Listen! Black Feminism and the Boundaries of Sisterhood," in Center for Contemporary Cultural Studies, ed., *The Empire Strikes Back: Race and Racism in 70s Britain* (London 1983); Ruth Frankenberg, *The Social Construction of White Women: Whiteness Race Matters* (Minneapolis 1993); bell hooks, *Talking Back: Thinking Feminist, Thinking Black* (Boston 1989).

[30]Dionne Brand, *No Burden to Carry: Narratives of Black Working Women in Ontario, 1920s-1950s* (Toronto 1991).

ity during the late depression and World War II era, Jennifer Stephen adeptly shows how such social variables were woven through and constitutive of perceptions of women's employment. Different female wage-earners had variant relationships with "the state, formal waged economy and labour market," depending on, among other things, racialized notions of domesticity and citizenship.[31] In the context Stephen explores, whiteness could also be a site of power and privilege for women. Most recently, Iacovetta has suggested that we more effectively de-centre the "WASP women worker" and the paradigms of female respectability and activisms derived from studies of primarily dominant majority women (WASP in English Canada, or Francophone in Québec), paradigms that, despite almost two decades of scholarship on "other" women workers, still provide the standard against which "other" women's experiences and actions are compared.[32] The intellectual trajectory of one of Canada's leading feminist historians, Ruth Pierson — from a women's historian to a race-critical gender scholar — offers a good illustration of the ways in which current debates about race and racialization have led to reassessments of women's relationship to the labour force, the state, and other institutions and to their experiences and identity formation. A "conception of interlocking and mutually constitutive character of social categories," Pierson writes in the introduction to *Nation, Empire and Colony: Historicizing Race and Gender,* "explodes the notion that gender rotates simply around a single axis of polar opposites."[33] It also provides an opportunity to reassess gender discrimination and the labour market participation of women during the Depression.

A case study of Toronto that uses oral history is particularly well suited to answer questions about identity and women's work experiences. Toronto was the second largest city in Canada during the Depression years.[34] Its economy supported significant female employment in a range of jobs in spite of gender restrictions and major economic stagnation; in fact, the city had a higher percentage of women in the labour market than any other metropolis in Canada at the time.[35] Toronto's population, though overwhelmingly Anglo- Protestant, did include, like Montréal and

[31]Jennifer Stephen, "Deploying Discourses of Employability and Domesticity: Women's Employment and Training Policies and the Formation of the Canadian Welfare State, 1935-1947," Ph.D. thesis, University of Toronto, 2000, 30.

[32]Iacovetta, "Feminist Transnational Labour History."

[33]Ruth Roach Pierson, "Introduction," in Ruth Roach Pierson and Nupur Chaudhuri, eds., *Nation, Empire, and Colony: Historicizing Gender and Race* (Bloomington and Indianapolis 1998), 2. Also see Sherene Razak's article in "Rigorous Feminist Standards!: A Panel in Honour of Ruth Roach Pierson," *Atlantis,* 28, 3 (Special Issue 2) (1994).

[34]The exact population statistic collected for Toronto in 1931 was 631,207. Canada, Bureau of the Census, *Summary Vol. I* (Ottawa 1931), 81.

[35]In Toronto women held 28 per cent of the jobs in the labour market, while in Winnipeg they held 26 per cent and in Montréal 25 per cent. Canada, Bureau of the Census, *Occupations and Industries Vol. VII* (Ottawa 1931), 226, 250, 190.

other major cities in the United States, various immigrant and racialized communities, especially Jews, Italians, and East Europeans, as well as African-Canadians and Francophones; women, including wage-earning women, could be found in all these communities.[36] The experiences of these women and those of people in immigrant and working-class communities more generally are not well reflected in the historical sources, which, more often than not, were produced by the city's Anglo-Protestant establishment — government officials, medical and psychological experts, and political élites.

Oral histories offer access to these voices and are particularly useful for exploring the issues raised by scholars like Cooper and Pierson.[37] They provide an opportunity to analyze how discrimination or privilege, or both for that matter, were established and experienced. In an effort to obtain a sample of female subjects who reflected Toronto's racial-ethnic mix, I made contact with several "ethnic" organizations and homes for elders and mined existing collections of oral histories.[38] Over 6 years, 85 women and men welcomed me into their homes and willingly shared their stories with me; in turn, I have made their stories central to this study.[39]

There are various approaches to interviewing and different ways of recovering and handling people's recollections of their lives, and their story-telling.[40] For ex-

[36]Canada, Bureau of the Census, *Cross-Classifications Vol. IV* (Ottawa 1931), 912-3.

[37]So too do foreign-language records of immigrant and ethnic organizations or individual diaries and journals, but that is not my focus here.

[38]I called every retirement home and religious organization listed in Toronto's *Yellow Pages*. I then mailed information packages to activity directors with flyers to be distributed to residents or congregants. This proved particularly fruitful as people felt more comfortable responding to my ad when there was an intermediary person. I also placed ads in the following newspapers: *Toronto Star, Corriere Canadese, Beeton Banner, Vaughan Weekly, King City Spectator,* and *The Bolton Enterprise*. The African Canadian, Italian Canadian and Jewish Canadian collections at the Multicultural History Society of Ontario have been invaluable to my research.

[39]To date I have completed 54 interviews with women and 29 interviews with men. The memories of both men and women are central to my understanding of the society in which women were working and living. Interview questions related to the following themes: family, schooling, neighbourhood, wage-earning, and leisure time. Participants responded on biographical information sheets and in conversations recorded by tape in 1 ½ and 2 hour interviews. Respondents had the option to remain anonymous. In these cases I have used different names. For the most part people have been happy to add their name and identity to an historical record burgeoning with the names (not the aliases) of famous people.

[40]Readers interested in the debates and recent important contributions to oral and memory history can usefully consult the following: Julie Cruikshank, *Life Lived Like a Story: Life Stories of Three Yukon Native Elders* (Lincoln 1998); Paula Draper, "Surviving their Survival: Women, Memory and the Holocaust," in Marlene Epp, Franca Iacovetta and Frances Swyripa, eds., *Sisters or Strangers? Immigrant, Ethnic and Racialized Women in Canadian History* (Toronto 2004), 399-414. Marlene Epp, *Women Without Men: Mennonite Refugees of the Second World War* (Toronto 2000); Epp, "The Memory of Violence: Mennonite Ref-

ample, many feminist studies of working-class women, especially of immigrant and racialized women, have used standard taped interview techniques to gather and reconstruct women's lives and subjectivities.[41] In doing so, these scholars have analyzed historical actors' voices, perspectives, recollections, and ideas to understand women's lived experiences, though they have rarely relied on this one source. Recognition of the limitations of retrospective interviews is important but it need not lead us to abandon the tape recorder any more than recognition of the limitations of archival holdings should prompt us to abandon the archives![42] Such studies have proven particularly fruitful for our understanding of the lives of women whose voices have generally been omitted from the historical record. Recent feminist scholarship dealing with refugee women, wartime rape victims, and Holocaust survivors, as well as feminist anthropologists collecting the stories and narratives of Aboriginal women and South American peasant women, have developed sophisticated understandings of the form, content, and silences of women's narratives and have also introduced us to female subjects who set the criteria and pace for telling their stories.[43] Here my focus on women's lived experiences in Toronto's labour market encourages a reading of memories as a source for women's voices and the events of their lives. While I have also incorporated critical issues flagged by scholars of women's oral traditions and memory history, I worked from the assumption

ugees and Rape in World War II," *Journal of Women's History*, 9, 1 (1997), 58-87; Luisa Passerini, *Fascism in Popular Memory: The Cultural Experience of the Turin Working Class* (Cambridge 1987); Raphael Samuel and Paul Thompson, *The Myths We Live By* (London 1990); Joan Sangster, "Telling Our Stories: Feminist Debates and the Use of Oral History," in Robert Perks and Alistair Thomson, eds., *The Oral History Reader* (New York 1998), 87-100.

[41]For Canadian examples see: Dionne Brand, *No Burden To Carry;* Frager, *Sweatshop Strife;* Iacovetta, *Such Hardworking People*; Lindström, *Defiant Sisters.*

[42]Franca Iacovetta, "Manly Militants, Cohesive Communities and Defiant Domestics: Writing About Immigrants in Canadian Historical Scholarship," *Labour/Le Travail*, 36 (1995), 217-52; Karen Flynn, "Experience and Identity: Black Immigrant Nurses to Canada, 1950-1980," in Epp, Iacovetta and Swyripa, eds., *Sisters or Strangers?*, 381-98.

[43]Julie Cruikshank, "Discovery of Gold on the Klondike: Perspectives from Oral Tradition," in Jennifer Brown and Elizabeth Vibert, eds., *Reading Beyond Words: Context for Native History* (Peterborough 1996); Cruikshank, *Life Lived Like a Story; The Social Life of Stories: Narrative and Knowledge in Yukon Territory* (Lincoln 1998); Epp, *Women without Men;* Gwendolyn Etter-Lewis, "Black Women's Life Stories: Reclaiming Self in Narrative Texts," in Sherna Berger Gluck and Daphne Patai, eds., *Women's Words: the Feminist Practice of Oral History* (London 1991), 43-58; Franca Iacovetta, "Post Modern Ethnography, Historical Materialism and Decentering the (Male) Authorial Voice: A Feminist Conversation," *Histoire sociale/Social History*, 64, 132 (November 1999), 275-93; Luisa Passerini, "Women's Personal Narratives: myths, experiences, and emotions," in Personal Narratives Group, ed., *Interpreting Women's Lives: Feminist Theory and Personal Narratives* (Bloomington 1989), 189-97.

that, as Joan Sangster and others suggest, interviews can provide important evidence for both "real" experiences and how people remember them.[44] Thus, like many other feminist historians who use oral interviews, when evaluating interviews I have examined the "facts" of women's memories by joining their narratives with historical evidence provided in sources such as contemporary newspapers, census data, and government documents; at the same time I have considered the recollection process and pondered not only what women remember, but also taken into account who was involved in the interview, in what context recollection occurred, and how memories were conveyed.[45] These memories provide access to stories about labour market participation that indicate that gender should not be conceptualized as the sole and dominant identity in women's lives: if gender inequality barred women from formal or institutional power, it did not preclude access to privilege that was created and maintained by a confluence of racial, ethnic, gender, and class forces and expectations, which determined whether some women made their way to employment in the city's classrooms and hospitals, while others had no choice but to toil in its sweatshops, to clean houses, or to take piecework into their homes.

Job options?:
Domestic Service, Clerical Work, the Garment Industry, and Teaching

The Depression-era working women discussed here came from various racial, ethnic, family, community, and socio-economic backgrounds. Together they belong to a generation of young women who in many instances lost time and opportunities. They were more likely to delay marriage, abandon educational aspirations, and find themselves constrained by economic insecurity than any generation after them. During the Depression years my female participants were single, between the ages of 15 and 25, and, with the exception of 3 who chose not to marry, all of them ended their participation in the labour market as wage earners when they married or bore their first child.

In this time between schooling and marriage, their experiences as breadwinners had many similarities. Often characterized as dutiful daughters, these young

[44] Sangster, "Telling our stories."

[45] Detailed field notes recorded before, during, and after the interview that reflect upon the interview context and the differences and similarities which exist between the interviewer and participant in areas like culture, age, and education, are the best way to reflect upon the shared process of memory generation. See for further discussion on this approach: Sherna Berger Gluck and Daphne Patai, eds., *Women's Words: The Feminist Practice of Oral History* (New York 1991); Trevor Lummis, *Listening to History: the Authenticity of Oral Evidence* (London 1987); Robert Georges and Michael Owen Jones, *People Studying People: The Human Element in Fieldwork* (Berkeley and Los Angeles 1980); Roy Rosenzweig and David Thelen, *The Presence of The Past: Popular Uses of History in American Life* (New York 1998); Raphael Samuel and Paul Thompson, eds., *The Myths We Live By* (London 1990).

single women contributed all or part of their wages to their families.[46] They also worked in a city that, unlike nearby "blue collar" Hamilton, enjoyed greater economic security because of its large financial, civil, and service sector.[47] The interwar years saw record numbers of Torontonians without homes and livelihood, dependent on the government for relief, but the city's unemployment rate was slightly below the national average.[48] Toronto's diversified economy, which included plenty of light industries, suffered less than those economies dependent on one form of industry for stability, such as manufacturing, agriculture, or exports. And, jobs traditionally performed by women such as domestic service, clerical work, manufacturing, and teaching were generally sheltered by the economic stability of Toronto's secondary and tertiary sectors.

A few men (0.06 per cent in 1931) worked as domestic servants in Toronto but the occupation was, as it was before and after these years, overwhelmingly female during the Depression.[49] The category of personal service included jobs such as boarding house keepers, waitresses, and general cooks; in 1931, more than 50 per cent of the women in personal service were domestics even though domestic service was the least desirable occupation choice for most women wage-earners.[50] It

[46]The term dutiful daughter was frequently used during the Depression to describe the young women who had forgone their individual desires for marriage or schooling to help their families economically and socially.

[47]For more information on the economic development in these areas of the city see: J.M.S. Careless, *Toronto to 1918: An Illustrated History* (Toronto 1984); Craig Heron, *Working in Steel: Early Years in Canada, 1883-1935* (Toronto 1988).

[48]Toronto's unemployment rate was 16.7 per cent in 1931 compared to the national average of 18.87 per cent. Canada, Bureau of the Census, *Unemployment Vol. VI* (Ottawa 1931), 1,267. In general, the provinces that relied upon the wheat market suffered the most in the early years. As a result Saskatchewan was particularly vulnerable while Ontario was relatively more stable. Beside P.E.I., Ontario had the lowest percentage of people not at work. Canada, Census, *Monographs Vol. XIII* (Ottawa 1931), 243. Western families often relied on assistance from "the Good Will, the Salvation Army or relatives in Ontario." Barry Broadfoot, *Ten Lost Years, 1929-1939: Memories of Canadians Who Survived the Depression* (Toronto 1973), 281.

[49]Canada, Bureau of the Census, *Occupations and Industries Vol. VII* (Ottawa 1941), 1,106. There were 10,758 female and 741 male domestics noted in Toronto in 1931. Canada, Census, *Occupations and Industries Vol. VII* (Ottawa 1931), 236. I could find no other indication of these men in the historical record; however, one man who worked as a launderer during the Depression did write an editorial in the *Evening Telegram* which discusses his job loss in the "old-fashioned trade" of blacksmithing and his subsequent employment in an occupation for which his "wife showed [him] the fine points." He had been doing it for four months, quite "fanc[ied] hand laundering and figured he was "ready anytime to go into a contest against the best fancy work laundresses in the world." *Evening Telegram*, 23 July 1932.

[50]Canada, Bureau of the Census, *Occupations and Industries Vol. VII* (Ottawa 1941), 1,106. Varpu Lindström's work on Finnish domestics makes the important observation that not all women accepted domestic work as negative. Indeed, the Finnish women she studied worked

had the lowest pay and among the worst working conditions. Consequently, it was generally women who had no other options who took up these jobs, particularly (though by no means exclusively) married and immigrant women. As Mabel Duncan noted in our 2001 interview, "a lot of women went into housework because that was the only kind of work they could get if they were married."[51] This memory is consistent with the experiences of women in this study whose qualifications for employment were moot because of their marital status. Joyce Cahill and Margaret McLean recall how their mother was forced to work as a domestic after her husband lost his job. "She couldn't do anything. Our mother was not schooled, and, well, she couldn't have got a job then anyhow as a married woman" recalled Cahill. "No, good heavens!" exclaimed McLean. Their mother had no schooling and she was married, which significantly limited her employment options. What she did start to do "was clean offices and so she would go, she'd leave about three o'clock in the morning ... for two hours come back get us kids ready for school or whatever, then go again."[52]

Advertisements in Toronto's newspapers also indicate the importance of identity, including ethnic identity, to personal service occupations. Frequently, potential employers indicated an ethnic preference, as in "Girl, Polish preferred, for Domestic Help"; "Capable girl Russian or Polish preferred for general housework, no cooking, references, sleep out."[53] Similar ads appeared for German, Finnish and "Negro" women. Some advertisements emphasized religion: "Domestic Help Wanted: Christian girl for general housework, with knowledge of cooking $5 weekly."[54] Still others reflected the fact that certain ethnic groups had a reputation or otherwise fit the image of a domestic in people's minds. Less well-known is Claire Clarke's recollection that Americans living in Toronto requested black women for service as they were so closely associated with this occupation south of the border.[55]

collectively to maintain a positive image and effectively resisted representations of themselves and treatment at the hands of employers which cast them as domestic slaves. See Lindström, *Defiant Sisters*; "'I Won't Be a Slave!': Finnish Domestics in Canada, 1911-1930," in Franca Iacovetta with Paula Draper and Robert Ventresca, eds., *A Nation of Immigrants: Women, Workers, and Communities in Canadian History, 1840s-1960s* (Toronto 1998), 166-86.

[51]Mabel Duncan, interview by Katrina Srigley, November 2001.

[52]Margaret McLean and Joyce Cahill, joint interview by Katrina Srigley, February 2002.

[53]*Mail and Empire*, 1 January 1931; *Evening Telegram*, 29 January 1935.

[54]*Evening Telegram*, 29 January 1935.

[55]Immigration policy has supported this association between ethnicity and domestic service. Though slowed to a trickle during the Depression years, immigration as a domestic was one of the few ways that single non-professional, particularly non-white, women gained entry to Canada. See for further discussion: Marilyn Barber, *Immigrant Domestic Servants in Canada*, Canadian Historical Association pamphlet, 1991; Barbara Roberts, *Whence They Came: Deportation from Canada, 1900-1935* (Ottawa 1988); Makeda Silvera, *Silenced* (Toronto 1989).

Depending on their class position, people, including women, experienced and recalled domestic service differently. Diana MacFeeters' family had household help during the Depression. "I remember," she said, that "my mother would interview them and they were live in. Their magnificent pay was $25 a month," but she quickly added, "they got a uniform."[56] When asked about the general feeling that conditions were poor for domestics MacFeeters disagreed: "You got all your food and lodging. You didn't have any other expenses ... unless you were sending money home to wherever you come from."[57] As historians have documented, many women were sending money home to family members, or supporting their own family who lived elsewhere in the city. That was true of Anne Hinsta, who arrived in Toronto from Finland in 1929 and worked at the Royal York and the Prince George Hotels. In an interview conducted for labour historian Wayne Roberts in the 1980s, she described her position: "I was a chamber maid and pay was small, but we used to get tips."[58] After her marriage in 1930 she stopped working, but when her husband lost his job in 1932 she hit the pavement looking for work. Her memory of that experience is noteworthy.

> They didn't have much work ... well they didn't have work at all ... we went on welfare ... city welfare, well I could not stand that. I started looking for a domestic job and I used to sit for days and days in the unemployment office. The ladies used to come and see you there if they want to pick you.[59]

Eventually, a woman from Forest Hill, a wealthy Toronto neighbourhood, hired both Hinsta and her husband but not before she asked "are you honest?" As Hinsta remembered "that hurt my feelings and I said if there is anything we guarantee it is that we are honest." She offered them employment for $35 a month; however, their two-year-old son Roy was not welcome. With few employment options they accepted the job and boarded their son for $25 a month elsewhere in the city.[60]

The exploitation experienced by people like the Hinstas was not uncommon. However, economic disenfranchisement did not mean domestic servants accepted their work conditions without comment. They voiced their discontent in local newspapers. One critical domestic who wrote to the *Evening Telegram* compared her situation to slavery:

[56]Ron and Diana MacFeeters, interview by Katrina Srigley, March 2002.

[57]MacFeeters, interview.

[58]Anne Hinsta, interview, *Wayne Roberts Collection,* Archives of Ontario (OA).

[59]Hinsta, interview.

[60]Hinsta does not indicate where she boarded her son Roy; however, she does say that boarding was common because so many Finnish women were domestics and Finnish men were off working in the bush. Hinsta, interview.

> The way domestics are treated in Toronto is shameful. My opinion is that free advertisements make it easier for people to exploit us. In most places there is work a plenty and skimmed milk, and the wage so small as to be not worth mentioning ... Cannot somebody act to cause an improvement? It's like buying and selling human beings.[61]

Another woman, after seeing a cartoon published in the same newspaper depicting "Mrs. Toronto" as a kind employer willing to pay $20 for a maid but unable to find any willing takers, was outraged by what she saw as an insulting misrepresentation. She wrote:

> I have answered every single advertisement for a housekeeper which appeared in the last nine months and the most I have been offered is 10 per month. The great majority offered me only a good home and perhaps a little pocket money. If I could get a pail of tar and some feathers I might be able to get along on this. How can anyone live decently on such wages?[62]

Connie Lancaster has vivid memories of the difficulties of domestic service. Lancaster immigrated to Canada as a foster child on a movement handled by the Salvation Army. But soon after arriving on her placement as a farm helper, she fled and found a job as a domestic in Toronto. Since childhood she had hoped to be a nurse but these opportunities were not open, at least initially, to an uneducated immigrant girl. In our 2002 interview, she shared with me her story of those years: "when I was eighteen my options were very limited, because of lack of education and I had no family to fall back on. I was homeless if I didn't make one, so I started as a domestic."[63] But the awful work conditions meant she did not keep this job for very long. "It was a job, I had an awful time because I didn't know electricity when I came to the city ... I got $25 a month for keeping a 14 room house clean." Although the literature on English immigrant women in Canada has said much about this sort of training, Lancaster received no training in the operation of household appliances. The first time she lit the stove she turned on the gas, went to find a match and returned several minutes later. The subsequent explosion did not endear her to her employers. "I lost my hair, my eyebrows and the dust off the floor. I went up and the family said: You could have blown us up! But nobody told me."[64] She soon found a job at another home in Toronto.

Luckily for Lancaster the Depression increased rather than decreased the middle-class demand for the household labour of certain groups of women, including white British-born ones. She found another job quickly. A *Chatelaine* journalist who covered this situation in a 1932 article marveled that,

[61] *Evening Telegram*, 30 April 1935.
[62] *Evening Telegram*, 23 April 1935. The cartoon was published in the *Evening Telegram* on 18 April 1935.
[63] Connie Lancaster, interview by Katrina Srigley, (2001). Eventually Lancaster did become a nurse with the Salvation Army. She worked in Toronto at the Grace Hospital.
[64] Lancaster, interview.

> despite unemployment figures which have long passed the astonishing stage and almost leave one stupefied, superintendents of women's employment bureaus report that domestic service is the one class of job for which vacancies always outnumber suitable applicants.[65]

Indeed, as the cost of living decreased more middle-class households could afford domestic help. Ron MacFeeters, a man from a middle-class Toronto family, remembers "that a lot of small, really small two and three bedroom houses ... had a funny little room off the kitchen called the maids room. It would have a sink in it and room for a bed and I guess a chest of draws."[66] Higher demand for domestics did not ease the job search of all women. The same *Chatelaine* writer noted that vacancies outnumbered "suitable applicants." Mrs. Hinsta and others certainly remembered the lack of jobs. At the time, some domestics noted the exploitation of the situation with anger. "Has it ever occurred to you, or anyone else," she wrote, "that a great number of Toronto's citizens (the average working class) who have not felt the 'pinch' of depression as others have, are taking a mean advantage of the present state of affairs."[67] When they had the option, many women protested by refusing to take domestic jobs, irrespective of demand.

As a consequence of vacancies and a perceived shortage of acceptable workers, an interesting tension emerged in the press between domestics who complained about working conditions and housewives who claimed that working-class women were shunning such jobs for a languid life on relief. In one editorial signed "ONE OF THOSE MOTHERS" a self-identified homemaker in search of a domestic insisted that authorities compel working-class women to take on this job. Otherwise, "[h]ow in the world can they succeed" in their role as household managers "when so many homes are looking for help?"[68] She claimed to be having a hard time finding a reliable girl despite the fact that she offered "$25 a month ... a good home, the best food, served at the same time the family [was] served, almost every night out, in addition to the regular full afternoon off each week and almost every Sunday afternoon [off]."[69] Not all people agreed with Toronto's housewives. Stories of poor wages, bad working conditions, and labour shortages did capture the attention of some reformers. In 1932 Constance Templeton of *Chatelaine* magazine wrote an article which proposed that if the home "were run on more businesslike lines, more women of the right type would be attracted to it...."[70] Who was the right "type" of woman? Well, Hudson noted, unlike in Europe where wealthy houses require large

[65] Constance Templeton, "Can Domestic Service Be Run on a Business Basis?" *Chatelaine*, December 1932, 17.
[66] MacFeeters, interview.
[67] *Evening Telegram*, 29 August 1932.
[68] *Evening Telegram*, 7 February 1935.
[69] *Evening Telegram*, 7 February 1935.
[70] Constance Templeton, "Can Domestic Service Be Run on a Business Basis?" *Chatelaine*, December 1932, 17.

staffs most Canadian houses only require a "cook general or houseworker."[71] But these workers had to be trained, indeed certified, and given a regular routine much like a stenographer. That way, Canadian housewives would get trained girls who knew what to expect at their workplace. Not surprisingly, these plans were never carried out, and domestic service remained a ghetto for married women, immigrants, and non-Anglo women.[72]

In certain sectors of the economy, such as office work, wages were more substantial and work conditions more favourable. Clerical workers in the city's financial sector and in the offices of industry did not experience widespread slow downs or job loss. And, as Graham Lowe's research demonstrates, the feminization of clerical occupations was well under way by the 1930s.[73] What had been a male occupation until the early 20th century became, with the expansion of the office and the invention of the typewriter, a space occupied by increasing numbers of women. Despite such feminization clear divisions between men's and women's jobs continued within offices. For instance, in 1931 men occupied more than twice as many accounting positions as women did in Toronto offices, while 93 per cent of stenographers were women.[74] In contrast to men who were more often lifetime breadwinners, women in clerical work, as in other occupations, earned wages at a particular stage in their life. Certainly, this was true for the overwhelming majority of clerical workers in this study; after completing the necessary schooling, they worked only until marriage. Of those who worked in offices, 71 per cent left work when they married, while approximately 29 per cent did not marry or continued to

[71]Constance Templeton, "Can Domestic Service Be Run on a Business Basis?" *Chatelaine*, December 1932, 17.

[72]In New York during the 1930s, training schools were organized for domestics by community associations like the Urban League and funded by the federal government. The School of Household Work was one of the better-known schools. Ultimately, Brenda Clegg concludes, despite their innovation such schools did little if anything to improve the working conditions of black domestics in New York during the Depression. Brenda Clegg, "Black Female Domestics During the Great Depression in New York City, 1930-1940," Ph.D. thesis, University of Michigan, 1983, 137.

[73]Graham Lowe, *Women in the Administrative Revolution: the Feminization of Clerical Work* (Toronto 1987). For a discussion of the American context see Margery Davies, *Women's Place is at the Typewriter: Office Work and Office Workers, 1870-1982* (Philadelphia 1982).

[74]Of the people employed as accountants and bookkeepers in Toronto in 1931, 3,124 were women and 9,520 were men. In 1941 little had changed. Men held 10,124 of the positions and women occupied 4,124 of them. In stenography there was a similar pattern. In 1931, 10,843 stenographers were women and 758 were men. In 1941, women and men held 12,888 and 659 positions respectively. Canada, Bureau of the Census, *Occupations and Industries Vol. VII* (Ottawa 1941), 1,106.

work after marriage.[75] Census statistics indicated that this situation was typical for the labour market as a whole: in 1931 four out of five female wage-earners were single.[76] The way in which Mildred Johnson remembers why women did not work after marriage in those years — "I don't think it entered their heads. I know women who had to work, but you see in those days we hadn't got to the place where women were tired of their homes" — does not, of course, speak to those married women who did work for pay. But her memories that working women were young and single women is borne out by statistics: the 1931 census also indicates that close to 64 per cent of working women in Toronto were between the ages of 18 and 34.[77] Moreover, it was common practice, and in some offices required, for women to leave work when they married. Matrimony meant the financial support of a husband but it also initiated greater household and family responsibilities. This "ideal" did not hold for jobs like domestic service, but in clerical occupations marital status affected access to employment, as did other sites of identity such as race.

Racist hiring practices and the implicit race-designations for employment and employability are well captured by the stories shared by Claire Clarke and Violet Blackman. These Canadian women of Caribbean descent were single and in their late teens and early twenties during the Depression. They lived in a city, which, unlike New York, had a tiny black community that included three churches, Mr. George's grocery store, mutual benefit and social organizations like the United Negro Improvement Association (UNIA), the Home Service Association and the Eureka Club, one medical doctor, Dr White, and two lawyers, the most well-known being B.J. Spencer Pitt.[78] Toronto's black neighbourhoods were viable communities but small black businesses and workplaces could not provide the women in their community with a range of jobs, or even a sufficient number of even very low-paying ones. In this regard, white ethnic women had access to more jobs within their (larger) immigrant or ethnic communities than was the case for black women

[75]Fourteen women in this study were clerical workers. Ten left their job when they married. Two did not marry and two continued to work after marriage. Neither of these women found this to be exceptional, though Helen Campbell did explain that she was a *private* secretary. She obviously felt this was an important factor in legitimizing her position as a married office worker.

[76]The percentage of married women in the workforce increased from 2 per cent in 1921 to nearly 4 per cent in 1931. Canada, Bureau of the Census, *Occupations and Industries Vol. VII* (Ottawa 1931), 37.

[77]Mildred Johnson, interview by Katrina Srigley, February 2002. Canada, Bureau of the Census, *Occupations and Industries Vol. VII,* (Ottawa 1931), 226.

[78]Spencer Pitt was a well-known lawyer and important role model for young West Indian and African Canadian women and men during this time. Claire Clarke, interview; J.E. Clarke, interview, (Multicultural History Society (MHS), BLA-5122-CLA) 1 August 1978. See also Dawn Moore, *Who's Who in Black Canada* (Toronto 2002), 81. The 1931 census suggests that there were 1344 people in Toronto's "negro" community. *Census*, Volume IV (Ottawa 1931), 912.

like Clarke and Blackman. As a result, they were compelled to search for jobs in mainstream white society where plenty of employers and businesses did not see black women as viable workers.[79]

Such views did not stop Claire Clarke from finishing her schooling, but after graduating she could not find a job that required her skills in stenography and typing. "I sent in applications, résumés and got one, I got a very nice response from ACME and I was so happy they were very pleased with my résumé and they invited me for an interview so I went for the interview but of course when they saw me...."[80] In her effort to find work Claire also went to visit an influential black professional man and remembered being snubbed. Her recollection also speaks to the tensions among blacks in a white-dominated world in which light or dark skin African Canadians could lead considerably different lives. With renewed anger, Claire shared the incident with me: "Well you might say he was a light coloured. He was married to a white so naturally he didn't have too much attachment to the black community. But he gave me an interview and he had just to tell me the white girls won't work with you. I got this from him!"[81]

Violet Blackman also had a clear sense of why she could not find employment in 1930s Toronto. Blackman, who had come to Toronto from Jamaica as a twenty year old in 1920, worked as a domestic during the Depression. When asked about employment options in the city, she responded with indignation and exasperation in her voice: "YOU COULDN'T GET office work and factory and hospital work and things like that you couldn't because they would not give you the job ... because of the colour of your skin because you were black you couldn't the only thing that you could get was a domestic."[82] Similarly, Halifax-born Isobel Bailey's hopes of becoming a nutritionist in Toronto were dashed; her memories capture her realization that her race would deny her access to the right courses at the city's schools. Instead, she worked as a domestic and eventually in a silk factory.[83] Most African and West Indian Canadians recall racial discrimination as subtle: Joseph Clarke recalled in a 1978 interview that it "got under your skin and you didn't know what the hell was irritating you," except for when it came to employment.[84] "It was the fun-

[79]Violet Blackman, interview, (MHS, BLA-6894-BLA); Daniel Braithwaite, (MHS, BLA - 5124 - BRA, BLA - 7986 - BRA); Rella Braithwaite, interview, (MHS, BLA - 7987 - BRA); Claire Clarke, interview; J.E. Clark, interview, (MHS, BLA - 5122 - CLA); Don Moore, *An Autobiography* (Toronto 1985).

[80]Claire Clarke, interview.

[81]For Canadian discussions of such tensions see Brand, *No Burden to Carry;* Shadd and Jones, eds., *Talking About Identity.*

[82]Blackman, interview. (I have added capitalization to reflect the tone of Blackman's voice). Brand, *No Burden to Carry,* 37-8.

[83]Isobel Bailey, interview, (MHS, BLA - 09686 - BAI)

[84]J.E. Clarke, interview. During the Depression, there were divisions in the black community between Canadians and immigrants from America and the West Indies. The Canadians tended to be more assimilated with the WASP community, have greater economic security

niest thing," Claire Clarke muses about blacks and whites in Depression Toronto, "we mingled together played together but we wouldn't work together at the time."[85]

Clarke also fit the profile of a "dutiful daughter." Moreover, she also possessed important signifiers of middle-class status in Toronto: she had a secondary education, her family owned their own home, and she and her sister took music lessons. But gender and class identities that she shared with white middle-class women did not for her translate into the same employment opportunities. For Clarke, as for Blackman and Bailey, race trumped education and marital status when she sought training and employment in Toronto's schools and workplaces.[86] These women's situation, and their memories of those years, stands in contrast to the access that young single women from similar class and educational backgrounds had to better paying clerical jobs.

Mildred Johnson and Thelma Plunkett, who were single Canadian women of Scottish and English descent, were in their late teens when they landed office jobs in the city. While Johnson chose not to marry and remained in an office throughout her working life, Thelma Plunkett left clerical work when she married. During our 2001 interview, Johnson, sitting tall and austere, her shoe heel rubbing methodically against her couch, remembered how she left school at eighteen to attend Shaw's Business school to earn the requisite training in stenography and typing:

> I didn't go right through. I only went to the fourth form Junior Matriculation and then father asked me what I was going to do, and I said I guess I'll go and work in an office. So I went to Shaw's business college, and I got a good training there in business....[87]

Access to clerical work depended upon education. There were differences in requirements (a file clerk required less education than a stenographer, for example), but most offices required training in commercial courses offered at high schools and private business schools around Toronto. The hierarchies within clerical work reflected skill level: secretaries who were expected to be stenographers and typists with a firm grasp of shorthand occupied the highest ranks, while clerks with filing responsibilities rounded out the bottom. The women themselves were well aware of these divisions. In discussing her employment as a secretary, Johnson, who is otherwise of humble demeanor and soft-spoken, confidently assured me "though I don't consider myself a secretary, I was a darn good typist if I do say so myself."[88]

and were often disparaging of, in particular, the West Indians. Claire Clarke, interview; Keith S. Henry, *Black Politics in Toronto since World War I* (Toronto 1981), 6; Harry Gairey, *A Black Man's Toronto, 1914-1980*, ed. Donna Hill, (Toronto 1981), 14.

[85]Claire Clarke, interview. Clarke continues to be a source of information and insight.

[86]For more on race and access to theatres see Backhouse, *Colour Coded.*

[87]Johnson, interview.

[88]Johnson, interview.

Among the women in this study, the most popular school in Toronto for such courses was Shaw's business school, which offered a range of courses and had locations all over the city. Their advertisements appeared regularly in the city's newspapers but, of course, not all women could take advantage of their offerings. This type of commercial training cost money in the form of wages, tuition, and books. Margaret McLean, and others, tell the story of education limited by the economic constraints of family responsibilities.[89] Malvern Collegiate, a school offering commercial courses, was minutes from their home, but the Tapp family could not afford the cost of books for sisters Ivy Phillips and Marg McLean. Phillips spoke movingly about her disappointment and envy:

> well I felt envious of the girls that went to Malvern and you'd see them the way they were dressed that bothered me. I hated going down that time of the morning and I had to pass all the girls all the kids going to Malvern ... I really HATED it. That's something that bothered me that I couldn't go on to high school.[90]

The Tapp sisters went to Danforth Technical High school which was located further away, but as it turned out, they could not remain there either. In sharing this story with me McLean began by saying "You speak of shame." She continued:

> Ivy, my sister, and I we wanted to go to Danforth Tech, a high school. Ivy loved sewing. But, eventually mother said I can't buy your books so you will have to go and tell the principal that you are on relief. Well Ivy and I stood outside the principal's office and we couldn't go in. We just couldn't go in. And we went home and told mother and she said, "I'm sorry."[91]

That working-class women were acutely aware that family difficulties hurt their chances of earning the clerical training that would have given them access to better paid jobs is born out not only by the stories that women shared with me but by their children, who grew with their parents' Depression tales. Speaking of his mother, Margaret, and aunt, Gladys Thompson, Ian Radforth understood well that these sisters had thought of extra education "as something they couldn't afford to do."[92] It was only after her marriage failed in the 1940s that Thompson eventually "learned the superior skills" of shorthand and typing to become a secretary, but to do so she had to keep her clerking job while taking "up-grading" courses at night and live cheaply in a rented room. During the Depression, the majority of young women and men did not finish high school let alone complete a university degree or a business school diploma. In 1935, a help wanted ad in the *Evening Telegram* requested a "stenographer and a dictaphone operator for [a] commercial office," stipulating

[89] McLean and Cahill, interview.
[90] Ivy Phillips, interview by Katrina Srigley, March 2002.
[91] McLean and Cahill, interview.
[92] Ian Radforth, interview by Katrina Srigley, December 2003.

that those without "sufficient education" need not apply.[93] Access to commercial education had an impact on job options, restricting access to employment in clerical occupations and to other jobs within the field.

Only certain women could take advantage of the necessary schooling for an office job, but far more women than men enrolled in business schools. Despite high rates of male unemployment, business courses continued to fill with young women receiving training in stenography, accounting, and typing. In fact, women occupied twice as many positions in business schools as men in 1930. In private business and commercial schools there were 3,777 women and 1,183 men enrolled in Toronto in 1930. In 1933, these numbers had dropped substantially; however, women still occupied well over two-thirds of the positions: 1,351 women and 540 men.[94] When asked about competing with men for jobs, Margaret McLean, who worked as a factory worker during the Depression responded: "GOODNESS no! Women were nothing until the war came!" Joyce Cahill concurred: "Yes, if a woman did it, then it was a job men wouldn't do." Similarly, census analysts explained the greater than 10 per cent difference in female and male unemployment rates by pointing to "the dissimilarity in the types of male and female employment."[95]

The ironies of this disparity between male unemployment and female employment did not go unnoticed by Toronto's citizens. In the letter-to-the-editor section of Toronto's *Evening Telegram* a correspondent noted, " that if fifteen [were] waiting at a car stop to board the car twelve [would] be well dressed girls, presumably office girls. Girls [were] in large numbers in offices. A large office looks more like a high-class school for stylish young ladies than a business office."[96] THE GOAT, the letter writer who had inspired this response, had written that he believed "that many women, now employed in various vocations should not hold these positions in the face of so much unemployment," but he was concerned that "it might be a difficult matter to find a male sufficiently qualified to take the places."[97] In Toronto's offices during the 1930s men and women sat behind desks. They filed, typed, and tabulated. At times, their close proximity caused concern among those who feared mixing would lead to immorality or that the presence of so many working women signaled an end to male breadwinning, but, in fact, men and women usually worked in different jobs. And notwithstanding the tough economic times, men were unwilling or ineligible for many positions in the city's offices.

[93] *Evening Telegram*, 29 January 1935.
[94] Canada, Dominion Bureau of Statistics, *Annual Survey of Education* (Ottawa 1930), 127; Canada, Dominion Bureau of Statistics, *Annual Survey of Education* (Ottawa 1933), 115. In 1937 there were seventeen different locations offering business courses in Toronto. The business school with the most schools around the city was Shaw's. Canada, Dominion Bureau of Statistics, *Annual Survey of Education* (Ottawa 1936), 158-9.
[95] Canada, Bureau of the Census *Monographs Vol. XIII* (Ottawa 1931), 235-9.
[96] *Evening Telegram*, 15 January 1932.
[97] *Evening Telegram*, 12 January 1932.

After completing her schooling at Shaw's, Mildred Johnson hoped to find a job. "For the first year I had a temporary [job] ... at the Faculty of Applied Science in the office there," she recalled, "but that only lasted till the end of June, the end of the university term proper." After that she noted with obvious disappointment, "I tried to get a job and I couldn't get a job for love nor money."[98] Then came a call from Shaw's, who contacted her, "because I was an Anglican you see they felt that I might apply for the job at the Anglican diocese on Jarvis."[99] In recalling her interview Johnson reminisced:

> [The Bishop] wasn't in a good humour because the hospital in Iqaluit had just gone up in flames ... he scared me out of my wits, anyway I came home and I said to my stepmother, I said, "oh I do like the girl in the office, but goodness I don't know about the bishop; but they're going to phone me around 5:30 tonight ..."And the phone rang, 'could I come in in the morning.' COULD I COME in in the morning! I was there before anybody (laughter).[100]

Landing a clerical position was an important economic and social achievement for young women in the context of the Depression. Clerical work, though hardly a ticket to prosperity, did give workers a degree of economic stability. In keeping with the minimum wage of $12.50 per week, Johnson's starting salary was $50 a month. This was significantly more than what men who frequented relief lines, women working as domestics, or doing piecework received. The latter earned as little as $3.80 per week.[101] Johnson shared with me an early story about the job that she would keep for 47 years: "As soon as I got my first cheque — we were paid monthly — I always paid board at home. Girls did in those days. I think I paid about five dollars a week and then as time went on and the salary increased, I increased it each time." A daughters' wage gave families greater financial security. Johnson too was a dutiful daughter but unlike her Caribbean-Canadian counterparts, her higher wages meant that she could give more to her family.

That clerical work might offer better conditions than domestic service or a garment shop does not mean all white-collar workers had good working conditions. Sitting on her sofa, surrounded by the objects of her daily life — cane, walker, pills, tissues, books, pens, crossword puzzle, water glass — Thelma Plunkett vividly remembered her job at H. Brown Silk Company when she was nineteen: "I worked there for five years and oh it was terrible the hours we had to put in ... I know one week I counted up and I had put in seventy-two hours!" She left her job as an invoice clerk, and paid eight dollars a week on the advice of her doctor after toxic dye

[98] Johnson, interview.
[99] Johnson, interview.
[100] Johnson, interview.
[101] In both 1931 and 1941 men earned, on average, 16 - 20 per cent more per year than women. Lowe, *Women in the Administrative Revolution,* 145; Canada, Royal Commission on Price Spreads, *Minutes of Proceedings and Evidence* 16 January 1935, 4,410.

fumes had caused her to faint.[102] However, she soon found another job at Aluminum Goods on York Street in Toronto. Her story of the job interview effectively conveys the willingness of women to take advantage of opportunities to land better-paying positions.

> When I went in there was quite a group of people, and I thought, oh, I will never get the position ... but anyhow when I went in and was interviewed I told them the different machines that I could use and, but of course there weren't anything like computers then but there were contometers ... and of course when he asked me I had to say that I didn't know how to use one ... so anyway at the end of the interview he said "Would you go to contometer school in the evening if we sent you and paid for it?" So I said OH YES![103]

In a time of relative job scarcity, Thelma Plunkett transferred jobs, albeit unpleasant ones, with ease. Although she lacked the necessary "contometer"[104] skills, Plunkett acquired the job at Aluminum Goods and the company gave her money to attend a course in the evenings. She accepted the job enthusiastically because, as she commented, "I was lucky to have a job." Indeed, Johnson and Plunkett were fortunate. Their access to education, their class, and their marital status made them suitable clerical workers. Still, as the experiences of women such as Claire Clarke clearly indicate, these social variables did not ensure employment across the racial divide; race also played a central role even if white women did not clearly articulate it in their memories of this time. In the Depression context, white femininity established racial privilege even as it created some gender disadvantages. It did not stand alone in creating the job market privilege of women such as Johnson and Plunkett, nor was it entirely Anglo-Protestant in construction. For instance, census analysts noted a significant number of Jewish and Italian women among clerical workers in the manufacturing industry in Toronto through the 1930s; their ethnicity was not as much of a liability as the blackness of Caribbean-Canadian women. Also, these women most likely would have been Canadian-born Jewish and Italian Canadians who did not confront the same language barriers as their parents. The presence of non-Anglo but nonetheless white ethnic women in the clerical industry points to the fluidity of employment boundaries and the complicated whiteness which bestowed

[102]Her doctor told her she had better leave "or they would be carrying her out of there." Thelma Plunkett, interview by Katrina Srigley, November 1997. For more on the unhealthy conditions of women workers in Toronto see Catherine Macleod, "Women in Production: The Toronto Dressmakers' Strike of 1931," in Linda Kealey, ed., *Women at Work: Ontario, 1850-1930* (Toronto 1974), 316-7.

[103]Plunkett, interview.

[104]A contometer is similar to a calculator. It is interesting that companies were willing to pay for their employees to attend school in a time of hardship. This points to the fact that Mrs. Plunkett was among the "desirable workers." Norma Langley also reported that her company promoted her when she finished night schooling. Norma Langley, interview by Katrina Srigley, October 1997.

privilege in the form of employment access.[105] Whiteness could also trump religious identities and the disadvantages of being Catholic and Jewish in Toronto.

Working in an industry that had long exploited its workers, female garment workers experienced greater vulnerability and insecurity than did clerical workers. As Henry Steven's 1934 Royal Commission on Price Spreads highlights, the textile industry, which employed 65 per cent of women in manufacturing in 1931, was an exploitative environment for wage-earners in the 1930s.[106] Characterized by stiff economic competition and instability, workers dealt with chronically low wages, poor working conditions, and deskilling. In the dry, blunt words of the Royal Commission, "the worker in the clothing industry can expect neither comfort nor security; in many cases he [sic] can indeed expect only hopeless poverty."[107] Despite efforts to unionize garment workers during the interwar years, the position of a labourer in the needle trades remained precarious. As Mercedes Steedman well documents, female garment workers were particularly vulnerable. Men maintained some control over the labour process because of their skilled positions as "cutters and trimmers, machine operators, finishers and pressers."[108] But, by the 1930s, women occupied very few skilled positions. Ready-made garments and piecework on sewing machines had replaced intricate hand sewing. In these low-paid positions, women were particularly vulnerable to mechanization and speed-ups.

Weak government regulations and the economic instability of the Depression worsened conditions. Several of the largest employers of women in Toronto increased hours and production requirements while simultaneously decreasing wages.[109] Timothy Eaton Company's exploitative policies received considerable publicity because of the Royal Commission. In order to compensate for the economic decline of the 1930s, Eaton's had decreased wages and increased production requirements so that by 1933, a dressmaker who had earned $3.60 a dozen for her work on voile dresses in the late 1920s now made only $1.75 for the same work. As

[105]Of the 17,457 teachers in Ontario in 1931, 14,394 were of British origin, 1,728 were French, 54 were Jewish, 46 were Italian, 14 were Indian [sic], and 12 were Asiatic. Canada, Bureau of the Census, *Occupations and Industries Vol. VII* (Ottawa 1941), 392-3.

[106]In manufacturing, 8,703 of 13,352 women worked in the textile industry. Canada, Bureau of the Census, *Occupations and Industries Vol. VII* (Ottawa 1931), 227-8.

[107]Canada, Royal Commission on Price Spreads, *Report on Findings*, 119.

[108]Mercedes Steedman, "Skill and Gender in the Canadian Clothing Industry, 1890-1940," in Ian Radforth and Laurel Sefton MacDowell, eds., *Canadian Working Class History: Selected Readings* (Toronto 2000), 453. Also see Mercedes Steedman, *Angels of the Workplace: Women and the Construction of Gender Relations in the Canadian Clothing Industry, 1890-1940* (Toronto 1997).

[109]Canada, Royal Commission on Price Spreads, *Evidence of Special Committee*, 28 February 1934, 129-30.

Mrs. Annie Wells testified, workers were being "badgered, harassed," and threatened with unemployment if they did not reach the expected production quota.[110]

Women workers faced specific barriers in their employment: vulnerable positions on the shop floor, male centered unions, not to mention the masculinist culture of the labour movement, and the added burden of traditional household responsibilities. The following memories underscore how religion, ethnicity, and class intersected in these factories. As Ruth Frager has extensively documented, the garment trade employed large numbers of immigrant women, particularly those who were Jewish. During the Depression, the Kensington Market area, situated on the border of Toronto's Spadina Avenue garment district, was the nucleus of this immigrant and working-class Jewish neighbourhood.[111] Here Yiddish was often the language of choice and all became quiet as the sun set on Shabbat. Many women, married and single, helped support their families; mothers haggled in the marketplace to stretch limited budgets, daughters and some wives too, worked in the ready-made clothing industry.

Toronto's Jewish women workers included women like Rose Edelist, who arrived on Baldwin Street in Kensington Market from Poland in 1928. During the Depression, she worked for several companies, each time changing jobs when conditions or wages worsened. She married in 1932 but continued to work until her daughter was born in 1935. The garment industry, along with jobs like domestic service, employed married women. When asked whether her marital status had forced her to abandon her job, Edelist stressed instead childcare responsibilities. "Well, who was going to look after my child?" she asked rhetorically in our 2002 interview.[112] Unable to afford childcare and without a large community of ex-

[110]Canada, Royal Commission on Price Spreads, *Evidence of Royal Commission*, 16, 17, 22 Jan 1935, 4,410, 4,462, 4,650; Royal Commission on Price Spreads, "Garment Industry: The Speed-Up at Eaton's," in Irving Abella and David Miller, eds., *The Canadian Worker in the Twentieth Century* (Toronto 1978), 185-93. By 1935 some women were earning as little as $6.00 to $7.00 a week despite the fact that $12.50 was the established minimum wage. The Minister of Trade and Finance Henry Stevens was forced to resign in October 1934 for exposing the exploitative practices of big business.

[111]There were approximately 45,305 Jewish people in Toronto in 1931. Canada, Bureau of the Census, *Cross-Classifications Vol. IV* (Ottawa 1931), 912. For more on Jewish women's experiences see Paula Draper and Janice B. Karlinsky, "Abraham's Daughters: Women, Charity and Power in the Canadian Jewish Community," in Franca Iacovetta, Paula Draper and Robert Ventresca, eds., *A Nation of Immigrants: Women, Workers, and Communities in Canadian History, 1840s-1960s* (Toronto 1998), 186-201; Frager, *Sweatshop Strife*.

[112]Rose Edelist, interview by Katrina Srigley, January 2002. This point was echoed by Mrs. R. Ducove, when asked why she stopped working after her first child was born. Mrs. R. Ducove, interview, (MHS, JEW - 1754 - DUC, 1977). Some women did not have a large family group to rely on for childcare and this, rather than cost, affected their employment choices. For Rose Edelist, it was a matter of affordability. Her immediate family, mother, father, and siblings all lived in Toronto.

tended family, Edelist abandoned the garment trade and breadwinning until her husband opened a delicatessen on College Street. In this situation, Edelist's wage-earning options depended where she worked and the cost and responsibility of childcare. Her story also reminds us that many women worked in small, family businesses that were more often seen as the husband's business. Nonetheless, Edelist's breadwinning experiences differed from those of single women who worked as teachers and nurses, as well as from those of middle and upper-class Jewish women who certainly faced discrimination in an Anglo-Protestant city, but did have greater economic security.[113] Some women, both Jewish and non-Jewish, could avoid the garment industry and find employment in other areas of Toronto's labour market. In the early 1930s, Edelist worked at the Walman Sportswear Company. Here she joined a garment workers union.[114] As her story shows, she still has vivid memories of the strike that her union called in 1931:

> The union wanted to have organized union shops. And then they called a strike and we had to leave. All my life I will never forget this strike. It was so terrible that the police protected the shops, and they treated the workers like garbage. It was so horrible. I tell you, I remember how they came so close by with the horses. The picketers they treated terrible. They protected the strikebreakers. So you know even [if] you didn't believe in unions ... you believed in unions when you saw what was doing [sic].[115]

When asked whether there was anyone who did not join the union, Edelist answered, "the gentile girls didn't join because they were happy with their employment situation. They were in a shop that men worked so they made decent wages."[116] Edelist insisted that she had no intention of being a scab. As Frager's work makes clear, the shared ethnicity and class exploitation of many of Toronto's Jewish garment workers, and a shared history of social activism and of anti-Semitism, shaped their union involvement. Edelist's memories also suggest

[113]There were several ways in which the immigrant working-class Jewish community was separated from the middle and upper class Jewish community in Toronto. Middle and upper class Jews may have shopped in the Kensington Market area, but they did not live there. The longer-established Holy Blossom synagogue had both Saturday and Sunday services and was attended by the older Jewish community. Rabbi Eisendrath, who presided over Holy Blossom for part of the 1930s, had a radio spot on a Toronto station and was often invited to speak at city functions. The Rabbis from synagogues around the Kensington Market did not seem to enjoy such acceptance or popularity. This separation may also have been related to country of origin and religious sect, such as the division between Chasidic Jews and other sects of Judaism.

[114]I presume it was the ILGWU, but she did not specify.

[115]Edelist, interview. For more on such strikes see Catherine MacLeod, "Women in Production: The Toronto Dressmakers' Strike of 1931," in J. Acton et al., eds., *Women at Work: Ontario, 1850-1930* (Toronto 1974), 309-29.

[116]Edelist, interview.

that while an activist heritage was certainly important, gentile women enjoyed access to jobs, which, in turn, gave them economic stability. They enjoyed the "privilege" to reject unionization, if they wished, or, to move jobs rather than stay and fight.[117]

By the 1930s, Toronto's Italian population, though by no means comparable to its post-World War II size, was the third largest ethnic group in the city: they numbered roughly 13,000 people.[118] During the early 20th century, a group of primarily sojourning men gradually became a settlement of Italian families: husbands, wives, children, and grandparents with a communal infrastructure replete with three parishes, grocery stores, and mutual aid societies.[119] Like Jewish women, Italian women frequently worked in the garment industry.[120] Mrs. Bassi emigrated from Italy's north-eastern Friuli region to Toronto after World War I. Many wage-earning Italian women took in piecework, but Mrs. Bassi found a job in the garment district on Spadina finishing men's suits.[121] There she encountered "English women or Canadian women" who took advantage of her language difficulties by blaming any faulty workmanship on "the immigrant." To resist this treatment, Mrs. Bassi drew upon the language skills of her husband and children; the story that her daughter, Evelina Bassi, shared with her interviewer also confirms the impressive resourcefulness of immigrant women who had so little to work with.

> She came home one night, and said "I want you to tell me how to say a couple of words" 'That's not my job.' So she wrote it on a piece of paper, 'That's not my job.' So the next day

[117]See Ruth A. Frager, "Class, Ethnicity, and Gender in the Eaton Strikes of 1912 and 1934," in Franca Iacovetta and Mariona Valverde eds., *Gender Conflicts: New Essays in Women's History* (Toronto 1992); Frager, *Sweatshop Strife.*

[118]Canada, Bureau of the Census *Cross-Classifications Vol. IV* (Ottawa 1931), 912. The numbers reported on the Italian community varied widely depending on who was recording the numbers. This is in part a consequence of seasonal work patterns and migration. For further tabulation see: Enrico Cumbo, "As the Twig is Bent, the Tree's Inclined": Growing Up Italian in Toronto, 1905-1940," Ph.D. thesis, University of Toronto, 1995, 461; John E. Zucchi, *Italians in Toronto: Development of a National Identity 1875-1935* (Montreal 1988), 44.

[119]Donna Gabbaccia and Franca Iacovetta, eds. *Women, Gender and Transnational Lives: Italian Workers of the World* (Toronto 2002); Robert F. Harney and Vincena Scarpaci, *Little Italies in North America* (Toronto 1981); Robert Harney, "Men without Women: Italian Migrants in Canada, 1885-1930," in Franca Iacovetta, Paula Draper and Robert Ventresca, eds., *A Nation of Immigrants: Women, Workers, and Communities in Canadian History, 1840-1960s* (Toronto 1998), 206-30; Zucchi, *Italians in Toronto.*

[120]Canada, Bureau of the Census *Summary Vol. I*, (Ottawa 1941), 338. In manufacturing in Canada 77 per cent of Italian women and 90 per cent of Jewish women were in the textile industry. Canada, Bureau of the Census, *Occupations and Industries Vol. VII* (Ottawa 1931), 418-27.

[121]Please note that I am using Mrs. Bassi because this was the only way she was referred to in her daughter's interview.

> when the jacket came back and she saw it wasn't hers she said, 'That's not my job!' She decided that she'd put — this was really clever — they had a punch clock, you know, and everybody had their own number, so she thought she is not going to fool me just because I can't speak. She thinks I'm stupid. So she put her number on every jacket.[122]

This memory of conflict underscores how language barriers and ethnic discrimination could enter and shape the workplaces of Italian women in the garment industry.[123] Like many women in this industry, Mrs. Bassi was married, suggesting that marital status was not always a determinant of employment, at least not if one was working in the "right" job ghetto. Both Edelist and Bassi's experiences also highlight some of the ways in which immigrant and ethnic working women of the Depression resisted and protested class exploitation and other forms of injustice, whether through unionization or smaller workplace protest.[124] More specifically, Mrs. Bassi's story offers yet another challenge to the stereotypes of Italian women as reluctant wage earners and docile workers.

Nora Windeatt and Agnes Trot began their wage-earning careers as single women in jobs similar to those of Edelist and Bassi, and they too earned meager wages for long hours of work. In contrast to Edelist and Bassi, however, Windeatt and Trot did not remain in their positions on the shop floor until they left work for marriage; rather both became managers of their departments. Nora Windeatt immigrated to Toronto just before the Depression. In May 1927, she arrived in Guelph, Ontario, from England, not Poland or Italy. Having left her family behind, Windeatt had to support herself. With obvious pride, she explained how she did so. For a year, she worked in several positions including a house-worker on a local farm and a food service employee in a hospital. As neither job appealed to her, and as she "refused to clean other people's houses for a living," she sought out different kinds of work.[125] Fairly soon she found a job at a hosiery company. Between 1929 and 1938, Nora Windeatt worked for Well Dress Hosiery in Mount Denis, a suburb of Toronto. Her first job at the company involved "transferring the stamps onto the hosiery" for twenty-five cents an hour, not a task that Windeatt was particularly fond of doing, but fortunately, "it wasn't too long before I received a promotion."

[122]Evelina Bassi, interview, (MHS, ITA - 0661 - BAS). For further discussion of this type of resistance see Angelo Principe, "Glimpses of Lives in Canada's Shadow: Insiders, Outsiders, and Female Activism in the Fascist Era," in Franca Iacovetta and Donna Gabaccia, eds., *Women, Gender and Transnational Lives* (Toronto 2003), 349-385.
[123]For more on the position of Italian women in the garment industry see Guglielmo, "Italian Women's Proletarian Feminism in New York City Garment Trades, 1890s-1940s."
[124]As Franca Iacovetta and Donna Gabaccia establish in their important collection *Women, Gender, and Transnational Lives: Italian Workers of the World,* the persistent stereotype of passivity does not hold for Italian women workers and must be replaced with a greater awareness of the different forms that resistance took in women's lives. Gabaccia and Iacovetta, *Women, Gender, and Transnational Lives.*
[125]Nora Windeatt, interview by Katrina Srigley, June 1998.

She advanced from her position on the shop floor to a salaried position as head of fifty men and women in the finishing, mending, and boarding department.[126]

When Agnes Trot, a Canadian of English and Irish descent, began earning wages as a domestic her family was on relief. At the age of sixteen, she abandoned personal service for a job sewing blinds at a curtain factory. It was 1935 and Trot was not happy with her wages or long hours, so when the International Ladies' Garment Workers' Union approached her to help unionize the factory she was more than happy to help. They succeeded in unionizing her floor in 1936. Although justifiably proud of her accomplishment, Trot had no other union stories to share with me. Sitting in her Scarborough home, her voice gravelly from years of smoking, she told me, "You see, I left the union shortly after they came. I was promoted to forelady and given $75 a month to oversee 40 women."[127] Interestingly, neither of these woman recalled whether their promotion or authority over men was considered abnormal in the 1930s. Still, their experiences point to the possibility that, notwithstanding dominant patriarchal structures and sentiments, certain women could attain higher status positions within manufacturing.

Mabel Duncan was born in England. When she was four months old her parents immigrated to Canada. Similar to Windeatt and Trot she started work on the shop floor of a factory when she was in her early teens. Hayhoe Tea Company employed Duncan from 1921 to 1962. She never married. Recalling her first job in our 2001 interview, she laughed perhaps a little self-consciously and said, "Well, I made boxes and packed jelly powders."[128] Not long after she started the company mechanized their tea line. She explained that "[w]ell you know machines came in and they started to put ... tea in bags so when I left there they had about four machines that they were using."[129] Duncan left the shop floor because she was promoted. "I got to the place where I was in charge of the female help." (By 1941 there were 17,993 women in the manufacturing sector, 340 of them Forewomen).[130] Like Windeatt, Trot, and Duncan, some women made higher wages and experienced authority over men and women. Ethnicity, religion, class, and language skills worked concurrently to privilege some women and exclude others in the garment industry. These social variables created situations of discrimination and resistance. And, un-

[126] For more information on women in management see G.L. Symons, "Her View from the Executive Suite: Canadian Women in Management," in Katerina Lundy and Barbara Warme, eds., *Work in the Canadian Context: Continuity Despite Change* (Toronto 1981), 337-53. Also of interest here is the power Nora Windeatt had over the men in her department. As she recalls it the men were from a similar ethnic and class background as Windeatt.

[127] Agnes Trot, interview by Katrina Srigley, December 2001.

[128] Duncan, interview.

[129] Duncan, interview.

[130] Canada, Bureau of the Census, *Occupations and Industries Vol. VII* (Ottawa 1941), 218-9.

like the situation in clerical work, marital status was less of a barrier to work on the shopfloor.

Race and class also influenced white-collar work. During the Depression, as before it, women teachers entered a semi-professional world marked by a very clear gender hierarchy. Most women teachers worked at the elementary level where they were paid less than their male colleagues who occupied the better paying jobs in high school and administration. They received, on average, only "two-thirds of the salaries offered to men" and were required to give up their positions at marriage or alternatively by first child.[131] When they left their classrooms, women teachers, much more so than men, could expect to have their behaviour scrutinized. While regular church attendance was a point in their favour, stepping out in the evening or taking a drink in public could result in harsh punishment, including dismissal.[132]

The number of female teachers declined slightly between 1931 and 1941 from 2,854 to 2,811, but only .03 per cent of employed women had these positions in Toronto.[133] If women school teachers faced serious gender discrimination, as white and British women, they enjoyed a racial privilege that did not extend to black women and even to some non-British immigrant or ethnic women. Moreover, in order to become teachers they had enjoyed access to Teacher's College or Normal School after high school.[134] The individual experiences of Mary Chenhall and Dora Wattie, single, white Canadian women of English descent, provide the opportunity to explore this interesting convergence of gender discrimination with racial and class privilege.

Mary Chenhall, a sprightly 90 year old who still lives in her own apartment and drives her own car, taught math at Markham District High School until she married in 1935. Sharing stories of her university education, Chenhall bitterly told the tale of she and other female classmates arriving at their Physics class at the University of Toronto one day only to find the door locked and their professor bellowing: "Go away, you little Victoria angels. Go back to Vic and enroll in the Household Eco-

[131]Erin Phillips and Paul Phillips, *Women and Work: Inequality in the Canadian Labour Market* (Toronto 1993), 28. Ruth Roach Pierson and Beth Light, eds., *No Easy Road: Women in Canada, 1920-1960s* (Toronto 1990), 209. Also see Alison Prentice, "Themes in the Early History of the Women's Teachers' Association of Toronto," in Paula Bourne, ed., *Women's Paid and Unpaid Work: Historical and Contemporary Perspectives* (Toronto 1985), 97-120; For the American experience see Lois Scharf, *To Work and to Wed* (Westport, Conn. 1980), 66-85.

[132]For an apt and very poignant fictional account of this situation see Richard Wright, *Clara Callan* (Toronto 2001).

[133]Canada, Bureau of the Census, *Occupations and Industries Vol. VII* (Ottawa 1931), 236; Canada, Bureau of the Census, *Occupations and Industries Vol. VII* (Ottawa 1941), 222.

[134]In the 1930s, teachers who taught in secondary school required Teacher's College while elementary school teachers went to Normal School. Margaret Gairns, interview by Katrina Srigley, November 2002.

nomics course. We don't want you in Math and Physics."[135] It was with great pride that Chenhall also recalled the successful completion of her degree. By the time she joined the teaching staff at Markham Collegiate in 1933, she had overcome a great deal of gender discrimination. Yet, class and race also shaped her access to a relatively high paying stable teaching position. First of all, Chenhall had a university education. This was an advantage enjoyed by only four of the women interviewed for this study, which reflects the small percentage of men and women enrolled in university during the Depression years.[136] (In 1936 the Annual Survey of Education indicated that on average between 1920 and 1936 just 4 per cent of young men and 1.5 per cent of young women in Canada became university undergraduates).[137] Indeed, as Paul Axelrod notes "to the vast majority of Canadians the universities were inaccessible...."[138] The Hall family could afford Chenhall's tuition and had the economic stability necessary to forgo her wages during her four-year degree program. They were never on relief. Nor was Mr. Hall, employed in management at Bell Telephone, ever without work. "It was a hard time, we were careful, but we always had good food to eat."[139] Chenhall occupied a privileged position in comparison to women and men without access to such schooling.

Dora Wattie taught at Weston Collegiate throughout the 1930s and her memories of those years certainly include examples of wage discrimination and cutbacks. However, our understanding of these restrictions, which were largely a result of her gender, must be tempered by the advantages that she enjoyed. At one point noting, rather imperiously, " I lost one hundred [dollars] when they cut the [teaching] salaries," she said of women teachers like herself, "we were just plain lucky, I had eighteen hundred dollars a year."[140] In the midst of a severe depression, some fellow citizens were also keenly aware of teachers' privileges. Using the pseudonym Sock

[135]Chenhall was enrolled at Victoria, an affiliated college at the University of Toronto. Mary Chenhall, *Memoirs: Forever in My Heart* (Toronto 1998),45; Mary Chenhall, interviews by Katrina Srigley, December 2001, April 2002. Mary Chenhall has generously allowed me to read the memoirs she wrote between 1988 and 1998 for her sons.

[136]The University of Toronto President's Report for 1931 conveys this reality. In a city of nearly 700,000 only 2,190 men and 1,680 women were enrolled in the Faculty of Arts. There were 1,385 graduates recieving, like Mary, a Bachelor of Science. 959 of these gradutes were men. In 1936-1937 4,007 people were enrolled at the University of Toronto. *President's Report*, Toronto, 1931, 99, 135, 161.

[137]Canada, Dominion Bureau of Statistics, *Annual Survey of Education*, 1936, p. xxvi. The University of Toronto had enrollments which generally hovered around 5,000 for men and 2,500 for women throughout the Depression years. See: *Annual Survey of Education* 1929-1939.

[138]Paul Axelrod, "Higher Education, Utilitarianism, and the Acquisitive Society: Canada, 1930-1980," in Michael Cross and Gregory S. Kealey, eds., *Modern Canada 1930- 1980* (Toronto 1985), 180.

[139]Chenhall, *Memoirs: Forever in My Heart.*

[140]Dora Wattie, interview by Katrina Srigley, November 1997.

Em Board, one writer to the *Telegram* complained that, "[t]eachers have had no wage-cuts or staff reductions," and added:

> can't they be sports and take their medicine like the rest of us who have not had cuts but annihilation of wages to the tune of well on to 50 per cent, which may surprise them ... Teachers get an abundance of holidays and have only to ask for six months leave of absence for personal sickness and it is granted.... Their work is sure because there are always children to teach. So there is no depression in their class.[141]

Indeed, Dora Wattie used her wages to help her father build a new house on Church Street in Weston (where she still lived at the time of our interview), a suburb of Toronto. Chuckling, she also related to me the following story: "I had an extra hundred so I bought some stock in Palace Pier, lost every cent. I could have had units in the Maple Leaf Gardens, but I hadn't the second hundred!" In 1935, Wattie spent the summer traveling in Europe with friends. "Can you imagine," she exclaimed, "it only cost three hundred and fifty dollars for two months!" To be sure, with a regular wage and the deflation of the Depression years, people like Wattie experienced a higher standard of living and in some cases, upward class mobility. With a good salary they were able consume much more for lower prices.[142] Dora Wattie and Mary Chenhall's memories confirm that class and race privileges shaped woman's employment options and economic stability. Both Chenhall and Wattie had families that supported their education. They were also single, white women, as were most employed teachers working in an overwhelmingly Anglo-Celtic city.

Conclusion

When the women in this study made their way home at the end of their workday, they brought wages that in many instances were essential to the survival of their family. Understanding their role as a group of young wage-earning women in a city dealing with significant levels of male unemployment is important. On the one hand, their experiences and memories of them reveal a great deal about familiar themes in women's labour history, including female job ghettos, gender inequality in wages and salaries, and sex discrimination based on marital status. But the stories of the women who feature prominently in this study tell us about more than that; they also reveal some of the ways in which race, class, and marital status created or sustained privilege and disadvantage. Whether one inclines toward Kessler-Harris' argument about the greater legitimacy of female employment in a context of massive male unemployment and grave economic crisis, or towards Hobbs' insistence that Depression-era arguments about economic justice for all did not reduce sexist opposition to working women, there can be no doubt, I argue, that gender based employment regulation must figure into our understanding of women's Depres-

[141] *The Evening Telegram*, 3 Feb 1932.
[142] Wattie, interview.

sion-era employment and their reactions to it. This Toronto case study confirms that finding. Yet there is more to "the story." An exclusive emphasis on gender can lead to a neglect or misunderstanding of the confluence of factors, including race, that served to privilege some women in the labour market while disadvantaging or indeed excluding others. As this study suggests, the labour market was not a cohesive whole but was variegated and uneven, and job options were determined in ways that gave some women the freedom to apply for relatively high-paying, stable positions as teachers, clerical workers, and managers and others the "choice" of jobs at the bottom of the heap. Furthermore, this study confirms the value of an oral history approach that pays very close attention to issues of subjectivity. My findings underscore the value of intersectional and dynamic modes of analysis; the intersectionality of class, gender and race-ethnicity, religion, and marital status, is not to be understood as a static equation with each ingredient (or social force) always weighing in equal parts. Instead, we need to make critical judgments about which identities emerge as more or less influential in shaping women's working lives in a given time and place, and at a particular phase of their life cycle.

In Toronto's labour market during the Depression domestic service continually occupied the lowest rung of the occupational ladder for women. It had the lowest pay, poor work conditions, and despite a labour shortage never drew the attention of the vast majority of Toronto's breadwinning women. Thus, it remained a job ghetto for women who had few other employment options. Clerical work on the other hand was a much more desirable occupation. It had more social caché and it provided greater economic stability to women and their families. But, unlike in domestic service, fewer women had access to these jobs. Claire Clarke had all of the necessary qualifications: she was educated and single; her family owned their own home, an important class signifier, but she could not find a job. Certainly, Thelma Plunkett's gender ensured that she would not have the privilege of working in a high power administrative job at Aluminum Goods Company, but it was more than luck that allowed her to transfer between clerical jobs with ease. Mildred Johnson found herself employed by the Anglican Church because Shaw's business school realized she had a similar religious affiliation. Both of these women also enjoyed a measure of economic stability that should not be discounted in our understanding of their wage-earning experiences. Rose Edelist and Evelina Bassi's memories underscore the importance of ethnicity, marital status, and class to our understanding of their work in the garment trade. Edelist and Bassi both resisted their poor working conditions, challenging conceptions of ethnic women, Italian women in particular, as passive. Nora Windeatt, Agnes Trot, and Mabel Duncan, white English and Canadian women, entered the manufacturing industry on the shop floor, but within years they had higher paying positions as managers of their departments. Dora Wattie and Mary Chenhall recognized and disliked the restrictions placed upon them because of their gender; but, in comparison to those for whom such jobs options were closed these limitations have a different impact on our understanding of their labour market experiences. Not only did these women not drive men out of work, at a time when rising numbers of men were unemployed, they had job ghettos which could in fact be assets. Moreover, Claire Clarke and other West-Indian and African Canadian women attribute employment discrimination to the colour of their skin.[143]

First of all, I would like to acknowledge the women and men who shared their memories with me. Without their kindness and generosity this project would never have come to fruition. Kimberly Berry, Heidi Bohaker, Heather DeHaan, and Carolyn Strange have all provided excellent feedback at different stages of the writing process. I would also like to thank the Toronto Labour Studies Group for their important assistance on various drafts of this paper. Several anonymous reviewers provided engaged and thoughtful responses to this article, thank you. All of the errors that remain are my own.

[143]Claire Clarke, interview.

Documents of Western History:

Experiences of a Depression Hobo

During the depression many of the unemployed in Canada took to the road and travelled about the country in an attempt to find work or better living conditions. Their chief mode of travel was "riding the rods" as non-paying passengers on the railway. In the course of the decade of depression many of these travellers crossed the country several times and became very knowledgeable about how to live the life of a hobo and survive in a society which did not seem to want them. Predictably they tended to become very bitter and cynical about society and to lean toward radical ideas which, if nothing else, at least offered some hope for change.

The following passages were taken from letters written to the late Mrs. Violet McNaughton by a young English immigrant who for a time was numbered among the single unemployed men in Canada. As far as can be determined the author of these letters had emigrated to Canada about 1930 and worked on a farm in Western Canada. When he joined the ranks of the unemployed he travelled first to Toronto and then to Vancouver. Eventually he again travelled east this time as far as Halifax and finally he worked his passage home. Unlike many others he managed by various stratagems to stay out of jail and out of the relief camps which were experiences shared by many of his fellow travellers. The passages have been selected from a few letters to illustrate some of the writer's experiences on the road. Names have been omitted but spellings remain as in the original.

THE EDITOR

[June 1932]

I arrived in Toronto a week ago but have not got work yet. The trip down took 5½ days and I did not visit any jails. My total expenses were 50 cents but I ate a [sic] slept well.

On the Saturday night of April 15 my friend and I took the last street car out to Sutherland having previously found out that a freight train was leaving for Winnipeg during the early hours of Sunday morning. We slunk around the yards till we came upon a brakeman and asked when the freight for the East was pulling out. Before he could reply a torch light beamed in our faces and the "bull" asked "Where are you guys going?" "East"—"Winnipeg." "Well that freight won't pull out till seven to-morrow morning." We thanked the policeman for this information and retired to the shadow of a nearby Pool Elevator, lighted cigarettes and attempted to keep warm. Even I, with 2 pairs underclothing, 2 shirts, a sweater, my brown suit, overalls, overcoat, winter cap & 2 pairs sox was getting chilly. Presently we became restless & walked out onto the tracks to espy an ancient looking empty coach with a light in it. Prowling lower we observed a notice on the side telling us it was for the use of stockmen only. A brakeman informed us that the coach was to be put on the freight to Winnipeg for the use of some stockman travelling. We entered the coach, found a fire burning in the stove, wiped the dust off the seats, spread them out bed fashion & were soon asleep. We were suddenly awakened by the guard who informed us that the train was pulling out in 5 minutes and that a "bull" was going to travel with the train. Observing the "bull" walking down the side of the train we waited till he rounded the end before ourselves, hopping out, walked after him & inspected the box cars. All but one were sealed, this "one" being half full of coal. There were already about ten other travellers sprawling in various positions amongst the coal.

The first division stop was Wynyard and here my friend turned back. He had a warm bed in Saskatoon, a mother, father and home—not work. He explained that he was a decent fellow, had never been in jail in his life &, did'nt like freight riding. What would his mother say if he was arrested? Besides, supposing there was no work in Toronto what would we do? We'd be arrested, vagrants. He had never been in a big city before, our money would not last long, we might even starve to death! In other words, he'd had enough—just chicken hearted.

The sun was warm and I rode on top of a box car all day. Towards evening the train pulled in at the next division stop, Bredenbury. I was hungry & made for the town semi-satisfying my appetite in a "Chinks". Returning to the train I fell in with two of my fellow passengers of the coal car who had been "bumming" the houses. They were lads of 23 also heading for Toronto—happy but broke. Arriving at the tracks we walked boldly towards the freight & walked right into the "bull" who instantly showed his ignorance. "What the hell d'you fellows want here." We put him right as to our wants whilst he accompanied us to the entrance of the yards and the freight steamed out. He informed us that should he see us around again he would put us all in "clink". One of my new-found confederates thanked him very much and suggested that as we had lost the freight and had nowhere to sleep we should very much appreciate his hospitality. But the "bull" was not so hospitable & we slept in the C.P.R. roundhouse beside a boiler. I slept well inspite of the sudden change from feather to concrete mattress. Following morning a pail & water from the boiler brightened our appearance & we made for town agreeing that the inhabitants should pay dearly for their ignorant railway cop. Meeting the oldest resident, I think he must have been, on "Main Street" we enquired as to the whereabouts of the local "town bull", the mayor, the residences of the station agent, the railway cop and the R.C.M.P. local. With this information we commenced our labours for breakfast. Seeing a man working in a garden we wondered whether he would like our aid or company. He was not impressed by either but gave us $1 for "eats". Entering the local hotel we explained our circumstances and gorged for 25 cents per head. During the morning we lay down on some open prairie & slept till roused by a crowd of children who had come to inspect us. One yelled "Hobo, hobo we've got some candy for you", but as I got up hopefully they took to their heals [sic] and ran for town. Our stomaches [sic] informed us dinner time had arrived, one of the boys set out for the mayors house and brought back a fine "hand out" which we consumed. The other set out for another of our addresses, split some wood & received a "sit-down". Then it was my turn to go "bumming". I set out for a large house set back from the town which looked hopeful. I tapped at the door nervously and a large man poked his head cautiously out of the door letting out an equally large dog as he did so. My knees knocked and I stuttered something about work & eat. The man told me he did not feed tramps & would set his dog on me. I moved towards the dog which instantly fled with its tail between its legs and the man slammed the door. As I was walking down the path the man popped his head out of an upstairs window and threatened to inform the police if I did not "get clear" immediately.

Towards evening the Winnipeg freight pulled in and we boarded it as it pulled out of the yards. There were no "empties" but a stock coach on the back, so we sat on the steps of this. As dusk fell we stopped for water at some place & the guard sighted us. He came up & inspected us, then unlocked the coach & told us to get in there for the night, we might go to sleep on the steps & fall off. Next morning we awoke to find our freight standing in the Portage La Prairie yards. Two "bulls" walked up the train, inspected the seals, glanced at the stock coach where we had assumed an attitude of sleep once more, walked off. We left the freight at a street crossing outside Winnipeg, yelled at a passing truck driver and were whirled into the city. The two lads I was with got a free shave at the Barber College and we learnt that the city was handing out meals to transients. After much walking and enquiring we obtained meal tickets and set out for the soup kitchens, which used to be the C.N.R. Immigration Hall where I stopped when first in Canada. The meal was awful! We walked down a counter gradually accumulating our ration which consisted of a piece of bread & square of butter, a small dish containing about a spoonful of sugar, a tin bowl containing a green fluid sometimes called soup, a tin plate on which had been dumped, dirty potatoes, two large hunks of fat, some carrots and thick gravy, and a mug contain [sic] hot water the same colour as weak tea. We sat on a bench containing males of all types, nationalities and descriptions and attempted to eat. The gentleman on my right had developed a strange habit of wiping a running nose with the back of his hand between each mouthful which did not increase the flavour of my meal. A large bowl of rice was placed on the table for desert but as I had my plate already filled with leavings I did not try any.

We left the soup kitchens and made enquiries about the times of freight trains. There was one leaving from the C.N.R. Transcona yards at around midnight for Toronto. We commenced the 9 miles walk to Transcona.

On the way out we passed over a bridge on the side of which some humorist had written with chalk "I'm fed up; for further information drag the river." Over the bridge is St. Boniface where there is a large catholic church, seminary, school, nuns home etc. etc. Whilst passing the seminary and admiring its size and beauty we espied the kitchen through a basement window. Thoughts concerning the higher arts vanished from our heads, we looked at each other, looked for the nearest door, and entered, coming upon a fat cook. I moved my hand over my chest and wore my most pious expression and one of the boys addressing the cook as "brother" explained that we were extremely undernourished and should be pleased with some bread. The cook prepared some sandwiches containing cold slabs of steak and we departed praising the Lord, the cook and ourselves.

Towards late afternoon we arrived at the yards, parked ourselves on the grass outside the fencing and built a fire of old ties—and commenced a 7 hour wait. We consumed our sandwiches which were delicious—I think I'll become a priest.

As time passed more "travellers" appeared and settled around our fire; soon we had about a dozen fellow "unionists" and grew to discussing "this world of ours" as men often do. In London there are cockney tales, in Scotland, Scotch tales and on the road, hobo tales. Hoboes also have quite a language of their own. The same as farmers but without the large variety of 'swear words' usually associated with the barnyard.

The depression, the railway companies and Bennett were our chief topics. We wisely listened to each others views on depression. Its due to tariffs, to immigration, the price of wheat, the U.S.A., Russia, war, their "big-bugs", religion, the "bohunks". Nothing but war will bring back prosperity; no cancellation of war debts; no socialism; no God;—let's have the good old days; scrap machinery, to hell with motor cars, deport the Reds, deport the "bohunks", oust Bennett . . .

[Later in commenting on his experiences in Ontario and in particular one incident in which he had been told to leave a town the author gave the following as his personal attitude toward the depression.]

Quite evidently there is no use for a penniless person in this land of opportunity; a person without work and money is considered an outcast, no town or city wants him but he can usually get two meals per day and exist because even Canadians do not usually let dogs starve. When a person has lost all his money and cannot get work he can either take to the road and become a bum or stop in his home town and get a free bed and two meals a day from the city relief for which he has to do as many hours work per week. I estimate that this scheme breaks the spirit of the average man within a year; hence I chose the road. My spirit is by no means broken I just feel angry and the harder Canada kicks me the more I'll retaliate. I do not consider myself an ordinary "bum". If there is any work to be done I'll do it providing I receive what I consider a decent living wage. I will certainly not work for my board and I will not work for the pittance many are receiving today.

Until such time as I get a decent job I intend to live well, dress respectably, eat all thats good for me, keep myself clean and have clean clothes. Canada generally will pay for this. I will obtain what I need by bumming and other comparatively honest methods. If such ways and means should fail I shall resort to thieving and other criminal ways of which I have some knowledge.

[In the fall of 1932 the author made an unplanned trip to Vancouver where he stayed for about a year. The following excerpt from a letter written in October 1932 describes this trip.]

I don't known whether you were worried by any unusual noises the night we left Saskatoon but the C.N.R. bull at Nutana Yards was suffering from throat trouble and was roaring at some hobo who annoyed him. I imagine his voice could be heard all through Saskatoon and should you have failed to hear him it is entirely due to the Saskatoon Street Car Service. Our freight left around midnight & we could have easily consumed more malted milk and pie. . . .

The journey to Edmonton was devoid of excitement; we just stayed in an empty box-car and talked, smoked, ate, slept. Diamond behaved like a veteran the way he slept in that jumping, rattling car was envious. We left him at Edmonton & spent the night in the Sally Ann. After a good dinner we returned to the tracks & learnt that a freight was leaving for the south at 11.55 that night. That day a store had been held up in the city consequently the bulls were active. We walked onto the tracks shortly before midnight to be instantly accosted by two bulls. A few questions & they decided we were not the fortunates who held up the store & merely ordered us "to get to hell out of the yards". A freight began to move & we shut ourselves in an empty refrigerator car, figuring it was the train going south.

Next morning we opened our bedrooms & observed mountains. We had jumped the wrong train & were bound for Vancouver. It was too late to turn back so we gave up any idea of more threshing.

There were about twenty other passengers on the train. We spent our days perched on top of the cars and nights inside the empty refrigerator. Only on top of a box-car can one enjoy the real thrill of constructing that line through the Rockies, enjoy the thrill of mountains towering almost vertically above on the one side and drops to distant valleys & creeks on the other; wondering why the rocks didn't roll down on the train & the train roll over the artificial ledge to the depths below.

The train took two days to cross B.C. Our supplies, gotten in Edmonton, lasted us the first & the second morning we arrived in the fruit district. The freight stopped for water early, conveniently close to an orchard. The free travellers disembarked en-mob and disappeared amongst the trees to emerge as the freight started with pockets, caps, shirts containing the forbidden fruit of Eden. I ate more fruit that day than I had consumed since leaving the Niagara Fruit Belt. Towards night we stopped at New Westminster and a brakeman warned us that the police were waiting on the freight in Vancouver. We jumped off 6 miles out of the city and walked in. . .

My present abode is a mission and I am pulling the religious stuff once more; last night I was presented with a New Testament by a well meaning gentleman who actually does believe in the stuff including Adams rib. . . .

This mission is known as the "Refuge" besides various illegal terms. Two stories above a garage comprise the institution. The top storey houses about 350 bunks built of wood in two tiers. The lower floor is used for feeding. Men lounge around here most of the day reading sensational trash in magazines, playing cards, smoking and generally trying to forget 'what might have been'. Men are only fed here if they can prove they have resided in B.C. more than so many months. Each day transients gather like wolves around the kitchen and eat up any food that is left over. The Refuge is only one of many similar relief kitchens. . . .

[February, 1933]

I am at present marvelling and gloating over the relief system, and my own ascent to the highest favor of single unemployed relief. You remember months ago my arriving in Vancouver and the daily scrounge for food and a bed. How I entered the 'Refuge' and stopped there for some weeks through excuses, work, and religion. How I obtained provincial relief, evaded the camps, and was transferred to the Central City Mission. One step accomplished.

Last Monday I arose early and made my way to Hamilton Hall where the single receive their relief tickets. A hawkish horn-rimmed faced gentleman is in charge there. I approached his desk and smiled sweetly. He looked up from an attempt to appear studious and carefully opened his mouth as if fearful that his upper false teeth might drop. Evidently Sunday and the spring weather humored him for his usual snarl had transformed to a polite, sane question. "Well, Blondie, what can I do for you, to-day?"

Encouraged by this show of sanity my lips remained spread and the smile expanded to my eyes, giving one the impression, I imagine, of a dog happily chewing razor blades. "Lots, if you want," I answered. "I am fed up with the Mission. Of course, Mr. Caldwell has treated me very courteously but I am studying, and its utterly impossible for me to concentrate in that environment. I can now get books from the library and I want to do about eight hours study per day."

The relief bloke seemed impressed, he studied my duplicate white card and my own card, looked stern and questioned. "What are you studying?"

"Er . . . hum," my brain groped for high sounding words, "Phrenology, psychology, entomology"—thinking of the mission stiffs and the beds.

He scowled as if to convince me that he did not believe in these new fangled religions. With a strange wiggle of his nose he allowed the horn windows to slip nearer the tip and gazed wisely and fatherly over them at me. He crossed the 'Central City Mission' stamp off my card and wrote a note which I took to another Johnny at another desk who handed me two weeks tickets on cafes, value $3.50, and two weeks bed tickets, value $2.10, for any rooming house in the city that takes relief men.

I am enclosing some cafe pamphlets that men hand the stiffs as they enter Hamilton Hall. There are so many on relief in Vancouver that the cafes actually advertise for the business. In fact, many cafes here only keep open through the business the relief men give them.

[July 1933]

Some weeks back I was finally cut off relief for refusing to go to camp. Since then I have been obtaining odd-jobs and manage to scrape by alright, but its a rotten existence. I never did have any ambition to cut lawns, clean windows, and chop wood.

5
"The War for the Common Man": The CIO's Narrative of a Fulfilled Democracy

THE SECOND WORLD WAR had fewer poets and memorials than the First World War and was fought with far less sentimentality.[1] Yet it produced at least one great myth: the myth of "the people's war," a notion created in Britain and taken up in Canada.[2] The original meaning of "the people's war" was that the war was total, demanding sacrifice from every citizen. But the CIO broadened that meaning, transforming it from a war *strategy* to a war *aim*. Victory in a people's war would mean a better country and a better life for workers. "Of all the wars fought in this world, not one has had so great a cause as the present conflict," said a CIO newspaper: "It is the war for the common man."[3] The CIO used the people's war rhetoric to mould workers' opinions about the meaning of the war, their place in it, and the postwar Canada that workers' wartime sacrifices should earn them. By appropriating the language of the people's war and by translating it to suit its own purposes, the CIO leveraged the strength the myth had with workers and the general public. The CIO's definition of the people's war helped shape political debates about Canada's future during wartime elections and thus contributed to the country's gradual movement towards the welfare state. In this way, the CIO, joining many other groups in Canadian society, participated in what one Canadian historian has called the "reconstruction culture."[4]

The CIO made strategic use of the nation's war effort by pairing the nation's heroes fighting overseas with workers fighting a less popular battle for unionization at home. The soldier on the battlefront overseas was fighting to defeat the anti-democratic, racist, and woman-repressing evil of Nazism, while the soldier on the "production front" was fighting for a new kind democracy in Canada, one that, in the postwar era, would extend far beyond mere political democracy to embrace economic democracy. This would be done through the "industrial democracy" of collective bargaining and the intervention in the economy of a more activist government, working in partnership with labour. Thus, the CIO argued, unlike after the Great War, the nation would keep faith with its returning soldiers by making the country a "fit" place for them to return. Canada would be transformed from a country of great natural wealth, but politically and socially backward, into a modern nation with modern laws and modern, democratic, social relations, including cooperation and partnership among labour, business, and government. Thus, the CIO argued, would the promise of democratic equality be fulfilled. The CIO story during wartime was a narrative that promised security and order in an insecure and disorderly world.

How workers and others received this message is a matter of speculation, although it can be argued that, in all probability, union writers, publicists, and orators would tend to use and re-use words, expressions, and metaphors that were persuasive and thus resonated positively with readers and audiences. This is not to say that CIO orators, writers, and publicists were not trying to "sell" a point of view to workers. They most definitely were, but they did so by leveraging the tropes, metaphors, and expressions used in mainstream discourses about the war to encourage workers to support the CIO's point of view.[5]

Courting Public Opinion: The CIO's Publicity Strategy

CIO leaders made their appeals not just to workers but also to the general public. They recognized early on their need for public relations, then referred to as "publicity." At a meeting in June 1939, the CIO Coordinating Committee discussed how the CIO had to produce "publicity on the need for industrial organization in our communities." Moral and financial support from the public was vital to the CIO's future organizing, its leaders believed, so publicity efforts had to be directed not just towards potential union recruits but also towards the community at large, as fellow Canadians. The committee reported: "We face the task of informing the public of our aims and through their understanding, enlisting their support, financial and moral, for improving the wages and benefits of our fellow Canadians."[6]

As the CIO unions grew in size and resources and thus came to have more members to organize and service, sentiment grew for establishing a permanent bureaucracy of staff specialists not necessarily drawn from the union's rank and file. CIO affiliates hired full-time educators, researchers, and even community liaison staff, but very often the first such appointment was a full-time publicity person.[7] One of the first recommendations of the CIO committee was that the CIO hire a full-time publicity director to help coordinate CIO organizing publicity.[8] In 1940, a Toronto Newspaper Guild resolution noted: "An efficient publicity apparatus is vital to the growth and development of a progressive labour organization both to keep its own members and the public fully informed of the aims of industrial democracy."[9] The CIO used advertising agencies as early as 1940 to assist with organizing campaigns.[10] So important was publicity thought to be that, when the UAW was considering laying off its public relations director in 1942, local union leaders, crediting him with a vital role in their organizing successes, advised George Burt to let one of the union's full-time organizers go instead.[11]

The Canadian media, during the war, were also more interested in labour than they are today, giving unions a better chance of garnering public attention. In the 1940s, daily newspapers hired staff reporters specializing in labour stories, carried reports on the monthly municipal labour councils meetings, and followed affairs of locals (especially large locals) closely. When the UAW presented a twenty-seven-page brief to a National War Labour Board inquiry into collective bargaining legislation in 1943, the *Windsor Star* devoted an entire page to it.[12] Labour understood that, given its burgeoning role in the local economy, publicity would follow. As George Burt said of the UAW local at Ford in Windsor, "Everything done in the local is the property of the public, it being such a large plant and of such importance."[13]

The union definition of publicity also included such union-produced material as union newspapers, which, for the most part, started publishing during the war. Furthermore, it was the war that gave CIO publicity the themes it used to link labour positively with the nation's war effort. CIO materials almost universally – and frequently – referred to the war, telling audiences that CIO unions were resolutely in support of the war effort, that their success in organizing workers was vital to winning the war, and that they shared the war aims and objectives of other Canadians.

There was nothing accidental about this. In March 1942, the UAW's Harry Rowe submitted a report to the union's district council advising the union to deploy the country's war effort in its publicity. He noted that, while the war would restrict labour's militancy (on account of public opinion against strikes), it would also give labour an alternative avenue to gain its objectives – namely, the positive publicity to be garnered by showing how labour stood shoulder to shoulder with other Canadians in support of the war. He urged that the union's publicity efforts be "largely integrated with the war effort."[14] "We have an opportunity only during wartime to show through group action the value of the labour movement and its contribution to the war effort," George Burt told his district council a year later.[15] Union publicists, including local union publicity committees, worked hard to ensure the mainstream media carried stories and photographs showing labour's contribution to the war effort. And, throughout the war, union records were filled with references to whether or not such initiatives had received the publicity union leaders felt they deserved.[16]

The CIO unions followed Harry Rowe's advice and took up war work with great energy. They bought Victory Bonds and urged their members to buy them as individuals, while union leaders such as George Burt spoke over the radio urging all Canadians to buy bonds, managing "to put in a plug for the union."[17] Unions cited the number of their members who had enlisted as proof of their contribution to the war effort.[18] Sergeant Gordon Fountain, a former member of UAW Local 89, had recruited an entire platoon for the Essex Scottish regiment, the *Automobile Worker* related proudly.[19] When union members, especially local labour leaders and well-known labour activists, joined the services, their enlistment was often front-page news for union papers.[20] New enlistees in the armed forces who had worked in plants were sent off with hearty congratulations from the local union papers. UAW Local 200, with about fourteen thousand members, persuaded 10,680 of them to donate blood for the troops and then broadly publicized its success in doing so.[21]

Local unions were energetic supporters of community war work efforts. UAW Local 222 in Oshawa, for example, contributed to the Red Cross, the Soldiers' Fund, the War Relief Committee, the British War Victims' Fund, and the Community Win the War Appeal. Its women's auxiliary was considered the most active group in the Oshawa war effort.[22] Union women's auxiliaries sometimes affiliated with local councils of women to help with their war work, and their leaders frequently served as representatives on local wartime prices and trade boards.[23] Unions even urged union members to help labour-short farmers with the harvest.[24]

Indeed, CIO unions deliberately sought to educate the public about the value of unions by having activists participate in local community groups that were aiding the war effort. The UE's C.S. Jackson told union supporters that, if labour wanted to educate the public about its mission and goals, it "must begin to play a basic community role … by … integrat[ing] … [its] Locals into the general stream of public activity in the community."[25] "We are becoming as broad as possible in our activities to spread the gospel of trade unionism," reported a UAW Local 200 activist after two of his local's activists were named to Windsor's war effort committee.[26] In some cases, the goal was explicit as well as strategic: union locals participated in community groups such as the Brantford Wartime Recreational Council because they did not want such committees "to become union busting organizations."[27]

Union papers provide a glimpse of how revolutionary it was to include unions in such community endeavours. It was a "celebrated occasion," according to an amused *Automobile Worker*, when a prominent citizen asked who the stranger was at the meeting of Brantford's Victory Bond committee and was told the newcomer was from the CIO. The stranger was put in charge of factory collections, and Brantford raised 45 percent more money than it had before.[28]

The CIO's Wartime Discourse

The CIO's strategy of linking itself with the nation's war effort went far beyond community war work. Its organizing materials – newspapers, leaflets, billboards, radio ads, speeches, and newspaper ads – used war-related themes to persuade workers and other citizens to advance CIO organizing drives and political views.

Using the "war for the common man" motif, the CIO countless times told a story about how working people would come into their own if they organized unions of such strength that the collective voice of labour would shape a peace in which workers would enjoy a life of prosperity, dignity, and, most important, security. If they unionized, the CIO told workers, they could force change not just from employers at the bargaining table but also from the political arena, pressuring government to respond not to the needs of Big Business but to the needs of workers. In telling this story, union speakers, educators, writers, poets, organizers, and publicists alike enlisted the war itself into the CIO cause, creating a heroic narrative in which workers and warriors, in shared sacrifice, were all soldiers fighting on different "fronts" for the same cause: the triumph of a fuller democracy, meaning a democracy that offered not just political egalitarianism but also economic egalitarianism.[29]

"Our Fighting Men Are Also Working Men"

The central theme in the CIO's wartime discourse was that the nation's working class was democracy's most stalwart defender. In the struggle to defend democracy, there were two kinds of fighters: the front-line soldier and the production-line soldier. The premise was that, since the bulk of Canada's armed forces were drawn from the working class, the interest and entitlement of workers was identical to that of soldiers. This worker-warrior partnership became a universal element in union literature. The men in the armed forces did not belong to "a different race from industrial workers," the *Inglis Steelworker* told its readers: "As a matter of fact the vast majority of officers and men came out of the factories and mines, they came from the homes of workers."[30] It was "the workers who were paying for the war, the workers who built the ships, the planes, the tanks, the guns, the workers who wore the uniforms both khaki and blue, that did the fighting and the dying," said a union editorial in the UAW paper at De Havilland Aircraft.[31]

The partnership of worker and warrior was rooted in the bitter memories of the treatment of the soldiers who took part in the First World War. As CIO writers emphasized, the promised "world fit for heroes" had not materialized after the First World War. A Great War veteran whose son was fighting overseas vowed the conditions in his plant would be improved for "my boy" when he returned, "not like when I came back." In this vein, the CIO urged workers to give the current war a higher purpose than that of merely defeating the enemy. They could do this by not allowing a repeat of the betrayal of the soldiers of the

Great War. "Our heroes came back to walk the streets, to sleep on park benches, to live on the dole," *Local 439 News* told readers and called for a new economic system that would make "the current war worth fighting."[32]

Indeed, CIO publicity implied a covenant between worker and warrior, with home-front soldiers owing a debt of honour to battlefield soldiers. Those fighting the war on the production lines had two battles: the first was to produce weapons for those fighting overseas to defeat Hitlerism and the second was to fight for a better workplace and a better Canada for those soldiers when they returned home. "We owe it to our loved ones overseas," a local union president told readers of his local's newsletter in January 1945: "We dare not fail them, we must see to it that those who have sacrificed much shall be rewarded by knowing that we at home are determined that Canada will be a home fit for her heroes to live in."[33] Moreover, as the UE's C.S. Jackson said, such benefits were indivisible within the working class: they were to be reaped by the home-front warriors as well as by their comrades overseas. "We owe a tremendous debt to our gallant comrades," he said: "This security and job opportunities must, however, be available to all our people ... The struggle for employment and security for the veterans is one and the same with the struggle for employment and security for all."[34]

"A Voice through Organization!"

The CIO told workers that they could best honour the worker-warrior partnership by joining unions. Unions would give worker-warriors the collective clout they needed to influence, for the first time, how and for whom Canada was to be run, thus achieving the home-front victory that was the promise of "the people's war." CIO writers usually expressed that clout as workers' acquiring a "voice" through collective action. Having a voice was a worker's right, the CIO said, and it would give them some control over their fate both in the private sphere of the shop floor and the public arena of politics.

Having a "voice" was more than just a fortunate benefit of unionization, the CIO said: it was a fundamental democratic right. The CIO extended the rights and privileges of citizenship to the workplace and argued that only unionization would give workers the workplace respect that their civic citizenship merited. As Charlie Millard told workers, using the discourse about freedom and equality so often heard during the war: "Collective bargaining is where labour meets management on equal terms, as free men."[35] As a Steelworkers organizing leaflet told Massey-Harris workers in 1941, a union meant that management would treat workers "as real people, as citizens of Canada, and [that] this [was] only possible by [means of its] union.[36]

By extension, the CIO maintained that a voice in the affairs of the nation was also a worker's right. Initially, in its 1939 brief to government, the CIO demanded representation on the agencies, boards, and commissions Ottawa had set up to run the national war effort. In 1939, however, there was no such reference to "voice" as a worker's right, one grounded in the natural rights of the country's working class. By 1943, however, as the CIO grew, its language changed to incorporate such notions. "As there are millions of us," said a UAW paper, "it is only natural that we should demand to have a rightful place in the seats of the mighty."[37] And, according to the CIO, unionization would give workers the voice they needed to take that rightful place. "Only through their union can workers gain a voice in determining that all the many difficult problems to be faced in the post-war world will be solved with full consideration for the wage earner," asserted a UAW organizing leaflet in late 1942.[38]

By late in the war, the CIO was claiming advocacy for all Canadians, not just wage earners. Labour's was the true voice of the nation, said the CIO. As the UAW's George Burt said, "The interests of labour and the basic effectiveness of the nation are intertwined and are alike in danger and in peril."[39] Union proposals for postwar full employment and a guaranteed annual income were described as a CIO mission on behalf of all Canadians.[40] The editor of the *War Worker* said the union's demands for postwar jobs and security were "only a few of the things we must demand for all Canadians."[41]

According to CIO writers – who exhibited great faith in the liberal democratic system – parliamentary politics would work to use its voice to effect labour-friendly laws as long as workers voted their interests. "We the people, by means of our ballot, can determine the destiny of Canada in the Post-War era," *Local 439 News* told its readers.[42] Arguing that governments would respond to ballot box pressure, a Steelworkers leaflet told workers at Inglis: "There are thousands in Canada who face the same 'after war' prospect that you do. It would be a foolish government that will not do something about it."[43] This sense of the potential of working-class power at the ballot box made voting an almost sacred obligation as far as the CIO was concerned, especially as its preservation was costing working-class blood. "To retain this privilege," wrote UAW Local 439 president George Goodwin, "we are now fighting the most costly and terrible War in history; to retain this privilege our sons, brothers and others dear to us are dying on foreign soil. You have a duty to perform: TO VOTE!"[44]

"Organize for Victory!"

Organizers told workers that unionization would lead to labour-management harmony, which would mean more war production (hence the much-used CIO slogan, "Organize for Victory"). The UAW credited Canada's 1943 output of 500,000 armoured vehicles to the union's being recognized at key automotive plants, which had increased cooperation between labour and management and so led to the "orderly settlement of grievances without loss of production time."[45] On the contrary, CIO organizers told workers, employer opposition to unionization caused dissension, which hurt production. According to one union leaflet: "When the UAW is recognized and collective bargaining established, Massey-Harris workers will be able to put their full energies into production and smashing Hitler. The war effort needs unions."[46] A 1943 Steelworkers leaflet quoted a company head who had stopped thwarting the union when he saw a 1,500 percent increase in production after unionization.[47]

Union organizers must address workers' concerns as workers, so the organizing literature distributed by CIO unions told workers how unionization would meet their workplace needs: higher wages, equal pay for women, safe working conditions, seniority, a grievance procedure.[48] But even when arguing for such material issues, CIO writers often used the war to rationalize union demands. "War entails the necessity of sacrifice," said the UE, "but we maintain that to allow wages which fail to provide a subsistence level of existence is in fact sacrificing the war effort itself."[49]

Often using strong language, the CIO argued that, by denying Canadian workers union rights, employers were undermining the war effort and, thus, abetting the enemy. A UAW editorial reacting to the failure of the Kirkland Lake strikers to win union recognition in 1942 stated: "Any act or policy which denies the right of labour … is subversive of the war effort. We brand it as subterfuge akin to treason."[50] "Measures that … curtail the rights of labour can only have an adverse effect upon our ability to fight against fascism … Those who are responsible for interfering with the democratic rights of labour are at the same time responsible for reducing the effectiveness of the war effort," declared a *UE News* editorial.[51] A CIO editorial accused both business and politicians of concentrating on defeating labour "instead of concentrating … on smashing Hitler." "We need to let Queen's Park know," wrote the editor, "that a good labour bill and defeating Hitler are indivisible."[52]

Not surprisingly, employers did not leave this CIO argument unanswered. They, too, warned that victory depended on workers and employers working together. Making collective bargaining compulsory, argued the Canadian Manufacturers' Association, would have a "disturbing effect on employer-employee relations and hence on the war effort."[53] Managers at Metallic Roofing, battling a UAW organizing drive in 1942, distributed a letter written by Stelco's president warning workers that the Allies were losing the war and that Canadians, including workers, had to put their duty above their rights or they would have no rights at all.[54]

"Democracy into the Very Homes and Souls of People"

As the nation's war effort against a dictatorial enemy became all-consuming, the CIO linked its goal of workplace democracy to the nation's defence of political democracy. As the war went on, the CIO's definition of democracy expanded to include talk about workers' rights in the workplace.[55] As one union editor wrote: "The democratic rights which [a worker] enjoys as a free citizen, vanishes when he enters the factory gates. Unless he has [union] protection he is subject to the arbitrary whims and rules of his employer, over whom he has no control whatever."[56] One union editorial asserted that a union would bring Franklin Roosevelt's famous "Four Freedoms" (which, for many people, encapsulated Allied war aims) to the workplace: "A union protects the worker in the exercise of his religious freedom, and prevents discrimination because of race or colour ... [I]t is a bulwark against freedom from want and provides workers with organization, whereby they no longer fear the economic strength and domination of their employer."[57]

As the war progressed, talk about rights entered the union discourse more explicitly and more frequently. In its 1939 conference paper, the CIO, with Canada still mired in depression, talked about the right to work as a fundamental democratic right, but its human rights demands were limited to CIO objections to employers' dismissing immigrant workers because of their foreign births.[58] As the war went on, however, references to human rights appeared increasingly in union literature, perhaps because the racist nature of the enemy had become clearer, perhaps because after June 1941 Communists in the labour movement, usually well-versed on issues of race and gender, became fully committed to the war effort.

The CIO included workplace rights in the scope of human rights. As Pat Conroy argued before the Ontario Select Committee, workers had a human right to organize and a right to sit across the bargaining table with their employers on an equal basis. Using the war as his moral lever, Conroy warned the committee that human rights could not be denied forever, that, just as human beings were resisting Hitler's classification of some people as inferior, so would workers resist employers' attempts to do the same: "[An employer] cannot grind individuals into a mechanism of his own choosing because human beings will rebel."[59] Before he shipped overseas, army private and former UAW organizer Jimmy Napier told De Havilland workers that he was "going over to fight for the democracy that was denied to [him] at home." Napier told workers that, after defeating fascism abroad: "We will have to defeat it at home ... [T]he interests of workers and soldiers, regardless of race, color or creed, must be united to defeat industrial dictatorship."[60]

Employers, however, were not prepared to cede to the CIO when it came to claiming "democracy." They argued that the democratic principle of freedom of association meant that the union shop and any automatic dues check-off were undemocratic. The same principle, they argued, supported recognition of company unions. They cited "freedom of speech" when they maintained that employers had the right to talk to workers about joining a union. They took out advertisements complaining about "CIO tyranny." They claimed secret ballot votes on union recognition were undemocratic because they allowed unions to mount propaganda campaigns of "false promises and misrepresentations," implying that majority votes in favour of a union were "illusory."[61]

On the other hand, government figures adapted to the growing strength of, and public sympathy towards, the CIO and began to use "democracy" when talking about labour, especially when public support for the pro-labour CCF began to grow.[62] By 1945, progressive government officials who were working at senior levels could safely espouse a more labour-friendly point of view. Jacob Finkleman, chair of the Ontario Labour Relations Board, gave a nod to democracy when he told employers that wartime pro-labour laws would outlast the conflict. Employers should stop "brooding" about their loss, he said, and "learn to accept the heavy burden of leadership in a democratic society lest [they] forfeit [their] claims to leadership."[63]

"Canadian Hitlers"

According to the CIO, if workers and their unions were the backbone of democracy, business and its friends in politics were the enemies of democracy. The CIO charged that business was not patriotic, that it was loyal only to its own interests and would use the nation's war effort as an excuse to roll back any advances workers had made. "Canadian industrialists would very much like to use the present war emergency to destroy gains made by workers over the past few years," said one Steelworkers organizing leaflet, which further accused companies of resisting unions in order to protect their war profits. [64] Suspicions of business's postwar plans also ran high, and labour papers warned readers about corporate Canada's postwar agenda. *Local 439 News* warned: "Industrialists hope to ... enter the post-war period in a condition of open shops and a surplus of labour to throw against established wage scales."[65] The *Automobile Worker* concurred, saying business would try to "bring back the pre-war years of misery and suffering after this war."[66]

A common motif in CIO wartime discourse involved linking business and its political sympathizers to the nation's fearsome enemy. A *UE News* editorial railed that the gains labour was seeking in Canada were "the first things denied by Hitler in the countries which he conquer[ed] and [that] these [were] the things which [were] opposed ... by the Canadian Manufacturers' Association."[67] "We may have political freedom, but we have industrial dictatorship," objected the UAW's George Burt after being jailed for walking a Chrysler picket line in 1940.[68] He continued: "We feel we have a responsibility of keeping Hitler doctrines from gaining a foothold in Canada through powerful corporations who use their strength against the democratic institutions of this country."[69]

The CIO's use of such hyperbole when characterizing business was frequent. When a Toronto local union pledged financial support for Kirkland Lake strikers, a union paper said that the local was showing "solidarity in face of a propaganda blitzkrieg by Canadian Hitlers."[70] When Massey-Harris laid off seventy-six union supporters during a 1942 organizing drive, the UAW accused the company of "Nazi-like methods" and likened the company's methods to a "blitzkrieg." When De Havilland fired four women UAW organizers, a union leaflet said that the company's actions gave "aid and comfort to the enemy ... [that] they hurt war production and destroy[ed] morale."[71] Company unions were favourite targets of such fevered CIO wartime rhetoric. Silby Barrett declared company unions to be "the same in principle as the fascist unions in Germany."[72] Company unions denied employees the right to freedom of association, argued the UE, contending: "[they create] suspicion and distrust in the minds of the workers – suspicion and distrust are the weapons of Hitler and it ill-behooves anyone in our country to provide him with those weapons."[73] When Ford proposed a union vote featuring only the company union on the ballot, the UAW fired back that the proposal was no better than "a Hitler plebiscite and [that] the company was engaging in typical Nazi tactics.[74]

"Security Is the Key to Happiness"

From the earliest days of the Second World War, what would happen to workers and their unions after the war was the central theme in CIO materials. At the CIO's inaugural conference in November 1939, CIO leaders, haunted by memories of the aftermath of the First World War, looked towards the postwar period of the latest conflict and pledged to "organize ... to meet the difficulties which beset labour following the last war." CIO leaders made postwar security – and an economic system that would provide it – their highest priority.

According to CIO literature, Canadian workers, after suffering through a decade of severe economic depression and then fighting a second global conflict within the space of a generation, wanted security above all else. The notion of "security" appeared countless times in CIO wartime records. In a letter to his local's newspaper, one worker explained what security meant to him: "The first thing I want is security for my wife and kids. To have that security, I've got to have a job ... [I want] my kids to have a decent break, decent education, a decent home, no more 'pogie,' the right to call a doctor if they get sick without worrying about the bill. I'd like to see the old folks get a decent break and a pension they can live on."[75] "Security is the key to happiness," wrote a contributor to a UE local union paper: "On this basis lies the future of our generation."[76]

The question uppermost in workers' minds was whether they would have a job after the war.[77] "The fear of unemployment is so great that it dominates everything else," Pat Conroy wrote in a 1944 edition of the *Automobile Worker*.[78] Union leaders warning against unemployment used the strongest terms. C.S. Jackson, for example, told the UE district council in 1944 that anything less than full employment would "set in motion forces which breed war and which [would] lead to another world conflict."[79] "Our armies are going to win this war on the battlefields," wrote UAW activist Margery Ferguson, "[but] if there [are] not jobs for all after the fighting stops, then I would say that we have lost the war."[80]

But with security as the goal, radicalism could not be the strategy. The CIO had a comparatively conservative view of the postwar economic system. As C.S. Jackson explained, "The majority of people in Canada from all walks of life and from all classes have the same general goal in mind, namely, security and a rising standard of living."[81] "We must as realists accept the fact that we are going to continue to live under the profit system known as capitalism, for many years to come," he told UE activists in 1945: "This is the thinking of the bulk of the people of Canada and the United States, and as such, it will of necessity be the prevailing mode of our economy." The goal was to change the way that system worked so that it provided "greater guarantees of security to the people."[82]

CIO writers often portrayed Canada as backward, especially with respect to labour relations. Governments everywhere were addressing the inequities created by modern industry, a UAW editor wrote in 1940, everywhere but in Canada. Pointing out that the United States, Great Britain, New Zealand, Australia, and France had all brought in labour relations legislation recognizing the right to organize, the writer emphasized that even "Germany, before the Nazis, had labour courts."[83] A UE editor described a Canadian labour movement "stymied by a government policy which fail[ed] to guarantee even a remote semblance of the rights accorded and guaranteed the workers of Britain and the United States."[84] Union editors pointed to the failure of Canadian governments to require equal pay for women, unlike jurisdictions in both the United States and Britain, which had done so as early as the First World War.[85]

The CIO told its readers just how backward working conditions were in Canada. The UE ran an editorial condemning Canada for failing to keep up with the United States and Britain in recommending shorter hours of work. Canadian workers were routinely working twelve-hour shifts, even in government-owned war plants.[86] Canada's low unionization rate led to another feature of backwardness: low wages. A UE editor told readers the wage difference between Canada and the United States was "so startling, it led an American commentator to describe Canada as a 'well-ordered game preserve' for industry."[87]

The CIO described itself as a modernizing force. As a modern labour movement, the CIO said, it matched modern developments in industry. A 1939 resolution read: "The self-organization of Canadian workers into modern labour unions capable of dealing with vast combines of industry and capital is the fundamental and unalterable purpose of the CIO."[88] Unlike the craft unions, CIO unions were better suited to the "modern, mass production plant which takes in all workers regardless of craft," a Steelworkers organizer told workers in 1942.[89]

Not surprisingly, the CIO described its demands on government and employers as demands for modernity. "Time to Modernize Collective Bargaining" was the headline for a story in the UAW newspaper, which pointed out that the 1907 Industrial Disputes Investigation Act was thirty-four years old.[90] The recognition of unions was described as "a modern conception of labour relations."[91] When labour supporters urged Ontario to enact collective bargaining legislation, they called for a "modern bill," one in line with the principles of the Allies' Atlantic Charter.[92] In a front-page story entitled "Modern Labour Policy Proposed in Ottawa Brief," the UAW's newspaper reported on the union's submission to National War Labour Board hearings in 1943. The CIO, it implied, was vital to a modern economic future that business's retrogressive opposition to the CIO was obstructing: "It is only due to the extreme patience of workers ... that attempts to hold their organizations static in a dynamic area of industrial society has not produced more work stoppages."[93]

Modern Labour Relations Means Cooperation

As the war progressed, the CIO tended to define modernity as "cooperation" and "partnership" with employers. As unions were the "culminating growth of a great industry," this meant that "labour and management could now cooperate," read a union editorial.[94] No doubt the CIO's emphasis on cooperation to some extent reflected the desire of Canadian workers to maintain war production during a hard-fought conflict and the consequent need for CIO organizers to be sensitive to that patriotism when making their appeals. CIO writers, orators, and publicists were nothing if not strategic in their propaganda efforts.

But the partnership motif was also a product of the strength of the Communist Party in the CIO.[95] After Hitler's invasion of the Soviet Union, Communists in both the Canadian and American CIO began to argue for labour-management cooperation in aid of an all-out war effort in defence of the Soviet Union. Canadian CIO affiliates had to play a delicate game that involved balancing the American CIO's no-strike pledge with the actualities of Canadian labour law and worker militancy. CIO unions trod a fine line between arguing for harmonious relations with management while also arguing for militancy and non-cooperation when employers proved obdurate. In spite of the strong language used in many organizing leaflets (e.g., comparing business and managers to Hitler and Nazism), cooperation was the dominant theme in the CIO's wartime literature pertaining to its vision of labour relations.[96] In the UAW's 1944 "Win the Peace Plan," the words "cooperation," "partnership," and "unity" appeared eighteen times in the three-and-a-half-page document.[97]

Indeed, the crusade, shared by Communist activists in all unions, for an "all-out war effort" and the incessant calls for an Allied second front in Europe may have moderated labour's views about both corporations and capitalism. The Communist-led UE told workers in all its organizing literature that it would adhere strictly to the no-strike pledge no matter what management provocation might be.[98] At times, UE literature read as though the real reason for joining a union was to help the war effort. "Will it help us win the war if I join the union?" asked UE organizer Dick Steele in an overseas letter to the *UE News*: "Will the union help to give our fighters more guns, planes, tanks, small arms, etc.?"[99] His letter made no reference to wages or working conditions. In 1942, UE district council delegates voted to boost production voluntarily by 10 percent to 15 percent "even if management opposed it."[100]

The UE was not alone in making pro-production appeals, however. When Pat Conroy, for example, who professed political non-partisanship, argued against suggestions that a general strike be called to support striking Stelco workers in the summer of 1943, he, too, invoked the war: "We are fighting a war for survival. Shall we let Hitler go ... and concentrate our fight against the employers? ... Above all else, we must see to it that this war is won."[101]

In fact, given that war production was their priority, some organizers' pro-production war rhetoric appeared designed to dampen worker militancy. A UAW leaflet to Metallic Roofing workers exhorted workers to exercise "production discipline" and not to use any "wildcat tactics" because the grievance procedure "recognized by the Company and the Union [would] make possible the peaceful settlement of every dispute."

Labour cooperation, however, did have a catch in that it was premised on business and government's entering into "partnership" with labour. That was the "deal" the UE was offering. The UE said it would adhere to its no-strike pledge in the interests of "total war," but it was explicit in its demand that, in return, business and government grant full "partnership" and recognition of labour rights.[102] As C.S. Jackson put it, the only guarantee of cooperation was for labour to be given "an important functional part to play in all the policy making bodies of the nation." CCL president Aaron Mosher, a CCFer, also alluded to a "deal" that traded off militancy for a place at the table. He said the majority of Canadian workers agreed with the CCL that winning the war was the first priority and that only by using the strike weapon as a last resort would CIO unions win the public support "essential to the attainment of [its] objectives."

Although the CIO in Canada did not adopt the American CIO's no-strike pledge, support for labour-management production committees (LMPCs) was official CIO policy in Canada. Organizers told workers that total war required total production, which could only be brought about by labour-management cooperation. But, as George Burt noted in 1942, few locals had set LMPCs up in spite of pressure from UAW headquarters, possibly because workers were not interested. Burt himself was ambivalent about the committees. "We may as well realize the fact that workers are more interested in protecting what they have and extending those benefits than in something which so far is only a popular theory," he told the union's Canadian district council in 1942, wondering out loud how many resources to divert to the project: "which in my opinion has doubtful organizational value."[103] Burt also worried that organizing workers into these committees as a means of eventually organizing them into a union would border on "company unionism."[104]

Significantly, the CIO believed the ethos of "cooperation" should survive the war. Long before such bureaucratizing measures as union security and government recognition laws may have, as some have argued, reduced the militancy of the labour movement, the CIO's proposals for the postwar social contract were already less than radical. Urging cooperation among management, government, and labour, the UAW's 1944 *Win the Peace Plan* reassured readers: "At no time do we challenge the right of the owners of industry to manage the plants in which our members are found."[105] "The worker does not seek to usurp management's function or ask for a place on the Board of Directors of concerns where organized," said the *Aircraft Worker.* "The worker through his union merely asks for his rights," which the writer defined as the right to negotiate wages and working conditions.[106] Union writers also assured workers that the union's goal was not to negotiate away all employer profits: "They will still make big profits, but it does mean that profits are more equally divided with the workers."[107]

Partnership, rather than an adversarial industrial philosophy in which relative bargaining power decided labour and management's essentially irreconcilable differences over the distribution of wealth and control, was the ethic of the day. "It is our job to help the worker," read the *War Worker* in 1943, "and in so doing we help production by bringing the worker and the employer closer together and showing them the great need they have for one another."[108] The paper went on to complain that management's failure to keep its promises was endangering "harmony" in the face of union efforts to create a "friendly and cooperative relationship that would accomplish more than continuous friction and table pounding." In fact, underlying the language of harmony and cooperation was the notion of "order," a commodity that CIO leaders appeared to value highly. In its submission to the NWLB hearings in 1943, the UAW called for labour relations legislation that would "permit the orderly growth of the labour movement."[109] The CCL's Pat Conroy argued that such legislation "would calm the excesses of both sides."[110]

Other forms of pragmatism were factored into the CIO's support for cooperation. The UE, for example, vowed to continue its wartime no-strike pledge after the war, reminding workers that unions had been "smashed" after the postwar strike wave in 1919. Cooperation would be the better path for workers to follow in the aftermath of the Second World War. "In the war period we have all gained through cooperation; in the postwar it is equally possible for all to continue that cooperation to our mutual benefit," the UE's director of organizing, Ross Russell, told union activists.[111] In late 1944, C.S. Jackson said that the war had changed social and class relations so completely that: "we must of necessity re-evaluate our relationships to employers in terms of the peace that lies ahead."[112] The labour movement should be prepared to make common cause with any group in society that wanted the same things labour wanted, including employers, Jackson said.[113]

But some activists were impatient with the cooperation line. Murray Dowson, a union activist at De Havilland Aircraft, complained in a letter-to-the-editor of the local union paper that the publication was too critical of workers who wanted the union to take a more aggressive policy vis-à-vis management. "The critical and militant tendencies in our union must be encouraged," he wrote: "Remember, the union movement was built on the dissatisfaction of the workers with rotten conditions. Our own CIO grew up on the criticisms of the inadequate methods and lack of militancy of the AF of L leadership."[114] Unlike some UAW locals, such as Local 439 at Massey-Harris in Toronto, the UAW unit at De Havilland had few Communist Party activists. That Dowson's letter was published by the De Havilland paper indicates that the union's official stance favouring partnership could be openly questioned, if not defied, at least at the local level.

"A Government with a Heart"

The CIO attitude towards government was ambivalent. On the one hand, government was seen as being captive of business and pro-business politicians were seen as being reactionary, advocating a world in which "pot-bellied millionaires control[led] everything and whose slogan [was] 'Billions for War but not a damn thing for Peace.'"[115] Government, furthermore, had been unsympathetic and unresponsive during the Great Depression. The *Aircraft Worker* printed a letter from a former member serving overseas, recalling how government had not taken action during the Depression. "Our government did nothing to protect us in those years," he reminded his readers: "To them we were a problem they did not care to solve."[116]

But while the CIO believed that big business controlled government, it did not believe that government was inherently hostile to labour. As one union editorial pointed out, referring to the New Deal's Wagner Act in the United States: "Our American cousins were much less harshly dealt with. They happen to have a government with a heart."[117] Examples of what government could and should do came not just from the prewar New Deal but also, and at least as important, from the wartime United Kingdom. Union newspapers carried frequent stories and references to government developments in Britain that were favourable to labour, including the 1942 Beveridge Report, considered the founding document of the British welfare state. Union papers often described the success of Britain's industrial war effort, which the CIO attributed to the Churchill government's "partnership" with labour, illustrated by the presence of Labour Party titan Ernest Bevan in its War Cabinet.

The CIO told workers that, through liberal democracy, it was possible for Canadians to elect a government more responsive to their needs. The Canadian people could vote for a government that would "administer Canadian affairs in the interests of the majority, not in the interests of the minority," which, as a UAW editorial averred, "is the case at present."[118] According to a contributor to *Local 439 News*: "Canada belongs to the people, so let us have a government in power who will see that we workers get a fair share of the things that are rightfully ours."[119]

The CIO's faith in government had grown with the nation's war effort. In 1939, the CIO's legislative program was minimal. It did not even include a demand for Wagner Act-type legislation but merely required that Ottawa insist that government war contractors recognize worker-chosen unions at their workplace. By the end of the war, however, the CIO's vision of government had expanded significantly. Using the Beveridge Report as a model, it included, in addition to comprehensive labour legislation, a wide range of social security measures;

state-run and financed full-employment programs; and national programs for health insurance, childcare, housing, fuel, transport, and food.[120] This new CIO vision of government was a far cry from its modest 1939 vision, and it was a direct result of what the war had wrought. New, even radical, demands on the state infused the CIO's views of postwar reconstruction, with the CCL's urging that Canada's banking and finance sectors be nationalized and that private broadcasting be brought under public ownership.

The CIO saw that the war had transformed Canada from being "primarily an agricultural nation [in]to one of the greatest industrial nations in the world," as Mosher told a 1944 CCL convention. "To convert this enormous national economy from wartime to peacetime basis," he said, "it will be necessary to place the financing and operation and control of the entire economic system under the control of the State."[121] The productive capacity that the nation had developed during the war should be utilized for the "common good" after the war, agreed the *Inglis Steelworker*, through public ownership and control of monopoly industry.[122] That ordinary workers were responding to this argument was indicated in a *Steelworker* letter-to-the-editor, which said: "[in Canada there is] enough wealth to go around, provided the Machinery of Government is used to organize and guide us to that end, not as now, in the manipulated interests of some few greedy individuals."[123]

The CIO argued that human rights were also government's responsibility, calling for laws counteracting racial and religious discrimination, making anti-Semitism a "punishable crime," extending full citizenship to Native peoples, and guaranteeing equal pay for women. In fact, the wartime language of "rights" infused the CIO's ideas about the proper role of government. The CCL's Political Action Committee used the language of rights in its 1944 legislative program. Canadians had "a fundamental right" to a job; they also had the right to an adequate income, decent housing, good health and adequate health care as well as the right to "complete social security" and education.[124]

The war had, to some extent, trained the CIO to look to government for support for its objectives. The IDIA, however irksome, had in fact allowed for the de facto and, eventually, the official recognition of unions, especially in workplaces in which, before the war, the IDIA had not been in place.[125] In 1941, George Burt was telling the UAW's International Executive Board that the union in Canada was calling strikes in order to wrest not just conciliation services (and therefore the possibility of union recognition) from government but also "more cooperation" from labour department officials.[126] In fact, as the war went on, many provisions in collective agreements – such as seniority clauses, union shop status, and dues check-off arrangements – were the result of the intervention of wartime labour boards and officials.[127] Over the course of the war, the CIO unions had learned how to use government mechanisms to reach key workplace objectives. As Burt pointed out in 1943, "before the war it was possible to settle most problems locally, but with the maze of procedure that is necessary to follow at the present time, it is all the more necessary for our membership to be conversant with the procedures of War Labour Boards and other Government agencies."[128] Other government regulations during the war had in many cases found strong support with the CIO; and resolutions to CCL conventions in the war's later years called for the continuation of many war-created programs, such as technical and training programs developed during the war, public ownership of some industries, and controls over the economy.[129]

As the CCL's Political Action Committee told workers in 1944, ensuring that government would continue to intervene positively for workers was why the CIO entered politics: "It has become increasingly clear that if workers are to enjoy freedom from want and freedom from fear, organized labour must once and for all definitely adopt a positive political attitude. It must take part in the political struggles of the day."[130] As CCL head Aaron Mosher told a 1944 CCL convention, "The primary purpose of a labour organization is to protect and promote the economic interests of workers." While this work would be done chiefly at the bargaining table, Mosher indicated that "the development of political machinery [was] nothing more than an extension of the general purpose of labour."[131] In other words, labour needed an expanded government regime in the public sector to bolster and ensure its successes in the private sector.

Its experiences during the war boosted the CIO's political activism. Its wartime failure to persuade government, through mere lobbying efforts, to bring in permanent labour legislation led the CIO to urge its locals and members to become involved in politics as it believed that such legislation was necessary if labour was to retain its wartime strength postwar. The ferocity of employer resistance to unionization and corporate plans to renew the assault on the CIO, once PC 1003 had expired with the conclusion of the war, was evidence of that need.[132] The CIO's incursion into politics, including its vocal support for labour-friendly candidates, made a difference in wartime elections, especially in urban working-class areas where CIO affiliates were strong. A Steelworkers editor, noting that both mainstream political parties were taking a leftward turn by 1943, wrote: "This ... speaks to the wisdom of the USWA going to direct political action to elect its own supporters and members."[133] There was some truth to this claim. In 1943, after a strong electoral showing by the labour-supported CCF in the Ontario election, the Ontario government introduced a labour bill that provided machinery for union recognition and that mandated employer obligation to enter into collective bargaining with recognized unions.

Labour was acutely aware that capital was entering the political fray, with company executives (such as John Inglis Co. vice-president Bert Trestrail) forming a committee to persuade Canadians of the value of private enterprise – "now cleverly referred to as 'free enterprise,'" a Steelworkers writer noted waspishly. "Canadian employers and THEIR union, the Canadian Manufacturers' Association are getting pretty scared," he wrote, referring to the growth of the CIO and swelling support for the CCF.[134] And so, as the labour movement turned to political action later in the war, it considered the strategic use of public relations ever more important. Noting that the Canadian Manufacturer's Association had opposed Ontario's proposed collective bargaining legislation, a UAW editor said it was "the weight of public opinion" that had led the government to bring in a genuine labour bill in 1943 and urged union members to become even more active in the public realm.[135]

Conclusion: A Successful Narrative Strategy

The CIO's narrative of the nation's workers and warriors fighting common enemies in order to win a modern, more compassionate country was integral to the young organization's early growth in Canada. It was a narrative that combined union militancy with submission to national duty. It was a story rooted in the Great Depression and two terrible global conflicts that had put security at the top of workers' needs. It was a tale that had to reconcile unionists' bitter experience of government as a hostile force with the wartime revelation of government's potential to help advance the CIO's agenda. As a result, this was not a story of revolution or radicalism but, rather, of reform, of parliamentarianism rather than syndicalism. It was a story told by union activists who were trying against fearsome opposition to organize workers in the middle of a massive national effort to prevail in a popularly supported and often desperately fought war. The narrative was virtually universal in all union rhetoric. Its themes, vocabulary, metaphors, and tropes were used by unions who supported the CCF and the CPC alike, demonstrating not just the resonance of the narrative with workers but also – in its reformist character – how much the wartime CPC wanted to be, or to be seen to be, part of a responsible labour movement. Given the CIO publicists' hard-headed appraisal of the primacy of the war effort for Canadian workers, it is likely the CIO used these discourses because it believed they would be effective; that is, that they would appeal to union members and the general public alike.

It remains unclear, however, whether the themes of "partnership" and "co-operation" that appeared in union newspapers represented the true beliefs of CIO leaders. It can be plausibly argued that, in the interests of labour's appearing reassuringly respectable and responsible, CIO leaders were more militant than the papers portrayed them. It can just as plausibly be argued that CIO leaders were less militant than workers and used themes of partnership and cooperation to inculcate in workers moderate views about labour ambitions and militancy.

The results of the Canadian UAW's no-strike-pledge vote, when elected union activists voted against a strike ban, however, could indicate that, during the war, union leaders were more militant than were union members. On the other hand, there is the evidence of workers' willingness to strike during the war – after all, one in three Canadian workers struck in 1943 – but seldom, if ever, in defiance of their leaders.[136] However, there is no ambivalence about the CIO leaders swiftly unsheathing the strike weapon as soon as the war was over and leading the hard-fought strikes of 1946-47. Indeed, as early as June 1945, only a month after V-E Day and even before the war in the Pacific had ended, the UAW's George Burt was musing out loud that, once the war was over and the Canadian UAW no longer constrained by its American division's no-strike pledge, his union could be less defensive about striking.[137] But at the very same time, in order to ensure that labour would be a full "partner" in redesigning the country, Burt and other labour leaders were lobbying government to appoint CIO representatives to the agencies and committees considering Canada's postwar reconstruction.

In sum, it is likely that, as trade unionists, CIO leaders had to tack in two directions simultaneously: (1) towards militancy and class struggle when they needed to strengthen their members' resolve to take on employers; and (2) towards responsible unionism and partnership when lobbying the power structure to enact legislative protection for unions and to give labour a seat at the tables of power.

It is also possible that, during the war, workers viewed their world in a similarly complex fashion: not wanting to interrupt the war effort, they were willing to "cooperate" to an extent while also having a sense when it was necessary to be militant. But when the war was no longer a factor, workers were as fiercely militant as were their leaders. The massive postwar strike wave in Canada was evidence of how CIO leaders and members worked together to take on the corporations, with the lines of union pickets swelled and strengthened by war veterans, sometimes wearing their service uniforms to assert their respectability and to stake a claim to what their wartime sacrifices had earned them.

The Cold War led to the purging or ostracism of Communists in the labour movement, put trade unionists on the defensive, and encouraged them to track mainstream political values. Thus, it was a factor in the CIO's becoming a moderate, pragmatic agent of change.[138] The CIO's wartime narrative strategy also

helped to produce the pragmatic labour movement of the postwar era. It was, nonetheless, a narrative that won workers' allegiance to industrial unions at a critical juncture, and it raised the ante for politicians to meet their own rhetoric regarding "the people's war" and its postwar aftermath.[139]

Origins of Canada's Wagner Model of Industrial Relations: The United Auto Workers in Canada and the Suppression of "Rank and File" Unionism, 1936-1953[1]

Donald M. Wells

Abstract. Focusing on the origins of the United Automobile Workers (UAW) in Canada during the 1940s, this study analyzes the evolution of a work-centred, "rank and file" model of unionism into a top-down model of economistic unionism centred on collective bargaining and the stabilization of labour-management relations in the workplace. In order to attain organizational security, UAW leaders turned to state elites. The main price of employer and state acceptance of such security was the union leaders' agreement to suppress worker "direct action." This tradeoff has helped to shape the current limits of trade union mobilization in Canada.

Résumé. Cette étude se concentre sur les origines du TUA (Travailleurs Unis de l'Automobile) au Canada pendant les années 1940 et analyse l'évolution d'un modèle de syndicalisme "s'appuyant sur la base" qui s'est transformé en un modèle pyramidal de syndicalisme de l'économie, centré sur la négociation collective et la stabilisation des relations industrielles sur le lieu de travail. Dans le but de parvenir à la sécurité organisationnelle, les dirigeants du TUA se sont tournés vers les élites d'État. Le prix principal à payer pour que les employeurs et l'État acceptent de donner une telle sécurité aux syndicats a été de faire promettre à leurs dirigeants d'interdire aux ouvriers de recourir à "l'action directe." Ce marché a aidé à marquer les limites actuelles imposées à la mobilisation des syndicats au Canada.

---

1. Funding for this research was paid for, in part, through an Arts Research Board Grant from McMaster University and a Henry Kaiser Family Foundation Award from the Walter Reuther Archives of Labor and Urban Affairs at Wayne State University. For their generous archival assistance, I thank Ray Boryczka, Archives of Labor and Urban Affairs, Wayne Sate University; Walter Neutel, National Archives of Canada; Kathy Bennett, Archives of the Canadian Auto Workers; and Sandra Notarianni, Historical Consultant, Ford Motor Company of Canada. I am grateful to Bob Russell, Larry Haiven, William Coleman, Wayne Lewchuk, Carl Cuneo, David Fraser, and three anonymous reviewers from the *Canadian Journal of Sociology* for many helpful suggestions. I thank Bill Walsh and Andy Maroko for sharing their UAW experiences, and John Napier for sending to me the memoirs of his father, the late James Napier. As usual, Ruth Frager provided much encouragement and advice.

> You know, there are really two UAWs. There is ... the UAW that wins pay raises, good pensions, more vacation pay, guaranteed wages.... Then there is the UAW we hear about in union locals — the UAW that can't make General Motors, Chrysler, and Ford stop driving workers like machines.
>
> *Indonesian trade unionist, 1960 (Marquart, 1975: 129)*

> The worker does not seek to usurp management's function....
>
> Preamble, *Constitution of the International Union, UAW-CIO* (1955)

Introduction

Since the 1970s, industrial unionism in Canada has been facing a growing crisis. In contrast to the "boom" years of the postwar era, real wage growth has stagnated and union density in the mining, manufacturing, and transportation sectors has declined. Overall, collective bargaining strength has weakened in the context of chronic high unemployment and a dual labour market characterized by increasing polarization between better-paid, "good" jobs and a burgeoning number of low-paid, part-time, temporary, contract, and other kinds of contingent "bad" jobs (Betcherman, 1992; McBride, 1992; O'Grady, 1992; Economic Council of Canada, 1990).

The causes of labour's crisis are partly economic: the rapid diffusion of skill-cutting and labour-displacing technologies, greater global competitiveness (cutting monopoly rents sustaining higher wages and job security), increased capital mobility (often to low wage, high repression areas), and a shift in the sectoral and occupational composition of the economy away from industrial unionism's base in mass production.

Labour's crisis is also in part political in origin. It is rooted, most fundamentally, in the declining willingness and capacity of governments to use Keynesian macroeconomic stabilization policies to foster employment. It is also rooted in deepening reductions in the social wage (e.g. public welfare, health care, education) and a series of state attacks on collective bargaining, including the deregulation of highly unionized sectors (e.g. communications, transportation) and restrictions on labour rights, including the suspension of strike rights, wage controls, and abrogation of public sector contracts (McBride, 1987; Panitch and Swartz, 1993; Russell, 1990b). Finally, labour's crisis is rooted in the implementation of international agreements (Canada-US Free Trade Agreement, North American Free Trade Agreement, General Agreement on Tariffs and Trade) which enhance the autonomy of transnational firms from state regulation.

These economic and political changes signify a shift away from Canada's postwar "Fordist" framework based on a state-regulated balancing of Taylorist mass production and mass consumption (Jenson, 1989; Wolfe, 1984; Mahon, 1991). It was this framework which helped to stabilize the industrial relations regime which emerged during and after World War II. With important carryovers from prewar industrial relations, Canada's postwar industrial relations regime was crafted on the 1935 US National Labor Relations Act (known as the Wagner Act) which grew out of mass strikes and sitdowns of the mid 1930s in the US and legalized the right to unionize and bargain collectively.[2]

The primary goal of this Wagner model of industrial relations was to ensure industrial peace (Tomlins, 1965). To this end, the model is centred on bureaucratic, economistic collective bargaining by union elites and precludes a politics of class mobilization, particularly in the workplace. Unions have bargaining jurisdiction over such issues as pay systems, fringe benefits, the length of the working day and week, and structures of union representation in the workplace. Particularly through their exercise of contractual seniority provisions, unions also have a limited role in the regulation of internal markets in areas such as promotions, layoffs, transfers, etc. However, under the Wagner model the main contours of the division of labour are established by management. Management reserves the right to make decisions in all areas that are fundamental to the control of the labour process, as well as decisions regarding the location and nature of investment and the choice and design of products and services. The union has a contractual obligation to uphold not only these management rights but all other powers of management that have not been specifically qualified by the contract or by law. Furthermore, the union is bound, both by contract and by statutory law to assist in the adjudication of workplace disputes through mandatory grievance and arbitration procedures. These constraints, together with a prohibition on strikes for the duration of the contract (in most jurisdictions), signify that union leaders are legally bound to repudiate and to either directly or indirectly suppress the workplace militancy of the workers they represent (Drache and Glasbeek, 1992: ch. 6, 7; Haiven, 1990).

This model of unionism was more or less coherent as long as the Fordist framework held. In effect, the macroeconomic stability of Canadian Fordism after World War II reinforced this model of labour relations at the microeconomic level. However, with the breakdown of Canadian Fordism during the past twenty or so years, the inadequacies of this industrial relations model are becoming increasingly apparent (Mahon, 1991).

I will attempt in this essay to come to an understanding of key elements of the crisis of contemporary Canadian unionism, in particular the failure of the unions to mobilize their members in response to "post Fordist" economic and political challenges. I will attempt this understanding by analyzing the *origins* of the confinement of workers' collective self-activity during and after World War II. The main thesis is that while Canada's Wagner model contained major gains for labour, it also contributed to fundamental, enduring weakness in the internal organization of industrial unionism. By severing mass militancy and solidarity, on the one hand, from contract bargaining and administration, on the

---

2. On the differences between the Canadian and US Wagner models, see Robinson (1993).

other, Canada's Wagner model became a Trojan horse: at once a token of victory and a breach of labour's defenses.

Moreover, the defeat of this "rank and file" unionism[3] was not simply imposed on union leaders, but, with the exception of a few local leaders, was sponsored by most of them. Indeed, this suppression of rank and file unionism was not addressed in any fundamental way by any major faction of the labour leadership in Canada, regardless of their ideological and other differences. After a lag of several years, by the 1950s Canadian industrial unionism converged (with some differences) toward the Wagner model developed earlier in the US, a model which also featured a marginalization of rank and file action.[4] This shift in the basic nature of Canadian unionism considerably predated the ascendancy of capital which began in the 1970s, and helps to account for it.

As will be seen, a critical goal of industrial workers before and during World War II was to limit management's right to control their jobs in areas such as speedup, discipline, hiring, and the allocation of work. By setting limits on managerial prerogatives in production, workers sought a form of industrial citizenship in which violations of workplace rules would be settled by grievance procedures rather than managerial fiat. To this end, they engaged in "direct action," including walkouts, sitdowns, sabotage, and slowdowns. Such direct action was largely local in character and often did not emerge beyond work group militancy. To become more effective as a vehicle of working class politics, this militancy required coordination across workplaces and between locals. As noted, however, this option was abandoned in favour of a more orderly, rule-bound regime based on contracts with grievance and arbitration procedures that substituted for worker militancy. The unions hoped that this would provide both institutional security and protection for workers by checking the power of employers and their political allies.

At stake was a change in the meaning of unionism from a political *movement* built out of class mobilization at work to *institutions* built around collective bargaining and contract administration. This parallels the main theme of Michels's *Political Parties*. Yet his "iron law of oligarchy" assumes the "rank and file are incapable of looking after their own interests" and that "a fighting party needs a hierarchical structure" (1962: 111, 79). In this case, however, the

3. Testimony to the hegemony of the kind of unionism the emerged out of the postwar compromise, the term "rank and file" today is typically used in the Canadian labour movement to refer to local *leaders*. The term itself is military in origin and refers to the disciplined mass of soldiers who take orders from the officers.
4. Basing their findings on research at union locals in the US from 1948-1952, Sayles and Strauss concluded that "good relations with management have been associated with a decline in democracy." They observed that the "greatest concentration of undemocratic unions exists where the union is strong enough to 'stabilize' the industry" (p. 256).

rank and file had often been demonstrably effective in pursuit of their interests. Moreover, in this case, the hierarchical structures were a precondition of industrial "peace." Contrary to Michels, the evidence here suggests that the oligarchic tendencies which developed were not simply inherent in unions but imposed by external forces acting reciprocally with bureaucratic *tendencies* (not imperatives) inside the union. These tendencies reflected a broader interplay of class forces than Michels analysed, since he focused almost entirely on leader-mass relations *inside* political parties and unions. Finally, as will be explained, Canada's Wagner model of unionism emerged out of particular and contingent historical circumstances rather than from any inherent imperative of organizational development. As a result, Michels's functionalist generalizations are inapplicable here.

The empirical focus of this analysis is the shift in the nature of leader-member relations at the largest industrial union in Canada, the United Auto Workers (UAW), from the late 1930s to the early 1950s. More than any other union, the UAW was central to the making of Canada's Wagner model. Most attention is devoted to the key UAW Local 200 at Ford of Canada in Windsor, Ontario, where the pivotal 1945 Ford strike and the critical Rand decision took place. Analytical emphasis is placed on changing relations between local leaders, especially in-plant leaders (substewards, stewards, committee persons, etc.) and the rank and file.

As the following section on the early history of union leader-member relations at Ford of Canada shows, UAW leaders in Canada initially were linked organically to rank and file militancy. However, by the middle years of the war a split emerged between leaders and members. Several sources of this division emerge from the historical evidence. These include attempts by some leaders to subordinate workers' immediate class interests to the war effort, the ways union representation privileged those who spoke English, and the role of political elites in enticing union leaders with promises of legal guarantees for union security if rank and file militancy were curbed. Most prominent of all was the role of the wartime state in the legal regulation of relations between union leaders and the rank and file.

This rise of a more authoritarian type of trade union leadership provides the basis for a more balanced perspective on the import of the postwar compromise in Canada. Whereas some have argued that the grievance procedure and other restrictions on managerial power embedded in the Wagner model were, in essence, democratic achievements by organized labour (MacDowell, 1978: 196), evidence presented here suggests a serious loss of democratic potential in the workplace and a manifest loss of democratic accountability in the UAW.

The evidence presented here also demonstrates that the modern collective bargaining system was not in any simple sense imposed by capital and the state. Canada's Wagner model was the product of complex reciprocal forces, including the contradictory role of wartime political elites and the intransigent opposition of Ford of Canada to such unionism right up to 1945. Not least in significance, it was the product of sustained, active support by organized labour at all levels, including most of the rank and file. The notion that the Wagner model was caused primarily by power-hungry or "sellout" or corrupt union leaders does no justice to what was a complicated historical and sociopolitical process. Instead, the evidence suggests that the Wagner model arose through piecemeal changes during the war, many of which were considered temporary at the time. Ottawa's concern to maintain war production was the main theme in the creation of a temporary wartime regulatory framework that only later emerged as a more permanent industrial relations system. Yet each of the key points marking the evolution of that labour regime empowered labour leaders at the expense of rank and file workers. It was this emerging legal framework that provided the most powerful institutional preconditions and incentives for the suppression of rank and file militancy by union leaders.

Although senior labour leaders understood the course industrial unionism was taking, it was not until the later 1940s that the fuller implications of that direction became clear. While the general tenor of the Wagner model was outlined during the war, the transformation of relations between union leaders and members took place afterwards over a period of several years. Moreover, that transformation was not wholly determined by the legal framework but was reinforced by a series of contingent factors, most of which were outside the control of UAW leaders in Canada. These included the rise of a single dominant leadership faction in the UAW in the US, the use of the Cold War as a convenient political atmosphere for stigmatizing worker militancy and "left" leadership, and the rise of anti-labour forces within the US Congress. Not least in significance, the Wagner model of unionism was sustained by the most powerful and sustained economic boom in history.

Workplace Militancy, State Regulation, and Union Leadership in the Canadian UAW, 1936-45

Throughout the 1930s, Ford of Canada's automobile assembly complex in Windsor, Ontario, was notorious for its draconian labour policies. The Trades and Labour Congress dubbed it "the citadel of reaction in Canada" for its blacklists, favouritism to "red apple boys" (who curried favour with supervisors), and for firing workers at "the whim of the bosses."[5] Because of these conditions and because the Ford plants in Windsor contained the largest concentration of industrial workers in Ontario west of Toronto, the UAW and the Communist Party made organizing it a priority. The presence of a large number

5. *Trades and Labour Congress Journal*, n.d. (George Burt Scrapbook, CAW).

of Eastern European immigrants in East Windsor was also considered a major advantage to the Party (Manley, 1986: 113). Although few in number, Communists played "a big part in organizing [the local]," the former principal Communist organizer at Windsor recalled.[6] He explained that they concentrated on skilled workers

> because they travelled around the plant to do maintenance work. Therefore they could have contact with workers all over the plant. Generally speaking the workers would look up to the skilled workers.... They were safer because they were highly skilled and [so] had less chance of the company booting them, but they had to be cautious.[7]

Although the UAW chartered its first Canadian local in Windsor at Kelsey Wheel in 1936, and another local at McKinnon Industries in St. Catharines in the same year, and followed with a breakthrough at General Motors in Oshawa in 1937, Ford of Canada proved to be a much more formidable challenge. Despite the combined efforts of the UAW, Communists,[8] and others, and despite their success in helping to build a pro-union core of skilled British immigrants, unionization at Ford of Canada in Windsor failed until after the UAW organized Ford in the US in 1941 (Cako, 1971: 21).[9]

In the context of wartime labour shortages, the 1941 UAW victory at Ford Windsor was also aided by Ford *management* in Detroit and by the Canadian *state*. Fearing that UAW sympathy strikes would disrupt its US production if workers struck Windsor, managers in Detroit stopped shipping parts to Ford Canada (Montero, 1979: 96). In order to avert threats to war production, Ottawa conducted a recognition vote (Moulton, 1974: 155) in which the UAW won sixty per cent of the votes against Ford's offer of a company union and generous economic terms (Veres, 1956: 47).

6. Interview with Bill Walsh, former union organizer for the Communist Party, 14 July, 1994. Communists had been trying to organize Ford Windsor since 1925 (Manley, 1986: 113).
7. Ibid.
8. After the Soviet-German Non-Aggression Pact of 1939, Stalin directed Communists around the world to oppose the war. In June 1940 an amendment to the Defence of Canada Regulations declared the Communist Party of Canada illegal. Communists were interned and jailed. After Hitler's invasion of the Soviet Union in 1941, the Communist Party of Canada supported the war but it took two more years before the party was legalized (Penner 1988: 179). The party's organizing and general credibility were severely hampered during this period.
9. Dependence on the US UAW is a major theme in the history of the Canadian UAW. James Napier, a former Communist organizer and auto worker, notes that a 1936 strike at Kelsey Wheel in Windsor failed because the US UAW did not support it. Reinstatement of fired Kelsey Wheel strikers in Canada was due to the intervention of the UAW at Kelsey Wheel in the US (1976: 15-18). Napier also credits union victories at Young Industries and Walker Metal in Windsor in the late 1930s to the UAW's victory at General Motors in Flint, Michigan (1976: 25). See also Veres (1956: 33-38, 52-54).

Ford thus became the first auto manufacturer in Canada officially to recognize the UAW. Unlike Ford-US, however, the company only "grudgingly consented" to the UAW "on a minimum basis."[10] And unlike the US government, which integrated the American UAW into a system of wartime corporatism (Gerstle, 1989: 311-12), both Ottawa and the government of Ontario refused labour any official public policy role during the war.[11] These differences help explain the closer relationship between Canadian UAW leaders and the rank and file during the early war years.[12]

The Canadian UAW's early support for direct action *in conjunction with* the grievance process was especially important to relations between leaders and members. Communist UAW organizer James Napier argued that winning such grievances "established the union." At the Kelsey Wheel local in Windsor, the UAW

> ... never signed a written contract until after the war nor had a written grievance procedure. When the members needed a raise or a problem settled, they got it-right away — by demanding it from management and getting it by relying on their own united strength. As new gains were won ... they were posted in minutes as union-management agreements and became the regular practice of the plants. (Napier, 1976: 20)

Nor did UAW staff receive salaries and cars which set them apart. Organizers were paid $40 a week plus expenses, not much more than a worker's pay (Napier, 1976: 20).

Not surprisingly, the number of work stoppages in the automobile industry far exceeded the average for the Canadian manufacturing sector as a whole throughout the 1940s (Herzenberg, 1991: 88) and the UAW's Local 200 at Ford Windsor was in the forefront. There were mass walkouts in 1942, 1943 and 1945, and numerous workgroup and department-wide stoppages. A frequent form of sabotage was dubbed "offset": "You had to look like you were working like hell and miss a bolt off some part," a worker explained (Fraser, 1982: 27). Because such resistance resulted in costly repairs, management would slow the work pace. By using such tactics, workers achieved unprecedented control in areas such as supervisory practices and workloads. Direct action was used even in areas such as pay and vacations (Millar, 1981: 251).

During the early war years, union stewards and committeemen were important allies of this resistance. Elected by groups of rank and file workers, they conducted informal negotiations with front line supervisors, and became the UAW's backbone as a workplace organization. This was partly due to dense representation: the 1942 contract provided 50 stewards and 13 committeemen for some 7,000 members. There was also a sub-steward for every 50 or so workers.[13] These latter played a critical role. While they collected dues and signed up new members, they communicated union policy to the members (and the members' concerns to the leaders) on a daily basis.

In-plant leaders also played a major role in bargaining. Because the UAW was new to Ford, key aspects of shop floor relations were still part of an unwritten "common law" of the workplace that was established day-to-day (Fraser, 1982: 63). Wage bargaining, for instance, was conducted by reclassifying jobs to get around the government wage freeze. The UAW's advocacy of job reclassification was a big factor in the constant drive to recruit union members[14] and maintain dues payments.

The UAW also strengthened the organizational ties between local and regional leaders in Canada. The main mechanism was the District Council which was created in 1937 to represent Canadian UAW locals (Benedict, 1992: 141-45; Veres, 1956: 172-73). Meeting regularly to discuss common problems, the Council consisted of delegates from each local, but it was not a rank and file body. Delegates were elected at annual meetings which, although open to all members, were attended mainly by local leaders and activists. Delegates thus tended to be local executive board members.[15]

Initially, the UAW leadership rode a wave of increasing worker militancy. Many workers were emboldened by the rapid decline in unemployment from over 11% at the start of the war to 4.4% in 1941. By 1943, labour was so scarce that Ottawa denied workers in essential industries the right to quit, and denied employers, such as Ford, the right to fire them at will (Roberts and Bullen, 1984: 112).

Because Ford-Windsor made military vehicles, Local 200 fell under federal jurisdiction. In order to limit potential threats to war production, Ottawa intervened directly. A 1939 federal order-in-council (PC 3495) made conciliation and "cooling off periods" mandatory. In 1941 Ottawa made strikes illegal.

---

10. Memorandum by Roy England, President of Local 200, UAW, 15 May, 1945 (NAC, Acc. MG 30 A94, vol. 44, File 3144).
11. For example, the President of Ford Canada threatened to resign from the War Supply Labour Board, which he chaired, if union representatives were named to serve on it (Whitaker, 197: 148).
12. Nevertheless, there was much direct action in many UAW plants in the US, and shop stewards often played a central role in it (Edsforth, 1987: 198-200; Lichtenstein, 1983: 295; Glaberman, 1980).
13. Report of Local 200, Minutes of District Council 26, 14-15 March, 1942, Box: "Canadian Council Minutes", CAW National Archives (hereafter DC 26, date, CAW).
14. Local 200 increased the percentage of workers receiving wage increases from 26% to 50%. Ford responded by reducing wages (Report of Local 200 to DC 26, 9-10 May, 1942, CAW).
15. Letter from H. Rowe to G. Parson, 6 March, 1946; List of Executive Officers, UAW Local 199; Miscellaneous Correspondence File, UAW Collection, CAW). Council by-laws do not specify how the representatives were elected or selected (Box, "Canadian Council Minutes", CAW).

even after conciliation, until a government-conducted vote showed a majority of *all* workers (not just those voting) favoured strike action.[16] This made legal strikes all but impossible. Moreover, a union that was deemed responsible for a wildcat could be declared illegal and have its funds seized.[17]

Nevertheless, the UAW pledged "full out aid" when St. Catharines' McKinnon workers went on strike in 1941.[18] The Canadian UAW also refused to take the unconditional no-strike pledge which the UAW in the US agreed to after Pearl Harbour in December 1941 (two years after Canada entered the war). The Canadian UAW continued to engage in recognition strikes, not only schooling workers in militancy but also cementing their links to leaders who picketed and then went to jail with them when police arrested them for contravening the Defence of Canada Regulations.[19]

The UAW leaders' relation to member militancy in this period is perhaps best illustrated by the first major walkout at Ford Windsor. In October 1942, Ford announced it would hire 1500 women at lower wages. Although the collective agreement obliged Ford to discuss such plans with the union,[20] management bypassed the UAW and made its request directly to the Regional War Labour Board on grounds that male labour was unavailable (Sugiman, 1992: 90-92). The Board agreed. When Ford hired 37 women, workers "took it upon themselves to settle this question" by walking out and shutting down production for a week.[21] This "equal pay for equal work" strike, with its sexist overtones, was supported by UAW leaders (Fraser, 1982: 58) until Ottawa persuaded the strikers to go back to work prior to arbitrating the issue.[22] Later on, Ford applied to the Regional War Labour Board to hire women in 1943, but withdrew its request in the face of union opposition.[23]

This strike proved to be the zenith of unity between the leaders and members at Local 200, however. In a walkout during the spring of 1943, local 200 leaders

16. Even workers locked out by their employers were jailed for picketing under these regulations (Minutes DC 26, 5-6 October, 1940). Yet C.D. Howe, Mackenzie King's "minister of everything," acknowledged military contractors went on strike with impunity, refusing to "let a wheel turn until the government removed its five per cent limit on profits" (Millar, 1981: 19).
17. Report of George Burt to DC 26, 29-30 March, 1941 (CAW).
18. Ibid.
19. DC 26, 5-6 October, 1940.
20. Agreement Between Ford Motor Company of Canada, Ltd., Windsor, Ontario, and Local 200 UAW-CIO, 15 January, 1942, as amended by Memorandum of Agreement dated 31 December, 1942, and as further amended by Memorandum of Agreement entered into on the 11th day of January, 1944, p. 18 (NA, MG30 A94, vol. 37, File 3073).
21. DC 26, 16-17 January, 1943 (CAW).
22. DC 26, 16-17 January, 1943 (CAW).
23. Report of speech by Roy England, President of Local 200, UAW, *Toronto Daily Star* 28 November, 1945.

"found it impossible to stop the men" from striking over management harassment. In another plant, UAW leaders halted a walkout over unsafe working conditions, but workers defied them and sat down on the job.[24] The president of the local eventually stopped the sitdown and chastised in-plant leaders for failing to follow the "established procedure of our local and the International Union" (Fraser, 1982: 61).

At other locals, UAW leaders were divided over such militancy. For example, in 1943, striking UAW members at Dominion Glass in Wallaceburg, Ontario, contacted UAW members at Dominion Glass in Hamilton, Ontario, who also wanted to strike to achieve union recognition. Although George Burt, Director of the Canadian UAW, wanted to strike both plants, the Canadian Congress of Labour, together with regional and local UAW leaders, including Local 200's president, opposed it.[25]

Meanwhile, rank and file direct action continued at Local 200. In the spring of 1944, 14,000 workers conducted a nineteen-day walkout. The immediate cause was Ford's attempt to weaken the grievance procedure,[26] and suspension of six stewards (Cako, 1971: 42). Workers were also frustrated by lack of progress in contract negotiations. When they resumed the strike after the government conciliators failed to devise an effective grievance procedure,[27] Ford cancelled the contract (Fraser, 1982: 62). Ford then demanded RCMP intervention to help workers cross picket lines,[28] arguing that the strike violated the contract the UAW had "pledged its members to uphold."[29] Many UAW leaders, including George Burt and Roy England, the Communist president of Local 200,[30] opposed the strikes, as did many other Communists (Abella, 1973: 142). The UAW sent its International Vice President to persuade the workers to end the strike, warning them that it played into the hands of those who wanted to break the union.[31] Although his view had some merit, some UAW

24. DC 26, 5-6 June, 1943 (CAW).
25. Special DC 26 Meeting, 9 February, 1943 (CAW).
26. Ford wanted workers to write grievances before a steward investigated. This threatened access to the procedure, especially for workers who could not write English (Russell, 1990: 216). Ford argued stewards were roving about the plant too much during work hours. The UAW replied this was standard practice (*Globe and Mail* 26 April, 1944), and argued Ford was trying to "break the union" (*Ford Facts*, Special Edition, UAW Local 200, Windsor, Ontario, 15 April, 1944, p. 1).
27. George Burt to Jerry Taylor, 5 January, 1949, WSU, UAW Canada Officers, Box 51, Folder 4, p. 2.
28. *Toronto Telegram* 8 May, 1944.
29. *Toronto Telegram* 24 April, 1944.
30. *Toronto Star* 8 May, 1944.
31. *Toronto Telegram* 11 May, 1944.

leaders, particularly in-plant leaders at Local 200 and other locals, supported the strike.[32]

The growing differences between most UAW leaders and members over strike action reflected several factors. Senior UAW leaders were encouraged by significant Ontario and Canadian government support for new laws providing unions with security in exchange for assurances labour relations would be stable. While still uncertain, such support was the major source of hope that wartime gains would be made permanent. In addition, with some exceptions, Communist UAW leaders tended to support their party's policy of subordinating workers' workplace concerns to the war effort.[33]

Ethnic differences were another factor distancing members from leaders. Many of the rank and file members were Finnish and Slavic (especially Ukrainian) immigrants, most of whom did not speak English well.[34] Most of these immigrants were also Roman Catholic. On the other hand, most union leaders had Anglo-Celtic or German backgrounds. They tended to be Protestant, to speak English as their first and only language, and to work in skilled trades. In addition, many were members of the Masonic Lodge, a largely Protestant (and middle class) fraternal organization. In these important respects, UAW leaders often had more in common with Ford supervisors than with their members.

These ethnic and religious differences were particularly relevant because Ford had a history of discriminatory hiring and promotion practices against Eastern Europeans (Millar, 1981: 252). With the coming of the UAW, many such immigrants traded dependence on one section of these dominant ethnic groups (supervisors) for another section (union leaders). One Eastern European immigrant who worked at Chrysler in Windsor during this period explained:

> The first [collective] agreements were short, a few pages of almost nothing. There was no grievance form. You argued everything orally.... when the government and the union became more sophisticated, everything had to be in writing. The more writing you got, the more restrictions you put on yourself. But the rank and file, especially the immigrants, would go on slowdown strikes and we got things. But once we got into the written agreements ... Anglo-Saxons would say 'it's in the book!' and our guys would tell them where to put it. So there was a cleavage. Our people became resentful of the Anglo-Saxon people.... A lot of our people got fired.[35]

The differences between leaders and members widened as militancy increased, but growing militancy also strengthened the hand of UAW leaders in pressing for labour law reform. The 1941-1943 strike wave was associated with increasing state intervention to settle disputes (Cruikshank and Kealey, 1987: 96). Furthermore, with a third of unionized labour on strike in 1943 (almost the same level as the record high in 1919-20), labour militancy was causing growing public concern about the industrial relations system. Furthermore, according to a 1943 Gallup poll, the Cooperative Commonwealth Federation (CCF) (supported by the 160,000-strong Canadian Congress of Labour), was the most popular party in Canada. That year, with only four seats fewer than the Tory government, the CCF became Ontario's official opposition. Clearly vulnerable, the Tories now promised "advanced and fair labour laws" including "comprehensive collective bargaining legislation" (Caplan, 1973: 101). Prior to their defeat, the Ontario Liberals also promised something akin to the Wagner Act.

Impressed by such promises, the President of Local 200 blamed the three-month strike in Wallaceburg in 1943 for labour's failure to attain them:

> We have given the anti-labour forces a golden opportunity in recent months to criticize the proposed Ontario Labour Act ... we have looked forward to the time we would have an act comparable to the Wagner Act and we ... have done more than any other union to have such an act placed on the statute books of Ontario, but ... chances of such an act passing ... have pratically [sic] been eliminated ... through our recent series of strikes.[36]

Despite — or because of — such militancy, however, the Tories passed the Collective Bargaining Act of Ontario, which obligated employers to bargain collectively and to give the union with a majority of the workers' votes exclusive bargaining rights, thereby precluding recognition strikes (Logan, 1956: 24; Matheson, 1989: 117). As well, thanks in no small part to the CCF's political threat and to massive strike activity,[37] when the federal Liberal government passed a Wage Control Order banning strikes related to wage controls, they also passed programs such as the family allowance, which helped alleviate worker discontent.

Most significantly, with the support of some employer groups, including the Canadian Chamber of Commerce, but against strong opposition from most

32. Letter from George Burt to Plant Chairmen, Local 195, UAW, 8 May, 1944 (File, "General Correspondence 1945-1947," CAW).
33. In line with the Communist Party's shift to a "popular front" policy after Hitler's invasion of the Soviet Union in 1941, the Communist-led United Electrical Workers, for example, took a no-strike pledge (Abella, 1973: 141). However, despite this policy change toward the war and worker militancy, discipline was not uniform. To varying degrees, Communists in the UAW and other unions sometimes defied the party's policy (Stepan-Norris and Zeitlin, 1991: 1184-88).
34. By 1931, Eastern Europeans constituted about a quarter of the population of East Windsor (Manley, 1986: 112). Manley suggests that this concentration of immigrants reflected "a conscious Ford policy to recruit a polyglot workforce, perhaps as a barrier to collective action" (ibid.).
35. Personal interview, Andrew Marocko, 13 December, 1993. I am indebted to Wayne Lewchuk for stressing the impact of ethnicity on relations between union leaders and members at Ford Windsor.
36. Minutes of Special DC 26 Meeting, February 9, 1943 (CAW).
37. From 1941 to 1943, 425,000 workers went out on strike (Palmer, 1992: 279); in 1943 a third of the unionized working class was on strike. There were more strikes and strikers in 1943 than in 1919 (Heron, 1989: 78).

major industrialists (Russell, 1990a: 207-10, passim) the federal cabinet replaced its core labour law, the Industrial Disputes Investigation Act (IDIA), with Order-in-Council PC 1003 in 1944. This order proved to be a turning point in relations among the state, capital and unions, and between UAW leaders and members. Designed to curb the growing industrial militancy that was threatening war production (Williams, 1964: 319), PC 1003 combined mandatory arbitration during collective agreements with compulsory conciliation before legal strikes (as in the IDIA) with the core of Wagner: the right to organize, automatic certification if a union gained the majority in a government supervised vote, the right to bargain collectively, and protection from certain unfair labour practices.[38] In addition, for the first time, unions gained equal representation with employers on labour boards.

Yet employers were still under no compulsion to bargain once a union was certified, and they could still avoid formal union recognition by negotiating with non-union worker representatives. Moreover, bargaining was to be done at individual work sites, thereby fragmenting collective union power. On top of this, because PC 1003 did not cover employees who worked in firms and sectors that were not directly engaged in war production, it legally segmented the Canadian working class, thus reinforcing divisions that would have longer term consequences.

Furthermore, unlike the US Wagner Act, strikes were made illegal for the duration of a contract. Even after a contract expired, strikes were made illegal until after conciliation. Slowdowns and any other form of direct action designed to restrict production were expressly forbidden. As a substitute for direct action, PC 1003 made it mandatory that all collective agreements it covered have a formal grievance procedure. Critical to the kind of unionism that was emerging, PC1003 gave all residual rights not limited by the contract or labour law to management: grievance arbitration was confined to "interpretation and application" of the contract (Fudge, 1990: 92). Also critical was the key condition that union leaders police their members to uphold these obligations. In particular, unions were forbidden to encourage direct action. Nevertheless, union leaders' reaction to PC1003 was appreciative (Logan, 1956: 31) and the Canadian Congress of Labour (CCL) did not oppose the limits on strike rights (Warrian, 1986: 112).

38. *Labour Gazette*, 1944, pp. 136-37.

The No-Strike Pledge

Although union certification was slow and penalties for employer non-compliance were inadequate,[39] PC 1003 helped keep industrial order for the duration of the war, and it encouraged the Canadian UAW to make a no-strike pledge only four months later. In June, 1944, shortly after the walkout at Local 200 which it opposed, the District Council unanimously pledged "uninterrupted maximum production" for the war's duration.[40] In October the Council adopted a "Win-the-Peace Plan" which referred to UAW members as "soldiers of production."[41] The Plan called for a tripartite Joint Council to promote a neo-mercantilist strategy based on a partnership among government, labour, and capital.[42] In November 1944, Local 200's president affirmed UAW support for the no-strike pledge, warning that "company stooges are being used to create strikes to mislead the membership."[43] Although fewer than 20% of the members voted on the no-strike pledge, and of these only 54% favoured it, the District Council reaffirmed the no-strike pledge in February 1945.[44]

Canadian UAW leaders adopted the pledge for several reasons. One was pressure from UAW leaders in the US who had taken a no-strike pledge shortly after the US entered the war. Canadian leaders also promoted the pledge for patriotic reasons and on the grounds strikes invited anti-labour legislation.[45] More fundamentally, however, as the Canadian District Council of the UAW had argued in 1942, the no-strike pledge was part of the price of a Canadian Wagner model:

> ... efforts of the Canadian trade union movement to give its utmost to production would be greatly aided if there was a legislation in Canada, such as the American Wagner Act.... Such action ... would establish a basis for greater harmony in industry and for co-operation to obtain greater war production.[46]

The pledge also reflected the influence of the Communist Party of Canada which, immediately after Hitler's 1941 invasion of the Soviet Union, became a

39. In late 1944 George Burt complained of the "injustices" and "inefficiencies" of PC 1003 in relation to arbitration (DC 26, 24-25 November, 1944.) The maximum penalty for unfair labour practices was prosecution in a Police Court and a $500 fine (Fraser 1982: 81).
40. DC 26, 22-25 November, 1944, CAW.
41. DC 26, 28-29 October, 1944 (CAW).
42. "The Canadian UAW-CIO "Win-the-Peace" Plan," DC 26, 28-29 October, 1944 (Box: Canadian Council Minutes, CAW). In 1942 all major UAW leadership factions in the US adopted an "equality of sacrifice program," including a commitment to speedup and not to strike, against rank and file opposition (Milton, 1982: 153).
43. DC 26, 24-25 November, 1944 (CAW).
44. DC 26, 17-18 February, 1945 (CAW); Glaberman, 1980: 117-18.
45. DC 26, 5-6 June, 1943 (CAW).
46. DC 26, 29-30 August, 1942 (CAW).

"firm advocate of industrial peace in the interests of victory"[47] and committed itself to "win the labour movement to a policy of sacrifice" (Penner, 1988: 188). With PC 1003 enacted, Communist arguments for a no-strike policy were more persuasive. Although its influence has been exaggerated by both the left and right,[48] the Communist Party's influence in the UAW and other industrial unions was substantial. This is a major reason the UAW refused to affiliate to the CCF, even after the CCL endorsed the CCF in 1943 (Horowitz, 1968: 78-82).[49] Labelling the CCF "irresponsible" for condoning strike rights during a "people's war,"[50] the Communist Party (now renamed the Labour Progressive Party) allied with the Liberals in the 1945 federal and provincial elections, supporting leaders of the UAW, such as George Burt, on a Liberal-Labour ticket.

The no-strike pledge also reflected the patriotism of the leadership and the rank and file. Although this patriotism was deeply felt during the war, it is also probable that many workers were ambivalent about the pledge. This would be consistent with Glaberman's analysis of the UAW's no-strike pledge in the US where a majority of the members voted for the pledge while, at the same time, a majority of them wildcatted.

The 1945 Ford Strike and the Rand Formula

By war's end, 700,000 workers, twice the prewar level, belonged to unions, and over 50,000 belonged to Canada's biggest union, the UAW. Yet even though PC 1003's wartime mandate was extended for two years into postwar reconstruction, many feared Ford would try to "bring back the conditions of the 1930's."[51] Indeed, the UAW considered Ford to be "the spearhead of the attack on the trade union movement" as a whole.[52]

Despite PC 1003's ban on strikes during a collective agreement, and despite the UAW's no-strike pledge and growing UAW opposition to direct action, Ford of Canada had never made peace with the UAW. Management used a loophole in PC 1003 to stipulate that it regarded the President of Local 200, not the UAW, to be the workers' official representative (Logan, 1956: 31). Even though the grievance procedure was the main substitute for direct action, Ford undermined it, defying the arbitrators' decisions.[53] Supervisors refused to deal with union grievances,[54] encouraging workers to deal directly with management. During conciliation in 1945, Ford wanted to gut the grievance procedure by disqualifying any grievance considered inconsistent with management functions (Warrian, 1986: 179). Ford also objected to the time stewards took to perform these union duties.

Considered "very hostile" by the UAW during contract bargaining, Ford submitted "drastic recommendations,"[55] and threatened major layoffs. After eighteen months of futile bargaining, Local 200 went on strike in September 1945, just after the war ended. On the plant floor the key issues were speedup and favouritism in job allocation.[56] However, the main bargaining issues were a dues checkoff and union security. War Labour Boards continued to decide most economic issues,[57] so wages were less significant as a contract issue.[58] Job security was a major concern, however. Feeding the spectre of a return to mass unemployment after the war, Ford proclaimed it would maintain the seniority of 5,000 workers who had joined the military and announced hundreds of layoffs to provide openings for returning veterans.[59] As in 1941, Ford offered a company union.

The 99-day strike by 10,000 Ford workers marked the start of the massive 1945-46 strike wave. The Ford strike was also important because of the solidarity of the mass picketers, the community, and much of the organized Canadian and American industrial working classes. At one point, Detroit supporters and

47. *Program of the Labor-Progressive Party* (Toronto: Eveready Printers, 1953), p. 6, quoted in Penner (1988: 194).
48. "Communist" was often used to label anyone opposed to the non-Communist leadership of the UAW or the CCF. Andrew Marocko, a former auto worker, said that in working class Windsor people who "wouldn't have recognized the Communist Manifesto if they ran over it" were called Communists for "striving to better their lives." (Interview 13 December, 1993).
49. Historian Desmond Morton argues that by 1944 the hostility of Communists toward the CCF had "almost annulled the impact of any CCL endorsement" of the CCF (1980: 204). Moreover, Communists had helped to push the more conservative Trades and Labour Congress toward a non-partisan position (Heron, 1989: 83).
50. In 1944, Communist leader Sam Carr wrote, "because this is a people's war, the working class has forgone the right to strike and is doing all in its power to produce without interruption for the fighting fronts" (Penner, 1988: 196).
51. Strike leaflet, *Which Shall it Be*, Drew Papers, RG3, Box 443, File 158-G, 1945 (OA).
52. DC 26, 23-24 June, 1945 (CAW).
53. Memorandum of R. England, President UAW Local 200, NAC, MG 30 A94, vol. 44, File 3144; DC 26, 29-30 August, 1942 (CAW).
54. DC 26, 27-28 June, 1942; DC 26, 19-20 February, 1944 (CAW).
55. "Brief History of UAW in Canada," p. 6, 26 January, 1948 (UAW Canada Officers, Box 51, Folder 3, WSU).
56. Letter from R. England, President UAW Local 200, to J. Cohen, 27 January, 1945; *Grievance Agenda* 17 January, 1945 (NA, MG 30 A94, v. 42, file 3122).
57. Letter from G. Burt to J. Taylor, 5 January, 1949 (WSU, UAW Canada Officers, Box 51, Folder 4).
58. Key demands were a union shop, dues checkoff, two weeks' paid vacation, more pay for work on holidays, seniority for veterans, lay-off pay, and no reduction in take-home pay. The most contentious were the first two (Moulton 1974: 134).
59. "Ford #4", scrapbook (CAW). The UAW also favoured veterans' seniority, making it a strike issue (*Which Shall it Be*, pamphlet, Local 200, UAW-CIO n.d. Drew Papers, RG3 Box 443, File 158-G, OA). Cumulative seniority for veterans was achieved (*Memorandum of Agreement between the Ford Motor Company and the UAW-CIO*, December 1944, art. 64, p. 18, MG 30 A94, v. 37, file 3073, NAC).

marching bands — about a thousand strong — paraded with the strikers through Windsor.[60] UAW Local 195 shut down Windsor's other auto plants, swelling the picket lines to 6,000 outside Ford's gates. Finally, and most important of all, the strike was important because its settlement set the contours of Canada's postwar Fordist industrial relations system.

While it appears that most UAW members were united in support of the strike, UAW leaders were not. The District Council[61] and the International UAW refused to authorize a sympathy strike by Local 195. Despite this, "it was impossible to restrain the membership," Burt reported.[62] The UAW issued anti-strike statements against Local 195, and the Canadian Congress of Labour (CCL) scotched a national sympathy strike on the grounds it would cause Ottawa to side with Ford (Cako, 1971). The CCL leadership called on the strikers to return to work and accept an arbitrated settlement. Similarly, the craft unions' Trades and Labour Congress warned of the kind of state repression which occurred after the 1919 strike wave (Russell, 1990a: 222). Indeed, reminiscent of Ottawa's response to the Winnipeg strike in 1919 (Borden called it an "attempt at revolution"), CCL leaders labelled the one-day sympathy strikes a "revolution" and warned there was a "Labour Progressive Party plot to seize power in our country."[63]

Meanwhile, powerful senior Tories and Liberals, including Drew, Howe, St. Laurent, and Mitchell, saw the UAW "insurrection" as a pretext for military intervention (Millar, 1981: 261). In November 1945 Ontario Premier Drew called on Ottawa to send in the army or the navy, claiming there were "probably two thousand active and vigorous communists at the core of this" who might be "reinforced with some thugs from across the [Detroit] river."[64] In a radio speech, Ontario's Attorney General called the strike an "open insurrection against the Crown." He threatened to respond with force and warned that "if this results in casualties, the fault will not lie with the government."[65] As in 1944, Ford of Canada also demanded military intervention (Russell, 1990a: 221) and warned of bloodshed.

Despite such threats and opposition from union leaders, 8,500 workers conducted about 30 sympathy strikes. Some UAW leaders, including George Burt, supported them.[66] Seventy-eight strike committees were set up,[67] and Burt claimed they collected more money than had been collected for any other strike in Canadian history.[68] As noted, there was much community support, including support from Windsor professionals[69] and credit and cash donations from Windsor merchants. Local churches were especially supportive. Thanks to such community solidarity, the strikers suffered only three evictions for non-payment of rent.[70]

By shutting down the Ford powerhouse, the strikers threatened to freeze the plants and cause massive damage. When Windsor police were unwilling to gain access to the powerhouse, both Ontario and Ottawa sent police to escort guards through the picket lines, despite the opposition of Windsor's mayor and MPP.[71] Workers then barricaded Ford with over two thousand cars, trucks, and buses. Other locals responded with sympathy strikes.[72] These tactics pressured the municipal, provincial and federal governments, Royal Canadian Mounted Police, Ontario Provincial Police, much of the public, and even Ford in the US, to call for an end to hostilities. Ottawa strongly urged Ford and the UAW to accept an arbitrated settlement.

At this point, the division between UAW leaders and rank and file militants widened. Mackenzie King's Labour Minister gave secret assurances to senior Canadian UAW leaders that he would appoint an arbitrator who favoured union security and the dues checkoff (Fraser, 1982: 113). Except for the assistant regional director, most leaders above in-plant level, including the president of Local 200, Burt, and Local 200's negotiating committee, favoured Ottawa's proposal.[73] However, shopfloor leaders and members of Local 200 were not told about the deal. Even after eleven weeks without strike pay, most Local 200 stewards voted down the offer, and a majority of 6,000 members at a meeting voted to reject their leaders' advice to end the strike.[74] UAW leaders had to force a second ballot before a majority of the members agreed.[75]

60. *Windsor Star* 17 November, 1945.
61. DC 26, 21 October, 1945 (CAW).
62. Report of the Canadian Director to DC 26, 19-20 January, 1946 (CAW).
63. DC 26, 19-20 January, 1946 (CAW). The CCL's broader goal was to establish tripartite (labour, business, and government) industry councils to plan postwar economic conversion (*Minutes of Proceedings and Evidence*, House of Commons Standing Committee on Industrial Relations, Ottawa, Monday 12 August, 1946, p. 1029).
64. Transcript of telephone conversation between Drew and J.L. Isley, federal cabinet minister, 2 November, 1945. See also transcript of telephone conversation between Drew and Isley on 5 November, 1945 (Drew Papers, RG3, Box 443, file 158-G, OA).
65. Drew Papers, RG3, Box 443, File 158-G (OA).
66. Scrapbook "Ford #4" (CAW).
67. DC 26, 19-20 January, 1946 (CAW).
68. Ibid.
69. Report of speech of Roy England, President of Local 200, in *Toronto Star* 28 November, 1945.
70. Telegram from J. Napier to H. Rowe, 19 November, 1945 ("Miscellaneous Correspondence" File, UAW Collection, CAW; *Toronto Daily Star*, 15 December, 1945.
71. *Windsor Star* 2 November, 1945; telegram from Alex Parent MPP for Windsor and President of UAW Local 195 to Premier George Drew, 2 November, 1945 (Drew Papers, RG3, Box 443, File 158-G, OA). Parent was also a leader of UAW Local 195.
72. After provincial police and the RCMP were sent to Windsor, UAW Local 199 in St. Catharines unanimously voted for a sympathy strike. (DC 26, 19-20 January, 1946, CAW).
73. Ibid.

The arbitration decision proved to be a watershed in Canadian labour history. Although he refused the union shop, Justice Rand, the arbitrator, granted the essence of union security: a dues checkoff. Because Ford would deduct dues from the pay of *all* workers, including the non-UAW members, Rand's award freed the UAW from continually having to organize new members where the union had already won certification elections. This removed the financial disincentive to joining the union and solved the major problem of "free riders" benefitting from the contract without paying dues.

Yet the union paid a big price for the checkoff. As noted, prior to Rand, the stewards (particularly sub-stewards) collected dues on the plant floor,[76] reinforcing the local leaders' ties to the members. Without their dues-collecting function, the substewards soon disappeared. Ironically, it is not clear how necessary the checkoff was to the union. UAW organizer James Napier argued, for example, that union security provisions were not required to maintain a de facto union shop if workers were imbued with the spirit of rank and file unionism. At Kelsey Wheel, they "dumped any newcomer who refused to join the union into a wheelbarrow and rolled him out to the scrap heap" (1976: 20).

The implications of his award for relations between union leaders and members were clear to Rand. He noted that if Ford collected dues directly from workers' pay, the company would be concerned about the "expense of the check-off and the strength which it may give to the union." He then made a compelling observation:

> But the expense can properly be taken as the employer's contribution toward making the union through its greater independence more effective in its disciplinary pressure even upon employees who are not members, an end which the Company admits to be desirable.[77]

Thus, in the same measure the UAW became financially independent of its members, it became dependent on management. Rand made continuation of the check-off was contingent on UAW repudiation of unauthorized strikes. Failure to do so would cost the union two to six months' dues. Participants in unauthorized strikes would also be fined three dollars for each day's absence from work and lose a year's seniority for each week's absence.[78] Rand stipulated no penalties for management's violations.

74. *Windsor Star* 29 November, 1945.
75. Letter from G. Burt to Jerry Taylor, 5 January, 1949, p. 6 (WSU, UAW Canada Officers, Box 51, Folder 4). For the best account see Moulton (1974: 143-47). See also Burt (1979).
76. Letter from Burt to Jerry Taylor, 5 January, 1949, p. 6 (WSU, UAW Officers Canada, Box 51, Folder 4). During the war, each steward had substewards "check on the backsliders" who had not paid their dues (DC 26, 29-30 August, 1942, CAW).
77. "Award on Issue of Union Security in Ford Dispute" (Rand Report), *Labour Gazette*, vol. 46, January-June 1946 (Ottawa: King's Printer, 1947), p. 128.
78. Ibid., p. 129.

Ford had argued during the strike that unless the UAW were forced to fulfill its disciplinary responsibility "the very failure of the Ford Motor Company [would be] at stake."[79] Management asked Rand to make the UAW take "enforceable responsibility" in return for security of union finances.[80] Rand delivered. The UAW was woven tightly into other legal and administrative obligations, as well. Added to the local's dependence on Ford for dues, the UAW's Constitution compelled local leaders to pressure workers to return to work if a strike violated the agreement, unless the International authorized it. The 1943 Ontario Collective Bargaining Act contained additional penalties for illegal strikes.[81]

Rand's decision divided union leaders from their members in other ways too. According to the award, stewards and committee persons were to enjoy superseniority during layoffs and in the allocation of overtime. Irrespective of their date of hire, they could not be laid off as long as a minimum number of workers in their jurisdictions were still on the job. Similar provisions gave stewards and committeepersons privileged access to overtime.[82] In 1942 Local 200 had won an arbitration that required the company to call stewards in when ten or more members were working.[83] This strengthened union representation, but at the same time, because in-plant leaders accumulated overtime at premium wages, it also widened the gap between the leaders and members. In hindsight, it became the genesis of "lost time unionism" in which in-plant leaders often gain considerable amounts of company-paid time to do union work in their offices. This provision, together with the privileges Rand gave to local leaders widened the status and income differences between local leaders and union members.

Rand's decision also enhanced the power of the local leaders by giving them more authority to bring grievances to arbitration (Young, 1952: 87). In order to compensate for blocking worker direct action, Rand expanded the role of local leaders in the use of the grievance and arbitration procedure in order to direct discontent into administrative channels while maintaining production.[84] This was consistent with the UAW's longstanding demand, against much employer opposition, for compulsory dispute arbitration.[85] More fundamentally, it was

79. "Facts from Ford about Union Security" *Windsor Daily Star* 24 November, 1945.
80. Brief by J. Aylesworth for the Ford Motor Company of Canada to the Arbitration Proceedings, v. 1, p. 214 (PAC, Rand File, MG30 E77).
81. Letter from G. Burt to Jerry Taylor, 5 January, 1949, p. 5 (WSU, UAW Canada Officers, Box 51, Folder 4).
82. *Text of Award*, Justice Rand, *The Labour Gazette*, January-June 1946, v. 46, clause 50, p. 130.
83. DC 26, 27-28 June, 1942 (CAW).
84. On the simultaneously empowering and disempowering nature of the grievance and arbitration procedure, see Drache and Glasbeek, 1992: 127-48 and Haiven, 1990.
85. *Brief Submitted to the People of Windsor by the UAW-CIO Dealing with the Existing State of Labour Relations in the Counties of Essex, Lambton, Kent*, p. 5, n.d. (NA, MG 30 A94, v. 44, file 3144).

consistent with the argument senior UAW leaders had long been making that union security was the key to workplace discipline. In a November 1945 radio broadcast, for example, the (Communist) president of Local 200 had argued that union security was equivalent to "production security" because with union security the union "is in a better position to assume responsibility and exercise discipline. Management cannot ask for discipline and responsibility on one hand and refuse machinery to guarantee it on the other."[86]

Despite these serious implications for the union's role as a demobilizer of militancy in the workplace, the Rand decision was seen as a major gain for labour. There is no evidence of opposition by UAW leaders, or by the rank and file. The benefits were considered to be well worth the costs. Union security implied a measure of relief from managerial tyranny and potential gains concerning control of the labour process, as well as material gains. It is thus inaccurate to see this compromise as simply serving the particular interests of UAW leaders. Support for the Rand award also reflected a general recognition that many industrial employers and their political allies were determined to suppress not only rank and file direct action but unions per se unless a compromise were worked out.

In summary, thanks to intervention by Ford-US and the Ontario and Canadian governments, as well as the solidarity of sizeable sections of the working class on both sides of the border, Ford-Canada reluctantly embarked on a unionized regime of labour relations. The peace obligations built into that regime widened the wedge between a militant, work-centred rank and file model of unionism and a more economistic, leader-centred unionism that evolved. As the basis of the labour relations system that was generalized throughout unionized mass industry after the war, this alternative to rank and file unionism became the heart of what Russell calls a "truly hegemonic" Fordism (1990a: 226).

The Postwar Convergence of the US and Canadian Wagner Models

After the war, the Big Three auto manufacturers began massive restructuring to meet enormous pent-up consumer demand. Labour stability was a critical precondition for these efforts. In the 1946 Ford contract negotiations in the US, senior UAW leaders gained more control over local leaders and the rank and file by giving managers the right to fire the leaders of illegal strikes, to suspend other participants for up to two weeks, fire them for a second offense, and to penalize the union if it were not able to reduce the stoppages (Selekman et al., 1964: 99). International UAW leaders also concentrated more power in their own hands in ways that further committed workers to channel direct action into the grievance procedure (Halpern, 1988: 196). In 1949, the UAW International Executive Board gained constitutional power to discipline workers if their own locals refused to do so (Jefferys, 1986: 31). With such power, the UAW was able to guarantee Ford that "the only kind of strike it need fear or expect would be the orderly mass walkout" (Harris, 1982: 146).

By centralizing control over contract bargaining and eliminating opposition elements, the dominant Reuther faction turned the UAW into a "one party union" that marginalized shop floor leaders, the UAW stratum with the strongest ties to the members.[87] According to his brother, Walter Reuther wanted to "take the ball out of the hands of the stewards and committeemen and put it back in the hands of the national leadership" (Lichtenstein, 1982: 226).

Allied to the Democratic Party in the US and the CCF in Canada, Reuther was also allied to the Roman Catholic Church in both countries. This political and religious coalition targeted dissidents deemed to be "Communists" or their sympathizers.[88] It was in this context that anti-Communists linked to Walter Reuther and the Associations of Catholic Trade Unions in the US (Hogan, 1988: 94; Benedict, 1992: 127-28) won the leadership of Local 195 in Windsor in 1946, and later of Local 200 (Veres, 1956: 77). These victories were facilitated by the International's electoral system which made it easier to suppress opposition elements. Instead of being elected by the members, top UAW leaders were elected at conventions they largely controlled. As well, the delegates to such conventions were elected at meetings open to all members of their respective locals but usually attended by a small core of local leaders who themselves became increasingly dependent on International UAW leadership and staff.

Reinforcing these internal union pressures stifling the power of the membership, in 1947 Congress passed the Taft-Hartley Act, which made collective agreements enforceable in federal courts and allowed employers to sue unions for illegal strikes. Taft-Hartley also permitted the banning of secondary boycotts and the enactment of "right to work" laws, thus limiting organizing and stigmatizing militancy as "radical" and "un-American." This fed into an anti-labour, anti-left Cold War atmosphere which provided a convenient rationale for attacks on militants in the name of "national" security. Since the US section dominated the UAW International, and since Canadian UAW members often worked for the

---

86. *Toronto Star* 28 November, 1945.

87. Steiber, 1962: 11. It became more difficult to coordinate opposition to Reuther as the automobile industry decentralized geographically, reducing the power of big locals in the Detroit area (Steiber, 1962: 13-14, 155). With few local exceptions, opposition to Reuther was eliminated by 1951 (Steiber, 1962: 131).

88. Napier writes that the Catholic president of UAW Local 195 in Windsor, who succeeded the Communist-aligned local president, was "knighted by the Pope for services rendered" (1976: 31). On the influence of the Catholic Church in Windsor in this period, see Hart (1949).

same companies as their US counterparts, these developments influenced the Canadian UAW, too.

As well as suppressing militancy and dissidence, the UAW, and CIO unions more generally, largely abandoned attempts to generalize union wage increases to the working class as a whole. They lost much of the sense that they were engaged in a larger class struggle. As in the US, the Canadian industrial relations system privatized and fragmented the wage relation. Since Canadian governments did not provide health care or pensions, these and benefits such as paid holidays based on seniority, became bargaining priorities. Although the social wage expanded during the early 1940s and in the 1950s, it remained paltry compared to the social wage in most other industrialized nations, and Canadian workers were only "marginally less dependent on ... employers' paternalism" (Tudiver, 1987: 199). In this context, UAW gains in non-portable company welfare provisions were a critically important response to the members' needs, but they also became "golden handcuffs," tying the workers and the union more closely to the employers rather than to the labour movement or the working class as a whole. Furthermore, since Canada's welfare programs expanded in large part through bureaucratic politics and elite federal-provincial accommodations, much of the social wage did not come through electoral mobilization (Pal, 1988; Banting, 1987). Consequently, and in the absence of a motivating vision of class politics, Canadian labour's public policy role became increasingly restricted to that of an interest group (Yates, 1990).

By negotiating multi-year contracts that committed it to support management control in return for automatic wage increases based on productivity improvements and changes in the cost-of-living, the International UAW also largely abandoned aspirations to gain more control over the labour process. Despite local demands for more job control, by 1946-1948 formal job rights at Ford in the US were more restricted than they had been during the war (Harris, 1982: 148). After failing to win a say over GM's pricing policy in the 1945-46 strike, the UAW made no further attempts to gain a serious role in decisions about production. In 1950, the UAW signed a five year contract, the "Treaty of Detroit," giving GM essentially unilateral control in return for greater economic benefits. At the time, eminent industrial relations pluralist Frederick Harbison noted that such a contract:

> calls for intelligent trading rather than table pounding, for diplomacy rather than belligerency, and for internal union discipline rather than grass roots rank and file activity. (Lichtenstein, 1983: 303)

The GM contract also became the model for Ford and Chrysler contracts. Added to the tradeoff between money and control issues, such multi-year contracts deprived workers of the mass politicization annual contracts tend to provoke.

In the meantime, similar trends were developing in Canadian industrial relations and in the Canadian UAW. In response to the massive strike wave in 1946, Ottawa had lifted its wartime wage controls and unions won collective bargaining rights over wages. Major strikes continued to erupt, however. In 1948, Ottawa passed the IRDIA (Industrial Relations and Disputes Investigation Act). Most provinces adopted equivalents. In addition to making the core of PC 1003 a permanent basis of Canadian industrial relations, the IRDIA outlawed company unions. The IRDIA did not rule out union or closed shops, but neither did it include Rand's Formula, so unions obtained the Formula in contract bargaining.[89] Like PC 1003, the IRDIA made grievance and arbitration procedures mandatory for settling disputes during the terms of collective agreements. In addition to making direct action in the workplace illegal, this precluded sympathy strikes, thus undermining the potential for broader solidarity. The IRDIA also strengthened central union leaders by certifying national or international unions, not local leaders, as bargaining agents (Logan, 1956: 31).

In sum, by the late 1940s, after a lag of about a decade, this Canadian Wagner model was well established and had much the same impact on relations between union leaders and members as it had earlier in the US[90] Events at Local 200 in the late 1940s and early 1950s illustrate this transition toward this new unionism.

For a few years after the 1945 strike and the Rand award, there was little direct action at Ford Windsor.[91] However, in 1950-51, stimulated by speedup, safety problems,[92] and inflation pressures due to the Korean War, and supported by in-plant leaders, direct action erupted once more.[93] Ford retaliated, firing twenty six workers, half of them in-plant leaders. Nine thousand responded by walking out. In response, UAW leaders, including Local 200's president, the Canadian Regional Director, and Reuther pressured them to return. After twelve days the workers voted to end the strike and returned to work pending arbitration. However, the arbitrators reinstated only ten of the twenty six workers, and Ford fired six more for cutting the plant's power during the strike.[94] This led to more wildcats, which the UAW District Council also

89. By 1949, 40 UAW contracts in Canada contained a Rand Formula (Letter from G. Burt to J. Taylor, 5 January, 1949, UAW Canada Officers, Box 51, Folder 4, WSU).
90. Such implications of the Wagner model in the US have been well documented (Tomlins, 1985; Lichtenstein, 1992; Harris, 1982; Brody, 1980; Goldfield, 1989; Klare, 1977-78).
91. In 1948, George Burt wrote that there had been no strikes, legal or illegal, at Ford of Canada ("Brief History of UAW Canada" p. 8, 26 January, 1948, UAW Canada Officers, Box 51, Folder 3, WSU) but there was at least one walkout in 1947, which the UAW officially repudiated (Fraser, 1982: 131).
92. UAW Canada Locals, Box 88, Folder 11, WSU.
93. Letter from G. Burt to K. Sachindranath, General Secretary, Auto Manufacturers Employees Association, Bombay, India, 12 February, 1952 (WSU, UAW Locals, Box 88, File 12); Fraser 1982: 137.

repudiated (Yates, 1988: 204). The animosity between the militants and their leaders became so great during these wildcats that in-plant leaders assaulted senior UAW leaders.[95] Nevertheless, Burt ordered the strikes stopped, arguing "UAW prestige had dropped" and that "contracts should not be signed if we do not intend to live up to them."[96]

The following anecdote indicates something of the relationship between the UAW and rank and file militants which had emerged by this point. Sometime after the wildcats, an experienced unionist was contacted by Local 200 leaders.

> They told me they had a wildcat strike. People in the boiler room had stopped work and cut the plant off. [Ford] fired the people in the boiler room. The people in Local 200 said ... guys had been fired for instigating a wildcat. The strike was settled but the boiler room guys were fired and would I be the union nominee on their arbitration board? And they told me that we want you to know there are some of these guys we don't want back. I think they made some comment about them being troublemakers.

Under the circumstances, he refused to serve on the arbitration board. A short time later, while he sat on another arbitration board, the chair of the board happened to refer to the same strike.

> He said, 'I was chair of an arbitration board for Local 200. There were a bunch of guys fired. The union let me know there were a number of guys they didn't want back.' I said, 'What did you do?' He said, 'I did what they wanted.' ... He didn't reinstate some of the people.[97]

In the subsequent contract negotiations in 1952, Local 200 members voted almost unanimously in favour of a strike.[98] Despite their militancy, the contract failed to resolve speedup and ventilation problems which had prompted the wildcats (Yates, 1988: 203). On top of this, the grievance procedure remained just as ineffective.[99] A group of dissatisfied members complained that all significant grievances had to go to arbitration.

> The membership nowhere has the opportunity to act. They have no recourse to appeal. Under the process labour is disarmed, bound and shackled. This is a skillfully devised procedure to completely circumvent and immobilize the membership.[100]

Most tellingly, after signing the 1952 contract, Ford announced a major partial closing of its Windsor operations and their removal to Oakville, a non-union town 350 kilometers away.[101] By 1955, Local 200 had less than half the fourteen thousand members it had during the war. That year Ford and the UAW negotiated a master contract bringing all locals under a standard wage and benefit agreement, thereby further reducing local autonomy and rank and file influence (Wells, 1995a).

As noted, the dominant Reuther faction of the UAW used the Cold War to stigmatize the opposition. Canada endured a milder version of this anti-Red fervor but the results were similar. Partly due to CCF efforts and the Roman Catholic Church, the opposition in Local 200, as well as elsewhere in the Canadian UAW were soon marginalized (Yates, 1993: 64-77). Workers continued rearguard actions for several years but mounted no serious challenge to the Reutherites. With no overall coordination, direct action continued and grew in the wake of the Auto Pact from the mid 1960s into the 1970s, but was unable to create an alternative to the bureaucratic, economistic unionism that developed out of World War II.

This suppression of rank-and-file unionism at Local 200 was not *fundamentally* different from that in the US (Lichtenstein, 1992; 1983; Jeffreys, 1986; Marquart, 1975) or at other locals in Canada (Yates, 1993: 81-106) in the 1950s. Although the Canadian UAW may have suppressed rank and file unionism less thoroughly than the rest of the UAW did, and although left elements were somewhat stronger in the Canadian UAW, it was still a top-down union in which relations between leaders and rank and file members were not qualitatively different, by this time, from those in the UAW south of the border. In both countries the UAW was enmeshed in multiyear contracts and master agreements. In Canada, this direction for the UAW evolved out of PC 1003, Rand, and the IRDIA. Indeed, in some respects Canada's new industrial relations framework was more restrictive of worker militancy and solidarity than the US Wagner model. Thus, while the origins and timing of the Wagner model in Canada and the US were not the same, by the 1950s UAW leaders in both countries had taken on essentially similar roles in demobilizing worker militancy.[102]

---

94. Letter from some Local 200 members to Emil Mazey, Secretary Treasurer of the UAW, 16 January, 1952 (WSU, UAW Canada Locals, Box 88, File 12); Fraser 1982: 187, 129-30.
95. Ibid.
96. Report of George Burt to DC 26, 5-6 January, 1952 (Box: "Canadian Council Minutes," CAW).
97. Personal interview, July 1994. Given the sensitivity of the interview material, the interviewee requested confidentiality.
98. Letter from G. Burt to K. Sachindranath, op. cit.
99. In 1949 the District Council criticized arbitration as costly, delay-ridden, and "highly legalistic" and called for less reliance on it (DC 26, 27 March, 1949, CAW).
100. Leaflet sponsored by "United progressive members of Local 200" n.d. (FMC).
101. Gonick (1965) emphasizes the punitive nature of the move as a response to worker resistance. The move was also part of a major reorganization after the war in which twenty-two new Ford plants were built in North America. (*Ford Facts* 2 November, 1951).
102. On the suppression of rank and file militancy at Canadian UAW locals in the 1970s and 1980s, see Johnson (1978) and Wells (1986).

Conclusion

Despite many differences between the history of organized labour in Canada and the US in the 1930s and 1940s, a very similar institutionalization of labour around Wagner model unionism occurred in both countries. At the centre of this model was an agreement to provide union security and a growing standard of living to unionized workers in return for union leaders taking on a key role in disciplining workers to keep the no-strike terms of the contract.

It is important to stress that this compromise centred on changes in industrial relations that the UAW leadership itself favoured. Even before PC1003, the war years saw a growing divergence between UAW leaders and rank-and-file militants concerning direct action on the shop floor. Regardless of formal left-right ideological differences, all major UAW leaders campaigned to obtain the Wagner model in Canada. In the 1945 Ford strike, they emphasized the goal of union security, and, without any apparent reservations, they regarded the Rand Formula as a major victory for labour. Leaders of other industrial unions throughout Canada then fought to win the Rand formula through contract bargaining.

The postwar industrial relations compromise was thus not simply imposed by capital and state forces. Indeed, as noted, it was initially opposed by most industrialists and by many Conservative and Liberal political leaders. In the context of management recalcitrance and the enmity of political elites, UAW leaders felt that these provisions (the Ontario Collective Bargaining Act, PC 1003, the Rand Formula, etc.) were gains guaranteeing union legitimacy and stability. Yet these same developments fundamentally transformed the nature of unionism by making union leaders responsible for disciplining their members and hence responsible for suppressing rank-and-file direct action. As the evidence indicates, Canadian UAW leaders took these responsibilities very seriously.

This legal structure was strengthened by Reuther's dominance, the Cold War, and a postwar economic boom which provided the basis for collective agreements that allowed most unionized workers to enjoy a "middle class" standard of living and prolonged job security for the first time in history. Under these conditions, despite continuing direct action and opposition from dissidents, the postwar Canadian UAW was restricted to a narrow, albeit frequently militant, economism. Wartime gains in worker control over the production process all but came to an end.

Although the Canadian UAW embarked on a more militant nationalist trajectory in the 1970s and 1980s, this has not meant a return to rank and file mobilization of the kind discussed here. The core terms of labour's commitment to the Wagner model continue to hold today, even as capital and the state have lost much of their commitment to it, and as its Keynesian foundations have crumbled. Fordist stability is now giving way to a "new world order" of heightened global competitiveness, labour "flexibility," and renewed class war against labour in Canada. In this context, the Wagner model is less congruent with politico-economic realities than it was during and after World War II (Wells, 1995b).

In retrospect it is clear that the war was an interregnum between the personal absolutism of Henry Ford and a state-sanctioned regulation of workplace industrial relations in which union leaders acted as disciplinarians of their own members. The shift away from a rank and file unionism with strong spontaneist elements to a state-sanctioned bureaucratic unionism was central to the compromise shaping Canada's postwar industrial relations system. Consequently, World War 2 was a critical juncture in the development of Canada's political economy. Although unions were not in any sense fully integrated into either state or employer apparatuses, the class compromise that emerged from it helped to create an essentially economistic, demobilizing and top-down unionism. This transformation contributed to the contemporary limits on worker self-activity and to enduring weakness in the core institution of the Canadian working class.

References to archival material:

NAC= National Archives of Canada, Ottawa.
WSU= Archives of Labor and Urban Affairs, Wayne State University, Detroit.
CAW= Archives of the Canadian Auto Workers, National Office, Toronto.
OA= Ontario Archives, Toronto.

References

Abella, Irving
1973 *Nationalism, Communism and Canadian Labour*. Toronto: University of Toronto Press.

Banting, Keith
1987 *The Welfare State and Canadian Federalism*. 2nd ed. Kingston and Montreal: McGill-Queen's University Press.

Benedict, Daniel
1992 "Good-bye to Homer Martin." *Labour\Le Travail* 29: 117-55.

Betcherman, Gordon
1992 "The Disappearing Middle," in Daniel Drache (ed.). *Getting On Track* Kingston and Montreal: McGill-Queen's University Press.

Brody, David
1980 *Workers in Industrial America* New York: Oxford University Press.

Cako, Stephen C.
1971 "Labour's Struggle for Union Security: The Ford of Canada Strike, Windsor, 1945." MA thesis, University of Windsor.

Caplan, Gerald
1973 *The Dilemma of Canadian Socialism*. Toronto: McClelland and Stewart.

Cruikshank, Douglas and Greg Kealey
1987 "Canadian Strike Statistics, 1891-1950." *Labour\Le Travail* 20: 85-145.

Drache, Daniel and Harry Glasbeek
1992 *The Changing Workplace*. Toronto: Lorimer.

Economic Council of Canada
1990 *Good Jobs, Bad Jobs*. Ottawa: Government of Canada.

Fraser, David
1982 "Years of Struggle: A History of Local 200 of the United Automobile Workers of America at Ford Canada, Windsor Ontario, 1941 to 1955." MA thesis, University of Western Ontario.

Fudge, Judy
1990 "Voluntarism, Compulsion and the 'Transformation' of Canadian Labour Law During World War II," in Gregory Kealey and Greg Patmore (eds.). *Canadian and Australian Labour History*. St. John's, NF: Memorial University.

Gerstle, Gary
1989 *Working Class Americanism*. Cambridge: Cambridge University Press.

Glaberman, Martin
1980 *Wartime Strikes*. Detroit: Bewick.

Goldfield, Michael
1989 "Worker Insurgency, Radical Organization, and New Deal Legislation." *American Political Science Review* 83(4): 1257-82.

Gonick, Cyril W.
1965 "Aspects of Unemployment in Canada." PhD dissertation, University of California-Berkeley.

Gramsci, Antonio
1971 "Americanism and Fordism," in Quintin Hoare and Geoffrey Smith, (eds.). *Selections from the Prison Notebooks of Antonio Gramsci*. New York: International.

Haiven, Larry
1990 "Hegemony in the Workplace," in Larry Haiven et al. (eds.). *Regulating Labour*. Toronto: Garamond.

Halpern, Martin
1988 *UAW Politics in the Cold War Era*. Albany: State University of New York Press.

Harris, Howell J.
1982 *The Right to Manage: Industrial Relations Policies and American Business in the 1940s*. Madison: University of Wisconsin Press.

Hart, C.W.M.
1949 "Industrial Relations Research and Social Theory." *Canadian Journal of Economics and Political Science* 15: 53-73.

Heron, Craig
1989 *The Canadian Labour Movement*. Toronto: Lorimer.

Herzenberg, Stephen
1991 "Towards a Cooperative Commonwealth? Labor and Restructuring in the US and Canadian Auto Industries." PhD dissertation, Massachusetts Institute of Technology.

Hogan, Fr. Brian
1988 "Catechising Culture: Assumption College, The Pius XI Labour School, and the United Automobile Workers, Windsor, 1940-1950." *Canadian Catholic History Studies* 55.

Horowitz, Gad
1968 *Canadian Labour in Politics*. Toronto: University of Toronto Press.

Houlahan, Raymond
1963 "A History of Collective Bargaining in Local 200 UAW." MA thesis, University of Windsor.

Jenson, Jane
1989 "'Different' But Not 'Exceptional': Canada's Permeable Fordism." *Canadian Review of Sociology and Anthropology* 26(1): 69-94.

Jefferys, Steve
1986 *Management and Managed*. Cambridge: Cambridge University Press.

Johnson, Walter
1978 "Strike: General Motors," in Walter Johnson. *Trade Unions and the State*. Montreal: Black Rose.

Klare, Karl
1977-78 "Judicial Deradicalization of the Wagner Act and the Origins of Modern Legal Consciousness, 1937-41." *Minnesota Law Review* 62: 265-339.

Lichtenstein, Nelson
1992 "Reutherism on the Shop Floor: Union Strategy and Shop-Floor Conflict in the UAW 1946-70," in Steven Tolliday and Jonathan Zeitlin (eds.). *Between Fordism and Flexibility*. Oxford: Berg.
1983 "Conflict Over Workers' Control," in Michael Frisch and Daniel Walkowitz (eds.). *Working Class America*. Chicago: University of Illinois.
1982 *Labor's War at Home: The CIO in World War II*. Cambridge: Cambridge University Press.
1980 "Auto Worker Militancy and the Structure of Factory Life, 1937-55." *Journal of American History* 67(2): 335-53.

Logan, Harold A.
1956 *State Intervention and Assistance in Collective Bargaining*. Toronto: University of Toronto Press.

Macdowell, Laurel S.
1978 "The Formation of the Canadian Industrial Relations System." *Labour/Le Travailleur* 3: 175-96.

Mahon, Rianne
1991 "Post Fordism: Some Issues for Labour," in Daniel Drache and Meric Gertler (eds.). *New Era of Global Competition*. Kingston and Montreal: McGill-Queen's University Press.

Manley, John
1986 "Communists and Auto Workers: The Struggle for Industrial Unionism in the Canadian Automobile Industry, 1925-36." *Labour/Le Travail* 17: 105-66.

Marquart, Frank
1975 *An Autoworker's Journal*. University Park: Pennsylvania State University Press.

Matheson, David
1989 "The Canadian Working Class and Industrial Legality, 1939-1949." MA thesis, Queen's University.

McBride, Stephen
1992 *Not Working: State, Unemployment and Neo-Conservatism in Canada*. Toronto: University of Toronto Press.
1987 "Hard Times and the 'Rules of the Game,'" in Robert Argue et al. (eds.). *Working People and Hard Times*. Toronto: Garamond.

Michels, Robert
1962 *Political Parties*. New York: Free Press.

Millar, Frederick D.
1981 "Shapes of Power: The Ontario Labour Relations Board, 1944 to 1950." PhD dissertation, York University.

Milton, David
1982 *Politics of US Labor*. New York: Monthly Review.

Montero, Gloria
1979 *We Stood Together*. Toronto: Lorimer.

Morton, Desmond
1980 *Working People*. Ottawa: Deneau.

Moulton, David
1974 "Ford Windsor 1945," in Irving Abella (ed.). *On Strike: Six Key Labour Struggles in Canada, 1919-1949*. Toronto: Lorimer.

Napier, John S.
1976 *Memories of Building the UAW*. Toronto: Canadian Party of Labour.

O'Grady, John
1992 "Beyond the Wagner Act, What Then?" in Daniel Drache (ed.). *Getting on Track*. Montreal: McGill-Queen's University Press.

Pal, Leslie
1988 *State, Class and Bureaucracy*. Kingston and Montreal: McGill-Queen's University Press.

Palmer, Bryan
1992 *Working Class Experience*. Toronto: McClelland and Stewart.

Panitch, Leo and Donald Swartz
1993 *The Assault on Trade Union Freedoms: From Wage Controls to Social Contract*. Toronto: Garamond.

Penner, Norman
1992 *From Protest to Power: Social Democracy in Canada 1900-Present*. Toronto: Lorimer.
1988 *Canadian Communism: The Stalin Years and Beyond*. Toronto: Methuen.

Roberts, Wayne and John Bullen
1984 "A Heritage of Hope and Struggle: Workers, Unions, and Politics in Canada, 1930-1982," in Michael Cross and Gregory Kealey (eds.). *Modern Canada, 1930-1980s*. Toronto: McClelland and Stewart.

Russell, Bob
1990a *Back to Work? Labour, State and Industrial Relations in Canada*. Toronto: Nelson.
1990b "Assault Without Defeat," in Larry Haiven et al. (eds.). *Regulating Labour*. Toronto: Garamond.

Sayles, Leonard and George Strauss
1953 *The Local Union*. New York: Harper and Bros.

Selekman, Benjamin et al.
1964 *Problems in Labor Relations*. New York: McGraw Hill.

Steiber, Jack
1962 *Governing the UAW*. New York: Wiley.

Stepan-Norris, Judith and Maurice Zeitlin
1991 "'Red' Unions and 'Bourgeois' Contracts?" *American Journal of Sociology* 96(5): 1151-1200.

Sugiman, Pamela H.
1992 "Labour's Dilemma: The Meaning and Politics of Worker Resistance in a Gendered Setting." PhD dissertation, University of Toronto.

Tolliday, Steven and Jonathan Zeitlin
1985 *Shop Floor Bargaining and the State*. Cambridge: Cambridge University Press.

Tomlins, Christopher T.
1985 *The State and the Unions*. Cambridge: Cambridge University Press.

Tudiver, Neil
1987 "Forestalling the Welfare State," in Allan Moscovitch and Jim Albert (eds.). *The Benevolent State*. Toronto: Garamond.

Veres, Louis J.
1956 "History of the United Automobile Workers in Windsor, 1936-1955." MA thesis, University of Western Ontario.

Warrian, Peter
1986 "Labour is Not a Commodity: A Study of the Rights of Labour in the Canadian Postwar Economy, 1944-48." PhD dissertation, University of Waterloo.

Wells, Donald
1995a "The Impact of the Postwar Compromise on Canadian Unionism." *Labour/Le Travail* (forthcoming).
1995b "New Directions for Labour in a 'Post-Fordist' World," in Ernest Yanarella and William Green (eds.). *Other People's Cars: Organized Labor and the Crisis of Fordism*. Albany: State University of New York Press (forthcoming).
1986 "Autoworkers on the Firing Line," in Craig Heron and Robert Storey (eds.). *On the Job*. Kingston and Montreal: McGill-Queen's University Press.

Whitaker, Reginald
1977 *The Government Party*. Toronto: University of Toronto Press.

Williams, C. Brian
1964 "Notes on the Evolution of Compulsory Conciliation in Canada." *Relations Industrielles* 19.

Wolfe, David
1984 "The Rise and Demise of the Keynesian Era in Canada," in Michael Cross and Gregory Kealey (eds.). *Modern Canada 1930-1980s*. Toronto: McClelland and Stewart.

Woods, H.D.
1955 "Canadian Collective Bargaining and Dispute Settlement Policy." *Canadian Journal of Economics and Political Science* 21(4): 447-65.

Yates, Charlotte
1993 *From Plant to Politics: The Autoworkers Union in Postwar Canada*. Philadelphia: Temple University Press.
1990 "Labour and Lobbying," in William Coleman and Grace Skogstad (eds.). *Policy Communities and Public Policy in Canada*. Mississauga, ON: Copp Clark Pitman.
1988 "From Plant to Politics: The Canadian UAW 1936-1984." PhD dissertation, Carleton University.

Young, F.J.L.
1952 "The Limits of Collective Bargaining in the Canadian Automobile Industry." MA thesis, Queen's University.

CHAPTER 23

Public Interest, Public Service

In the first half of the twentieth century, Parliament and provincial legislatures had grudgingly established machinery for collective bargaining between private employers and their workers. The public sector was different. Unlike other employees, the public's servants performed work too vital to be left to the vagaries of the free market in either prices or wages. Moreover, a constitutional principle was at stake. In 1885, Manitoba's first Civil Service Act had made it clear that any request for a raise "shall be considered as a tendering of the resignation of such member." Little changed. "The Queen does not negotiate with her subjects," proclaimed Quebec's premier, Jean Lesage, in 1964. A more democratic argument was that, since Parliament was supreme, elected members could not be compelled to ratify spending decisions reached at some remote bargaining table. Consultation and discussion might be contemplated, and even welcomed, but to strike against a government was tantamount to civil war. Police strikes in Quebec, Toronto and other cities in 1919–20 had been followed by wholesale dismissals. Postal workers who joined Winnipeg's general strike in 1919 or who walked out in Toronto in 1922 were sternly disciplined. When Joe Davidson went to work as a sorter in Toronto in 1957, some of the older workers who went over to greet him were accompanied by soft calls of "Cuckoo, cuckoo." They were still shunned as the "scabs" of 1922.

In principle, civil servants in Canada traded the benefits of unionization for blessings few working people enjoyed: the prospect of superannuation at the end of a working life and, provided they did not fall victim of a partisan purge after a change of government, relatively secure employment. The proposition that governments should, somehow, be model employers was much slower to

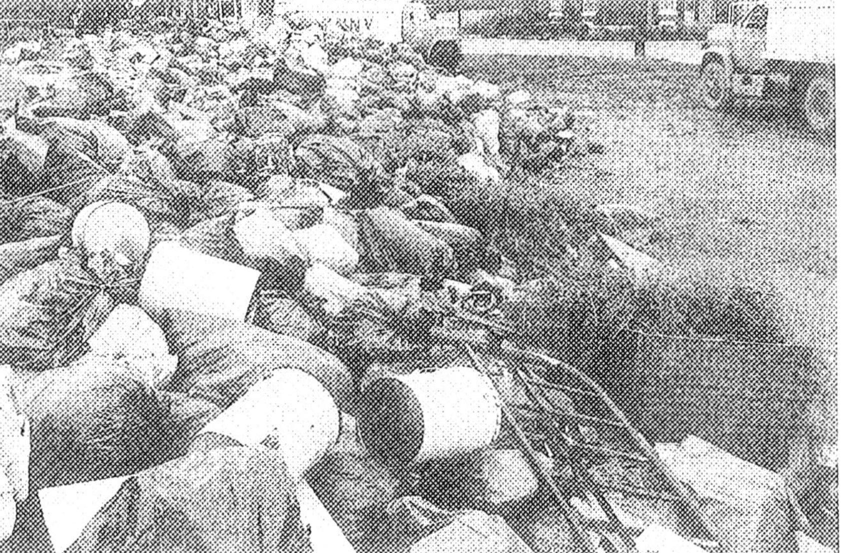

Top

With the era of public service strikes, Canadians began to revise some assumptions about what was indispensable. Plastic garbage bags stacked in a nearby park could make a strike of sanitation workers barely tolerable even during the summer. Most people even adjusted to postal strikes although some businesses were driven to bankruptcy by unfilled orders and uncollected bills. (Labour Gazette)

One of the major transformations of the 1960s was the emergence of federal and provincial employees as militant members of the union movement. Civil servants, once the victims of political patronage and later strictly aloof from politics, returned in the seventies as a force in their own right, fighting cutbacks and pay restraint policies. (Public Service Alliance of Canada)

emerge. The "fair wages" resolution of 1900 established that federal government contracts would be performed for the "prevailing rate" of wages in a locality. No government wished to annoy local employers by overpaying their workers.

The Post Office had the longest experience of employee organization. The Railway Mail Clerks Association was born in 1889 under the wing of the railway brotherhoods. The Federal Association of Letter Carriers followed in 1891, and the Canadian Postal Employees' Association (for inside workers) in 1911. The Winnipeg militants of 1919 were part of a breakaway Western Federation of Postal Employees. To broaden its appeal, the western group evolved into the Amalgamated Postal Workers and, still later, the Amalgamated Civil Servants of Canada.

In 1909, members of other federal government departments in Ottawa linked their associations in a Civil Service Federation, insisting that they intended no more than to serve social and benevolent functions and to make occasional polite representations to their employer. They were as good as their word. Several provincial and municipal employee associations formed in the same period shared the same spirit. They reminded their members of the dignity of public service and their obligations to the taxpayers. In 1911 two hundred Ontario civil servants met at Queen's Park to consider "the necessity of a Civil Service Association, pointing out its possibilities in the way of improving the Service, promoting social togetherness, urging healthy athletics and co-operating with one another in the purchasing of supplies." Members agreed that they needed the government's permission to proceed. It was cheerfully granted. It was in much the same spirit that many historic and effective unions had been formed in the previous century. Indeed, by 1919, the new CSAO had opened discussions with the government on pensions and, since wartime inflation cost salaries half their value, on wages too. Never forgotten was the realization that, even after civil service reforms in the 1920s, political patronage played a major part in appointments, promotions, salaries and dismissals. Incorporated in 1920 as a charitable organization, Manitoba's Civil Service Association, organized months after Winnipeg's 1919 general strike, promised that its goal was "the largest possible measure of joint action between the government and its employees." Most early MCSA leaders were senior government officials; five of the first 24 officers were women.

Across Canada, public services remained modest in size, income and competence. In 1941, even with a war on, 342,934 men and women worked in education, health or government service, barely 8 percent of the Canadian workforce. The Second World War brought changes. The example of industrial unionization was contagious. By 1944, Montreal city employees, including police and firefighters, not only had organized unions but had struck successfully. Unhampered by tradition, the new CCF government in Saskatchewan extended its new Trade Union Act to cover provincial employees and offered them the right to strike. Most of them formed a union and affiliated with the TLC. Ottawa and other provinces were unpersuaded. Mackenzie King had another model, Britain's "Whitley Councils," a post-1919 development for unorganized industries and civil servants. In 1944, Ottawa authorized a Whitley-style Joint National

Council, so that an "official" side of deputy ministers and personnel experts could discuss hours, overtime, leave entitlements and kindred matters with a "staff side" chosen from the civil service associations. The cabinet could accept, alter or ignore Joint Council advice as it preferred.

Postwar prosperity initially undermined civil service bargaining power. Anyone who complained of a low salary or poor prospects could easily find a better job. Inflation and the growing size and complexity of government gradually rebuilt the pressure for better salaries and benefits. By 1951, salaried public employment absorbed 12 percent of the workforce. The share grew as hospitals, schools and suburbs exploded with population growth and affluence. By the 1960s, two in ten Canadian workers depended on public funds for all or part of their income. Years of full employment and rising wealth for most Canadians, and the advent of younger, less grateful employees, brought a mood of militancy that fed on the frustration of more obsequious elders. Governments felt the heat.

In 1957, with an election approaching, the Liberal government appointed a veteran diplomat, Arnold Heeney, to head the Civil Service Commission and to report on wages, working conditions and job classifications. Heeney recommended pay raises and a Pay Research Bureau to establish rates comparable with private sector wages, but his report was delivered to a Conservative government deeply suspicious of an overgrown and Liberal-infected civil service. The new finance minister, Donald Fleming, simply announced that pay raises would be frozen until further study. He needed the money for his unavailing efforts to balance the federal budget. The Tories' new Civil Service Act in 1961 agreed that the Pay Research Bureau would share its data with civil service organizations.

By then, federal civil servants and their provincial counterparts had a lot to discuss. Frustration levels varied with rank, but professionals and trades alike shared a bitter sense of betrayal. Generous pay increases to federal employees on the eve of the 1962 election did not make them grateful. By the 1963 election, leaders of three of the major parties had pledged their support for the once-revolutionary notion of collective bargaining for government employees. Narrowly victorious, the Liberals asked Heeney to serve as chairman of a Preparatory Committee on Collective Bargaining. A Bureau of Classification appeared in the fall of 1964 to unravel the baffling tangle of salary scales. Heeney's final report in 1965 recommended what the Civil Service Federation and its rivals had wanted since 1958: a process of negotiation that led to compulsory arbitration. Governments would be free to reject an award – but only by a vote of Parliament.

By the time Heeney reported, events had again bypassed him. As early as 1960, British Columbia civil servants had gone on strike against their Social Credit government. Like Saskatchewan's public employees, they affiliated with the TLC and then with the CLC.

A powerful impetus for change came from Quebec. In 1960, the Catholic unions had reversed their drift to the CLC, shed the last vestiges of clerical control, and emerged as the Confederation of National Trade Unions (*Confédération des syndicats nationaux*). One motive was political. While Catholic unions

Public sector unions gradually came to dominate the Canadian labour movement in the 1970s and, in return, union involvement politicized public employees. Demonstrations of political concern did not prevent governments from creating recessions, wiping out jobs, and wrecking the economy, if not Canada. (Ontario Federation of Labour)

and the CCL's industrial unions had fought Duplessis, much of the former TLC in Quebec had backed him in return for favours. A Liberal victory in 1960 changed the players. Gérard Picard, the last president of the Catholic confederation, had backed the New Party movement and became the NDP's first associate leader. His successor, Jean Marchand, had backed the Liberals in opposition. He would share the fruits of victory.

In 1963, Quebec Liberals finally delivered a promised Labour Code, complete with a requirement for union check-off and a sharp reduction in government meddling with collective bargaining decisions. However, there was no mention of unions for civil servants. Marchand exploded. The province, he warned, would be set on fire. The rival Quebec Federation of Labour called a special convention and talked of a general strike. Underpaid hospital workers staged illegal walkouts. In August, 1963, the once conservative teachers' federation insisted that any right of association would be meaningless without the right to strike. The Lesage government finally listened. In 1964, a revised Code emerged, covering all workers, with the exception of police, firefighters and a few narrowly-defined categories of essential workers.

There was a small wrinkle in the Code; civil servants could affiliate with any labour organization that did not openly back a political party. By no coincidence, only Marchand's CNTU qualified. The arrangement seemed an enormous bonus to an ambitious organization. It seemed unlikely that civil servants, hospital workers or liquor store employees would be very militant or need much service. Instead, their dues would cover the CNTU's mounting costs. In practice, like the industrial workers of the 1940s, Quebec's public employees had abysmal wages and a huge backlog of grievances. Almost as soon as the new law was proclaimed, Quebec Liquor Commission workers tested it with a prolonged strike. Highway workers and hospital employees soon followed.

In the 1940s, Quebec's French-speaking Catholic teachers had defied the Duplessis government and lost. In 1959, they reappeared in the guise of a dutiful professional association, but a few years of the Quiet Revolution restored the old militancy. Illegal walkouts in 1963 and 1964 persuaded the Lesage government to add teachers to the growing list of Quebeckers who could legally strike. In 1966, under the leadership of Raymond Laliberté, teachers dropped the word "Catholic" from their title. Three years later, they dropped an old commitment to "social Christianity" and pledged instead to uphold the "Rights of Man." By 1970, when Yvon Charbonneau was elected president, the *Corporation des enseignants du Quebec* (CEQ) was a union by any standard, and Quebec workers, public- and private-sector, had moved from the back row to the front rank in labour militancy.

If Jean Lesage's government struggled to stay ahead, Ottawa seemed to have lost control. Fed up with low pay and a host of mean little injustices that stemmed from political patronage and low-level supervisors, postal workers were the angriest federal workers. Post Office officials ignored warnings that only a big wage increase would keep employees on the job during the summer of 1965. Negotiations dragged on, month after month. Finally, on July 23, the government announced that it had handed the problem to Judge J.C. Anderson for a solution. That day, Montreal postal workers walked out. Next day the strike spread to Vancouver, Toronto and other cities. Union officials were helpless. On July 27, they announced a settlement only to have it decisively rejected by the Montreal local. Only on August 7, under the threat of sending troops and students to do their work, did Montreal workers return. Instead of a government offer of $300, the strikers settled for $550 and Judge Anderson's strong advice that the Post Office become a crown corporation, subject to the IRDIA.

The 1965 postal strike was as decisive as the Algoma strike of 1943. Canadians discovered that they could live without postal service, but at a high price. Postal workers discovered that public sympathy ended the moment they struck for their rights – but only by striking could they budge the government. Bitter and resentful, they sought leaders like Toronto's Joe Davidson and Montreal's Jean-Claude Parrot, tough and uncompromising enough to fight Ottawa and the Post Office. Meanwhile Post Office managers planned vengeance, not adjustment. New technology and soaring volumes of mail offered a solution. Instead of being a low-wage, labour-intensive industry, the Post Office would become the most automated in the world. If corporations wanted a lesson in how to combine radical technological change with a maximum of rancour, disruption and delay, Canada Post would be the model.

Despite the turbulent, strike-ridden atmosphere of 1966, Liberals, Conservatives and New Democrats worked in surprising harmony to create a public service bargaining structure which offered the hitherto unthinkable option of the strike. With the Post Office strike and Quebec as cautionary tales, experts and politicians agreed that federal employees would have the right to choose between compulsory arbitration, mediation or a strike. Both the experts and the Civil Service Federation president, Claude Edwards, agreed: the vast majority of public employees would never even think of walking out. On February 20, 1967, the Public Service Staff Relations Act (PSSRA) and two companion bills became law.

Designed by the veteran Ontario labour lawyer Jacob Finkelman, the PSSRA gave the government more rights than the IRDIA allowed private employers. The armed forces, the RCMP and senior officials were excluded, and bargaining rights were extended to only 260,000 of Ottawa's 400,000 employees. The Treasury Board, the department that monitored government spending, became the employer, though effective authority was so widely dispersed among departments and levels of supervisors that union negotiators soon complained that they bargained chiefly with phantoms. A host of issues, from working conditions to staffing levels, were excluded from negotiation. For groups that chose them, strikes were possible only after conciliation and a waiting period – a near-guarantee that serious bargaining would occur only in the final days before a walkout. A Public Service Staff Relations Board would serve as a labour relations commission, defining bargaining units, settling incidental disputes, and operating with as much independence as it could manage when the employer paid the bills.

In its way, the PSSRA was as significant as the Trade Unions Act of 1872 and P.C. 1003. Canada's labour movement had organized virtually all it could of a predominantly male, blue-collar and shrinking industrial workforce, and, like its U.S. counterpart, which had begun to decline in the 1950s, it was losing its share of the labour market. With the public sector – now a fifth of the Canadian workforce – open to be organized, Canadian unionism began to grow, from a quarter of the non-agricultural labour force at the beginning of the decade to well over a third by 1970. Other jurisdictions followed the lead of Quebec and Ottawa. In Ontario, a tradition of charter flights, a Christmas singsong and intimate chats between the premier and the manager of the Civil

Frequent postal strikes during the 1970s sometimes left employees themselves deeply divided. Though the Letter Carriers' Union was far less militant than the inside workers of the Canadian Union of Postal Workers, they bore the brunt of public indignation. (Canadian Press)

Service Association of Ontario dissolved in bitter internal battles between conservatives and young militants. The turning point came after sweeping recommendations from a Committee on Government Productivity, eagerly embraced by a new premier, William Davis. Designed to end ad hoc, politically motivated decision-making, the COGP supplanted paternalism with the bureaucratic rule of experts.

With some reluctance on both sides, government workers and their association found that they needed each other. Productivity demands, downsizing and privatization turned the CSAO into a union. The process included some bitter fights, including the firing of some key CSAO staff by general manager Harold Bowen, and his ouster a year later by his opponents. The battle coincided with debate on the notorious Crown Employees' Collective Bargaining Act, a law that guaranteed the CSAO full bargaining rights for Ontario government employees and then barred the right to strike and to negotiate on twenty-one different issues, from training to pensions. Judge William Little, advisor to Ontario's Conservative government, dismissed public service strikes as a form of incipient insurrection: "I cannot accept the proposition that anyone who joins the public service would have the right, in conjunction with others, to withdraw his services with the sole object of compelling a duly-elected government to meet his demands." Ontario left its employees to the mercy of three-member arbitration commissions.

The struggle to repair hostile legislation turned the CSAO into a union. Flamboyant tactics by Bowen's public relations-conscious successor, Jake Norman, helped. Norman let his staff bargain outrageously, raising expectations which no government could have matched, but which left unhappy workers feeling robbed. Without the right to strike, the CSAO was as free as the government to be unreasonable. Jim "Foghorn" Fuller, a meat inspector, delighted delegates to the last CSAO convention by roaring, "I am seldom civil and I am a servant to no man." In 1974, the old CSAO became the new Ontario Public Service Employee Union.

In Manitoba, the combination of militant new civil servants in the 1960s and election of Ed Schreyer's NDP government in 1969 produced a catalytic reaction. By opposing Schreyer's offer of the right to strike and to political action, the old-guard leaders made themselves vulnerable to a harsh arbitration award. The MGEA's counterpart to "Foghorn" Fuller was John Pullen, a labour department inspector, who brought down the house at the critical 1973 convention by railing: "We got the bloody crumbs off the table, that's all we got, we got the crumbs off the table." By the end of 1974, the MGEA had affiliated to the Canadian Labour Congress.

By the early 1970s, every province had accepted some form of collective bargaining with its employees, though Alberta and Ontario had refused to concede the right to strike. As legal barriers crumbled, so did obstacles of tradition, status and suspicion. Hospital and social workers, teachers, librarians, university employees, municipal workers, even professional engineers with Ontario Hydro and other big public utilities, demanded the right to bargain collectively. While some groups, such as teachers, preferred to work through erstwhile professional associations and federations, many welcomed the expertise

The decision by Montreal firemen and police to conduct a "study session" to press for early settlement of contract demands led in 1969 to wild riots, looting, and a violent assault on the Murray-Hill Bus Lines garage. For the first time since 1933, troops were called out to help restore order in a strike situation. The experience was a prelude to the October crisis of 1970. (Canadian Press)

and resources that only unions could give them. The Canadian Union of Public Employees was the product of a 1963 merger between 53,000 members of the National Union of Public Employees and the 30,000-member National Union of Public Service Employees, its former CCL rival. In a decade, CUPE doubled its membership, surpassing the United Steelworkers as Canada's biggest union organization. Low dues, an openness to modern public relations style, and a host of eager young organizers gave CUPE an inside track on municipal and hospital workers, but legislation and the public mood helped clear the way. Under pressure to adapt to the new environment, the major federal employee organizations, the Civil Service Association and the Civil Service Federation, cautiously accepted a merger, though old departmental components, such as

the National Defence Employees and the Customs and Excise Officers were carefully preserved. In November, 1966, the 120,000-member Public Service Alliance of Canada became the country's third largest union, with Claude Edwards as president. The CLC eagerly embraced it as an affiliate.

Unionization of Canada's public employees changed more than membership statistics. Labour in Canada had always been a predominantly male and blue-collar institution. Public sector unions added hundreds of thousands of members who were women, middle-class or both. People from a wide gamut of trades and occupations, many with no private-sector counterparts, such as lighthouse keepers and air traffic controllers, became part of the labour movement. The newcomers threatened a number of traditions. As members of Canadian-based organizations, they threatened the traditional dominance of international unions in the Canadian labour movement. One potential issue, the CLC's commitment to its own political party, caused problems in some provinces, particularly British Columbia and Ontario, where government employees were banned from affiliating with a political party. In practice, CLC affiliates were free to decide their own political stance, and there were many that cheerfully ignored Congress policies. The leaders who emerged in the new public-sector unions tended to have NDP sympathies and even an imprudent yearning to mobilize their members for the cause. NDPers could boast that the CCF had made Saskatchewan a pioneer in unionizing public employees without significant friction. Hidden in the future were the strains that would develop when NDP governments faced tough bargaining and even strike-ridden relations with their employees.

The biggest change for unions was barely perceived in the sixties: the advent of large numbers of women, ranging from professionals to unskilled workers, in a male-dominated labour market. During the decade the female share of the workforce grew from 27 to 34 percent, and to 43 percent by the end of the 1970s. Few noticed at first, because women initially crowded into the ill-paid, non-union jobs they had always dominated. Memories of the Eaton Drive and other failures had convinced organizers that women in sales, secretarial and service work would never be unionized. In industries like clothing and textiles, where women had been organized, union leadership was routinely dominated by men.

By illuminating coincidence, Canada's centennial, the PSSRA, and the appointment of the Royal Commission on the Status of Women all happened in 1967. Judy LaMarsh, the Pearson government's sole female cabinet minister, pressured her colleagues to launch an investigation into every aspect of the lives and prospects of Canadian women. Unions and how they served women were part of the mandate. Summoned to testify, most unions had nothing to say. Women unionists, insisted the Quebec Federation of Labour, enjoyed equality with men in most but not all respects: "It has unfortunately been impossible, we must admit, to secure real implementation of the principle of equal pay for equal work in certain sectors." Since equal pay for equal work was enshrined in law, a union movement which cared profoundly about the issue might have made more impact. Of course, unionists guarded their hard-earned differentials, and employers sheltered behind narrow definitions of

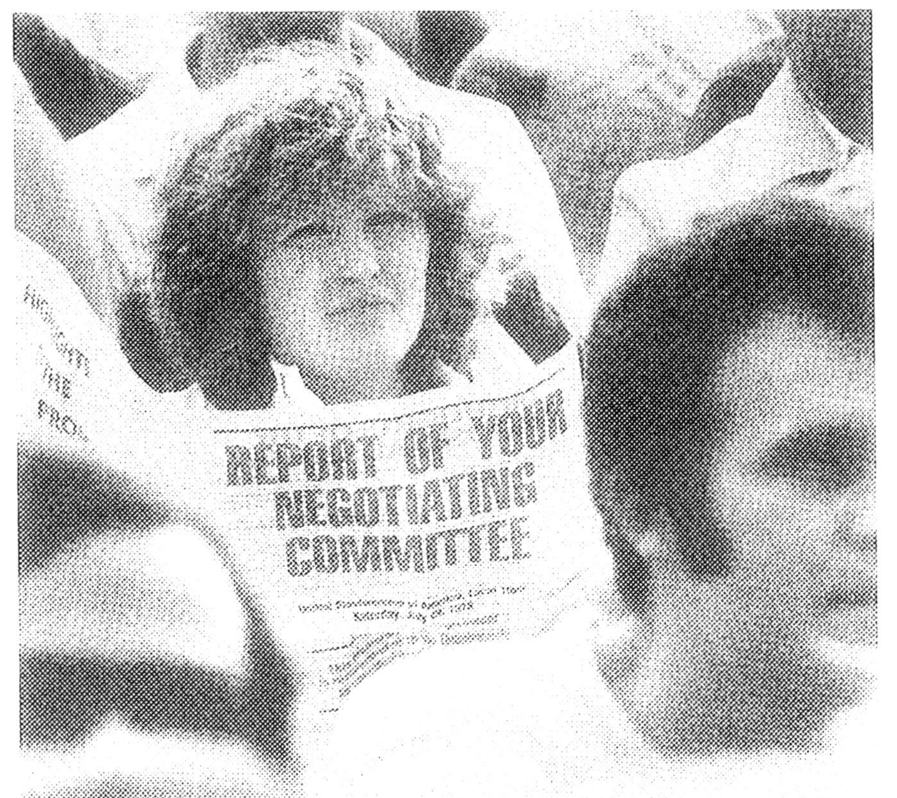

One consequence of rank-and-file rejection of settlements was a more sophisticated attempt by union leaders to explain to their membership what had been accomplished during bargaining. (United Steelworkers)

"equal work," and laws which banned women from working on night shifts, lifting heavy weights or labouring underground in a mine. In the absence of better evidence, the Royal Commission accepted the cautious judgement of Sylvia Ostry at Statistics Canada that, other things being equal, a Canadian woman earned 75–85 percent of a man's wage. Better evidence soon proved that the estimate was far too generous.

The male leadership of most unions had regarded women's concerns with some sympathy, little understanding and low priority at bargaining time. Maternity leave and equal pay for equal work seemed a reasonable agenda. Expectations began to change with surprising rapidity. In the 1960s, as more women went to work, even more expected to stay for a career. By the 1970s, as inflation drained family purchasing power, economic motives were as pressing as changing social values: supporting a family on a single income became a fair prescription for poverty. Women not only insisted on escaping from traditional

low-wage job ghettos, they demanded new respect and income levels for nurses, office staff and homemakers. Equal pay must be for work of equal value, as defined by complex formulas. Like politicians and business executives, union leaders could no longer judge these needs from the comfort of a nearly all-male club. In the labour movement, the advent of public service unions meant that women would have a new and growing constituency of sympathetic voters. In 1970, a woman named Shirley Carr persuaded fellow office employees at the Niagara Falls city hall to form a local of CUPE. They made her their president. Fourteen years later, she was president of the Canadian Labour Congress.

Public-sector unionization and the 1960s revival of French-English tensions embittered relations between the CLC and its far smaller Quebec rival, the CNTU. In 1960, about a quarter of the CNTU's members worked in the public sector; by 1971, barely 40 percent of its 206,000 members worked for private companies. With its enlarged membership and financial base, its political connection and its appeal to Quebec pride, the CNTU carried new weight in Ottawa as well as Quebec City. In 1965, it demanded the right to represent workers in the CPR's Angus Shops in Montreal. The Canada Labour Relations Board said no: with seventeen unions already involved in railway bargaining, there was no room for another. The CNTU was indignant; the CLC, with a majority of labour nominees on the Board, was smug. But in 1965, the CNTU's Jean Marchand became a federal cabinet minister. By 1968, the government had framed legislation to reshape the CLRB to suit the CNTU. Now the CLC was outraged at "one of the most blatant expressions of political partisanship which we have observed." The bill died with the premature dissolution of Parliament and the Woods Task Force inherited another issue.

It was easier to agree that public employees had the right to organize, bargain and even to strike than to foresee the practical consequences that soon followed. In urging a national health insurance system, for example, the Hall Royal Commission had estimated the costs on the unspoken assumption that nurses, orderlies and other health employees would continue to accept modest wages. Many other public services, from operating grain elevators to snow removal, tended to be low-wage, labour-intensive activities. The public could sympathize with low-paid workers without realizing that either the remedy had to come from its own pockets or it would suffer the consequences in unshipped grain or blocked highways. Unless an employer dominated a community, few citizens were affected by private-sector labour disputes. They had no such immunity when hospitals, schools or government liquor stores were surrounded by pickets or when wage settlements increased taxes.

By the late 1960s, there were many issues in the once-tranquil labour relations scene, and several governments sought academic or judicial wisdom. In Ontario, where picket-line violence and defiance of *ex parte* injunctions had invaded the 1967 election, Mr. Justice Ivan Rand was summoned from retirement. Those who remembered his ingenious formula for union check-off would be disappointed. The price of banning injunctions, Rand insisted, was that unions must become legal entities, able to sue and be sued. Mass pickets, boycotts and sympathetic walkouts were intolerable. Above all, Rand urged an

Australian-style labour court, with power to end strikes and lockouts. The Ontario government thanked Rand, listened to the uproar from the labour movement, and buried the report. British Columbia's Social Credit government sent Mr. Justice Nathan Nemetz to Europe to find solutions for the province's labour turbulence. Nemetz came home with arguments for labour-management committees, better-trained mediators and a permanent industrial inquiry commission. The government created a Mediation Commission, with power to impose its own settlements on disputes referred by the government. Within months, the Commission was suspect among employers and detested by unions. By 1972, anger at the Commission helped defeat the Social Credit regime.

The Woods Report, presented in March, 1969, was different. To those who had dreamed of clever solutions to labour strife, Woods and his colleagues offered little comfort. Conflict had no mysterious cause. Inflation, fuelled by prosperity and by Washington's decision to finance the Vietnam War by borrowing, sent prices climbing. Armed with the right to strike, employees would use it to pressure their bosses. Once both sides had measured their strength, relations would settle down. Whatever its problems, the adversarial system fitted "our heritage of western values," and there were no better alternatives. The rights of workers were integral to the values of liberal democracy.

As befitting a group of academics, Woods and his colleagues had ideas. Employer associations should be encouraged as a counter to labour organizations. The government must do more to protect individual union members. The CLC-CNTU battle over the CLRB might be solved by replacing it with an appointed, independent board. A three-member public interest disputes commission could tackle strikes in essential services, with power to help work out solutions and, if necessary, to recommend "seizure, trusteeship, partial operation, statutory strikes and compulsory arbitration ..."

The work of the Woods Task Force, modified by labour and management critics, was embodied in the Canada Labour Code of 1972, the first real revision of federal bargaining legislation since 1948. For the first time a Canadian statute declared that "the common well being" was promoted "through the encouragement of free collective bargaining and the constructive settlement of disputes." Woods's pleas for a new non-partisan labour relations board was respected; so was his concern for the democratic rights of individual union members. The right to collective bargaining was extended to professionals, to owner-operators of trucks and to fishermen in "share of catch" operations.

The sharpest debate over shaping the new Code was how far workers would be consulted about technological change. For the first time, a narrow, carefully-guarded breach was opened in the inviolability of a valid collective agreement. Accepting more from Mr. Justice Freedman than from Woods, the new Code demanded ninety days' notice of "any technological change likely to affect the conditions or security of employment of a significant number of employees" and allowed negotiations and even the possibility of a legal strike. Management decisions would be exempt if they were shared before a contract was signed. Predictably, employers and editors worried that Canada would lose a valued tradition of secure labour contracts. The Canadian Chamber of Commerce raged that the government was "legalizing Luddite-like conduct, aimed at arbitrarily stopping progress and promoting feather bedding."

Missing from the new Code was Woods's proposed "public interest disputes commission." Quiet lobbying by both unions and employers had buried the idea. Politicians and their official advisors would be left to their common sense. That may have been a mistake. Adding almost a million workers to the labour movement and fuelling their militancy with a huge surge of inflation guaranteed that the 1970s would see even more labour turmoil than the 1960s, and in areas where Canadians had little experience of, or tolerance for, labour's traditional tactics.

The true public interest needed a sensible interpretation. Common sense is always scarce.

Excerpts from "Women and OPSEU"

THE STEREOTYPE OF WOMEN

MANY MALE MANAGERS HAVE A STEREOTYPED VIEW OF WORKING WOMEN . . .			. . . BUT THE PICTURE IS INACCURATE				
Men generally believe that women . . .	In particular, they think that women . . .	They are often heard to say . . .	But most of these beliefs are, at best, "half truths" . . .				. . . according to the available evidence
			True	"Half true"	"Quarter true"	False	
. . . Are not career-oriented	Have limited aspirations for advancement	"Women are happy where they are; they just want 9 to 5 jobs so that they can get home to their families"			X		. In recent studies, roughly half of all women say they want to be promoted, compared to two-thirds of men . Researchers attribute the difference to women's scaling down their ambitions to avoid repeated disappointments
	Are unwilling to relocate	"Her husband has a good job here in Regina; she couldn't move to Saskatoon to take a promotion"		X			More women than men are unwilling to relocate, but: . Difference between single men and single women is small . Increasing numbers of husbands move to follow wives
	Have little need for money	"She doesn't need the extra dough; all women work for pin money"			X		. 43 percent of working women are single, and presumably work to support themselves . 50 percent of working wives either have children or have husbands making less than $8,000 per year; wife's income is therefore necessary
. . . Are less suited than men for many jobs	Lack required education and experience	"There is just no hope of finding a woman with the education and experience needed for that job"		X			Significantly more men than women hold degrees or diplomas in business, the sciences, and technical disciplines, but: . More women than men finished high school . Women now receive 44 percent of all bachelor's degrees awarded
	Are more often absent	"I need somebody reliable for that position — I can't use a woman who would be sick or away looking after her kids all the time"				X	All recent studies have found that difference in days worked per year is negligible — e.g.: . 0.5 percent in Public Service . 1.2 percent at CBC . No difference in United States
	Quit too frequently	"It's a bad investment to promote a woman; she's liable to get married, have a baby and quit"			X		. While women leave more often in lower paying jobs, they quit less frequently in higher status positions . Difference between men and women who stay is minimal — e.g., gap in retention rates in Public Service is 6 percent.
	Are unable to travel	"This position requires a week of travelling every month; how could she handle it and still raise her three kids?"			X		Overall, more men than women are willing to travel, but: . Small difference between single men (88 percent willing) and single women (74 percent willing) . Smaller difference for higher job levels
	Won't be accepted as supervisors	"I'd like to promote her, but the men in the department would never accept her authority"		X			. In nationwide survey, percentage of people expressing reluctance at prospect of a female supervisor declined from 82 percent in 1954 to 45 percent in 1974 . Men who have been supervised by a woman are 40 percent less likely to prefer a male supervisor than men who have not
	Are unable to do strenuous physical work	"A woman couldn't climb up a ladder with that equipment"			X		Men are on average stronger than women by at least one-third, but: . Most jobs do not require physical strength . For those that do, what counts is the strength of the individual candidate, and there are strong women and weak men
. . . Are better suited than men for many jobs	Have greater manual dexterity	"Women have the manual dexterity it takes for typing; men don't"				X	All available research suggests that there is no difference in inherent manual dexterity between men and women, but that dexterity is acquired
	Are more tolerant of repetitive detail	"Women don't mind repetitive and boring jobs; they are born not wanting a life of challenge"				X	. Studies have found that women and men holding identical unstimulating jobs express equal dissatisfaction . Women quit these jobs at a greater rate than men
. . . And are too emotional	Cry frequently	"I have a lot of women working for me and they are quite good; but they cry so much"				X	Women and men have come to express their emotions in different ways: Women cry and men shout; neither sex understands how the other reacts
	Are incapable of fact based decision making	"She couldn't handle the job; she'd base tough decisions on her intuition"				X	. Researchers have failed to show any difference in problem-solving capability . Studies have shown that women tend to be more conservative in their business decisions

Source: Adapted from Women in the CBC, the report of the Canadian Broadcasting Corporation's Task Force on the Status of Women.

This is International Women's Year—as good a time as any for every working woman to examine her conditions of employment for examples of discriminatory practices. (Men must get involved in this issue too—injustice is everyone's business.)

Discrimination often works in subtle ways. It's usually rooted in preconceived notions about what women can, or should, do. Many employers and employees still cling to ideas that should have been retired long ago.

In an attempt to focus attention on this problem, the CUPE Education Department offers the following guidelines for investigating conditions at your workplace.

Apply the questions posed in this checklist to your work situation, to the best of your knowledge. If you answer "yes" more often than not, you're getting a raw deal. Any "yes" answer, in fact, should be grounds for action—a grievance or an improvement in the collective agreement.

Keep this leaflet and discuss it with your fellow local union members. Having located the problem areas, discuss at union meetings how to correct them through bargaining or by other means.

- 8 -

ARE YOU BEING DISCRIMINATED AGAINST?

1 Wages

1. Are women paid less for substantially the same work as men?

To test whether jobs are comparable, use the following five criteria: Working Conditions, Complexity of Work, Physical Effort, Responsibility, Education and/or Experience.

2. Is the average rate of pay for women less than that for men?

...to obtain salary information for all employees and check ... of men and women on the same job.

2 Entrance Tests

Do a significantly greater proportion of men sc... tests than do women?

Check with personnel to see how many women and ... particular jobs and what their scores on entrance tes... is a significant difference between the men and wo... step would be to check whether or not tests are j... measure things that have nothing to do with job pe...

3 Hiring

Have women been told they would not be hire... transferred or given certain jobs because:

a. They have children?
b. They might miss too much work?
c. They might quit if their husbands are transferred
d. They might not take their work seriously because the "primary bread winner" of the family?

Check with women to see if they were told any of th... asked about them.

4 Classification and Promotion

1. Are jobs classified as light or heavy, and are light and automatically assigned to women, with no tes... mine if women could do the heavier work if they so ...
2. Are certain jobs or departments all or nearly all m... female?
3. Are females denied the same promotion opportuni...
4. Is there failure to promote women to so-called "...
5. Do women occupy the bulk of dead-end jobs?

Check with shop stewards and personnel departmen... job classifications and with female employees conce... tional opportunities.

5 Pregnancy and Maternity Benefits

1. Is seniority during maternity leave treated differently from seniority during other temporary disabilities?
2. Are women denied the guarantee to return to the same job or a job of the same level after maternity leave?
3. Are women denied any welfare plan benefits while disabled by childbirth or by complications arising from pregnancy?
4. Are female employees denied pregnancy benefits available to the wives of male employees?
5. Are policies on accumulated sick leave during pregnancy more restrictive than the sick leave policies for other temporary disabilities?
6. Are women required to take maternity leave at a fixed point in their pregnancy?

- 6 -

6 Pensions

1. Does the pension plan have a provision in which age is a qualification for participation and men may join the plan at an earlier age than women?
2. Does the pension plan provide for a lower mandatory retirement age for women than for men?
3. Are there differences in premiums or benefits between male and female employees and/or their dependants or spouses?

7 Insurance Plans

1. Are a man's dependants covered, but not a woman's dependants?
2. Are better benefits available to employees who are the "head of the household" or the "principal wage earner"?
3. Are spouses of women employees not eligible to receive the same benefits as spouses of male employees?

Check with the personnel department for regulations covering insurance and pension benefits. If your department or institution ublishes a booklet on employee benefits, get it and compare for men and women.

8 Protective Laws or Regulations

Do provincial laws or employer rules exist which suppose protect women (from things such as heavy lifting) but in pract limit the opportunities available for women?

9 Training

1. Do opportunities for on-the-job training differ for men women?
2. Are women denied equal consideration for educational a tance?

Try to obtain personnel department data on participation in trai programs. Check with men and women to see if their applicat for educational assistance have been refused unequally.

10 Discrimination against Men

1. Are single male parents denied day care privileges norr afforded to females?
2. Have male applicants been refused jobs that are held t traditionally female (such as qualified male nurses)?

There's so much to be done

Education Department,
Canadian Union of Public Employees,
233 Gilmour St., Suite 800, Ottawa.

A FIST FULL OF DOLLARS

A guide to pay equity

Excerpts from "A Fist Full of Dollars"

A supplement to PASSWORD

Ontario Public Service Employees Union

Agenda for change

Spring, 1985: OPSEU's "Setting the Agenda" campaign makes pay equity an important part of the provincial election. The issue is part of the pact signed by the Liberals and NDP which leads to the fall of the Conservative government. The new government consults OPSEU, other unions, business and women's groups about their ideas for a pay equity law. The Ontario Federation of Labour drafts a model law.

Fall, 1985: OPSEU and the labour and women's movement press for one law covering all workers in Ontario. Despite this, the government publishes two discussion papers. One is the "Options Paper for Pay Equity in the Ontario Public Service." The other, a "Green Paper on Pay Equity," deals with the issue outside the OPS--in the rest of the public sector (including community colleges and areas organized by OPSEU under the Ontario Labour Relations Act) and in the private sector.

January, 1986: The government appoints a panel to hold hearings on the Green Paper. The panel is made up of two company presidents and a business economist. The Ontario Federation of Labour appoints an "alternate commissioner" to monitor the panel and receive submissions the panel will not hear. OPSEU decides to organize presentations to the Green Paper panel from OPS, community college and OLRA locals, to increase the union's input into the legislation.

February, 1986, and beyond: The panel begins hearings. The government introduces legislation into the provincial parliament covering pay equity in the OPS. Union representatives will have other opportunities to influence the law before it is adopted. After adoption, it will take time to set up mechanisms to make the law work. Then the union will sit down with the employer to bargain wage increases based on pay equity.

Did you know?

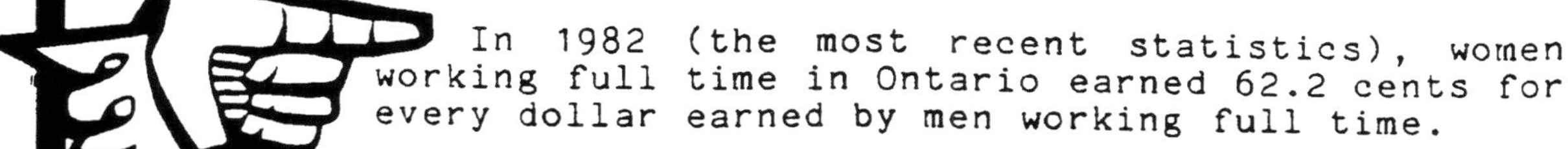

In 1982 (the most recent statistics), women working full time in Ontario earned 62.2 cents for every dollar earned by men working full time.

In the community colleges, a Technician 2 and a Library Technician 1 make the same wages ($11.67 per hour after 3 years). The Technician 3 classification (86% male) makes $13.78 per hour after three years. But a Library Technician 2 (97% female) makes $1.14 less.

In the Ontario Public Service, women's wages were about 83% of men's in 1984. The gap declined by about one-half of one per cent between 1980 and 1984. At this rate, the gap would be eliminated in the year 2120.

Food service workers (level 1) in one local organized by OPSEU under the Ontario Labour Relations Act earn $11,165 for cooking and serving food, operating a cash register and cleaning. They are all women. Mail room workers, all men, make $14,000 for sorting, distributing and processing mail.

In 1984, the 5,722 women in the Office Services category of the Public Service had a mean salary of $19,290. The 310 men in the same category had a mean salary of $22,617, 17.25% greater.

Did you know?

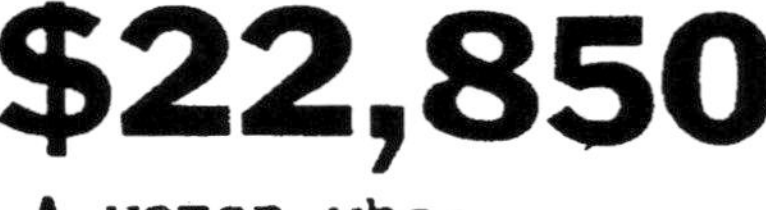

A woman who:
- Has completed high school.
- Has about 6 years experience.
- Works a 36 1/4-hour week.
- Is likely to stay at this level.
- Earns 5.2% more than the average for her wage category.
- Has some supervisory responsibility.
- 82% of her co-workers are women.

makes about $22,850 per year.

$26,925

A man who:
- Has completed high school and has some technical training.
- Has about 4 years experience.
- Works a 36 1/4-hour week.
- Is likely to stay at this level.
- Earns 3.4% less than the average for his wage category.
- Checks the work of subordinates.
- 96% of his co-workers are men.

makes about $26,925 per year.

Pay equity laws have already been passed by Canada's federal government and in Manitoba, Quebec, the European Economic Community, Australia, New Zealand and some states in the U.S.

%

86% of OPSEU members polled in 1985 think their union bargaining teams should place a high priority on negotiating wage increases based on pay equity to overcome the wage gap between men and women.

Business representatives are waging an all-out campaign against proposals to enact pay equity legislation. Here are some of their arguments. Think how you would answer them.

They say / We say

Women choose low-paying jobs:

They say	We say
"Yet many more are still reluctant to invest the requisite amount of time, energy and money in themselves and their future.... Workers affect their pay prospects by choosing or not choosing to enter particular professions." (Joan Breckinridge, Report on Business Magazine, Dec., 1985)	Most women don't have real choices when they need a job. Only a few hav enough "time, energy and money" to buck the system and prepare for a professional career. So most women are channelled into traditionally female occupations. These jobs are important to society. But they are low-paid. Not because they are useless, but because they have traditionally been done by women, and society has undervalued women's work. So a zookeeper earns more than a childcare worker.

Pay equity means armies of bureaucrats:

They say	We say
"... an army of job evaluators ... nightmarish bureaucracy ...." (John Crispo, Influence, Dec. 1985/Jan. 1986) "... nosey bureaucrats into everyone's private business ...." (Barbara Amiel, Toronto Sun, Dec. 3, 1985) "... would require an enormous bureacracy ...." (Toronto Star editorial, October 11, 1985)	This is a scare tactic. Many Ontario employers already have job evaluation systems. These can be changed to eliminate biases against women. Where there is a union, pay equity can be bargained. Some unions have been doing it for decades. Overall job evaluation is only one method for comparing value and equalizing pay. Other clear, uncomplicated approaches include: comparing benchmark jobs; raising minimum wage rates; and equalizing entry-level wages. These other methods are important to OPSEU members because an overall job evaluation scheme that covered the entire Public Service would undermine the system of bargaining by categories now in place.

They say — We say

Pay equity will hurt the economy:

"... equal value legislation could have a disastrous effect. Higher wages without any rise in productivity would for example push up prices across the board ... economic growth would be impeded .... Canada will alienate both foreign and domestic investors ..." (Breckinridge)

"... it would be astonishing, therefore, to find employers not moving aggressively to reduce their dependence on women .... They will substitute capital in the form of mechanization, automation and robotics for the labour that is increasing in cost...." (John McCallum, Toronto Star, November 22, 1985)

These arguments make it seem that the whole economy would fall apart if women were paid what they are worth. Similar arguments were made against the abolition of slavery and child labour.

In fact, pay equity can lead to higher productivity, because women will feel they've been treated fairly. Paying women fairer wages will put money back into the economy. Women will have more buying power. And higher wages will also mean better pensions for women.

Pay equity will hurt women:

"... employers will reduce the number of women employees through attrition and make more use of part-time labour ...." (Breckinridge)

"Women who gain equal pay for work of equal value increases could, therefore, find their jobs in time no longer exist ...." (McCallum)

"The very women who need our help will be without jobs." (Laura Sabia, Toronto Sun, Dec.3, 1985)

It's just not true. After Australia, for example, brought in pay equity laws in the 1970s, female employment continued to grow faster than male employment. Women's relative earnings grew by 30 per cent.
Pay equity means wages are based on jobs, not gender. So employers won't stop hiring women. If they did, they'd have trouble finding men to work those jobs, especially at the old, low rates.

On The Fastrack

3

THE GREAT COMPRESSION

In 1953 *Time* magazine, declaring that "the real news of the nation's political future and its economic direction lies in people who seldom see a reporter," sent one of its contributing editors, Alvin Josephy, on a national tour. His mission was to get a sense of America.

The portrait he painted bore little resemblance to the America of 1929. Where the America of the twenties had been a land of extremes, of vast wealth for a few but hard times for many, America in the fifties was all of a piece. "Even in the smallest towns and most isolated areas," the *Time* report began, "the U.S. is wearing a very prosperous, middle-class suit of clothes. . . . People are not growing wealthy, but more of them than ever before are getting along." And where the America of the twenties had been a land of political polarization, of sharp divides between the dominant right and the embattled left, America in the fifties was a place of political compromise: "Republicans and Democrats have a surprising sameness of outlook and political thinking." Unions had become staid establishment institutions. Farmers cheerfully told the man from *Time* that if farm subsidies were socialism, then they were socialists.[1]

Though the *Time* editor's impression that America had become a middle-class, middle-of-the-road nation wasn't based on hard evidence, many others shared the same impression. When John Kenneth Galbraith called his critique of postwar American values *The Affluent Society*, he was being sardonic; yet its starting point was the assertion that most Americans could afford the necessities of life. A few years later Michael Harrington wrote *The Other America* to remind people that not all Americans were, in fact, members of the middle class—but a large part of the reason he felt such a book was needed was because poverty was no longer a majority condition, and hence tended to disappear from view.

As we'll see, the numbers bear out what all these observers thought they saw. America in the 1950s *was* a middle-class society, to a far greater extent than it had been in the 1920s—or than it is today. Social injustice remained pervasive: Segregation still ruled in the South, and both overt racism and overt discrimination against women were the norm throughout the country. Yet ordinary workers and their families had good reason to feel that they were sharing in the nation's prosperity as never before. And, on the other side, the rich were a lot less rich than they had been a generation earlier.

The economic historians Claudia Goldin and Robert Margo call the narrowing of income gaps that took place in the United States between the twenties and the fifties—the sharp reduction in the gap between the rich and the working class, and the reduction in wage differentials among workers—"the Great Compression." Their deliberate use of a phrase that echoes "the Great Depression" is appropriate: Like the depression, the narrowing of income gaps was a defining event in American history, something that transformed the nature of our society and politics. Yet where the Great Depression lives on in our memory, the Great Compression has been largely forgotten. The achievement of a middle-class society, which once seemed an impossible dream, came to be taken for granted.

Now we live in a second Gilded Age, as the middle-class society of the postwar era rapidly vanishes. The conventional wisdom of our time is that while this is a bad thing, it's the result of forces beyond our control. But the story of the Great Compression is a powerful antidote to fatalism, a demonstration that political reform can create a more equitable distribution of income—and, in the process, create a healthier climate for democracy.

Let me expand on that a bit. In the thirties, as today, a key line of conservative defense against demands to do something about inequality was the claim that nothing *can* be done—that is, the claim that no policies can appreciably raise the share of national income going to working families, or at least that none can do so without wrecking the economy. Yet somehow Franklin Delano Roosevelt and Harry Truman managed to preside over a dramatic downward redistribution of income and wealth that made Americans far more equal than before—and not only wasn't the economy wrecked by this redistribution, the Great Compression set the stage for a great generation-long economic boom. If they could do it then, we should be able to repeat their achievement.

But how did they do it? I'll turn to possible explanations in a little while. But first let's take a closer look at the American scene after the Great Compression, circa 1955.

Portrait of a Middle-Class Nation

By the mid-1950s, Long Island's Gold Coast—the North Shore domain of the wealthy during the Long Gilded Age, and the financial hub of the Republican Party—was no more. Some of the mansions had been sold for a pittance, then either torn down to make room for middle-class tract housing or adapted for institutional use (country clubs, nursing homes, and religious retreats still occupy many of the great estates.) Others had been given away to non-profit institutions or the government, to avoid estate tax.

"What killed the legendary estates?" asks *Newsday*, the Long Island newspaper, in its guide to the structures still standing. Its answer is more or less right: "A triple whammy dealt by the advent of a federal income tax, the financial losses of the Great Depression and changes in the U.S. economic structure that made domestic service a less attractive job for the legions of workers needed to keep this way of life humming."[2]

If the Gold Coast mansions symbolized Long Island in the Long Gilded Age, there was no question what took its place in the 1950s: Levittown, the quintessential postwar suburb, which broke ground in 1947.

William Levitt's houses were tiny by the standards of today's McMansions: the original two-bedroom model had only 750 square feet of living space and no basement. But they were private, stand-alone homes, pre-equipped with washing machines and other home appliances, offering their inhabitants a standard of living previously considered out of reach for working-class Americans. And their suburban location presumed that ordinary families had their own cars, something that hadn't been true in 1929 but was definitely true by the 1950s.

Levitt's achievement was partly based on the application to civil-

ian housing of construction techniques that had been used during the war to build army barracks. But the reason Levitt thought, correctly, that he would find a mass market for his houses was that there had been a radical downward shift of the economy's center of gravity. The rich no longer had anything like the purchasing power they'd had in 1929; ordinary workers had far more purchasing power than ever before.

Making statistical comparisons between the twenties and the fifties is a bit tricky, because before the advent of the welfare state the U.S. government didn't feel the need to collect much data on who earned what, and how people made ends meet. When FDR spoke in his second inaugural address of "one third of a nation ill-housed, ill-clad, ill-nourished," he was making a guess, not reporting an official statistic. In fact the United States didn't have a formal official definition of poverty, let alone an official estimate of the number of people below the poverty line, until one was created in 1964 to help Lyndon Johnson formulate goals for the Great Society. But despite the limitations of the data, it's clear that between the twenties and the fifties America became, to an unprecedented extent, a middle-class nation.

Part of the great narrowing of income differentials that took place between the twenties and the fifties involved leveling downward: the rich were significantly poorer in the fifties than they had been in the twenties. And I literally mean poorer: We're not just talking about relative impoverishment, a failure to keep up with income growth further down the scale, but about a large absolute decline in purchasing power. By the mid-fifties the real after-tax incomes of the richest 1 percent of Americans were probably 20 or 30 percent lower than they had been a generation earlier. And the real incomes of the really rich—say, those in the top tenth of one percent—were less than half what they had been in the twenties. (The real *pre*tax income of the top 1 percent was about the same in the mid-fifties as it was in 1929, while the pretax income of the top 0.1 percent had fallen about 40 percent. At the same time, income tax rates on the rich had risen sharply.[3])

Meanwhile the real income of the median family had more or less doubled since 1929.[4] And most families didn't just have higher income, they had more security too. Employers offered new benefits, like health insurance and retirement plans: Before the war only a small minority of Americans had health insurance, but by 1955 more than 60 percent had at least the most basic form of health insurance, coverage for the expenses of hospitalization.[5] And the federal government backed up the new security of private employment with crucial benefits such as unemployment insurance for laid-off workers and Social Security for retirees.

So working Americans were far better off in the fifties than they had been in the twenties, while the economic elite was worse off. And even among working Americans economic differences had narrowed. The available data show that by the 1950s unskilled and semiskilled workers, like the people manning assembly lines, had closed much of the pay gap with more skilled workers, like machinists. And employees with formal education, like lawyers and engineers, were paid much less of a premium over manual laborers than they had received in the twenties—or than they receive today.

Economic statistics are useful, of course, only to the extent that they shed light on the human condition. But these statistics do tell a human tale, that of a vast economic democratization of American society.

On one side the majority of Americans were able, for the first time, to afford a decent standard of living. I know that "decent" isn't a well-defined term, but here's what I mean: In the twenties the technology to provide the major comforts and conveniences of modern life already existed. A modern American transported back to, say, the time of Abraham Lincoln would be horrified at the

roughness of life, no matter how much money he had. But a modern American transported back to the late 1920s and given a high enough income would find life by and large tolerable. The problem was that most Americans in the twenties couldn't afford to live that tolerable life. To take the most basic comfort: Most rural Americans still didn't have indoor plumbing, and many urban Americans had to share facilities with other families. Washing machines existed, but weren't standard in the home. Private automobiles and private telephones existed, but most families didn't have them. In 1936 the Gallup organization predicted a landslide victory for Alf Landon, the Republican presidential candidate. How did Gallup get it so wrong? Well, the poll was based on a telephone survey, but at the time only about a third of U.S. residences had a home phone—and those people who didn't have phones tended to be Roosevelt supporters. And so on down the line.

But by the fifties, although there were still rural Americans who relied on outhouses, and urban families living in tenements with toilets down the hall, they were a distinct minority. By 1955 a majority of American families owned a car. And 70 percent of residences had telephones.

On the other side F. Scott Fitzgerald's remark that the rich "are different from you and me" has never, before or since, been less true than it was in the generation that followed World War II. By the fifties, very few Americans were able to afford a lifestyle that put them in a different material universe from that occupied by the middle class. The rich might have had bigger houses than most people, but they could no longer afford to live in vast mansions—in particular, they couldn't afford the servants necessary to maintain those mansions. The traditional differences in dress between the rich and everyone else had largely vanished, partly because ordinary workers could now afford to wear (and clean) good clothes, partly because the rich could no longer afford to dress in a style that required legions of servants to help them get into and out of their wardrobes. Even the traditional rich man's advantage in mobility—to this day high-end stores are said to cater to the "carriage trade"—had vanished now that most people had cars.

I don't think it's romanticizing to say that all this contributed to a new sense of dignity among ordinary Americans. Everything we know about America during the Long Gilded Age makes it clear that it was, despite the nation's democratic ideology, a very class-conscious society—a place where the rich considered themselves the workers' "betters," and where workers lived in fear (and resentment) of the "bosses." But in postwar America—and here I can speak from my personal memory of the society in which I grew up, as well as what we can learn from what people said and wrote—much of that class consciousness was gone. Postwar American society had its poor, but the truly rich were rare and made little impact on society. A worker protected by a good union, as many were, had as secure a job and often nearly as high an income as a highly trained professional. And we all lived material lives that were no more different from one another than a Cadillac was from a Chevy: One life might be more luxurious than another, but there were no big differences in where people could go and what they could do.

But how did that democratic society come into being?

What Happened to the Rich?

Simon Kuznets, a Russian immigrant to the United States who won the Nobel Prize in Economics in 1971, more or less invented modern economic statistics. During the 1930s he created America's National Income Accounts, the system of numbers—including gross domestic product—that lets us keep track of the nation's income. By the 1950s Kuznets had turned his attention from the

overall size of national income to its distribution. And in spite of the limitations of the data, he was able to show that the distribution of income in postwar America was much more equal than it had been before the Great Depression. But was this change the result of politics or of impersonal market forces?

In general economists, schooled in the importance of the invisible hand, tend to be skeptical about the ability of governments to shape the economy. As a result economists tend to look, in the first instance, to market forces as the cause of large changes in the distribution of income. And Kuznets's name is often associated (rather unfairly) with the view that there is a natural cycle of inequality driven by market forces. This natural cycle has come to be known as the "Kuznets curve."

Here's how the Kuznets curve is supposed to work: In the early stages of development, the story goes, investment opportunities for those who have money multiply, while wages are held down by an influx of cheap rural labor to the cities. The result is that as a country industrializes, inequality rises: An elite of wealthy industrialists emerges, while ordinary workers remain mired in poverty. In other words a period of vast inequality, like America's Long Gilded Age, is the natural product of development.

But eventually capital becomes more abundant, the flow of workers from the farms dries up, wages begin to rise, and profits level off or fall. Prosperity becomes widespread, and the economy becomes broadly middle class.

Until the 1980s most American economists, to the extent that they thought about the issue at all, believed that this was America's story over the course of the ninteenth and twentieth centuries. The Long Gilded Age, they thought, was a stage through which the country had to pass; the middle-class society that followed, they believed, was the natural, inevitable happy end state of the process of economic development.

But by the mid-1980s it became clear that the story wasn't over, that inequality was rising again. While many economists believe that this, too, is the inexorable result of market forces, such as technological changes that place a growing premium on skill, new concerns about inequality led to a look back at the equalization that took place during an earlier generation. And guess what: The more carefully one looks at that equalization, the less it looks like a gradual response to impersonal market forces, and the more it looks like a sudden change, brought on in large part by a change in the political balance of power.

The easiest place to see both the suddenness of the change and the probable importance of political factors is to look at the incomes of the wealthy—the top 1 percent or less of the income distribution.

We know more about the historical incomes of the wealthy than we know about the rest of the population, because the wealthy have been paying income taxes—and, in the process, providing the federal government with information about their financial status—since 1913. What tax data suggest is that there was no trend toward declining inequality until the mid-1930s or even later: When FDR delivered his second inaugural address in 1937, the one that spoke of one-third of a nation still in poverty, there was little evidence that the rich had any less dominant an economic position than they had had before World War I. But a mere decade later the rich had clearly been demoted: The sharp decline in incomes at the top, which we have documented for the 1950s, had already happened by 1946 or 1947. The relative impoverishment of the economic elite didn't happen gradually—it happened quite suddenly,

This sudden decline in the fortunes of the wealthy can be explained in large part with just one word: taxes.

Here's how to think about what happened. In prewar America the sources of high incomes were different from what they are now. Where today's wealthy receive much of their income from employment (think of CEOs and their stock-option grants), in the twenties matters were simpler: The rich were rich because of the returns on the capital they owned. And since most income from capital went to a small fraction of the population—in 1929, 70 percent of stock dividends went to only 1 percent of Americans—the division of income between the rich and everyone else was largely determined by the division of national income between wages and returns to capital.

So you might think that the sharp fall in the share of the wealthy in American national income must have reflected a big shift in the distribution of income away from capital and toward labor. But it turns out that this didn't happen. In 1955 labor received 69 percent of the pretax income earned in the corporate sector, versus 31 percent for capital; this was barely different from the 67–33 split in 1929.

But while the division of *pre*tax income between capital and labor barely changed between the twenties and the fifties, the division of *after*-tax income between those who derived their income mainly from capital and those who mainly relied on wages changed radically.

In the twenties, taxes had been a minor factor for the rich. The top income tax rate was only 24 percent, and because the inheritence tax on even the largest estates was only 20 percent, wealthy dynasties had little difficulty maintaining themselves. But with the coming of the New Deal, the rich started to face taxes that were not only vastly higher than those of the twenties, but high by today's standards. The top income tax rate (currently only 35 percent) rose to 63 percent during the first Roosevelt administration, and 79 percent in the second. By the mid-fifties, as the United States faced the expenses of the Cold War, it had risen to 91 percent.

Moreover, these higher personal taxes came on capital income that had been significantly reduced not by a fall in the profits corporations earned but in the profits they were allowed to keep: The average federal tax on corporate profits rose from less than 14 percent in 1929 to more than 45 percent in 1955.

And one more thing: Not only did those who depended on income from capital find much of that income taxed away, they found it increasingly difficult to pass their wealth on to their children. The top estate tax rate rose from 20 percent to 45, then 60, then 70, and finally 77 percent. Partly as a result the ownership of wealth became significantly less concentrated: The richest 0.1 percent of Americans owned more than 20 percent of the nation's wealth in 1929, but only around 10 percent in the mid-1950s.

So what happened to the rich? Basically the New Deal taxed away much, perhaps most, of their income. No wonder FDR was viewed as a traitor to his class.

Workers and Unions

While the rich were the biggest victims of the Great Compression, blue-collar workers—above all, industrial workers—were the biggest beneficiaries. The three decades that followed the Great Compression, from the mid-forties to the mid-seventies, were the golden age of manual labor.

In fact, by the end of the 1950s American men with a high school degree but no college were earning about as much, adjusted for inflation, as workers with similar qualifications make today. And their relative status was, of course, much higher: Blue-collar workers with especially good jobs often made as much or more than many college-educated professionals.

Why were times so good for blue-collar workers? To some extent

they were helped by the state of the world economy: U.S. manufacturing companies were able to pay high wages in part because they faced little foreign competition. They were also helped by a scarcity of labor created by the severe immigration restrictions imposed by the Immigration Act of 1924.

But if there's a single reason blue-collar workers did so much better in the fifties than they had in the twenties, it was the rise of unions.

At the end of the twenties, the American union movement was in retreat. Major organizing attempts failed, partly because employers successfully broke strikes, partly because the government consistently came down on the side of employers, arresting union organizers and deporting them if, as was often the case, they were foreign born. Union membership, which had surged during World War I, fell sharply thereafter. By 1930 only a bit more than 10 percent of nonagricultural workers were unionized, a number roughly comparable to the unionized share of private-sector workers today. Union membership continued to decline for the first few years of the depression, reaching a low point in 1933.

But under the New Deal unions surged in both membership and power. Union membership tripled from 1933 to 1938, then nearly doubled again by 1947. At the end of World War II more than a third of nonfarm workers were members of unions—and many others were paid wages that, explicitly or implicitly, were set either to match union wages or to keep workers happy enough to forestall union organizers.

Why did union membership surge? That's the subject of a serious debate among economists and historians.

One story about the surge in union membership gives most of

the credit (or blame, depending on your perspective) to the New Deal. Until the New Deal the federal government was a reliable ally of employers seeking to suppress union organizers or crush existing unions. Under FDR it became, instead, a protector of workers' right to organize. Roosevelt's statement on signing the Fair Labor Relations Act in 1935, which established the National Labor Relations Board, couldn't have been clearer: "This act defines, as a part of our substantive law, the right of self-organization of employees in industry for the purpose of collective bargaining, and provides methods by which the government can safeguard that legal right." Not surprisingly many historians argue that this reversal in public policy toward unions caused the great union surge.

An alternative story, however, places less emphasis on the role of government policy and more on the internal dynamic of the union movement itself. Richard Freeman, a prominent labor economist at Harvard, points out that the surge in unionization in the thirties mirrored an earlier surge between 1910 and 1920, and that there were similar surges in other Western countries in the thirties; this suggests that FDR and the New Deal may not have played a crucial role. Freeman argues that what really happened in the thirties was a two-stage process that was largely independent of government action. First the Great Depression, which led many employers to reduce wages, gave new strength to the union movement as angry workers organized to fight pay cuts. Then the rising strength of the union movement became self-reinforcing, as workers who had already joined unions provided crucial support in the form of financial aid, picketers, and so on to other workers seeking to organize.

It's not clear that we have to decide between these stories. The same factors that mobilized workers also helped provide the New Deal with the political power it needed to change federal policy. Meanwhile, even if FDR didn't single-handedly create the conditions for a powerful union movement, the government's shift from agent of the bosses to protector of the workers surely must have helped the union drive.

Whatever the relative weight of politics, the depression, and the dynamics of organizing in the union surge, everything we know about unions says that their new power was a major factor in the creation of a middle-class society. According to a wide range of scholarly research, unions have two main effects relevant to the Great Compression. First, unions raise average wages for their membership; they also, indirectly and to a lesser extent, raise wages for similar workers, even if they aren't represented by unions, as nonunionized employers try to diminish the appeal of union drives to their workers. As a result unions tend to reduce the gap in earnings between blue-collar workers and higher-paid occupations, such as managers. Second, unions tend to narrow income gaps among blue-collar workers, by negotiating bigger wage increases for their worst-paid members than for their best-paid members. And nonunion employers, seeking to forestall union organizers, tend to echo this effect. In other words the known effects of unions on wages are exactly what we see in the Great Compression: a rise in the wages of blue-collar workers compared with managers and professionals, and a narrowing of wage differentials among blue-collar workers themselves.

Still, unionization by itself wasn't enough to bring about the full extent of the compression. The full transformation needed the special circumstances of World War II.

The Wages of War

Under ordinary circumstances the government in a market economy like the United States can, at most, influence wages; it doesn't set them directly. But for almost four years in the 1940s important parts of the U.S. economy were more or less directly controlled by the government, as part of the war effort. And the government used its influence to produce a major equalization of income.

The National War Labor Board was actually created by Woodrow Wilson in 1918. Its mandate was to arbitrate disputes between labor and capital, in order to avoid strikes that might disrupt the war effort. In practice the board favored labor's interests—protecting the right of workers to organize and bargain collectively, pushing for a living wage. Union membership almost doubled over a short period.

After World War I the war labor board was abolished, and the federal government returned to its traditional pro-employer stance. As already noted, labor soon found itself in retreat, and the war-time gains were rolled back.

But FDR reestablished the National War Labor Board little more than a month after Pearl Harbor, this time with more power. The war created huge inflationary pressures, leading to government price controls on many key commodities. These controls would have been unsustainable if the labor shortages created by the war's demands led to huge wage increases, so wages in many key national industries were also placed under federal controls. Any increase in those wages had to be approved by the NWLB. In effect the government found itself not just arbitrating disputes but dictating wage rates to the private sector.

Not surprisingly, given the Roosevelt administration's values, the rules established by the NWLB tended to raise the wages of low-paid workers more than those of highly paid employees. Following a directive by Roosevelt that substandard wages should be raised, employers were given the freedom to raise any wage to forty cents an hour (the equivalent of about five dollars an hour today) without approval, or to fifty cents an hour with approval from the local

office of the NWLB. By contrast increases above that level had to be approved by Washington, so the system had an inherent tendency to raise wages for low-paid workers faster than for the highly paid. The NWLB also set pay brackets for each occupation, and employers were free to raise any worker's wage to the bottom of the pay bracket for the worker's occupation. Again this favored wage increases for the low paid, but not for those with higher wage rates. Finally the NWLB allowed increases that eliminated differences in wages across plants—again raising the wages of those who were paid least.

As Goldin and Margo say, "Most of the criteria for wage increases used by the NWLB served to compress wages across and within industries." So during the brief period when the U.S. government was in a position to determine many workers' wages more or less directly, it used that power to make America a more equal society.

And the amazing thing is that the changes stuck.

Equality and the Postwar Boom

Suppose that Democrats in today's Congress were to propose a rerun of the policies that produced the Great Compression: huge increases in taxes on the rich, support for a vast expansion of union power, a period of wage controls used to greatly narrow pay differentials, and so on. What would conventional wisdom say about the effects of such a program?

First, there would be general skepticism that these policies would have much effect on inequality, at least in the long run. Standard economic theory tells us that attempts to defy the law of supply and demand usually fail; even if the government were to use wartime powers to decree a more equal structure of wages, the old wage gaps would reassert themselves as soon as the controls were lifted.

Second, there would be widespread assertions—and not only from the hard right—that such radical equalizing policies would wreak destruction on the economy by destroying incentives. High taxes on profits would lead to a collapse of business investment; high taxes on high incomes would lead to a collapse of entrepreneurship and individual initiative; powerful unions would demand excessive wage increases, leading to mass unemployment, and prevent productivity increases. One way to summarize this is to say that the changes in U.S. policies during the Great Compression look like an extreme form of the policies that are widely blamed today for "Eurosclerosis," the relatively low employment and (to a lesser extent) economic growth in many Western European economies.

Now, maybe these dire predictions would come true if we tried to replicate the Great Compression today. But the fact is that none of the bad consequences one might have expected from a drastic equalization of incomes actually materialized after World War II. On the contrary, the Great Compression succeeded in equalizing incomes for a long period—more than thirty years. And the era of equality was also a time of unprecedented prosperity, which we have never been able to recapture.

To get a sense of just how well things went after the Great Compression, let me suggest dividing postwar U.S. economic history into three eras: the postwar boom, from 1947 to 1973; the time of troubles, when oil crises and stagflation wracked the U.S. economy, from 1973 to 1980; and the modern era of reasonable growth with rising inequality, from 1980 until the present. (Why start in 1947? For two reasons: The Great Compression had been largely accomplished by then, and good data mostly start from that year.)

During the postwar boom the real income of the typical family roughly doubled, from about $22,000 in today's prices to $44,000. That's a growth rate of 2.7 percent per year. And incomes all through the income distribution grew at about the same rate, preserving the relatively equal distribution created by the Great Compression.

The time of troubles temporarily brought growth in median income to a halt. Growth resumed once inflation had been brought under control—but for the typical family even good times have never come close to matching the postwar boom. Since 1980 median family income has risen only about 0.7 percent a year. Even during the best of times—the Reagan-era "morning in America" expansion from 1982 to 1989, the Clinton-era boom from 1993 to 2000—family income grew more slowly than it did for a full generation after the Great Compression.

As always these are just numbers, providing at best an indication of what really happened in peoples' lives. But is there any question that the postwar generation was a time when almost everyone in America felt that living standards were rising rapidly, a time in which ordinary working Americans felt that they were achieving a level of prosperity beyond their parents' wildest dreams? And is there any question that the way we feel about the economy today is, at best, far more cautious—that most Americans today feel better off in some ways, but worse off in others, than they were a couple of decades ago?

Some people find the reality of how well the U.S. economy did in the wake of the Great Compression so disturbing, so contrary to their beliefs about the way the world works, that they've actually rewritten history to eliminate the postwar boom. Thus Larry Kudlow, who preaches his supply-side doctrine every weekday night on CNBC, tells us that thanks to Ronald Reagan's tax cuts, "for the first time since the post–Civil War period (but for the brief

Coolidge-Mellon period in the 1920s), the American economic system became the envy of the world." I guess the prosperity reported by that *Time* editor, not to mention all the available economic data, was simply an illusion.

But it was no illusion; the boom was real. The Great Compression, far from destroying American prosperity, seems if anything to have invigorated the economy. If that tale runs counter to what textbook economics says should have happened, well, there's something wrong with textbook economics. But that's a subject for a later chapter.

For now let's simply accept that during the thirties and forties liberals managed to achieve a remarkable reduction in income inequality, with almost entirely positive effects on the economy as a whole. The men and women behind that achievement offer today's liberals an object lesson in the difference leadership can make.

But who were these men and women, and why were they in a position both to make such large changes in our society and to make those changes stick?